Jane Austen:
The Complete Juvenilia
Text and Critical Introduction

Edited by
Ray Moore M.A.

**Watercolor of Jane Austen by her
sister Cassandra Austen (1804).**

(The original is in the possession of the Austen Family. This
image is from Wikimedia Commons where it is described as
being in the public domain.)

Dedication:

To Janeites everywhere.

Acknowledgements:

I am indebted to the work of numerous reviewers and critics. Where I am conscious of having taken an idea or used a phrase from a particular author, I have cited the source in the text. Any failure to do so is an omission which I will correct if it is drawn to my attention.

I believe that all quotations used fall under the definition of 'fair use.' If I am in error on any quotation, please notify me.

Thanks are due to my wife, Barbara, for reading the manuscript, offering valuable suggestions, and putting the text into the correct formats for publication. Any errors which remain are my own.

A Note on the Text

I have based the text of the juvenilia largely on digital and print facsimiles of Jane Austen's final handwritten version of these works (see Bibliography). Because my aim in editing the text has been to produce a readable version, the text is presented in Modern Standard English, as is normal practice with editions of Austen's novels. That means that I have: modernized archaic spellings and corrected obvious spelling errors (Austen never mastered the "'i' before 'e' except after a 'c'" rule); revised the punctuation where necessary to make the author's meaning clearer; and used lower case in place of upper case letters when the latter appear now to be redundant.

Austen makes frequent use of the dash, sometimes to indicate excitement (particularly in direct speech) and sometimes simply as an alternative to using a period. Where dashes seem to have the former function, I have retained them; where they seem only to have the latter function I have added periods. In terms of layout, my aim has been to produce a clear and consistent format, not to try to render in print the layout in the original manuscripts.

These are all of the words that Jane Austen wrote in the order in which she wrote them. None of Austen's original words has been removed. I have made no attempt to 'correct' the grammar nor to 'improve' the author's style. Anyone wishing to appreciate exactly *how* Austen wrote these words should consult the facsimile version of the notebooks which is readily available both in print and on the Internet.

As with most handwritten manuscripts, these texts show evidence of correction and editorial revision. Some of these changes were obviously made by Austen at the time of transcription, but others were done later, sometimes years later, and not all appear to be in Austen's handwriting. Sometimes words were erased and written over; sometimes words were simply crossed through and new words inserted above the line. I have only indicated these when I felt that a reader (as opposed to a manuscript scholar) might find the changes interesting.

Quotations from texts contemporary with Jane Austen are presented exactly as written in the sources I used. Because these are generally quite short, I have retained the archaic spelling and punctuation whenever they occur in the original.

My own text is in American Standard English because I live and write in the USA.

A Note on the Typeface

My text is presented in Times New Roman. For ease of differentiation, the text of Austen's notebooks is presented in Bookman Old Style.

Contents

Preface...1

Chapter One: Jane Austen: Novelist...3

Chapter Two: The Juvenilia...23

Volume the First 31

   Frederic and Elfrida – a novel... 32
   Jack and Alice – a novel... 44
   Edgar and Emma – a tale.. 64
   Henry and Eliza – a novel 69
   The Adventures of Mr. Harley.. 78
   Sir William Montague 79
   Memoirs of Mr. Clifford – an unfinished tale 82
   The Beautiful Cassandra.. 85
   Amelia Webster 90
   The Visit – a comedy in two acts 93
   The Mystery – an unfinished comedy 100
   The Three Sisters – a novel 102
   A Fragment Written to Inculcate the Practise of Virtue[5] 121
   A Beautiful Description of the Different Effects of Sensibility on Different Minds.. 121
   The Generous Curate 123
   Ode to Pity.. 127

Volume the Second 129

   Love and Friendship – a novel in a series of letters 130
   Lesley Castle - an unfinished novel in letters........................ 169
   The History of England 200
   A Collection of Letters.. 215
   Scraps.. 237

Volume the Third 248

   Evelyn.. 248
   Kitty Catharine[1]*, or the Bower*[2] 266
   Appendix: Guide to Further Reading...................................... 318
   Bibliography.. 320
   About the Author 324

Preface

The items of juvenilia that are contained in three notebooks and written in Jane Austen's own hand were never intended for publication; they were originally written and subsequently transcribed by the teenage Austen for the amusement of members of her immediate family and of close friends. Of course, these early efforts at authorship are an invaluable resource for academics studying the evolution of a great novelist. They are also a source of delight to all Janeites, whose credo E. M. Forster somewhat self-deprecatingly stated: "I am a Jane Austenite, and therefore slightly imbecile about Jane Austen … She is my favourite author! I read and reread, the mouth open and the mind closed. Shut up in measureless content, I greet her by the name of most kind hostess, while criticism slumbers." However, why the rest of us should take the slightest interest in the adolescent scribblings of a teenager some two hundred and thirty years ago is a valid question.

The answer is very simple: Austen's apprentice pieces, uneven and unfinished as they are, contain some of the best comic writing in all English Literature. I am reminded of the high school student (a young man who, like most young men, had decided that he would hate *Pride and Prejudice* because it was 'chick-lit') who raised his hand after I had read Chapter One to the class and said reproachfully, "Mr. Moore, you didn't tell us this book was going to be falling-down funny!" Austen's juvenilia retain their capacity to delight readers today. Peter Sabor makes the same point in more scholarly terms when he writes, "they represent not an embryonic form of the later novels but a major achievement in their own right" (xxiv).

In these dedications, stories, essays, squibs and skits, Austen satirizes the sentimental novels of her day, the plays of her day, the history writing of her day, and (increasingly) the social values and mores of her day. Of course, it helps to understand a little about these things in order fully to appreciate just what Austen is getting at (and I have tried to give some of that background in this book), but silly is silly, snobby is snobby, and vicious is vicious whether it happens in the last decade of the eighteenth century or the early decades of the twenty-first. The great paradox of Austen's fiction is that, whilst the characters wear Regency clothes, speak in rather archaic English, and are constrained by what passed at that time for good manners, we recognize their emotions, their reactions and their motivations as our own. Austen's fiction does not date; she is the first modern novelist writing in English – which accounts for the fact that her novels are still selling well while those of her more illustrious contemporaries are largely forgotten.

Prepare to laugh out loud as the beautiful Cassandra falls in love with a bonnet and elopes with it for a day of anarchic adventures in London; or while Elizabeth and Fanny hop delightfully from Hereford to their home by the side of their horse-riding mother because they only have one pair of blue satin slippers between them; or while Captain Harley, returned from his first sea voyage, encounters a beautiful young wife in a stage coach and suddenly recollects that he had himself had married the lady a few weeks before leaving England.

Chapter One: Jane Austen: Novelist

> ... there seems almost a general wish of decrying the capacity and undervaluing the labour of the novelist, and of slighting the performances which have only genius, wit, and taste to recommend them. "I am no novel-reader – I seldom look into novels – Do not imagine that I often read novels – It is really very well for a novel." Such is the common cant. "And what are you reading, Miss — ?" "Oh! It is only a novel!" replies the young lady, while she lays down her book with affected indifference, or momentary shame. "It is only *Cecilia*, or *Camilla*, or *Belinda*"; or, in short, only some work in which the greatest powers of the mind are displayed, in which the most thorough knowledge of human nature, the happiest delineation of its varieties, the liveliest effusions of wit and humour, are conveyed to the world in the best-chosen language. (Jane Austen, *Northanger Abbey*, Ch. 5)

> I will run the risk of asserting, that where the reading of novels prevails as a habit, it occasions in time the entire destruction of the powers of the mind: it is such an utter loss to the reader, that it is not so much to be called *pastime* as *kill-time*. It is filling the mind with a little mawkish sensibility, instead of encouraging and cultivating the more noble faculties. (Coleridge, *Lectures on Shakespeare and Milton*, 1811)

The Eighteenth Century Novel

Jane Austen (1775-1817) was neither the first significant woman novelist in English literature, nor the most commercially successful woman novelist of her time. She had no personal contact with any of the major literary figures of her day, either male or female, yet her works are still in demand whilst theirs are largely forgotten. The reason is that, despite their Regency setting and archaic expression, Austen's novels have not dated in the way that the novels of her contemporaries and rivals, such as Fanny Burney (1752-1840), Ann Radcliffe (1764-1823), Maria Edgeworth (1768-1849) and Sir Walter Scott (1771-1832), undoubtedly have. Claire Harman defines Austen's unique contribution to the development of the novel thus, "No one had reproduced dialogue so naturalistically before, no one had reined in so skillfully from caricature to character, no one had been as honest about female motivations or so efficient in telling a story" (26). Put simply, Austen was the first modern English novelist; virtually single-handed she invented the novel of psychological realism.

Ian Watt, describing the evolution of the novel genre, terms the second half of the eighteenth century a period of "quantitative increase ... not in any way matched by an increase in quality ... [which] reveals only too plainly the pressures towards literary degradation which were exerted by the booksellers and circulating library operators in their efforts to meet the reading public's uncritical demand for easy vicarious indulgence in sentiment and romance" (*Rise* 290). A Walton Litz concurs, writing:

> During the fifty years from 1740 to 1790 the annual production of works of fiction increased from approximately twenty to over eighty, and this accelerated production was matched by a decline in quality. As the reading audience rapidly widened, the influence of the few intelligent commentators waned, and popular taste fell under the control of those readers (mainly women) who patronized the sentimental fiction of the circulating libraries ... [which] catered to the lowest denominator of taste. (5-6)

The Juvenilia

As a child, Austen was an avid reader having unrestricted access to her father's library of five hundred books and to the various subscription libraries to which the family subscribed. In an age when novels were seen as inferior to poetry, history and essays, the Austens loved reading them – even the bad ones. Josephine Ross writes, "Even as a child she was an astute observer of social and literary conventions – and in particular, those of trashy popular fiction: the elopements and lurid deathbeds; the improbably rediscovered rich relations and fainting, virtuous heroines" (12). No one in the Austen family would have agreed with Lady Sarah Pennington (?-1783) who wrote in *An Unfortunate Mother's Advice to Her Absent Daughter* (1761):

> *Novels and Romances*, very few of them are worth the trouble of reading; some of them do perhaps contain a few good morals, but they are not worth the finding where so much rubbish is intermixed. Their moral parts are indeed like small diamonds amongst mountains of dirt and trash, which, after you have found them, are too inconsiderable to answer the pains of coming at ... The most I have met with in these writings, to say no worse, is little better than the loss of time to peruse – but some of them have more pernicious consequences ... they are apt to give a romantic turn to the mind, which is often productive of great errors in judgment, and of fatal mistakes in conduct – of this I have seen frequent instances, and therefore advise you scarce ever to meddle with any of them.

When an acquaintance, Mrs. Martin, advertised the setting up of a subscription library, she went out of her way to make it clear that it would not

4

consist only of novels. Writing to inform her sister Cassandra of this proposal, Austen commented rather archly, "She might have spared this pretention to *our* family, who are great Novel-readers & not ashamed of being so; – but it is necessary, I suppose, to the self-consequence of half her Subscribers" (December 18th, 1798).

Novel reading in the evenings at Steventon Rectory was a family activity, and here Austen found an enthusiastic audience for her own manuscripts. In his *Biographical Notice of the Author* (1817), Jane's brother Henry noted, "She read aloud with very great taste and effect. Her own works, probably, were never heard to such advantage as from her own mouth; for she partook largely in all the best gifts of the comic muse" (Southam *Heritage* 76). That Austen was no uncritical reader is proved by the fact that at the age of twelve, she began writing parodies and satires of the works she had been reading giving them titles such as *The Adventures of Mr. Harley*, *Love and Friendship*, and *The Beautiful Cassandra*. Margaret Anne Doody asserts, "Jane Austen was not a child as a writer when she wrote these early pieces. She possessed a sophistication rarely matched in viewing and using her own medium" (Baker ed. 554).

When, in the 1790s, Austen made a revised copy of her early works in three quarto notebooks, she selected twenty-seven pieces, the earliest perhaps having been written in late 1786 or early 1787 when she was eleven or twelve, and the latest in June 1793 when she was seventeen. The selection includes a wide range of genres: novels, short stories, letters, moral homilies, dramatic sketches and one verse. *Volume the First* contains sixteen, *Volume the Second* nine, and *Volume the Third* just two – a clear indication that, as her writing matured, her texts became longer and more detailed. We must assume that in this process of making a fair copy Austen chose not to include some of her early writings, which have consequently been lost. Even of those texts transcribed into the notebooks, no original manuscripts survive.

On December 5th, 1794, Austen's father purchased in Basingstoke "a Small Mahogany Writing Desk with 1 Long Drawer and Glass Ink Stand Compleat." Although it is not absolutely certain that this was intended for Jane, the description accurately matches the 'writing-box' that Austen is known to have used. The portable desk was probably a present for his daughter's nineteenth birthday (Le Fave 83). When opened, it provides a sloping surface on which to write and a small compartment for an ink pot. A lockable drawer allows the owner to store paper and so ensure privacy. Austen's desk, which was kept after her death as a family heirloom, now resides in the British Library.

That Rev. George Austen encouraged his daughter's writing is clear because the white vellum notebook which became *Volume the Second* was inscribed by Austen as a gift from her father ("Ex Dono Mei Patris"), and because he described the contents of *Volume the Third* as, "Effusions of Fancy / by a very Young Lady / Consisting of Tales / in a Style entirely new."

Although following Austen's death the family sought vigorously to *downplay* the importance of authorship in her life, the mock dedications and even mock payments which preface the juvenilia give the impression of a young woman who set out from an early age to become a published novelist, and the publication history of her novels fully supports this view.

Austen's First Appearance in Print?

The 1780s and 1790s saw an unprecedented growth in university journalism. While they were together at St. John's College, Oxford, James and Henry Austen produced a humorous weekly periodical which they called *The Loiterer*. It ran for sixty issues, from January 31st, 1789, to March 20th, 1790, and received wide distribution outside of Oxford through booksellers in London, Birmingham, Bath and Reading. (The London distributor was Richard Egerton who would, perhaps not coincidentally, become Jane's first publisher.)

The ninth issue of the *Loiterer* (Saturday, March 28th, 1789) contains a letter signed "Sophia Sentiment" – a comic pseudonym – in which the writer criticizes the absence of material of interest to women in the publication. She suggests that "some nice, affecting stories" about lovers should be included, and proceeds to describe the type of stories that she believes women would appreciate. However, the real target of the journal's satire is Sophia herself – or rather the kind of women she represents. From her own words, she comes across as silly, frivolous, absurdly sentimental and entirely lacking in discrimination when it comes to the reading of novels.

It has been suggested that this letter was written by Jane. The only evidence for such an identification is that the kind of novels that Sophia describes in such glowing terms are precisely those that the young Jane was parodying in her early stories. Thus, Li Ping Geng writes, "what is urged in the letter – the false tastes of Gothicism and sentimentalism currently in vogue – is precisely what the fourteen-year-old Jane Austen was satirizing, along with her brothers, at about the same time, in her juvenilia" (588). The main argument against the identification (other than Jane's youth in 1789) is that the style of the letter is very different from that of Jane's early stories. Natalie Tyler, however, suggests another possibility which meets this objection: perhaps Jane "wrote the letter and … it was heavily edited by her brothers before publication" (36). Put simply, we do not know whether Jane had any hand in writing Sophia's letter. What is clear, however, is that Austen grew up in a family whose members dearly loved to laugh at the absurdity of bad novels and that her brothers James and Henry contributed significantly to shaping both Jane's literary tastes and her satiric wit. At the very least, we can assume that Austen was familiar with *The Loiterer* whose period of publication coincided with the composition of some of her early stories and skits, and that her brothers' "*Loiterer* essays offer the earliest inspiration to Jane as a precocious and aspiring writer of fiction" (Li Ping Geng 580).

The exchange in *The Loiterer* is rather long, but since it may well represent Jane's first appearance in print, it is worth quoting in full:

> The following letter was brought us the last week, while we were deliberating on a proper subject for the Loiterer; and as it is the first favour of the kind we have ever received from the fair sex (I mean in our capacity of authors) we take the earliest opportunity of laying it before our readers, and hope the fair writer of it will consider our present eagerness to comply with her commands as some expiation for our past neglect, and will no longer condemn our paper as a pedantic performance, or set its authors down for old bachelors.

To the AUTHOR of the LOITERER.
Sir,

I write this to inform you that you are very much out of my good graces, and that, if you do not mend your manners, I shall soon drop your acquaintance. You must know, Sir, I am a great reader, and not to mention some hundred volumes of Novels and Plays, have, in the last two summers, actually got through all the entertaining papers of our most celebrated periodical writers, from the Tatler and Spectator to the Microcosm and the Olla Podrida. Indeed I love a periodical work beyond any thing, especially those in which one meets with a great many stories, and where the papers are not too long. I assure you my heart beat with joy when I first heard of your publication, which I immediately sent for, and have taken in ever since.

I am sorry, however, to say it, but really, Sir, I think it the stupidest work of the kind I ever saw: not but that some of the papers are well written; but then your subjects are so badly chosen, that they never interest one. – Only conceive, in eight papers, not one sentimental story about love and honour, and all that. – Not one Eastern Tale full of Bashas and Hermits, Pyramids and Mosques – no, not even an allegory or dream have yet made their appearance in the Loiterer. Why, my dear Sir – what do you think we care about the way in which Oxford men spend their time and money – we, who have enough to do to spend our own. For my part, I never, but once, was at Oxford in my life, and I am sure I never wish to go there again. – They dragged me through so many dismal chapels, dusty libraries, and greasy halls, that it gave me the vapours for two days afterwards. As for your last paper, indeed, the story was good enough, but there was no love, and no lady in it, at least no young lady; and I wonder how you could be guilty of such an omission, especially when it could have been so easily avoided. Instead of retiring to Yorkshire, he might have fled into France, and there, you know, you might have made him fall in love with a French Paysanne, who might have turned out to be some great person. Or you might have let him set fire to a convent, and carry off a nun, whom he might afterwards have converted, or any thing of that kind, just to have created a little bustle, and made the story more interesting.

In short, you have never yet dedicated any one number to the amusement of our sex, and have taken no more notice of us, than if you thought, like the Turks, we had no souls. From all which I do conclude, that you are neither more nor less than some old Fellow of a College, who never saw any thing of the world beyond the limits of the University, and never conversed with a female, except your bed-maker and laundress. I therefore give you this advice, which you will follow as you value our favour, or your own reputation. – Let us hear no more of your Oxford Journals, your Homelys and Cockney: but send them about their business, and get a new set of correspondents, from among the young of both sexes, but particularly ours; and let us see some nice affecting stories, relating the misfortunes of two lovers, who died suddenly, just as they were going to church. Let the lover be killed in a duel, or lost at sea, or you may make him shoot himself, just as you please; and as for his mistress, she will of course go mad; or if you will, you may kill the lady, and let the lover run mad; only remember, whatever you do, that your hero and heroine must possess a great deal of feeling, and have very pretty names. If you think fit to comply with this my injunction, you may expect to hear from me again, and perhaps I may even give you a little assistance: – but, if not – may your work be condemned to the pastry-cook's shop, and may you always continue a bachelor, and be plagued with a maiden sister to keep house for you.

Your's, as you behave,
SOPHIA SENTIMENT.

As we well know how much the success of a periodical work, and the reputation of its authors, depend on the opinion of the fair; it gives us no small uneasiness to be informed, that we have involuntarily offended any of our fair countrywomen; whose smiles, whatever my correspondent may think of us, we are not yet old enough, either as authors or men, to be indifferent to. Our alarm, however, on this account is not lessened by the consciousness that we may perhaps appear to have deserved it.

To have written eight papers indeed, without formally dedicating any one to their service, is a very serious accusation; and, if literally true, and fully proved against us, would be sufficient at once to ruin our production in the opinion of the world. We, however, trust to the candour of our fair readers, and hope they will acknowledge, that if one or two of our numbers have, from the nature and place of this publication, been on subjects uninteresting or unintelligible to them, yet in general our labours have been directed as much to the amusement of their sex as ours; and that if the Loiterer has not been eminently conspicuous for wit and humour, he has at least been free from the sententious gravity of the adviser, or the solemn dullness of the pedant. We flatter ourselves also, that our protestations will meet with their belief, when we assure them, that we have hitherto been deterred from addressing ourselves more particularly to them, and devoting our labours to their amusement, by reflecting on our own incapacity to fulfill an attempt, where to succeed would be difficult, and to fail dishonourable. – Situated indeed as we are, at this place, by various causes cut off from the agrêmens [i.e., delights] of female society, alike removed from the enlivening mirth of public festivity, and the endearing charms of domestic comfort, it cannot be easy to find subjects worth the attention of our fair friends. What however can be done, we shall be most happy to do; and whenever any subject occurs (either from our correspondents or ourselves) which shall appear proper to engage their notice, we shall gladly seize the opportunity of adding to their amusement, and encreasing our own popularity.

To do this exactly in the way which my correspondent points out, we do not pledge ourselves, and (though it is always with diffidence we contradict a lady) must doubt whether the generality of our female readers would be much amused with Novels, Eastern Tales, and Dreams. The first mentioned species of production, has of late years increased so much, as to render the necessity, or even the propriety of adding to the number rather doubtful, and which might perhaps be considerably lessened without any great diminution of our knowledge, wit or taste. Eastern Tales indeed have had their admirers; and our illustrious ancestor, the Adventurer, has often employed them as vehicles of instruction, and endeavoured to make the Ladies of Britain wise and good from the lessons of some venerable Dervise, whose greatest recommendations are a white beard, and a long name. The thought seems to have been a good one, for his fair readers soon found the precepts of an illiterate Turk or Persian excessively edifying, and were vastly attentive to the lectures of these turban'd teachers – nay, though sometimes taken in for a great deal more advice than they liked – even forgave the moral for the sake of the story, and could tolerate its heroes being virtuous, provided he was not a Christian. But this invention, though at the time successful, was in a great measure indebted for its success to its novelty, and must therefore cease to please, because it has ceased to be new. For the fine ladies of the present age are much too wise to be entrapt into virtue by such underhand means, and I should fear would turn in disgust from an Eastern Tale, when they know that a Dervise and a Mosque mean, in plain English, a Parson and a Church, two things that have been so long and so justly voted bores, that one circumstance only can make the company of the former, or an entrance into the latter, desirable. Still less are we inclined to imitate some of our predecessors, and dream for the entertainment of our friends, having often observed sleeping to be infectious, and consequently extremely liable to be transferred from the author to the reader. After this it may possibly be asked, with what subjects we do intend to treat those of our fair friends, whom curiosity, or desire of amusement, may incline to read our work? To give a particular answer to this question is not in our power. In a work of this kind, the matter must of course vary with the complexion of the times, and the temper of the writers. But in general it may be said, that, in the papers more particularly devoted to their service, we shall carefully select such subjects as may captivate the imagination, without offending the judgment, and interest the feelings, without misleading the heart.

S.

The letter and the commentary which follows it share the desire to satirize sensational novels and those who read them uncritically, but while the letter employs the device of parodying that which is being criticized, the commentary is a direct attack, witty enough, but not half so funny. The method of the letter is Austen's method in the juvenilia.

In *The Loiterer* 43 (Saturday, November 21st, 1789), the author confides in his readers that "I at this moment feel the ill effects of possessing an extensive reputation." He continues by referring to two letters that he "received last week, and which prove incontestably, that in some cases it is equally dangerous to please as to displease." The first letter, written by "Benj. Bluster," a man who acknowledges himself to read little, criticizes the author because, in his commendable efforts "to reform the World," he has dared to criticize boxing. After a series of preposterous arguments in support of the "noble Science," the correspondent concludes with a threat that, should the author not recommend the exercise of boxing to his fellow students, he will "give you a good drubbing." The second letter, from Margaret Mitten, the impoverished "daughter of a [late] country Clergyman" who outspent his income, is not so much a proposal of marriage as a threat of marriage. Miss Mitten describes herself as tall, slim, upright and not "flushed with the vulgar glow of health," and as having "few failings, and … wanting in no virtue except Candour, Generosity, and Truth." The threat of the first correspondent the author hopes to have averted by having published his letter and that of the second by pointing out that as "a Fellow of a College" he cannot marry (and, I suspect, by giving an incorrect address for future correspondence).

Emily Auerbach has suggested that Jane Austen might also have written this letter arguing that Miss Mitten's boastful description of herself and her qualities sound very like some of the heroines of the juvenilia. In fairness, other critics have found the humor of the letter somewhat too labored to be Jane's. This letter is also worth quoting in full.

> To the AUTHOR of the LOITERER.
> My dear Sir,   Precincts, Canterbury.
>   You will perhaps be surprised, both at the receipt and the contents of this letter; but do not let your amiable modesty incline you to doubt the sincerity of the Writer, for merit, like yours, deserves to meet every encouragement; and under some particular circumstances the Poet tells us, "A Maid, unasked, may own a well placed Flame." But it is necessary I should tell you who and what I am. Take then the following account of the person who is destined to be your future Helpmate.
>   I am, Sir, the daughter of a country Clergyman, who having lived, what is called up to his income, that is a good deal above it, left me when he died nothing more than a small annuity, which was secured to me by my Mother's marriage articles. With this I retired to the place whence I date this letter, and where, between prayers and scandal, sermons and cards, I lead a tolerably happy life, and seldom find my time hang heavy on my hands.
>   One circumstance alone has occasionally interrupted my tranquillity, which is the strange neglect I have experienced from your sex, who seem extremely averse to any acquaintance with me, notwithstanding I have been very far from carrying myself in a reserved and haughty manner

towards them, but have on the contrary always demeaned myself with the most open and conciliating complacency. – I am sure, Mr. Loiterer, you are too much a man of sense to pay any regard to mere external beauty; otherwise I would tell you, that I am in person of the very tallest size, not encumbered with the coarse redundance of plumpness, or flushed with the vulgar glow of health; and that I have preserved my figure in the unbending Majesty of prim perpendicular, uncorrupted by the present fashionable lounge of our modern Girls, who always appear to me as if they were going to tumble on their noses. – Such is my person, nor is my mind unworthy of it, for except an unfortunate propensity for tittle tattle, and an hereditary love of the bottle, I have few failings, and am wanting in no virtue except Candour, Generosity, and Truth. Such, Mr. Loiterer, as I am, and in my thirty – but no matter of my age, I am ready to become yours. – Don't, my dear Sir, object my never having seen you; for since I am perfectly acquainted with your better part, your writings, that is of small consequence. And indeed I have as perfect an idea of your figure as if I had seen you. – I imagine, for instance, you are a little square broad shouldered squat man, with a sallow complexion, dark eyes, black eye-brows and beard. – But I shall soon see if I am right, as I intend shortly paying you a visit at Oxford; where your Publisher will direct me to your Rooms, and where I trust we shall quickly settle matters to our mutual satisfaction; for, as I before told you, I am sure that it is destined by fate, that I am to be Mrs. Loiterer: in hopes of which I remain,

Your's, affectionately,

MARGARET MITTEN

Once again, there is simply no way of knowing what part, if any, Jane had in the composition of the above letter. I have, however, printed both *Loiterer* letters in their entirety because I detect in them the voice of the juvenilia.

The Unpublished Author

First Impressions (begun October 1796 and completed August 1797) was Austen's "first attempt at writing a full length novel in a straightforward narrative form" (Le Fave 93), the earlier drafts of *Elinor and Marianne* (begun 1795) and *Lady Susan* (1795) having been written in epistolary form after the manner of Richardson. (*Elinor and Marianne* would be entirely re-written in 1797-8 as *Sense and Sensibility*, while *Lady Susan* would remain an unpublished manuscript.) As with all of her writings, *First Impressions* was read aloud by the family where it quickly became a firm favorite. Austen's niece, Anna Lefroy, recalled later that, being only three and a half at the time, the adults wrongly presumed that she would not pay much attention to the readings, "one of her earliest Novels was read aloud in the Parsonage at Dean whilst I was in the room & not expected to listen – Listen however I did with such interest, & with so much talk afterwards of 'Jane & Elizabeth' that it was resolved, for prudence sake, to read no more of the story aloud in my hearing." The problem was that Austen had used so many family names in the novel that the young child's talk about the various characters falling in and out of love might have been misunderstood (Le Fave 93).

On January 8th, 1799, whilst staying at Godmersham, Cassandra asked her sister to send the manuscript. Austen replied ironically, "I do not wonder at your wanting to read first impressions again, so seldom as you have gone through it, & that so long ago –." Six months later, on June 11th, 1799, when she was in Bath, Austen wrote to her sister in the same ironic vein, "I would not let Martha [Lloyd] read First Impressions again upon any account, & I am very glad that I did not leave it in your power. – She is very cunning, but I see through her design; she means to publish it from Memory, & one more perusal must enable her to do it –."

On November 1st, 1797, a manuscript which is generally assumed to have been *First Impressions* was offered by Rev. George Austen, acting on his daughter's behalf, to the London publisher Thomas Cadell to whom he wrote:

> Sir,
>
> I have in my possession a Manuscript novel, comprised in three Vols. about the length of Miss Burney's *Evelina*. As I am well aware of what consequence it is that a work of this sort should make its first appearance under a respectable name I apply to you. Shall be obliged therefore if you will inform me whether you chuse to be concerned in it; what will be the expense of publishing at the Author's risk; and what you will advance for the Property of it, if on perusal it is approved of? Should your answer give me encour-agement I will send you the work.
>
> I am, Sirs, Yr. obt. Hbl, Sevt.
> GEO AUSTEN

The offer was rejected by return of post and the manuscript never left home.

In 1803, having been approached by a business associate of Austen's brother Henry, the publisher Crosby paid £10 for *Susan* (begun 1789). Although Crosby promptly advertised the publication of "Susan: a Novel in 2 Volumes," the book did not appear. It has been suggested that, since Crosby's list was largely composed of precisely the kind of Gothic romances that *Susan* satirized, "he ran the double risk of on the one hand offending his established authors and on the other of losing money if the new book were ignored by unsympathetic critics and failed to sell" (Le Fave 128). It was not until April

5th, 1809, that Austen wrote to Crosby, reminding him that, "Six years have passed … and this work of which I avow myself the Authoress, has never to the best of my knowledge, appeared in print, tho' an early publication was stipulated at the time of Sale." With much more than a hint of sarcasm, she added, "I can only account for such an extraordinary circumstance by supposing the MS by some carelessness to have been lost," and offered to supply a replacement. Austen also threatened to submit the novel to another publisher if Crosby made no reply. The letter ended with another example of Austen's caustic humor since she signed herself:

> I am Gentlemen andc andc
> M.A.D.-
> Direct to M/rs Ashton Dennis
> Post office, Southampton

There is no indication that Crosby appreciated either the facetious suggestion that he had lost the manuscript or the significance of the initials at the end of the letter. His son's reply was firmly business-like, pointing out that when the copyright was purchased, "there was not any time stipulated for its publication, neither are we bound to publish it. Should you or anyone else [attempt to publish the novel] we shall take proceedings to stop the sale. The MS shall be yours for the same as we paid for it."

Despite Crosby's perfectly reasonable offer to re-sell the copyright at cost, Austen, whose annual allowance for the previous year was only £50, was unable or unwilling to raise the necessary £10. She suffered another disappointment when, in June of the same year, the publisher John Booth brought out a novel entitled *Susan* by an anonymous author. Although the coincidence of the title was the only similarity, it must have been clear to Austen that "her own story, if it were ever to appear in print, would now have to have the heroine's name altered throughout, as well as the title" (Le Fave 153-4). It was not until 1816 that Austen was able to buy back the rights to *Susan* following Crosby's bankruptcy, and it would be published only posthumously as *Northanger Abbey*.

Although anxious to have *Susan* published, Austen had, for most of the first decade of the nineteenth century virtually stopped writing. As Tyler explains, "Perhaps the biggest mystery of Jane Austen's life … [is that] for almost ten years she wrote virtually nothing. Between [the ages of] twenty-five and thirty-five, Austen for all practical purposes was silent" (59). This is the period of her life between leaving the childhood home at Steventon Rectory, following her father's unexpected decision to retire to Bath (December 1800), and moving with her widowed mother, her sister, and Martha Lloyd into Chawton Cottage (July 7th, 1809) where she would spend the last, highly productive, eight years of her life.

Attempts to account for Austen's relative silence during this period (the unfinished *The Watsons* falls into the first half of the decade) range from her being too depressed by the move away from her beloved Steventon to write, to being too busy enjoying an active social life in Bath to find either the time or the motivation to write. To put it another way: we do not know. However, shortly after settling into Chawton Cottage, Austen was re-reading and revising the three volumes of her juvenilia and making revisions to *Sense and Sensibility*. Responding to an inquiry by Cassandra about her progress on the novel, Austen wrote in a letter dated April 25th, 1811, "I am never too busy to think of S & S. I can no more forget it, than a mother can forget her sucking child; & I am much obliged to you for your enquiries."

The Published Author

Austen's brother Henry, at the time a London banker, acted as Austen's literary agent for her third attempt to become a published author, and in November 1811 *Sense and Sensibility* was issued by Thomas Egerton in a three volume edition priced at fifteen shillings. Egerton, who advertised himself as "Tho. Egerton Bookseller, successor to Mr. Millan ... Military books in all languages," seems a strange choice of publisher for a lady novelist, but presumably Henry was making use of his military connections.

A notice appeared in *The Morning Chronicle* on October 31st announcing "A New Novel by a Lady" – probably it was on the advice of Cassandra that the author was simply described as "a Lady." *Sense and Sensibility* was published on commission; that is, Austen did not sell the publisher the copyright. She was to receive ten percent commission on each sale; however, there was a clause in the contract which made Austen liable to reimburse the publisher for any copies left unsold, and she is known to have reserved funds for this purpose. Fortunately, this clause was never invoked, for the novel was positively received by reviewers and readers. The first edition of something less than one thousand copies sold out in twenty months, and a second edition would be published in October 1813.

Austen next turned to revising *First Impressions*: she later described herself as having "lop't and crop't" the original. In 1812, the copyright of *Pride and Prejudice* was bought by Egerton for £110, a sum which disappointed Austen. In a letter to her friend Martha Lloyd dated November 29th-30th, she wrote, "P. & P. is sold. – Egerton gives £110 for it. – I would rather have had £150, but we could not both be pleased, & I am not at all surprised that he should not chuse to hazard, so much. – Its' being sold will I hope be a great saving of Trouble to Henry, & therefore must be welcome to me. – The Money is to be paid at the end of the twelvemonth." The title page of *Pride and Prejudice*, which was published on January 28th, 1813, in a three volume edition priced at eighteen shillings, identified the writer only as "the Author of *Sense and Sensibility*." The change of title probably resulted from the publication in 1801 of the novel *First Impressions* by Margaret Holford.

By January 29th, 1813, Austen reported in a letter to Cassandra that the first copy of the novel had arrived at Chawton, "I want to tell you I have got my own darling Child from London," and that it had been read aloud by the family and Miss Benn, a neighbor to whom the authorship was entirely "unsuspected." Fortunately, Austen was able to report that Miss Benn "really does seem to admire Elizabeth." Austen states that the first night's reading covered half of the first of the three volumes, so it must have taken several hours. In a subsequent letter to Cassandra dated February 4th, she wrote:

> Our second evening's reading to Miss Benn had not pleased me so well [as the first], but I believe something must be attributed to my mother's too rapid way of getting on: and though she perfectly understands the characters herself, she cannot speak as they ought. Upon the whole, however, I am quite vain enough and well satisfied enough.

The letter continues to make an ironic 'apology' for the novel:

> The work is rather too light, and bright, and sparkling; it wants shade; it wants to be stretched out here and there with a long chapter of sense, if it could be had; if not, of solemn specious nonsense, about something unconnected with the story; an essay on writing, a critique on Walter Scott, or the history of Buonaparte [sic], or anything that would form a contrast, and bring the reader with increased delight to the playfulness and epigrammatism of the general style. I doubt your quite agreeing with me here. I know your starched notions.

Here Austen is anticipating those readers and critics who would find the novel lacking in seriousness and moral improvement. The kind of insertion which she pretends to feel necessary reminds one, for example, of Fielding's Prefaces to each book of *Tom Jones*. In fact, this passage amounts to an assertion of Austen's confidence in her own conception of what a novel should be – a conception which she is sure Cassandra shares.

From the start, *Pride and Prejudice* sold well. It "became the fashionable novel of the spring of 1813," and the question of the author's identity was a topic of lively speculation, Austen's brother Henry reporting a literary friend of his remarking, "I should like to know who is the author, for it is much too clever to have been written by a woman" (Le Faye 175). The first edition of one thousand five hundred sold out by July 1813, by which time the identity of the writer was generally known within literary circles mainly because Henry, full of pride in his sister, could not resist telling people. The result was, as Austen reported to her brother Frank, "the truth is that the Secret has spread so far as to be scarcely the Shadow of a secret now – and that I beleive whenever the 3d [i.e., the third novel] appears, I shall not even attempt to tell Lies about it. – I shall rather try to make all the Money than all the Mystery I can of it. – People shall pay for their knowledge if I can make them" (September 25th, 1813).

Austen enthusiastically informed her brother Frank in a letter written on July 3rd, 1813, that *Sense and Sensibility* had sold out its first edition, adding, "it has brought me £140 – besides [the fact that I still own] the Copyright, if that shd ever be of any value. – I have now written myself into £250 – which only makes me long for more. – I have something in hand [*Mansfield Park*] – which I hope on the credit of P. and P. will sell well, tho' not half so entertaining." Selling the copyright to *Pride and Prejudice* proved to be a business error (one which Austen would never repeat) since Egerton was free to publish a second edition in November 1813 and a third edition in 1817 for which Austen received nothing. Claire Harman states that, "[a] conservative estimate of these sales (based on the print runs of other Austen novels) would be 1,500 copies – and of the gross profit to Egerton about £575: £465 more than he had paid for the rights" (42).

Contemporary readers of *Pride and Prejudice* appreciated that Austen was doing something very different from the popular Gothic romances and novels of sentiment. The following opinion from Miss Milbanke (later Lady Byron) speaks for those readers delighted by this new kind of novel:

> I have finished the *Novel* called *Pride and Prejudice*, which I think is a very superior work. It depends not on any of the common resources of novel writers, no drowning, no conflagrations, nor runaway horses, nor lap-dogs and parrots, nor chambermaids, nor rencontres and disguises. I really think it is the most <u>probable fiction</u> I have ever read. It is not a crying book, but the interest is very strong, especially for Mr. Darcy. The characters which are not amiable are diverting, and all of those are consistently supported. (Southam *Heritage* 8)

Of course, there were others who either did not understand what Austen was doing or simply did not appreciate it. Lady Darcy, writing May 1813, speaks for those:

> I do not very much like [*Pride and Prejudice*]. Want of interest is the fault I can least excuse in works of mere amusement, and however, natural the picture of vulgar minds and manners is there given, it is unrelieved by the agreeable contrast of more dignified and refined characters occasionally captivating attention. Some power of new character is, however, ably displayed, and Mr. Bennett's indifference is in truth not exaggerated. (Southam *Heritage* 9)

Mansfield Park, probably begun in the spring of 1812, was published by Egerton on May 9th, 1814, and appeared as three volumes priced at eighteen shillings in a first edition of 1,250 copies. Neither Austen herself nor Egerton anticipated that this book would achieve the same popularity as *Pride and Prejudice* due to its more serious subject and tone. Thus, although Egerton "praised it for it's Morality, and for being so equal a Composition – No weak parts" (Le Faye 185), he did not offer to buy the copyright. However, despite not having received a single review, the first edition sold out in November, earning Austen £350.

Egerton, feeling that *Mansfield Park* had achieved its potential sales, was reluctant to print a second edition. As a result, Austen offered *Emma* to John Murray whose reader, William Gifford, the editor of the influential *Quarterly Review*, reported:

> Of Emma I have nothing but good to say ... The MS though plainly written has yet some, indeed many little omissions, and an expression may now and then be amended in passing through the press. I will readily undertake the revision. (Le Faye 201).

Gifford also commented on *Pride and Prejudice* (which Murray could not publish since Egerton owned the copyright):

> I have for the first time looked into 'P and P'; and it is really a very pretty thing. No dark passages; no secret chambers; no wind-howlings in long galleries; no drops of blood upon a rusty dagger – things that should now be left to ladies' maids and sentimental washerwomen. (Southam *Heritage* 8)

On October 17th, 1815, Murray offered Austen £450 for the copyright to *Sense and Sensibility, Emma,* and *Mansfield Park,* which would have been very good business for him. In a letter to Cassandra, Austen called Murray "a rogue of course, but a civil one." Brother Henry, writing to Murray from his sickbed on November 3rd, commented tartly that, "The terms you offer are so inferior to what we had expected that I am apprehensive of having made some great error in my mathematical calculation" and went on to claim (somewhat inaccurately) that Murray's offer was less than his sister had received for the single, limited edition of *Mansfield Park.* The caustic irony of this letter sounds so like that of Austen's earlier letter to Crosby (and so unlike a man who had been seriously ill for some time though now recovering) that it is likely that Austen herself drafted or dictated the contents. Although unwilling to increase his offer for the copyrights, Murray did publish two of the novels in December 1815. *Emma* had a first edition of two thousand copies and sold 1,250 copies in the first year, making Austen a profit of £221, but *Mansfield Park*, in a second edition of only seven hundred and fifty, did not sell so well, and Austen's losses of £182 on that novel reduced her earnings from *Emma* to just less than £39. In contrast, Hannah More's novel *Coelebs in Search of a Wife*, first published in 1808, was "so sensational a success [that] it ran through fourteen editions in five years" (Cronin, *Context* 290).

Persuasion, begun on August 8th, 1815, was finished almost exactly a year later, by which time Austen's health was in decline. On January 27th,

1817, she began writing a new novel (the unfinished *Sanditon*), but with twelve chapters completed worsening health forced her to abandon the project. *Persuasion* would be published in December 1817, five months after her death, in a four-volume set, together with *Northanger Abbey*. Murray printed 1,750 copies at £1.4s.0d. for the set, and sales were good during 1818, but then fell away sharply in 1819 leaving 282 copies remaindered by 1820. Nevertheless, this final publication made a profit of £515.17s.7d., which was paid, by the terms of Austen's will, to her surviving sister, Cassandra. However, by 1821 Jane Austen was no longer fashionable and "remaindered copies of Jane Austen's *Emma* [of which Murray had 535] and *Mansfield Park* were advertised by John Murray at the bargain prices of 2s and 2s 6d [respectively]" (Ross 44).

The taste of the novel-reading public had changed, and the works of Jane Austen were out of print and largely forgotten. However, in the years 1832-3, the publisher Richard Bentley paid Egerton £40 for the copyright of *Pride and Prejudice* and Henry and Cassandra £210 for the copyrights to the five other novels which he published in his low-cost Standard Novels series so that, for the first time, all six of Austen's novels were in print at the same time. From this point on, the Austen family no longer had any financial or business interest in the publication of Jane's novels, though they continued to guard her reputation fiercely.

Ross estimates that "in her lifetime, her writing had earned her less than £1,000" (44), while Fergus writes that, "Austen's six novels earned only £1,625 through 1832," a figure which includes earnings from the posthumously published *Persuasion* and *Northanger Abbey* (Todd *Context* 11). Fergus comments that, "This sum compares unfavourably to the earnings of other contemporary women writers, Maria Edgeworth (more than £11,000) or Frances Burney (more than £4,000)" (Todd *Context* 11).

Critical Reception

At the time when Austen began writing with the intention of becoming a published author, the novel was still an emerging genre hardly taken seriously by critics. Two myths perpetuated this sense of the novel's inferiority to poetry, the medium of sublime utterance: firstly, that the only readers of novels were women, and secondly, that the only justification for writing a novel was to exemplify a moral lesson. In contrast to the prevailing opinion, Austen (who grew up in a predominantly male household) was an avid reader and a staunch defender of novels, and as a writer she did not subscribe to the need to point a moral in her novels. This did not, however, prevent the reviewer of *Sense and Sensibility* in the *Critical Review* (February 1812) from commending the novel as being one "from which both amusement and instruction may be derived," and his counterpart in the *British Critic* (May 1812) from praising the novel as exemplifying Elinor's virtues of "sober exertion of prudence and judgement." Both writers, assuming that readers of the novel would be women, patronizingly termed them "our fair readers" and "our female friends" respectively.

Pride and Prejudice was more widely and even more positively reviewed. The *British Critic* (February 1813) found the novel:

> very far superior to almost all the publications of the kind which have lately come before us. It has a very unexceptionable tendency ... Of the characters, Elizabeth Bennett, the heroine, is supported with great spirit and consistency throughout; there seems no defect in the portrait; this is not precisely the case with Darcy her lover; his easy unconcern and fashionable indifference, somewhat abruptly changes to the ardent lover ... It is unnecessary to add, that we have perused these volumes with much satisfaction and amusement, and entertain very little doubt that their successful circulation will induce the author to similar exertions. (Southam *Heritage* 41-2)

The *Critical Review* (March 1813) stated:

> [*Pride and Prejudice*] rises very superior to any novel we have lately met with in the delineation of domestic scenes. Nor is there one character which appears flat, or obtrudes itself upon the notice of the reader with troublesome impertinence. There is not one person in the drama with whom we could willingly dispense; – they all have their proper places; and fill their several stations, with great credit to themselves, and much satisfaction to the reader. (Southam *Heritage* 47)

The writer, however, felt it necessary to establish the moral tendency of the novel by adding:

> [It] shows the folly of letting young girls have their own way, and the danger which they incur in associating with officers, who may be quartered in or near their residence ... The sentiments which are dispersed over the work, do great credit to the sense and sensibility of the authoress. The line she draws between the prudent and the mercenary in matrimonial concerns, may be useful to our fair readers ... (Southam *Heritage* 46)

Strangely, *Mansfield Park* was not reviewed at all, which is something of a mystery. Even in his (anonymous) review of *Emma* in *The Quarterly Review* (1815), Sir Walter Scott contrived to mention all of Austen's published novels except *Mansfield Park* which drew from Austen an expression of disappointment. The eight reviews of *Emma* published between March and September 1816 were mixed: some praised the realistic depiction of social interaction, but others found the novel to be lacking in incident. In his review of *Emma* for their joint publisher John Murray, Sir Walter Scott commended Austen's novels as having gone beyond the romances which had dominated the genre since its inception and having substituted:

> the art of copying from nature as she really exists in the common walks of life, and presenting to the reader, instead of the splendid scenes of an imaginary world, a correct and striking representation of that which is daily taking place around him. (Southam *Heritage* 63)

He went on to compliment Austen for creating a new kind of fiction:

> keeping close to common incidents, and to such characters as occupy the ordinary walks of life, she has produced sketches of such spirit and originality, that we never miss the excitation which depends upon a narrative of uncommon events, arising from the considerations of minds, manners, and sentiments, greatly above our own. In this class, she stands almost alone … The narrative of all her novels is composed of such common occurrences as may have fallen under the observation of most folks; and her dramatis personæ conduct themselves upon the motives and principles which the readers may recognize as ruling their own and most of their acquaintances. (Southam *Heritage* 63-4)

By the early 1820s, however, Austen's novels were out of print and she was all but forgotten by the novel-buying public. Claire Harman comments that, "In the mid-nineteenth century – heyday of the Victorian triple-decker novel – Austen's restrained Regency romances looked old-fashioned and irrelevant" (xix). Nevertheless, Austen had her advocates even in these decades. Writing "Modern Novels" in *The Quarterly Review* (January 1821), Archbishop Whately praised Austen as having the "essential" merit "of being evidently a Christian writer." In line with the prevailing view that novels needed to be justified by their ethical tendency, he commented:

> The moral lessons of this lady's novels, though clearly and impressively conveyed, are not offensively put forward, but spring incidentally from the circumstances of the story; they are not forced upon the reader, but he is left to collect them (though without any difficulty) for himself … On the whole, Miss Austen's works may safely be recommended … as combining, in an eminent degree, instruction with amusement, though without the direct effort at the former, of which we have complained, as sometimes defeating its object. (Southam *Heritage* 95)

Scott also continued to be enthusiastic about her work. On March 14th, 1826, he wrote in his Journal:

> Also read again, for the third time at least Miss Austen's finely written novel of Pride and Prejudice. That young lady has a talent for describing the involvement and characters of ordinary life which is to me the most wonderful I have ever met with. The Big Bow-wow strain I can do myself like any now going, but the exquisite touch which renders ordinary common-place things and characters interesting from the truth of the description and the sentiment is denied to me. What a pity such a gifted creature died so early! (Southam *Heritage* 106)

Interestingly, both Scott and Whately used the male pronoun to identify Austen's readers – perhaps a sign of the changing status of the novel since the time Austen had begun writing.

The first significant resurgence of interest in Austen's novels was prompted by the publication of James Edward Austen-Leigh's *Memoir of Jane Austen* in 1870, though ironically the saintly Aunt Jane described there appears to be unrelated to the iconoclastic teen who wrote the juvenilia.

Chapter Two: The Juvenilia

The History of the Juvenilia

Jane Austen had the advantage of growing up in a tolerant household whose members loved to laugh at silliness and absurdity whether they found it in life or in literature. Le Faye writes of the family theatricals which were a regular feature of life at Steventon parsonage during Jane's childhood, "the Austens were not in the least prudish, for some of the comedies performed in succeeding years, dealing as they did with the eternal battle between the sexes, were quite outspoken in their dialogue" (47). From her mother, Cassandra, Jane inherited her ironic wit, and far from locking her in the coal hole for the anarchic, irreverent, iconoclastic stories that she wrote as an adolescent, her father, as we have seen, actively encouraged her.

Jane probably began writing short sketches and skits in late 1786 when she was eleven. This may strike the modern reader as improbably young given the sophistication of the earliest of her juvenilia, but we must remember that childhood was an invention of the Victorians. (As an illustration, the eldest sibling, James, was able to matriculate at St. John's College, Oxford, in 1779 at the age of fourteen.) Jane, like all of her siblings (except the unfortunate George who suffered some unknown handicap) began her education early. In 1783, at the age of seven, she went away to Mrs. Ann Cawley's school in Oxford with her sister Cassandra, who was ten. After a period of home-schooling, from the spring of 1785 until the autumn of 1786, the two sisters (aged nine and twelve respectively) attended the Abbey House School in Reading. Although that marked the end of Jane's formal education, she returned to Steventon parsonage where her father taught boarding pupils, and with his guidance, and that of her brothers James and Henry, she educated herself, reading widely and indiscriminately, but never without discernment. What Josephine Ross says of the adult Jane Austen was already becoming true of the apprentice writer of the juvenilia:

> [T]hough she lacked the classical education, bestowed, as of right, on her brothers, and claimed brightly to know nothing of "science and philosophy", Jane Austen was better informed, and far better read, than most women of her day, having good French and some Italian, a love of history, considerable skill in both music and drawing, and an extensive, intelligent knowledge of some of the greatest writers in the English language, from Johnson, Richardson and Fielding, to Goldsmith, Hume and Crabbe. (9)

Beginning in the summer of 1793, Jane began to compile in three volumes texts which had, presumably, existed previously only on separate sheets of paper. It is safe to assume that the process of compilation involved a certain amount of selection, so that some works (now lost) did not make it into the collected juvenilia, and that in transcribing her earlier works she also edited and revised them, a process that would continue into her adulthood. Kathryn Sutherland concludes that "Though we cannot date [most of] these revisions, they point to the continuing service provided even by the slightest of the early sketches as a means to refine style and narrative skills over time" (*Vol.1* 10). It may be that the later works were written directly into the notebooks.

The arrangement of the pieces in the three volumes is not strictly chronological, nor does it appear that the transcription was a sequential process, since Austen clearly began the second and third volumes before she had completely filled the first. Thus, the Contents page of *Volume the Third* is dated "May 6th 1792," while the final entry in *Volume the First*, "Ode to Pity, is dated "June 3rd 1793," and *Love and Friendship* is the first story in *Volume the Second* simply because there was not sufficient room for it after *The Mystery*; instead, *The Three Sisters*, a slightly later work, is fitted into the remaining blank pages at the back of *Volume the First*. The "Detached Pieces" and "Ode to Pity" appear to have been added (again simply because there were blank pages on which to write them) after the transcription of volumes two and three had been completed. In all, these three notebooks contain approximately 75,000 words (estimates vary).

These notebooks were designed to be shared with family members and close friends, and their well-worn condition attests to their having been read and re-read. There is also some evidence that, while most of the revisions made to the original transcription were done by Austen herself, others may also have contributed. Indisputably, there is additional material in *Volume the Third* written some time after Jane's original transcription, and presumably with her approval, by her nephew James Edward Austen Leigh (1798-1874) and, probably after Austen's death, by her niece Jane Anna Austen Lefoy (1793-1872), both of whom knew their Aunt Jane well in their youth. This shows that the three volumes were a shared family artifact.

Following Jane's premature death in 1817, Cassandra inherited the three volumes, and following her own death in 1845 they were willed to her surviving brothers: *Volume the First* went to the youngest Charles Austen (1779-1852); *Volume the Second* went to Francis (Frank) Austen (1774-1865); and *Volume the Third* to James Edward Austen (1798-1874). These much-loved volumes were valued by family members and passed on to each succeeding generation, which is how they came to survive. However, the Austen-Leigh family took great pains to keep their contents from the public. In his *Biographical Notice of the Author* which prefaced the first edition of *Northanger Abbey* and *Persuasion* (1818), Austen's favorite brother Henry made no mention of her having written stories in her adolescence though he must certainly have been aware of the existence of the three volumes. There was nothing sinister in this decision: Henry's aim was to draw to the attention of readers (and potential purchasers) his sister's published novels, and for the same reason he made no mention of her unfinished (and therefore unpublished) novels *Lady Susan*, *The Watsons* and *Sanditon*.

Half a century later, James Edward Austen-Leigh does make reference to one of these collections of juvenilia in his *Memoir of Jane Austen* (first edition 1869, second enlarged edition 1871), writing that there exists a "copy-book, containing several tales, some of which seem to have been composed while she was quite a girl." Since he describes the stories in this book as being "of a slight and flimsy texture," he was probably referring to *Volume the First*. At this date, the remaining family members had obviously discussed the possibility of publishing some of Jane's juvenilia because he goes on to write, "the family have, rightly, I think, declined to let these early works be published." James Edward does not state the reasons behind this decision, so we can only speculate that it was felt that releasing these texts would somehow damage Jane Austen's literary reputation. As Litz comments, "a young lady of under fifteen years old who could write knowingly of theft, deformity, drunkenness, and bastardy was subversive to the Victorian cult of the child" (Tyler 34). To this list might be added: unmarried unions, male homosexuality, violence, murder, suicide, gluttony, and swearing.

Support for Litz's conclusion comes in a letter from James's sister Caroline whom he consulted over which specimens from the juvenilia might be included in his *Memoir*. Caroline thought that *Evelyn*, though "all nonsense, might be used." She added:

> I have always thought it remarkable that the early workings of her mind should have been in burlesque, and comic exaggeration, setting at nought all rules of probable or possible – when of all her finished and later writings, the exact contrary is the characteristic. The story I mean [Evelyn] is clever nonsense but one knows not how it might be taken by the public, tho' something must ever be risked. What I should deprecate is publishing any of the 'betweenities' when the nonsense was passing away, and before her wonderful talent had found it's proper channel. (Le Faye 276-77)

Evidently the comic genius of Jane and Cassandra's generation had vanished in the succeeding generation. Not only does Caroline fail to understand the satirical intention of the juvenilia, but she fails to see the continuity between Jane's early burlesques and her later realistic fiction.

Certainly publishing these irreverent, ironic, anarchic, 'politically incorrect' stories would have completely exploded the image of 'saintly Aunt Jane' that the family had, from the moment of her death, striven so single-mindedly to construct. The sanitization (one might almost say 'sanctification') of Jane was begun, with the very best motives, by her beloved sister, Cassandra, who, "[a]fter Jane's death … sifted jealously through her correspondence and destroyed all intimate, or indiscreet, references, especially those concerning love-affairs…" (Ross 19). Emily Auerbach comments, "As readers of the complete juvenilia, we know that Jane Austen was an irreverent, impudent, caustic, and funny rebel, as satirical as they come, delighting in silly and severe expressions ridiculing the faults of others" (67). That was the reality that the Victorian James Edward was so desperate to conceal. He did include in the second edition of his *Memoir* one example of the juvenilia, but it was carefully chosen. *The Mystery* is a very brief, very funny dramatic skit, which has the merit of having nothing in the way of either language, values or action that could possible offend anyone. In this it is atypical and does not in the least (as James claims), provide "a specimen of the kind of transitory amusement which Jane was continually supplying to the family party," since most of the stories involve the most outrageous conduct (murder, drunkenness, theft, etc.) and the most ridiculous sentiments (running mad, fainting, pining away, etc.).

The reading public did not gain access to the juvenilia until transcriptions of the three notebooks were finally published: *Volume the Second* in 1922, *Volume the Third* in 1933, and *Volume the First* in 1951.

The Voice of the Juvenilia

> In *The Borough* (1810) Crabbe condemned the average novel's lifeless characters as "creatures borrow'd and again convey'd / From book to book - the shadows of a shade"; and in his review of Emma Scott observed that the reader of popular novels gradually "became familiar with the land of fiction, the adventures of which he assimilated not with those of real life, but with each other." … [This 'land of fiction'] was a strange and absurd world, in which the actions of the characters obeyed the 'laws' of fiction rather than probability, and the author's point-of-view was determined by literary habit … By 1790 the typical English novel was almost a parody of itself, and the way lay open for Jane Austen's cleansing irony. (Litz 6)

The juvenilia are in three volumes, mimicking the structure of the three-volume novel of the period, with mock dedications and pleas for patronage that show Austen's "familiarity with book production and distribution, and a tacit acknowledgment of her own ambitions [to be a writer]" (Ibid. 5). The individual pieces in these volumes are by no means uniform in terms of content, style or artistic intention. In general terms, the earlier texts (1786 to 1790) are hilarious parodies, burlesques and satires of the language, characters, and plot devices of the sentimental, romantic and Gothic novels which she and members of her family devoured enthusiastically. Her plots are full of coincidental meetings, improbable escapes, terrible accidents, 'flexible' handling of chronology, and contrived happy endings. In contrast, the later texts (*Evelyn*; *Kitty, or the Bower*; and *The Three Sisters*) show a move *toward* more detailed and sustained narratives that develop believable characters in order to mock the absurd values and behaviors in society rather than in bad novels. Isobel Grundy writes that, "From an early age, she read like a potential author. She looked for what she could use – not by quietly absorbing and reflecting it, but by actively engaging, rewriting, often mocking it" (quoted in Harman 3-4). Her heroines are either the very opposite of the young lady of sensibility (that is, girls who behave badly, their unrestrained behavior breaking every rule of good manners and law), or they are young ladies in whom sensibility has been heightened to an absurd level (that is, girls who form life-long friendships with young women at first meeting; feel compelled to tell their life stories whenever requested to do so; fall in love at first sight; pride themselves on their superior sensibility, which they prove by fainting and running mad on the slightest provocation; and despise the judgment of parents and all those in positions of authority).

Emily Auerbach describes the voice of the Juvenilia as displaying "irreverence towards authority" (58) indicating a writer who was an "irreverent, impudent, caustic, and funny rebel, as sarcastic as they come, delighting in silly and severe expressions ridiculing the faults of others" (67). Thus, in *Frederic and Elfrida*, the heroine, "the lovely Charlotte," wakes up one morning to the recollection that she has agreed on the previous day to marry two men. Oppressed by her folly, she determines on a yet greater act of folly, and "to that end threw herself into a deep stream which ran through her aunt's pleasure grounds in Portland Place." Against the rules of geography and gravity, Charlotte's body floats all the way to her home in Crankhumdunberry where she is buried with an epitaph of "sweet lines, as pathetic as beautiful."

The voice of these texts is ironic and occasionally satirical as in the description of Sir George and Lady Harcourt who at the start of *Henry and Eliza* "were superintending the labours of their haymakers, rewarding the industry of some with smiles and approbation, and punishing the idleness of others, by the cudgel…" The humor here comes from the ironic disjunction between the picture of the benevolent Harcourts in the first part of the sentence and their use of a cudgel (a deliberately extreme weapon) in the second half.

Claire Harman describes Austen's stories as "pastiches of sentimental literature … knockabout comedies full of abductions, abandonments, exotic accidents, adultery, and death (all the sort of spicy drama that is absent or carefully backgrounded in her adult fiction)" (12-13). Brian Southam, however, points to a serious purpose behind the knockabout comedy, "the impulse behind Jane Austen's attack [on the novel of sentiment] was not merely that of amused contempt. With many eighteenth century critics she believed that the indulgence of emotion was a dangerous example in literature as in life. She also believed that literature is properly a means to truth, and that truth is to be found in the realms of common sense and real life, not in the romantic delusions of sentimentalism" (*Manuscripts* 9). Her heroines are either of such heightened sensibility that they self-destruct, like Laura and Sophia who "fainted alternately on a sofa," until the latter faints once too often on the damp ground and dies of "galloping consumption" (*Love and Friendship*), or so opposite to the socially acceptable feminine stereotype as to satirize the conduct books which prescribed appropriate behavior for young women, like the sixteen-year-old Cassandra who steals a bonnet, refuses to pay for the six ices she consumes, hires a carriage she has not money to pay for, and finally returns home after a day she considers to have been well spent. Or Anna Parker who explains at the start of her story, "I murdered my father at a very early period of my life, I have since murdered my mother, and I am now going to murder my sister" (*A Letter from a Young Lady*). These rebellious young women say and do the things that all teenagers merely dream of.

Halperin points to a change in the later *Juvenilia* (1791 to 1793) towards social satire in which Austen's "ridicule ... mockery ... contempt even, which emphasizes the faults and vices of others" is turned upon the real world rather than the world of fiction (36). The heroine of *Kitty, or The Bower* thus laments the fate of her friend Miss Wynne who being, on the death of her father, left without an inheritance is shipped off by her relatives to the East Indies where she is "[s]plendidly, yet unhappily married. United to a man of double her own age, whose disposition was not amiable, and whose manners were unpleasing, though his character was respectable." Later, the voice of the narrator uses similar irony to describe the conventional education of Miss Stanley who "was not inelegant in her appearance, rather handsome, and naturally not deficient in abilities; but those years which ought to have been spent in the attainment of useful knowledge and mental improvement, had been all bestowed in learning drawing, Italian and music ... and she now united to these accomplishments, an understanding unimproved by reading and a mind totally devoid of taste or judgement." Here we see the young Austen turning her attention to the same social and personal issues which are central to *Pride and Prejudice*. Kathryn Sutherland describes the themes of *Kitty* as:

> the criticism of fashionable accomplishments over proper education for women; the limited prospects for middle-class girls without fortune; and the championship of the novel as the legitimate vehicle for the expression on women's views ... After the freakish comedy of the earlier juvenilia, where active heroines, by force of energy and will, turn their little worlds upside down, we sense in 'Kitty, or the Bower' a satire more reflective of things as they are and, in consequence, more effective. (Vol.3 5-6)

By the time she had completed *Volume the Third*, Jane Austen had passed her apprenticeship; she still had much to learn, but she was ready to begin writing novel-length works that really were, as her father wrote in *Volume the Third*, "Effusions of fancy by a very young lady consisting of tales in a style entirely new." It was a style that would change the course of the English novel.

The Voice of the Letters – A Digression

Readers who are not familiar with the letters of Jane Austen will find in them the closest parallel to the comic voice of the juvenilia. The surviving letters were written to Austen's sister Cassandra, to her brothers, or other close relatives and friends. Readers are often disappointed by their triviality since they contain no great wisdom about either art or life and very few references to the events of her times, while we learn exactly who was at every ball Austen attended and how many times she danced, and what dress material she bought and for whom.

A more substantial objection to the letters (and one that is more relevant to our purpose) is that Austen's delight in mocking absurdity, arrogance, ugliness, mannerisms, pretention, and affectation, which so delights the reader of her novels, is seen to be less acceptable when it refers to real people and real suffering. Her tone (except, of course, when she is writing about serious matters such as the death of her father) is ironic, sarcastic, cynical, caustic, and occasionally downright malicious. The reader can innocently smile at the cynical humor of the generalized assertion that, "Single Women have a dreadful propensity for being poor – which is one very strong argument in favour of Matrimony…" (to her niece, Fanny Knight, March 13th, 1817). However, when Austen focuses upon named individuals, some readers feel guilty about laughing. Here are five examples, taken from letters to Cassandra, in descending order of acceptability and taste:

> Dr. Hall is in such deep mourning that either his mother, his wife or himself must be dead. (May 17th, 1799)
> Only think of Mrs. Holder being dead! Poor woman, she has done the only thing in the world she could possibly do to make one cease to abuse her. (October 14th, 1813)
> Mr. Waller is dead I see;-I cannot greive about it, nor perhaps can his Widow very much. (June 20th, 1808)
> Kill poor Mrs. Sclater if you like it while you are at Manydown. (9th February 1813)
> Mrs. Hall of Sherbourne, was brought to bed yesterday of a dead child, some weeks before she expected, owing to a fright. I suppose she happened unawares to look at her husband. (October 27th, 1798)

If the comedy of such remarks (and they are *very* funny) makes the reader uncomfortable because it appears not to be consistent with his/her image of Aunt Jane, who "never uttered either a hasty, a silly, or a severe expression" (Henry Austen "Biographical Note," Southam *Heritage* 75), then it is that image which is at fault and not the real Austen.

It is well to remember that Austen's letters were never intended to be seen by anyone other than their recipients, and that Austen's most outrageous statements are in letters to her sister. On September 1st, 1796, Austen praises Cassandra writing, "The letter which I have this moment received from you has diverted me beyond moderation. I could die of laughter at it, as they used to say at school. You are indeed the finest comic writer of the present age." Remember too that Cassandra, traditionally regarded as more straight-laced than her younger sister, who destroyed so many of the letters and cut portions from others, saw nothing to object to in such passages. It should also be noted that Austen turned the same wit against herself. In her last illness, she wrote, "Sickness is a dangerous Indulgence at my time of Life" (to Caroline Austen, March 23rd, 1817), and "I am now really a very genteel, portable sort of Invalid" (to Anne Sharp, May 22nd, 1817).

Both the letters and the *Juvenilia* serve as evidence of Mitton's conclusion that "Jane Austen stands absolutely alone, unapproached, in a quality in which women are usually supposed to be deficient, a humorous and brilliant insight into the foibles of human nature, and a strong sense of the ridiculous" (1).

Volume the First

The first notebook contains sixteen pieces. It is impossible to date the original composition of most of these texts with any certainty, nor is it particularly helpful to do so. However, they appear to be arranged in a generally chronological sequence and to fall into three periods:

> 1787-1789: *Frederic and Elfrida, Edgar and Emma, Henry and Eliza, Sir William Montague, Memoirs of Mr. Clifford, The Beautiful Cassandra, Amelia Webster, The Visit, The Mystery;*
> 1790-1791: *Jack and Alice, The Adventures of Mr. Hartley, The Three Sisters;*
> 1793: *A Fragment, A Beautiful Description, The Generous Curate, Ode to Pity.*

The handwriting of the first eleven texts is immature suggesting that transcription was begun shortly after the works were first completed. The remaining five texts are in a more mature hand. Describing the earliest juvenilia, Brian Southam writes:

> [They are] the work of a high-spirited child set on amusement, delighting in knockabout farce, fanciful extravagance, solemn nonsense, and word-play … the wit is shrewdly applied in exposing the false values and absurd conventions of sentimental fiction, and in general the flaws of bad writing … the abundance of confidants, the recital of life-stories, the melodramatic succession of catastrophes, the interpolation of songs and poems, the egotistic heroines, the rhapsodical style, the technical weakness of clumsy plotting, improbable action, neglect of time scale, inconsequence and digression. (*Manuscripts* 21)

[Dedications]

For my brother Charles: I think I recollect that a few of the trifles in this volume were written expressly for his amusement. C.E.A.[1]

To Miss Lloyd[2]
My Dear Martha,

As a small testimony of the gratitude I feel for your late generosity to me in finishing my muslin cloak, I beg leave to offer you this little production of your sincere friend

The Author

Frederic and Elfrida – a novel

Chapter the First

The uncle of Elfrida was the ~~mother~~ father of Frederic; in other words, they were first cousins by the father's side[3].

Being both born in one day and both brought up at one school, it was not wonderful that they should look on each other with something more than bare politeness. They loved with mutual sincerity, but were both determined not to transgress the rules of propriety by owning their attachment, either to the object beloved, or to anyone else. They were exceedingly handsome and so much alike, that it was not everyone who knew them apart. – Nay, even their most intimate friends had nothing to distinguish them by, but the shape of the face, the colour of the eye, the length of the nose, and the difference of the complexion.

Elfrida had an intimate friend to whom, being on a visit to an aunt, she wrote the following letter:

To Miss Drummond

Dear Charlotte,

I should be obliged to you, if you would buy me, during your stay with Mrs. Williamson, a new and fashionable bonnet, to suit the complexion of your

E. Falknor

Charlotte, whose character was a willingness to oblige everyone, when she returned into the country, brought her friend the wished-for bonnet, and so ended this little adventure, much to the satisfaction of all parties.

On her return to Crankhumdunberry (of which sweet village her father was Rector[4]), Charlotte was received with the greatest joy by Frederic and Elfrida, who, after pressing her alternately to their bosoms, proposed to her to take a walk in a grove of poplars which led from the parsonage to a verdant lawn enameled ~~by~~ with a variety of variegated flowers and watered by a purling stream, brought from the Valley of Tempé[5] by a passage underground.

In this grove they had scarcely remained above nine hours, when they were suddenly agreeably surprised by hearing a most delightful voice warble the following stanza.

SONG

That Damon[6] was in love with me
I once thought and believ'd

But now that he is not I see,
I fear I was deciev'd.

No sooner were the lines finished than they beheld by a turning in the grove two elegant young women leaning on each other's arm, who immediately on perceiving them, took a different path and disappeared from their sight.

Chapter the Second

As Elfrida and her companions had seen enough of them to know that they were neither the two Miss Greens, nor Mrs. Jackson and her daughter, they could not help expressing their surprise at their appearance; till at length recollecting, that a new family had lately taken a house not far from the grove, they hastened home, determined to lose no time in forming an acquaintance with two such amiable and worthy girls, of which family they rightly imagined them to be a part.

Agreeable to such a determination, they went that very evening to pay their respects to Mrs. Fitzroy and her two daughters. On being shown into an elegant dressing room, ornamented with festoons of artificial flowers, they were struck with the engaging exterior and beautiful outside of Jezalinda, the eldest of the young ladies; but ere they had been many minutes seated, the wit and charms which shone resplendent in the conversation of the amiable Rebecca enchanted them so much that they all with one accord jumped up and exclaimed:

"Lovely and too charming fair one, notwithstanding your forbidding squint, your greasy tresses and your swelling back, which are more frightful than imagination can paint or pen describe, I cannot refrain from expressing my raptures, at the engaging qualities of your mind, which so amply atone for the horror with which your first appearance must ever inspire the unwary visitor.

"Your sentiments so nobly expressed on the different excellencies of Indian and English muslins[7], and the judicious preference you give the former, have excited in me an admiration of which I can alone give an adequate idea, by assuring you it is nearly equal to what I feel for myself."

Then making a profound curtsey to the amiable and abashed Rebecca, they left the room and hurried home.

From this period, the intimacy between the families of Fitzroy, Drummond, and Falknor daily increased, till at length it grew to such a pitch, that they did not scruple to kick one another out of the window on the slightest provocation.

During this happy state of harmony, the eldest Miss Fitzroy ran off with the coachman and the amiable Rebecca was asked in marriage by Captain Roger of Buckinghamshire.

Mrs. Fitzroy did not approve of the match on account of the tender years of the young couple, Rebecca being but thirty-six and Captain Roger little more than sixty-three. To remedy this objection, it was agreed that they should wait a little while till they were a good deal older.

Chapter the Third

In the meantime, the parents of Frederic proposed to those of Elfrida a union between them, which being accepted with pleasure, the wedding clothes were bought and nothing remained to be settled but the naming of the day.

As to the lovely Charlotte, being importuned with eagerness to pay another visit to her aunt, she determined to accept the invitation and in consequence of it walked to Mrs. Fitzroy's to take leave of the amiable Rebecca, whom she found surrounded by ~~rouge~~ patches[8], powder[9], pomatum[10], and paint[11], with which she was vainly endeavouring to remedy the natural plainness of her face.

"I am come, my amiable Rebecca, to take my leave of you for the fortnight I am destined to spend with my aunt. Believe me, this separation is painful to me, but it is as necessary as the labour which now engages you."

"Why to tell you the truth, my love," replied Rebecca, "I have lately taken it into my head to think (perhaps with little reason) that my complexion is by no means equal to the rest of my face and have therefore taken, as you see, to white and red paint which I would scorn to use on any other occasion, as I hate art[12]."

Charlotte, who perfectly understood the meaning of her friend's speech, was too good-temper'd and obliging to refuse her what she knew she wished – a compliment – and they parted the best friends in the world.

With a heavy heart and streaming eyes did she ascend the lovely vehicle[13] which bore her from her friends and home; but grieved as she was, she little thought ~~of~~ in what a strange and different manner she ~~would~~ should return to it.

On her entrance into the city of London, which was the place of Mrs. Williamson's abode, the postilion[14], whose stupidity was amazing, declared and declared even without the least shame or compunction, that having never been informed, he was totally ignorant of what part of the town he was to drive to.

Charlotte, whose nature we have before intimated was an earnest desire to oblige every one, with the greatest condescension and good humour informed him that he was to drive to Portland Place[15], which he accordingly did and Charlotte soon found herself in the arms of a fond aunt.

Scarcely were they seated as usual, in the most affectionate manner in one chair, than the door suddenly opened and an aged gentleman with a sallow face and old pink coat[16], partly by intention and partly through weakness was at the feet of the lovely Charlotte, declaring his attachment to her and beseeching her pity in the most moving manner.

Not being able to resolve to make any one miserable, she consented to become his wife; where upon the gentleman left the room and all was quiet.

Their quiet, however, continued but a short time, for on a second opening of the door a young and handsome gentleman with a new blue coat[16] ~~and~~ entered and entreated from the lovely Charlotte, permission to pay to her his addresses.

There was a something in the appearance of the second stranger that influenced Charlotte in his favour, to the full as much as the appearance of the first: she could not account for it, but so it was.

Having therefore, agreeable to that and the natural turn of her mind to make everyone happy, promised to become his wife the next morning, he took his leave and the two ladies sat down to supper on a young leveret, a brace of partridges, a leash of pheasants and a dozen of pigeons[17].

Chapter the Fourth

It was not till the next morning that Charlotte recollected the double engagement she had entered into; but when she did, the reflection of her past folly operated so strongly on her mind, that she resolved to be guilty of a greater, and to that end threw herself into a deep stream which ran through her aunt's pleasure grounds in Portland Place.

She floated to Crankhumdunberry where she was picked up and buried; the following epitaph, composed by Frederic, Elfrida and Rebecca, was placed on her tomb.

EPITAPH
Here lies our friend who having promised
That unto two she would be married

Threw her sweet body and her lovely face
Into the stream that runs through Portland Place.

These sweet lines, as pathetic as beautiful, were never read by anyone who passed that way, without a shower of tears, which if they should fail of exciting in you, Reader, your mind must be unworthy to peruse them.

Having performed the last sad office to their departed friend, Frederic and Elfrida together with Captain Roger and Rebecca returned to Mrs. Fitzroy's, at whose feet they threw themselves with one accord and addressed her in the following manner:

"Madam,

"When the sweet Captain Roger ~~must~~ first addressed the amiable Rebecca, you alone objected to their union on account of the tender years of the parties. That plea can be no more, seven days being now expired, together with the lovely Charlotte, since the Captain first spoke to you on the subject.

"Consent then Madam to their union and as a reward, this smelling bottle which I enclose in my right hand, shall be yours and yours forever; I never will claim it again. But if you refuse to join their hands in three days' time, this dagger which I enclose in my left shall be steeped in your heart's blood.

"Speak then, Madam, and decide their fate and yours."

Such gentle and sweet persuasion could not fail of having the desired effect. The answer they received was this:

"My dear young friends,

"The arguments you have used are too just and too eloquent to be withstood; Rebecca, in three days' time, you shall be united to the Captain."

This speech, than which nothing could be more satisfactory, was received with joy by all; and peace being once more restored on all sides, Captain Roger entreated Rebecca to favour them with a song, in compliance with which request, having first assured them that she had a terrible cold, she sung as follows:

SONG

When Corydon[6] went to the fair
  He bought a red ribbon for Bess,
With which she encircled her hair
  And made herself look very fess[18].

Chapter the Fifth

At the end of three days Captain Roger and Rebecca were united, and immediately after the ceremony set off in the stage wagon[19] for the Captain's seat in Buckinghamshire.

The parents of Elfrida, although they earnestly wished to see her married to Frederic before they died, yet knowing the delicate frame of her mind could ill bear the least exertion and rightly judging that naming her wedding day would be too great a one, forbore to press her on the subject.

Weeks and fortnights flew away without gaining the least ground; the clothes grew out of fashion and at length Capt. Roger and his lady arrived, to pay a visit to their mother and introduce to her their beautiful daughter of eighteen.

Elfrida, who had found her former acquaintance were growing too old and too ugly to be any longer agreeable, was rejoiced to hear of the arrival of so pretty a girl as Eleanor, with whom she determined to form the strictest friendship.

But the happiness she had expected from an acquaintance with Eleanor, she soon found was not to be received, for she had not only the mortification of finding herself treated by her as little less than an old woman, but had actually the horror of perceiving a growing passion in the bosom of Frederic for the daughter of the amiable Rebecca.

The instant she had the first idea of such an attachment, she flew to Frederic and in a manner truly heroic[20], spluttered out to him her intention of being married the next day.

To one in his predicament who possessed less personal courage than Frederic was master of, such a speech would have been death; but he, not being the least terrified, boldly replied:

"Damn me, Elfrida, you may be married tomorrow, but I won't."

This answer distressed her too much for her delicate constitution. She accordingly fainted and was in such a hurry to have a succession of fainting fits that she had scarcely patience enough to recover from one before she fell into another.

Though in any threatening danger to his life or liberty, Frederic was as bold as brass, yet in other respects his heart was as soft as cotton and immediately on hearing of the dangerous way Elfrida was in, he flew to her and finding her better than he had been taught to expect, was united to her forever. —

Finis

Notes

1. "For my brother Charles … C.E.A.": These words are written in ink on a slip of paper pasted to the inner cover that largely obscures the words "For my brother Charles" written beneath in pencil. Cassandra Elizabeth Austen (1773-1845) left *Volume the First* to the youngest of the six Austen brothers, Charles John Austen (1779-1852). Charles was a favorite with the sisters; writing to Cassandra on January 21st, 1799, Jane referred to him as, "Our own particular little brother." In 1801, Charles earned a bounty of £40 for taking an enemy ship and used some of it to purchase for his sisters two gold chains and topaz crosses. In a letter to Cassandra, Jane wrote, "I shall write again by this post to thank and reproach him. We shall be unbearably fine" (May 27th).

2. "Miss Lloyd": Martha Lloyd (1765-1843) was the sister of James Austen's wife. Martha became friends with the Austen sisters in the spring of 1789. In 1805, after her own mother died, she came to live permanently with Mrs. Austen, Cassandra, and Jane, first in Southampton and later in Chawton. This dedication was added later on a page which had been left blank for the purpose. The handwriting is noticeably more mature than that of the novel. Muslin was fashionable in the late 1780's and 1790s.

3. Being cousins on the father's side, the two have the same family name, Falknor. Had they been cousins on the mother's side, their surnames would have been different. Marriage between first cousins was quite common. Notice that the names of the two lovers are near anagrams. Since schools for the sons and daughters of gentry were always single-sex, it is an impossibility that the two had "one school" – unless they went to a village Dame school catering for the sons and daughters of ordinary laborers.

4. "Rector": A rector (or vicar) was an Anglican clergyman in charge of a parish and in receipt of the annual parish tithes.

5. "Valley of Tempé": A mock-grandiose classical reference to Tempe in Thessaly, Northern Greece, which was associated with the god Apollo.

6. "Damon … Corydon": Names associated with the classical pastoral literary tradition. Damon was a peerless youth whose death Corydon mourned (see: "A Pastoral Between Thirsis And Corydon, Upon The Death Of Damon, By Whom Is Meant Mr. W. Riddell" by James Thomson). In *Little Dorrit* (1855-1857) Charles Dickens described songs such as Jane Austen is satirizing here, as "pale and vapid little songs, long out of date, about Chloe, and Phyllis, and Strephon being wounded by the son of Venus [i.e. Cupid]" (Ch. 31).

7. "'Indian and English muslins'": Muslin, a light cotton cloth, was traditionally manufactured in Bengal from where it was exported to Europe during the seventeenth century. In the 1770s and 1780s, Bengal suffered a number of natural disasters (famine and floods), and high tariffs were imposed on textiles coming from Bengal to Britain. In the same period, the Industrial Revolution had boosted the production of high quality cotton cloth in Britain.

8. "patches": Beauty patches became popular in the seventeenth century originally to cover a defect in the complexion and then to accentuate a point of facial beauty. Made from expensive fabrics such as silk or velvet and coated with adhesive to hold them in place, patches came in decorative shapes such as crescents, hearts and stars.

9. "powder": For the hair.

10. "pomatum": Pomade, a perfumed hair-styling cream.

11. "paint": Rouge, used not only on the lips but to give the face a ruddy complexion. White was used on the neck.

12. "art": Artifice, artfulness.

13. "vehicle": Austen's own footnote: "1. A post-chaise" – that is a four-wheeled carriage with one seat that could accommodate one to three passengers. Post chaises could be hired, with driver and horses which were changed at intervals (or posts). This is meant to be a comic anti-climax. In *Northanger Abbey*, Austen writes: "A heroine in a hack post-chaise is such a blow upon sentiment, as no attempt at grandeur or pathos can withstand" (Ch. 29).

14. "postilion": A man who rides the leading near-side horse of a team pulling a carriage to guide it.

15. "Portland Place": An exceptionally wide street of elegant, exclusive Georgian terraced houses in Central London originally designed and built by the Adams brothers for the Duke of Portland in the 1770s. The houses did not, however, have pleasure gardens and there was no stream running through as the story later describes.

16. "old pink coat … new blue coat": A blue coat was considered the height of masculine fashion – in contrast with an "old pink coat" which is a sure sign of her first lover being dressed in the foppish manner of decades before. In *Pride and Prejudice*, when Bingley first visits Mr. Bennet, he "wore a blue coat and rode a black horse" (Ch. 3), and Lydia says, "'I was thinking, you may suppose, of my dear Wickham. I longed to know whether he would be married in his blue coat'" (Ch. 51).

17. This is a very large amount of game for two just ladies. Gluttony and over-eating is a theme throughout the juvenilia.

18. "fess": Hampshire dialect meaning: gay, lively, elated, in high spirits.

19. "stage wagon": A cheap but slow form of public carriage with rows of benches for the occupants.

20. "heroic": Austen used the word 'heroic' mockingly to describe the absurd histrionics of women given to an excess of sentiment. In *Northanger Abbey*, when Catherine Morland, "who had by nature nothing heroic about her," sees Henry Tilney with another woman, she does not turn to "a deathlike paleness" or fall "in a fit on Mrs. Allen's bosom," she merely blushes (Ch. 1). On another occasion, we are told that "Feelings rather natural than heroic possessed her" (Ch. 12). Similarly, when Emma discovers that Mr. Knightley loves her, not Harriet Smith, we read "of that heroism of sentiment which

might have prompted her to entreat him to transfer his affection from herself to Harriet ... – Emma had it not" (Ch. 49). For Austen, the heroic was one of those false virtues promoted by the sentimental novel, about which her views were similar to those expressed by Clara Reeve in *The School for Widows* (1791):

> The word [sentimental], like many others, seems to have degenerated from its original meaning; and, under this flimsy disguise, it has given rise to a great number of whining, maudlin stories, full of false sentiment and false delicacy, calculated to excite a kind of morbid sensibility, which is to faint under every ideal distress, and every fantastical trial; which have a tendency to weaken the mind, and to deprive it of those resources which Nature intended it should find within itself. (Quoted in Litz 8)

Commentary

Frederic and Elfrida is a parody of the absurdities of the sentimental and heroic literary conventions to be found in (bad) novels of the period. The narrative skips from one improbable scene to the next with only the most perfunctory effort to link them with plausible causality. The point is the individual scenes, and sometimes the individual jokes, to which characterization and plot are sacrificed.

The novel begins with comic understatement and circumlocution. Instead of simply saying that Frederic and Elfrida are in love, the narrator writes, "Being both born in one day and both brought up at one school, it was not wonderful that they should look on each other with something more than bare politeness." We are then told that the lovers, aware of "the rules of propriety," keep knowledge of their love not only from their friends but from each other! Notice that Austen adds this comic detail as an afterthought. Joke number three is that the two lovers are "so much alike" that even their closest friends cannot tell one from the other, since the only differences between them are: gender, shape of face, eye color, and complexion. In other words, everything!

Quite arbitrarily, Charlotte is introduced. Her key character trait is that she has "a willingness to oblige everyone." Charlotte's character is a parody of the way in which young women are taught to behave – all good temper and willingness to please. This will later lead to comic tragedy, but here it extends only to purchasing for Elfrida a bonnet – which is, indeed, a very "little adventure." These characters lead quiet and sheltered lives!

Chance meetings are the staple of sentimental fiction, and here the three friends enter what appears to be a magical landscape straight from Classical Greek literature. Austen delights in writing something absurd as though it were the most normal thing in the world, and so she tells us that, having been in the grove "scarcely ... above nine hours," they hear a beautiful, melancholy song of lost love. The three friends are intrigued to discover the singer, and the reader is intrigued to discover the singer, but no sooner are two elegant ladies seen than, aware of having been seen, they take "a different path and disappeared."

Thus are introduced the two Miss Fitzroys, Jezalinda and Rebecca, which provides an opportunity to parody social conventions because, of course, Frederic, Elfrida and Charlotte must pay a formal visit on the family that has just moved into the neighborhood. (Remember the etiquette of visiting from Chapter 1 of *Pride and Prejudice*.) Ironic juxtaposition [i.e., placing two contrasting things side by side] is a device Austen uses repeatedly for comic effect. Here we have the elegant language of excessive compliment juxtaposed with the blunt language of insult, "Lovely and too charming fair one, not withstanding your forbidding squint, your greasy tresses and your swelling back, which are more frightful than imagination can paint or pen describe, I cannot refrain from expressing my raptures at the engaging qualities of your mind, which so amply atone for the horror with which your first appearance must inspire the unwary visitor."

Once again, Austen delights in presenting the absurd as though it were commonplace. Thus she writes, "From this period, the intimacy between the two families ... daily increased till at length it grew to such a pitch that they did not scruple to kick one another out of the window upon the slightest provocation." Similarly, we are told that "During this happy state of harmony, the eldest Miss Fitzroy ran off with the coachman and the amiable Rebecca was asked in marriage by Captain Roger of Buckinghamshire." Jezalinda's shockingly inappropriate action rather puts into question the "harmony" that the narrator has described, and coupling her scandalous elopement with a servant with the socially appropriate proposal that her sister receives implies that they are comparable, which they are certainly not.

The absurd humor of Mrs. Fitzroy's objection to the match between Rebecca (aged 36) and Captain Roger (aged 63) on the ground of their youth is emphasized by the comic oxymoron [i.e., putting two contradictory words or ideas side by side for comic effect] that the two lovers "should wait a *little* while till they were a *good deal* older" (emphasis added). Fairly obviously, if they only wait a little while, they can become only a little older!

The narrative now switches quite arbitrarily to the story of Charlotte's visit to London. Before Charlotte leaves, she bids farewell to Rebecca, which allows the narrator, as Emily Auerbach puts it, "to expose the discrepancy between what people say and what they mean, what they proscribe for others and what they practice themselves, what they pretend and what they know to be true" (57). First the narrator herself implies that no amount of cosmetics can improve the face of Rebecca who is described as "surrounded by patches, powder, pomatum, and paint, with which she was vainly endeavouring to remedy the natural plainness of her face." Notice here how the alliteration of the letter 'p' weighs four cosmetics against the single plainness of the lady's face. When Charlotte tells her friend, "this separation is painful to me, but it is

41

as necessary as the labour which now engages you," she seems unaware of how insulting she is being, just as Rebecca seems unaware of being self-deceptive in declaring that, but for concern for her plain complexion, she would never use cosmetics since she hates "art." Everything about the encounter is comically false including Rebecca's final fishing for a compliment which Charlotte is obliging enough to give her, thus ensuring that "they parted the best friends in the world."

The narrator mocks Charlotte's pretentions by naming the vehicle in which she travels to London and describing the postilion's stupidity in not knowing to where in London he is going. Charlotte's "greatest condescension and good humour" in putting him right is praised, yet the intention is ironic, for it is Charlotte who should have told him where he was going in the first place!

The black comedy of her death rests on the poor girl's willingness to please others at the expense of her own feelings and desires The proposal scene begins with the absurd description of Charlotte and her aunt sitting "as usual in the most affectionate manner in one chair." There is nothing "usual" about it. Almost grotesquely comic is the vision of the old suitor falling at Charlotte's feet in the prescribed manner, but doing so only "partly by intention and partly through weakness." Poor Charlotte takes her compliance with the wishes of others to the absurd length of accepting two proposals of marriage within minutes of each other without realizing that in doing so she has made promises that she cannot keep.

Josephine Ross says of Austen that "The tempering of profound sensibility with sound good sense – the balancing of the Romantic with the rational – remained … her formula for ultimate feminine happiness and fulfillment" (136). This is illustrated in the negative by the fate of Charlotte. When the narrator tells us that "the reflection of [Charlotte's] past folly operated so strongly on her mind, that she resolved to be guilty of a greater," we realize that "mind" has nothing, and feeling everything, to do with her decision to commit suicide which "shows the menaces of sensibility taken to an extreme" (Tyler 37). In defiance of all we know about geography, Charlotte's body floats to her home parish. The mock-pathetic lines of the epitaph are a triumph of mawkishness, but the narrator denounces any reader who is not driven to tears as having a "mind … unworthy to peruse them."

Abruptly, the narrative returns to Captain Roger and Rebecca. The four friends throw themselves at the feet of Mrs. Fitzroy in the approved manner of supplicants and argue that her sole objection to the marriage (the youth of the two lovers) can no longer be valid "seven days being now expired, together with the lovely Charlotte." Notice how the verb "expired" applies both to the passing of a week and to the passing of Charlotte, two events with very different emotional connotations. (The term for this rhetorical device where one word, usually a verb, is made to apply to two different words, usually nouns, with comic effect is syllepsis.) This 'argument' is supported by a bribe

42

and a threat – a bottle of smelling salts as a gift and a dagger ready to be "steeped" in the mother's "heart's blood" as the threat With tongue firmly in cheek, the narrator comments, "Such gentle and sweet persuasion could not fail of having the desired effect," and Mrs. Fitzroy similarly calls the "arguments" used "too just and too eloquent to be withstood." All is well, and Rebecca, despite admitting to a "terrible cold" sings a song which appears to have nothing to do with anything except that a character like her in a situation like this is expected to burst into song.

The final chapter returns to the lovers who give the novel its title. Elfrida's parents wish her to marry Frederic, which given her love for him (and his for her) ought to be just what she wants. However, we *now* learn that Elfrida has a "delicate frame of her mind [that] could ill bear the least exertion" which makes her incapable of deciding on a marriage day. Clearly, the implication is that Elfrida fears the sexual "exertion" of the wedding night quite as much as she fears the "exertion" of preparing for the wedding itself. "Weeks and fortnights flew away" without a decision, but the reader is shocked to discover that, when Captain Roger and his lady arrive on their first visit to Mrs. Fitzroy since their marriage, they bring with them Eleanor their "beautiful daughter of eighteen."

Elfrida, who has noticed her friends "growing too old and too ugly to be any longer agreeable," plans (in the manner of sentimental heroines) to make Eleanor her special, confidential friend. What Elfrida has not understood, however, is that *she* herself has aged; she is shocked when Eleanor treats her "as little less than an old woman." Worst still, she detects in Frederic "a growing passion" for the attractive young woman.

Forgetting her aversion to "the least exertion," Elfrida flies to her lover's side and "in a manner truly heroic, spluttered out to him her intention of being married the next day." This comic inversion of gender roles is completed when Frederic takes the female part and rejects the lover's proposal – though his language is much more forceful that lovers normally use in novels, "Damn me, Elfrida, you may be married tomorrow, but I won't." Elfrida instantly reverts to the role of the female of excessive sensibility by fainting. The narrator implies something contrived in the performance by saying that Elfrida "was in such a hurry to have a succession of fainting fits that she had scarcely patience enough to recover from one before she fell into another." Frederic, ever tender-hearted to the fair sex, falls for her gambit and does not even recognize her emotional manipulation when he finds her "better than he had been taught to expect." The two marry and presumably live happily ever after.

Jack and Alice – a novel

Is respectfully inscribed to Francis William Austen
Esq., Midshipman on board his Majesty's Ship the
Perseverance[1] by his obedient humble servant
The Author

Chapter the First

Mr. Johnson was once upon a time about fifty-three; in a
twelve-months afterwards he was fifty-four, which so much
delighted him that he was determined to celebrate his next
birthday by giving a masquerade[2] to his children and friends.
Accordingly, on the day he attained his fifty-fifth year, tickets[3]
were dispatched to all his neighbours to that purpose. His
acquaintance indeed in that part of the world were not very
numerous, as they consisted only of Lady Williams, Mr. and
Mrs. Jones, Charles Adams and the three Miss Simpsons, who
composed the neighbourhood of Pammydiddle[4] and formed the
masquerade.

Before I proceed to give an account of the evening, it will be
proper to describe to my reader the persons and characters of
the party introduced to his acquaintance.

Mr. and Mrs. Jones were both rather tall[5] and very
passionate[6], but were in other respects good tempered, well-
behaved people. Charles Adams was an amiable, accomplished,
and bewitching young man; of so dazzling a beauty that none
but eagles could look him in the face.

Miss Simpson was pleasing in her person, in her manners,
and in her disposition; an unbounded ambition was her only
fault. Her second sister, Sukey[7], was envious, spiteful, and
malicious. Her person was short, fat and disagreeable. Cecilia
(the youngest) was perfectly handsome, but too affected[8] to be
agreeable pleasing.

In Lady Williams every virtue met. She was a widow with a
handsome jointure[9] and the remains of a very handsome face.
Though benevolent and candid, she was generous and sincere;
though pious and good, she was religious and amiable; and
though elegant and agreeable, she was polished and
entertaining.

Such was The Johnsons were a family of love, and though a
little addicted to the bottle and the dice[10], had many good
qualities.

Such was the party assembled in the elegant drawing room

of Johnson Court, amongst which the pleasing figure of a Sultana[11] was the most remarkable of the female masks. Of the males, a mask representing the Sun was the most universally admired. The beams that darted from his eyes were like those of that glorious luminary, though infinitely superior. So strong were they that no one dared venture within half a mile of them; he had therefore the best part of the room to himself, its size not amounting to more than three quarters of a mile in length and half a one in breadth. The gentleman at last finding the ~~inconvenience~~ fierceness of his beams to be very inconvenient to the concourse[12] ~~of masks~~ by obliging them to crowd together in one corner of the room, half shut his eyes, by which means the company discovered him to be Charles Adams in his plain green coat, without any mask at all.

When their astonishment was a little subsided, their attention was attracted by two Dominos[13] who advanced in a horrible passion; they were both very tall, but seemed in other respects to have many good qualities.

"These," said the witty Charles, "these are Mr. and Mrs. Jones," and so indeed they were.

No one could imagine who was the Sultana! Till at length, on her addressing a beautiful Flora who was reclining in a studied attitude on a couch with, "Oh Cecilia, I wish I was really what I pretend to be," she was discovered by the never failing genius of Charles Adams to be the elegant but ambitious Caroline Simpson, and the person to whom she addressed herself, he rightly imagined to be her lovely but affected sister Cecilia.

The company now advanced to a gaming table where sat three Dominos (each with a bottle ~~by his side~~ in their hand) deeply engaged; but a female in the character of Virtue fled with hasty footsteps from the shocking scene, whilst a little fat woman, representing Envy, sat alternately on the foreheads of the three gamesters[14]. Charles Adams was still as bright as ever; he soon discovered the party at play to be the three Johnsons, Envy to be Sukey Simpson, and Virtue to be Lady Williams.

The masks were then all removed and the company retired to another room, to partake of an elegant and well-managed entertainment, after which, the bottle being pretty briskly pushed about by the three Johnsons, the whole party (not excepting even Virtue) were carried home, dead drunk.

Chapter the Second

For three months did the masquerade afford ample subject for conversation to the inhabitants of Pammydiddle; but no character at it was so fully expatiated[15] on as Charles Adams. The singularity of his appearance, the beams which darted from his eyes, the brightness of his wit, and the whole *tout ensemble* of his person had subdued the hearts of so many of the young ladies, that of the six present at the masquerade but five had returned uncaptivated. Alice Johnson was the unhappy sixth whose heart had not been able to withstand the power of his charms. But as it may appear strange to my readers, that so much worth and excellence as he possessed should have conquered only hers, it will be necessary to inform them that the Miss Simpsons were defended from his power by ambition, envy, and self-admiration.

Every wish of Caroline was centered in a titled husband; whilst in Sukey such superior excellence could only raise her envy not her love, and Cecilia was too tenderly attached to herself to be pleased with anyone besides. As for Lady Williams and Mrs. Jones, the former of them was too sensible to fall in love with one so much her ~~inferior~~ junior, and the latter, though very tall and very passionate, was too fond of her husband to think of such a thing.

Yet in spite of every endeavour on the part of Miss Johnson to discover any attachment to her in him, the cold and indifferent heart of Charles Adams still, to all appearance, preserved its native freedom; polite to all but partial to none, he still remained the lovely, the lively, but insensible Charles Adams.

One evening, Alice finding herself somewhat heated by wine (no very uncommon case) determined to seek a relief for her disordered head and love-sick heart in the conversation of the intelligent Lady Williams.

She found her Ladyship at home, as was in general the case, for she was not fond of going out, and like the great Sir Charles Grandison[16] scorned to deny herself when at home, as she looked on that fashionable method of shutting out disagreeable visitors as little less than downright bigamy[17].

In spite of the wine she had been drinking, poor Alice was uncommonly out of spirits; she could think of nothing but Charles Adams, she could talk of nothing but him, and in short spoke so openly that Lady Williams soon ~~per~~ discovered the unreturned affection she bore him, which excited her pity and compassion so strongly that she addressed her in the following manner.

"I perceive but too plainly, my dear Miss Johnson, that your heart has not been able to withstand the fascinating charms of this young man and I pity you sincerely. Is it a first love?"

"It is."

"I am still more grieved to hear that; I am myself a sad example of the miseries in general attendant on a first love, and I am determined for the future to avoid the like misfortune. I wish it may not be too late for you to do the same; if it is not, endeavour, my dear girl, to secure yourself from so great a danger. A second attachment is seldom attended with any serious consequences; against *that* therefore I have nothing to say. Preserve yourself from a first love and you need not fear a second."

"You mentioned, Madam, something of your having yourself been a sufferer by the misfortune you are so good as to wish me to avoid. Will you favour me with your life and adventures?"

"Willingly, my love."

Chapter the Third

"My father was a gentleman of considerable fortune in Berkshire[18]; myself and a few more his only children. I was but six years old when I had the misfortune of losing my mother, and being at that time young and tender, my father, instead of sending me to school, procured an able-handed governess to superintend my education at home. My brothers were placed at schools suitable to their ages and my sisters, being all younger than myself, remained still under the care of their nurse.

"Miss Dickins was an excellent governess. She instructed me in the paths of virtue; under her tuition I daily became more amiable, and had not might perhaps by this time have nearly attained perfection, had not my worthy preceptoress been torn from my arms, e'er I had attained my seventeenth year. I never shall forget her last words. 'My dear Kitty,' she said, 'Good night t'ye.' I never saw her afterwards," continued Lady Williams, wiping her eyes. "She eloped with the butler the same night.

"I was invited the following Xmas year by a distant relation of my father's to spend the winter with her in town[19]. Mrs. Watkins was a lady of fashion, family, and fortune; she was in general esteemed a pretty woman, but I never thought her very handsome, for my part. She had too high a forehead, her eyes were too small, and she had too much colour."

"How can that be?" interrupted Miss Johnson, reddening with anger. "Do you think that anyone can have too much colour?"

"Indeed I do, and I'll tell you why I do, my dear Alice; when a person has too great a degree of red in their complexion, it gives their face, in my opinion, too ~~much colour~~ red a look."

"But can a face, my Lady, have too red a look?"

"Certainly, my dear Miss Johnson, and I'll tell you why. When a face has too red a look it does not appear to so much advantage as it would were it paler."

"Pray Ma'am, proceed in your story."

"Well, as I said before, I was invited by this lady to spend some weeks with her in town. Many gentlemen thought her handsome, but in my opinion, her forehead was too high, ~~his~~ her eyes too small, and she had too much colour."

"In that, Madam, as I said before, your Ladyship must have been mistaken. Mrs. Watkins could not have too much colour, since no one can have too much."

"Excuse me, my love, if I do not agree with you in that particular. Let me explain myself clearly; my ~~ideas~~ of the case ~~are these~~ is this. When a woman has too great a proportion of red in her cheeks, she must have too much colour."

"But Madam, I deny that it is possible for anyone to have too great a proportion of red in their cheeks."

"What, my love, not if they have too much colour?"

Miss Johnson was now out of all patience, the more so, perhaps, as Lady Williams still remained so inflexibly cool. It must be remembered, however, that her Ladyship had in one respect by far the advantage of Alice; I mean in not being drunk, for heated with wine and raised by passion, she could have little command of her temper.

The dispute at length grew so hot on the part of Alice that "from words ~~they~~ she almost came to blows," when Mr. Johnson luckily entered, and with some difficulty forced her away ~~his daughter~~ from Lady Williams, Mrs. Watkins, and her red cheeks.

Chapter the Fourth

My readers may perhaps imagine that after such a fracas, no intimacy could longer subsist between the Johnsons and Lady Williams, but in that they are mistaken; for her Ladyship was too sensible to be angry at a conduct which she could not help perceiving to be the natural consequence of inebriety, and Alice had too sincere a respect for Lady Williams, and too great a relish for her claret, not to make every concession in her power.

A few days after their reconciliation, ~~her Ladyship~~ Lady Williams called on Miss Johnson to propose a walk in a citron grove[20] which led from her Ladyship's pigsty to Charles Adams's horsepond[21]. Alice was too sensible of Lady Williams's kindness in proposing such a walk, and too much pleased with the prospect of seeing at the end of it a horsepond of Charles's, not to accept it with visible delight. They had not proceeded far before she was roused from ~~a~~ the reflection of the happiness she was going to enjoy, by Lady Williams thus addressing her:

"I have as yet forborne, my dear Alice, to continue the narrative of my life, from an unwillingness of recalling to your memory a scene which (since it reflects on you rather disgrace than credit) had better be forgot than remembered."

Alice had already begun to colour up, and was beginning to speak, when her Ladyship, perceiving her displeasure, continued thus:

"I am afraid, my dear girl, that I have offended you by what I have just said; I assure you I do not mean to distress you by a retrospection of what cannot now be helped; considering all things, I do not think you so much to blame as many people do; for when a person is in liquor, there is no answering for what they may do." ~~, a woman in such a situation is particularly off her guard because her head is not strong enough to support intoxication."~~

"Madam, this is not to be borne; I insist–"

"My dear girl, don't vex yourself about the matter; I assure you I have entirely forgiven everything respecting it; indeed I was not angry at the time, because as I saw all along, you were nearly dead drunk. I knew you could not help saying the strange things you did. But I see I distress you; so I will change the subject and desire it may never again be mentioned; remember it is all forgot – I will now pursue my story; but I must insist upon not giving you any description of Mrs. Watkins; it would only be reviving old stories and as you never saw her, it can be nothing to you, if her forehead was too high, her eyes were too small, or if she had too much colour."

"Again! Lady Williams: this is too much.–"

So provoked was poor Alice at this renewal of the old story, that I know not what might have been the consequence of it, had not their attention been engaged by another object. A lovely young woman lying apparently in great pain beneath a citron tree was an object too interesting not to attract their notice. Forgetting their own dispute, they both with sympathizing tenderness advanced towards her and accosted her in these terms.

"You seem, fair nymph, to be labouring under some misfortune which we shall be happy to relieve, if you will inform us what it is. Will you favour us with your life and adventures?"

"Willingly, ladies, if you will be so kind as to be seated."

They took their places and she thus began.

Chapter the Fifth

"I am a native of North Wales and my father is one of the most capital tailors in it[22]. Having a numerous family, he was easily prevailed on by a sister of my mother's, who ~~was~~ is a widow in good circumstances and keeps an alehouse in the next village to ours, to let her take me and breed me up at her own expense. Accordingly, I have lived with her for the last eight years of my life, during which time ~~some~~ she provided me with some of the first rate masters, who taught me all the accomplishments requisite for one of my sex and rank. Under their instructions I learned dancing, music, drawing and various languages[23], by which means I became more accomplished than any other tailor's daughter in Wales. Never was there a happier creature than I was, till within the last half year – but I should have told you before that the principal estate in our neighbourhood belongs to Charles Adams, the owner of the brick house, you see yonder."

"Charles Adams!" exclaimed the astonished Alice. "Are you acquainted with Charles Adams?"

"To my sorrow, madam, I am. He came about half a year ago to receive the rents of the estate I have just mentioned. At that time I first saw him; as you seem, ma'am, acquainted with him, I need not describe to you how charming he is. I could not resist his attractions–"

"Ah! Who can?" said Alice with a deep sigh.

"My aunt, being in terms of the greatest intimacy with his cook, determined, at my request, to try whether she could discover, by means of her friend, if there were any chance of his returning my affection. For this purpose she went one evening to drink tea with Mrs. Susan, who in the course of conversation mentioned the goodness of her place and the goodness of her

50

master; upon which my aunt began pumping her with so much dexterity that in a short time Susan owned, that she did not think her master would ever marry, 'For,' said she, 'he has often and often declared to me that his wife, whoever she might be, must possess youth, beauty, birth, wit, merit, and money. I have many a time,' she continued, 'endeavoured to reason him out of his resolution and to convince him of the improbability of his ever meeting with such a lady; but my arguments have had no effect, and he continues as firm in his determination as ever.' You may imagine, ladies, my distress on hearing this; for I was fearful that though possessed of youth, beauty, wit and merit, and though the probable heiress of my aunt's house and business, he might think me deficient in rank, and in being so, unworthy of his hand.

"However I was determined to make a bold push and therefore wrote him a very kind letter, offering him with great tenderness my hand and heart. To this I received an angry and peremptory refusal, but thinking it might be rather the effect of his modesty than any ~~other reason~~ thing else, I pressed him again on the subject[24]. But he never answered any more of my letters and very soon afterwards left the country. As soon as I heard of his departure, I wrote to him here, informing him that I should ~~soon~~ shortly do myself the honour of waiting on him at Pammydiddle, to which I received no answer; therefore, choosing to take silence for consent, I left Wales, unknown to my aunt, and arrived here after a tedious journey this morning. On enquiring for his house, I was directed through this wood, to the one you there see. With a heart elated by the expected happiness of beholding him, I entered it, and had proceeded thus far in my progress through it, when I found myself suddenly seized by the leg and on examining the cause of it, found that I was caught in one of the steel traps so common in gentlemen's grounds[25]."

"Ah!" cried Lady Williams, "How fortunate we are to meet with you; ~~as~~ since we might otherwise perhaps have shared the like misfortune.–"

"It is indeed happy for you, ladies, that I should have been a short time before you. I screamed, as you may easily imagine, till the woods resounded again and till one of the inhuman wretch's servants came to my assistance and released me from my dreadful prison, but not before one of my legs was entirely broken."

Chapter the Sixth

At this melancholy recital, the fair eyes of Lady Williams were suffused in tears, and Alice could not help exclaiming:

"Oh! Cruel Charles, to wound the hearts and legs of all the fair."

Lady Williams now interposed, and observed that the young lady's leg ought to be set without farther delay. After examining the fracture, therefore, she immediately began and performed the operation with great skill, which was the more wonderful on account of her having never performed such a one before. Lucy then arose from the ground, and finding that she could walk with the greatest ease, accompanied them to Lady Williams's house at her Ladyship's particular request.

The perfect form, the beautiful face, and elegant manners of Lucy so won on the affections of Alice, that when they parted, which was not till after supper, she assured her that except her father, brother, uncles, aunts, cousins and other relations, Lady Williams, Charles Adams, and a few dozen more of particular friends, she loved her better than almost any other person in the world.

Such a flattering assurance of her regard would justly have given much pleasure to the object of it, had she not plainly perceived that the amiable Alice had partaken too freely of Lady Williams's claret.

Her Ladyship (whose discernment was great) read in the intelligent countenance of Lucy ~~on~~ her thoughts on the subject, and ~~when~~ as soon as Miss Johnson had taken her leave, thus addressed her:

"When you are more intimately acquainted with my Alice, you will not be surprised, Lucy, to see the dear creature drink a little too much; for such things happen every day. She has many rare and charming qualities, but sobriety is not one of them. The whole family are indeed a sad drunken set. I am sorry to say too that I never knew three such thorough gamesters as they are, more particularly Alice. But she is a charming girl. I fancy ~~though~~ not one of the sweetest tempers in the world; to be sure I have seen her in such passions! However, she is a sweet young woman. I am sure you'll like her. I scarcely know any one so amiable. – Oh! that you could but have seen her ~~yesterday~~ the other evening! How she raved! And on such a trifle too! She is indeed a most pleasing girl! I shall always love her!"

"She appears, by your Ladyship's account, to have many good qualities," replied Lucy.

"Oh! A thousand," answered Lady Williams, "though ~~I may be partial; indeed, I believe I am; yes I am very partial to her~~ I am very partial to her, and perhaps am blinded, by my affection, to her real defects."

Chapter the Seventh

The next morning brought the three Miss Simpsons to wait on Lady Williams, who received them with the utmost politeness and introduced to their acquaintance Lucy, with whom the eldest was so much pleased that at parting she declared her sole *ambition* was to have her accompany them the next morning to Bath, whither they were going for some weeks.

"Lucy," said Lady Williams, "is quite at her own disposal and if she chooses to accept so kind an invitation, I hope she will not hesitate from any motives of delicacy on my account. I know not indeed how I shall ever be able to part with her. She never was at Bath[26], and I should think that it would be a most agreeable jaunt to her. Speak, my love," continued she, turning to Lucy, "what say you to accompanying these ladies? I shall be miserable without you – t'will be a most pleasant tour to you – I hope you'll go; if you do I am sure t'will be the death of me – pray be persuaded.–"

Lucy begged leave to decline the honour of accompanying them, with many expressions of gratitude for the extreme politeness of Miss Simpson in inviting her. Miss Simpson appeared much disappointed by her refusal. Lady Williams insisted on her going – declared that she would never forgive her if she did not, and that she should never survive it if she did, and in short, used such persuasive arguments that it was at length resolved she was to go. The Miss Simpsons called for her at ten o'clock the next morning and Lady Williams had soon the satisfaction of receiving from her young friend the pleasing intelligence of their safe arrival in Bath.

It may now be proper to return to the hero of this novel, the brother of Alice, of whom I believe I have scarcely ever had occasion to speak; which may perhaps be partly owing to his unfortunate propensity to liquor, which so completely deprived him of the use of those faculties nature had endowed him with, that he never did anything worth mentioning. His death happened a short time after Lucy's departure and was the natural consequence of this pernicious practice. By his decease, his sister became the sole inheritress of a very large fortune, which as it gave her fresh hopes of rendering herself acceptable as a wife to Charles Adams, could not fail of being most pleasing to her – and as the effect was joyful, the cause could scarcely be lamented.

Finding the violence of her attachment to him daily augment, she at length disclosed it to her father and desired him to propose a union between them to Charles. Her father consented and set out one morning to open the affair to the young man. Mr. Johnson being a man of few words, his part was soon performed and the answer he received was as follows:

"Sir, I may perhaps be expected to appear pleased at and grateful for the offer you have made me: but let me tell you that I consider it as an affront. I look upon myself to be, sir, a perfect beauty – where would you see a finer figure or a more charming face. Then, sir, I imagine my manners and address to be of the most polished kind; there is a certain elegance, a peculiar sweetness in them that I never saw equaled and cannot describe. – Partiality aside, I am certainly more accomplished in every language, every science, every art and everything than any other person in Europe. My temper is even, my virtues innumerable, myself unparalleled. Since such, sir, is my character, what do you mean by wishing me to marry your daughter?

"Let me give you a short sketch of yourself and of her. I look upon you, sir, to be a very good sort of man in the main; a drunken old dog to be sure, but that's nothing to me. Your daughter, sir, is neither sufficiently beautiful, sufficiently amiable, sufficiently witty, nor sufficiently rich for me. – I expect nothing more in my wife than my wife will find in me – perfection[27]. These, sir, are my sentiments and I honour myself for having such. One friend I have, and glory in having but one. – She is at present preparing my dinner, but if you choose to see her, she shall come, and she will inform you that these have ever been my sentiments."

Mr. Johnson was satisfied: and expressing himself to be much obliged to ~~him~~ Mr. Adams for the characters he had favoured him with of himself and his daughter, took his leave.

The unfortunate Alice, on receiving from her father the sad account[28] of the ill success his visit had been attended with, could scarcely support the disappointment. – She flew to her bottle and it was soon forgot.

Chapter the Eighth

While these affairs were transacting[28] at Pammydiddle, Lucy was conquering ever[y] heart at Bath. A fortnight's residence there had nearly effaced from her remembrance the captivating form of Charles. – The recollection of what her heart had formerly suffered by his charms and her leg by his trap, enabled her to forget him with tolerable ease, which was what she determined to do; and for that purpose dedicated five minutes in every day to the employment of driving him from her remembrance.

Her second letter to Lady Williams contained the pleasing intelligence of her having accomplished her undertaking to her entire satisfaction; she mentioned in it also an offer of marriage she had received from the Duke of —, an elderly man of noble fortune whose ill health was the chief inducement of his journey to Bath.

> "I am distressed," she continued, "to know whether I mean to accept him or not. There are a thousand advantages to be derived from a marriage with the Duke, for besides those more inferior ones of rank and fortune, it will procure me a home, which of all other things is what I most desire. Your Ladyship's kind wish of my always remaining with you is noble and generous, but I cannot think of becoming so great a burden on one I so much love and esteem. That one should receive obligations only from those we despise, is a sentiment instilled into my mind by my worthy aunt, in my early years, and cannot in my opinion be too strictly adhered to. The excellent woman of whom I now speak is, I hear, too much incensed by my imprudent departure from Wales, to receive me again. – I most earnestly wish to leave the ladies I am now with. Miss Simpson is indeed (setting aside ambition) very amiable, but her second sister, the envious and malevolent Sukey, is too disagreeable to live with. I have reason to think that the admiration I have met with in the circles of the great at this place has raised her hatred and envy; for often has she threatened, and sometimes endeavoured to cut my throat. – Your Ladyship will therefore allow that I am not wrong in wishing to leave Bath, and in wishing to have a home to receive

me, when I do. I shall expect with impatience your advice concerning the Duke and am your most obliged

andc. Lucy."

Lady Williams sent her her opinion on the subject in the following manner:

"Why do you hesitate, my dearest Lucy, a moment with respect to the Duke? I have enquired into his character and find him to be an unprincipled, illiterate man. Never shall my Lucy be united ~~be united~~ to such a one! He has a princely fortune, which is every day increasing. How nobly will you spend it! What credit will you give him in the eyes of all! How much will he be respected on his wife's account! But why, my dearest Lucy, why will you not at once decide this affair by returning to me and never leaving me again? Although I admire ~~the~~ your noble sentiments with respect to obligations, ~~but yet me beg you not to suffer their preventing your from them to prevent~~ yet, let me beg that they may not prevent your making me happy. It will, to be sure, be a great expense to me, to have you always with me – I shall not be able to support it – but what is that in comparison with the happiness I shall enjoy in your society? – 'twill ruin me I know – you will not therefore surely, withstand these arguments, ~~and~~ or refuse to return to yours most affectionately andc. andc.

C. Williams."

Chapter the Ninth

What might have been the effect of her Ladyship's advice, had it ever been received by Lucy, is uncertain, as it reached Bath a few hours after she had breathed her last. She fell a sacrifice to the envy and malice of Sukey who, jealous of her superior charms, took her by poison from an admiring world at the age of seventeen.

Thus fell ~~Lucy~~ the amiable and lovely Lucy, whose life had been marked by no crime, and stained by no ~~plot, but~~ blemish but her imprudent departure from her aunt's, and whose death was sincerely lamented by everyone who knew her. Among the most afflicted of her friends were Lady Williams, Miss Johnson and the Duke; the two ~~last~~[29] first ~~having~~ of whom had a most sincere regard for her, more particularly Alice, who had spent a whole evening in her company and had never thought of her since. His grace's affliction may likewise be easily accounted for, since he lost one for whom he had experienced, during the last ten days, a tender affection and sincere regard. He mourned her loss with unshaken constancy for the next fortnight, at the end of which time, he gratified the ambition of Caroline Simpson by raising her to the rank of a Duchess. Thus was she at length rendered completely happy in the gratification of her favourite passion. Her sister, the perfidious Sukey, was likewise shortly after exalted in a manner she truly deserved, and by her actions appeared to have always desired. Her barbarous murder was discovered, and in spite of every interceding friend, she was speedily raised to the gallows. – The beautiful but affected Cecilia was too sensible of her own superior charms, not to imagine that if Caroline could engage a Duke, she might without censure aspire to the affections of some Prince – and knowing that those of her native country were chiefly engaged, she left England and I have since heard is at present the favourite Sultana of the great Mogul[30].

In the mean time, the inhabitants of Pammydiddle were in a state of the greatest astonishment and wonder, a report being circulated of the intended marriage of Charles Adams. The lady's name was still a secret. Mr. and Mrs. Jones imagined it to be Miss Johnson; but she knew better; all her fears were centered in his cook, when to the astonishment of every one, he was publicly united to Lady Williams. –

Finis

Notes

1. "Francis William Austen": Frank (1774-1865) joined the Royal Navy in April 1786 and served on the frigate *HMS Perseverance* from December 1788 to December 1789 when he was promoted. This dedication is squeezed between the title and the first chapter in handwriting more mature than that of the novel.

2. "masquerade": A dance party at which guests wear masks and extravagant costumes. Masquerades had a reputation for being rather daring and subversive of the established order (since no one knew who anyone else was).

3. "tickets": One would hardly need tickets to so small a private function.

4. "Pammydiddle": 'Pam' is a reference to a playing card and to 'diddle' is to cheat. "The name 'Pam, denoting the J♣ in its full capacity as permanent top trump in Five-Card Loo, represents an old medieval comic-erotic character called Pamphilus (Latin for a Greek word, meaning 'beloved of all') or

'Pamphile', in French, described as 'an old bawd' by the New Zealand-born English lexicographer Eric Partridge" (Wikipedia article on "Lanerloo").

5. "rather tall": Being tall was, then as now, seen as an advantage (provided one was not *too* tall), indicating superior breeding and beauty.

6. "passionate": Subject to intense emotions, particularly anger.

7. "Sukey": Susan.

8. "affected": Artificial, contrived, pretentious.

9. "a handsome jointure": Money and/or property set aside for a widow for the period she survives her husband.

10. "addicted to the bottle and the dice": That is, they drank and gambled.

11. "a Sultana": The wife, or mistress, of a sultan.

12. "the concourse": The ability of people to interact and socialize.

13. "two Dominos": A 'domino' is a loose cloak, worn with a mask for the upper part of the face at masquerades in default of a symbolic costume.

14. "gamesters": That is 'gamblers'.

15. "expatiated": 'Expatiate' means to speak or write about something or someone in great detail.

16. "Sir Charles Grandison": The eponymous protagonist of Samuel Richardson's epistolary novel *The History of Sir Charles Grandison* (1753), which was a favorite of Austen.

17. "downright bigamy": Since bigamy is the act, and crime, of marrying a person who is already legally married, Lady Williams is guilty of malapropism (i.e., the erroneous the use of a word because it sounds similar to the right word). I suggest the word she meant to use is 'bigotry' (intolerance of people who hold different opinions to one's own – and are therefore disagreeable). Alternatively, this may be another reference to Sir Charles Grandison, who does instruct his servants to tell visitors that he is not at home in order to avoid them. The relevance of "bigamy" to Sir Charles is that he is a man torn between the desire to marry two different women.

18. "Berkshire": A county in south-central England to the west of London.

19. 'in town": That is, in London where the rich went to spend the winter months.

20. "citron grove": The citron is a shrubby Asian tree that bears large fruits similar to lemons. They do not grow in England but at the start of Book Five of *Paradise Lost* by John Milton (1608-1674), Adam asks Eve, "how blows [i.e., blooms] the Citron Grove[?]" This links Charles Adams with Adam and his grounds with Paradise. Groves were popular settings in romantic fiction.

21. "pigsty ... horsepond": Ironic juxtaposition of two of the least attractive features of the countryside with the exotic Citron Grove. A horsepond is a pond where horses drink or are washed.

22. "capital tailors in it": A comic oxymoron to link North Wales, a wildly beautiful place, with tailors, an occupation more associated with cities and culture. A girl adopted by the widow of the local innkeeper would hardly receive the privileged education that Lucy describes.

23. Lucy describes the fairly standard curriculum of girls from the gentry class whose aim was to make them desirable wives. Note the absence of topics from the curriculum of boys such as Latin, Greek, French, history, geography, theology and philosophy. This disparity in education is satirized in *The Loiterer* 27 where Henry Austen satirically sets out "some rules for the Education of a fine Lady":

> As soon as she can understand what is said to her, let her know that she is to look forwards to matrimony, as the sole end of existence, and the sole means of happiness; and that the older, the richer and the foolisher her Husband is, the more enviable will be her situation. Having taught her this truth, it will be easy to make her act accordingly.

He then, with tongue firmly in cheek, suggests a curriculum for girls to include: card playing, gambling, posture, scandal, and self-interest. The author concludes:

> By minutely pursuing this system of Prudence, She will reap praise and pleasure in every station of life; She will be an accomplished Coquette, and a Successful Gamester; she will be an unfeeling Daughter, a Childless Wife, and a tearless Widow.

24. The entire courting process is a comic inversion of the accepted norms in which the male pursues the female. Attributing Charles's refusal to "modesty" reminds one of Mr. Collins's refusal to take Elizabeth's refusal of his offer of marriage. He tells her:

> "Believe me, my dear Miss Elizabeth, that your modesty, so far from doing you any disservice, rather adds to your other perfections. You would have been less amiable in my eyes had there not been this little unwillingness ... I am not now to learn ... that it is usual with young ladies to reject the addresses of the man whom they secretly mean to accept, when he first applies for their favour; and that sometimes the refusal is repeated a second, or even a third time. I am therefore by no means discouraged by what you have just said, and shall hope to lead you to the altar ere long." (*Pride and Prejudice* Ch. 19)

Mr. Collins may be a pompous ass, but in this matter, he is merely stating convention.

25. "steel traps": These spring-loaded traps were not, as the modern reader might suppose, simply to catch wild animals. Owners of country estates often set such traps to discourage trespassers and poachers. In *The Loiterer* 50 (January 9th, 1790), Mr. Humphrey Discount informs the author, "as for

preserving my garden, I have just bought a couple of steel-traps, and I warrant the young rascals will keep clear of my premises by the time I have broke two or three of their legs."

26. "Bath": So far as is known, Austen did not herself visit Bath until November 1797. However, she would have known of the delights of the spa (i.e., taking the waters, enjoying walks in and around the town, attending its balls, and generally meeting the very best people) from acquaintances.

27. Charles's praise of himself is entirely inappropriate. Most significant is that it includes no mention of his performing any acts of service to his fellow man; it is all about his appearance and accomplishments.

28. "account ... affairs were transaction": Austen frequently uses the language of business to describe marriage negotiations.

29. The original text excludes Lady Williams from having "a most sincere regard" for Lucy, which is perhaps more consistent with the way Lady Williams is portrayed throughout.

30. "the great Mogul": The emperor of the Mogul Empire in India which covered most of India in the seventeenth century, but had by Austen's time been reduced to the area around Delhi.

Commentary

Jack and Alice is a parody of the novel of romance which Olivia Murphy describes as "a tale of unrequited love, officious advice, and grotesque vanity" ("From Pammydiddle to *Persuasion*: Jane Austen Rewriting Eighteenth-Century Literature"). Each of the major characters represents a particular vice or virtue. Joseph Wiesenfarth comments, "'Jack & Alice' is something of a morality play that never breaks free of the masquerade that sets it in motion. Charles Adams is Perfection and seeks Perfection in a woman. The closest he gets to having it is marrying Lady Williams or Virtue in the masquerade. But Lady Williams proves to be no more than a masquerade of Virtue. For virtue demands brains, and Lady Williams has none" ("Jane Austen's Family of Fiction: From Henry and Eliza to Darcy and Eliza").

The expectations generated by the title are never fulfilled since Alice, the novel's heroine, is not in love with Jack (who turns out to be her drunken brother and makes no actual appearance in the story) but with the "bewitching" Charles, who does not return her love, breaks hearts along the way, and finally (inexplicably) marries Lady Williams, the woman Alice supposed to be her best friend. Alice is herself an untypical heroine since though she "'has many rare and charming qualities ... sobriety is not one of them'" as Lady Williams tells Lucy with typically snide understatement. Alice is the antithesis of Chase Amos's prescription that "Delicacy of manners and purity of speech are so much expected from an amiable, modest female" (*The Excellent Female*, 1791). She is the first of Austen's young women who behave badly.

The narrative begins with absurdity: Mr. Johnson is so "delighted" to reach his fifty-fourth birthday that he decides to celebrate his fifty-fifth birthday with a masked ball – an admirable example of deferred gratification! There are only nine people at the masquerade, Pammydiddle being a small place, yet they have prodigious difficulty recognizing each other behind their masks, though from the descriptions the reader has none. Ironically, Charles Adams, who blinds everyone with his sun mask, is discovered to be "in his plain green coat with no mask at all." Unfortunately, the room in which the ball is held "not amounting to more than three quarters of a mile in length and half a one in breadth," it is hard for the other guests to stay away from his shining countenance. Notice how Austen delights in presenting the absurd proportions of the room as though they were commonplace.

Every character appears flawed except Lady Williams who is described only in terms of her qualities, "Though benevolent and candid, she was generous and sincere; though pious and good, she was religious and amiable; and though elegant and agreeable, she was polished and entertaining." Contemporary readers may not know that Austen is parodying the balanced sentence structure of Samuel Johnson by offering three pairs of antithetical qualities, the joke being that the reader understands them not to be antithetical at all; the word "though" is out of place since the qualities named are complements not opposites. However, even this paragon of virtue, who flees the gambling table in shock, ends up with the other party-goers being "carried home, dead drunk."

Our heroine, the alcoholic Caroline Johnson, has fallen in love with the captivating Charles at the masquerade – a fairly conventional romantic plot. With irony, the narrator tells us that Charles's attraction is so great that "of the six present at the masquerade but five had returned uncaptivated. Alice Johnson was the unhappy sixth whose heart had not been able to withstand the power of his charms." We have to read this twice, because it is has the opposite meaning to that the reader has been led to expect. The theme has been set: Caroline's unrequited, disastrous love for "the lovely, the lively, but insensible Charles Adams."

Already a little the worse for wine, Alice goes to talk to Lady William's about her desperate love for Charles. Lady Williams is at home because she never goes out; she does not stint herself at home in order to discourage visitors because she regards this method of "shutting out disagreeable visitors as little less than downright bigamy." 'Bigamy' is obviously the wrong word (see Notes above). Lady Williams gives Alice some absurd advice, "'Preserve yourself from a first love and you need not fear a second.'" She speaks as though one can avoid a first love and go straight to the second! The narrator now turns to a staple of romance fiction – the willingness of people to tell their life and adventures at the drop of a hat.

Lady William's story of her early youth is conventionally pathetic: she lost her mother at the age of six and her "excellent governess" Miss Dickins was "torn from" her arms before she was seventeen with the final words,

"'My dear Kitty … Good night t'ye.'" The truth is, however, a comic anticlimax: this paragon of virtue, dispenser of such wise moral advice to her pupil, "eloped with the butler the same night."

There follows an absurd argument between the inebriated Alice and Lady Williams over the ruddy complexion of Mrs. Watkins, a lady with whom Alice is not acquainted. Lady Williams opines that "when a person has too great a degree of red in their complexion, it gives their face, in my opinion, too red a look'" (a comic example of tautology, the saying of the same thing twice in different words), but Alice, whose own complexion is no doubt reddened by drink, disputes that this is possible. The narrator explains that the two ladies are soon reconciled, Lady Williams excusing Alice's conduct because of her being drunk and Alice having too much "respect for Lady Williams, and too great a relish for her claret" (note the comic juxtaposition of two incongruous motives) to wish to end their friendship. The next day, Lady Williams assures her friend that she has "'entirely forgiven everything'" about their quarrel but goes on to rehearse the quarrel in detail; she desires that the subject "'may never again be mentioned'" and in her next breath mentions again the fault of Mrs. Watkins's complexion.

A further quarrel is prevented by the discovery of Lucy, a "'fair nymph … labouring under some misfortune'" who, despite her pain (we later discover she has a broken leg!), responds appropriately to Lady Williams's request that she relate her "'life and adventures'" – a conventional phrase in the novels of the day. This allows Austen to make fun of the conventional education of women whose sole aim was to make them marriageable. Ross writes, "The affectation of accomplishments, with a view to ensnaring a husband, is a device with which Jane Austen … has no patience" (139). Lucy's aunt provides her with "first rate masters, who taught me all the accomplishments requisite for one of my sex and rank … I learned dancing, music, drawing and various languages." This is precisely the kind of education that Mary Wollstonecraft criticizes in *Rights of Woman* as neglecting the development of reason and understanding in women.

Charles Adams emerges as a typical male chauvinist who wants everything from a wife except the companionship of an equal. His cook reports, "'he has often and often declared to me that his wife, whoever she might be, must possess youth, beauty, birth, wit, merit, and money.'" The absurd conventions of courtship under such circumstances are mocked by comic inversion: it is Lucy who proposes to Charles in a "'very kind letter,'" and having received an "'angry and peremptory refusal,'" she refuses to take no for an answer explaining away the rejection as "'the effect of his modesty than anything else.'" (One cannot help but think of Mr. Collins's putting Elizabeth's rejection of him down to conventional modesty.)

As Kathryn Sutherland points out, Austen delights in the comic juxtaposition of discordant details as when Lady Williams says of the irresistible Charles, "'Oh! Cruel Charles to wound the hearts and legs of all the fair.'" The comedy of this syllepsis is that the handsome Charles is equally capable of making women suffer by falling in love with him and by snapping their legs in one of his traps. Later, Lucy repeats the same joke recalling that "her heart had formerly suffered by his charms and her leg by his trap."

Alone with Lucy, Lady Williams now sets about blackening the character of Alice whilst appearing to praise her. To do so, she constantly negates praise with criticism, "'I scarcely know any one so amiable. – Oh! that you could but have seen her the other evening! How she raved!'" Lady Williams repeatedly contradicts herself and fails to give anyone a straight answer. Thus, when taken with that instant devotion upon a first meeting, so common to the novel of sentiment, the three Simpson sisters invite Lucy to accompany them to Bath, Lady Williams replies with a series of contradictory statements, "'I hope you'll go; if you do I am sure t'will be the death of me.'" Ironically, the narrator comments that these "persuasive arguments" finally persuade Lucy to accept the invitation.

At this point, in an entirely unmotivated plot change, Jack, "the hero of the novel" who has been so drunk that he "never did anything worth mentioning," makes his one contribution to the plot by dying and leaving Alice a substantial legacy. So armed, Alice persuades her father to negotiate an engagement with Charles Adams, but his haughty rejection of this proposal merely sends Alice back to alcohol to relieve her pain, "She flew to the bottle and it was soon forgot." At this point, she virtually disappears from the novel.

Meanwhile, Lucy has conquered every heart in Bath, particularly that of an aged and ill Duke who has proposed. Lucy feels no love for the man (how could she?) but calculates the advantages of such a match, "besides those more inferior ones of rank and fortune, it will procure me a home, which of all other things is what I most desire." The need for a home is urgent, for she cannot stay longer with the Simpson sisters since, as she writes to Lady Williams, "the envious and malevolent Sukey ... [has] threatened, and sometimes endeavoured to cut my throat." Lucy feels that she cannot accept Lady Williams's offer of a home with her because of her aunt's absurd maxim that "one should receive obligations only from those we despise" – a comic inversion of conventional wisdom. This is Austen's first foray into a topic which will fascinate her: the marriage of financial convenience.

Lucy's request for Lady Williams's advice leads to more self-contradiction: Lucy should not marry the Duke because he is "an unprincipled, illiterate man" whom Lucy should not hesitate to marry; Lucy should return to live with Lady Williams who cannot possibly afford to have her live with her.

Perhaps fortunately, Lucy's dilemma is resolved by her being murdered. The narrator states that her "death was sincerely lamented by everyone who knew her, particularly Alice, who had spent a whole evening in her company and had never thought of her since," and the Duke who "mourned her loss with unshaken constancy for the next fortnight" and then marries the ambitious Caroline Simpson. In Austen's juvenilia, life-long loves and friendships develop instantly upon meeting and evaporate as quickly upon death and parting. With a delightful play on words, the narrator reports on Caroline's marriage "raising her to the rank of a Duchess" while "Sukey, was likewise shortly after exalted" by being hanged! Cecile sets her sights higher and becomes the "favourite Sultana of the great Mogul," while to everyone's astonishment Charles Adams marries the much older Lady Williams who has perhaps been manipulating events to this end all along. Of Alice, we hear nothing; she is, presumably, seeking consolation in the bottle.

Edgar and Emma – a tale

Chapter the First

"I cannot imagine," said Sir Godfrey to his lady, "why we continue in such deplorable lodgings as these, in a paltry market-town, while we have three good houses of our own situated in some of the finest parts of England, and perfectly ready to receive us!"

"I'm sure, Sir Godfrey," replied Lady Marlow, "it has been much against my inclination that we have stayed here so long; or why we should ever have come at all ~~is~~ indeed, has been to me a wonder, as none of our houses have been in the least want of repair."

"Nay, my dear," answered Sir Godfrey, "you are the last person who ought to be displeased with what was always meant as a compliment to you; for you cannot but be sensible of the very great inconvenience your daughters and I have been put to, during the two years we have remained crowded in these lodgings in order to give you pleasure."

"My dear," replied Lady Marlow, "how can you stand and tell such lies, when you very well know that it was merely to oblige the girls and you, that I left a most commodious house situated in a most delightful country and surrounded by a most agreeable neighbourhood, to live two years cramped up in lodgings three pair of stairs[1] high, in a smoky and unwholesome town[2], ~~and~~ which has given me a continual fever and almost thrown me into a consumption[3]."

As, after a few more speeches on both sides, they could not determine which was the most to blame, they prudently laid aside the debate, and having packed up their clothes and paid their rent, they set out the next morning with their two daughters for their seat in Sussex.

Sir Godfrey and Lady Marlow were indeed very sensible people and though (as in this instance) like many other sensible people, they sometimes did a foolish thing, yet in general their actions were guided by prudence and regulated by discretion.

After a journey of two days and a half they arrived at Marlhurst in good health and high spirits; so overjoyed were they all to inhabit again a place they had left with mutual regret for two years, that they ordered the bells to be rung and distributed ninepence among the ringers.

Chapter the Second

The news of their arrival being quickly spread throughout the country, brought them in a few days visits of congratulation from every family in it.

Amongst the rest came the inhabitants of Willmot Lodge, a beautiful villa not far from Marlhurst. Mr. Willmot was a younger the representative of a very ancient family and possessed besides his paternal estate, a considerable share in a lead mine[4] and a ticket in the lottery[5]. His lady was an agreeable woman. Their children were too numerous to be particularly described; it is sufficient to say that in general they were virtuously inclined and not given to any wicked ways. Their family being too large to accompany them in every visit, they took nine with them alternately. When their coach stopped at Sir Godfrey's door, the Miss Marlows' hearts throbbed in the eager expectation of once more beholding a family so dear to them. Emma the youngest (who was more particularly interested in their arrival, being attached to their eldest son) continued at her dressing-room window in anxious hopes of seeing young Edgar descend from the carriage.

Mr. and Mrs. Willmot with their three eldest daughters first appeared – Emma began to fear tremble. Robert, Richard, Ralph, and Rodolphus followed – Emma turned pale. Their two youngest girls were lifted from the coach – Emma sunk breathless on a sofa. A footman came to announce to her the arrival of company; her heart was too full to contain its afflictions. A confidante was necessary. – In Thomas she hoped to experience a faithful one – for one she must have[6], and Thomas was the only one at hand. To him she unbosomed herself without restraint and after owning her passion for young Willmot, requested his advice in what manner she should conduct herself in the melancholy disappointment under which she laboured.

Thomas, who would gladly have been excused from listening to her complaint, begged leave to decline giving any advice concerning it, which ~~must~~ much against her will, she was obliged to comply with.

Having dispatched him therefore with many injunctions of secrecy, she descended with a heavy heart into the parlour, where she found the good party seated in a social manner round a blazing fire.

Chapter the Third

Emma had continued in the parlour some time before she could summon up sufficient courage to ask Mrs. Willmot after the rest of her family; and when she did, it was in so low, so ~~faultering a manner~~ faltering a voice that no one knew she spoke. Dejected by the ill success of her first attempt, she made no other, till on Mrs. Willmot's desiring one of the little girls to ring the bell for their carriage, she stepped across the room and, seizing the string, said in a resolute manner:

"Mrs. Willmot, you do not stir from this house till you let me know how all the rest of your family do, particularly your eldest son."

They were all greatly surprised by such an unexpected address and the more so, on account of the manner in which it was spoken; but Emma, who would not be again disappointed, requesting an answer, Mrs. Willmot made the following eloquent oration:

"Our children are all extremely well, but at present most of them [are] from home. Amy is with my sister Clayton. Sam at Eton[7]. David with his Uncle John. Jem and Will at Winchester[8]. Kitty at Queen's Square[9]. Ned with his grandmother. Hetty and Patty in a convent at Brussells[10]. Edgar at college[11], Peter at nurse[12], and all the rest (except the nine here) at home."

It was with difficulty that Emma could refrain from tears on hearing of the absence of Edgar; she remained, however, tolerably composed till the Willmots were gone when having no check to the overflowings of her grief, she gave free vent to them, and retiring to her own room, continued in tears the remainder of her life.

Finis

Notes

1. "three pair of stairs": That is, three flights of stairs, so they are living on the fourth floor (the English would call it the third floor). Generally, rooms got smaller and less desirable the higher up in a house one went, culminating in

the servants' quarters at the top.

2. "a smoky and unwholesome town": Austen probably had Bath in mind.

3. Consumption (tuberculosis) is an infectious bacterial disease, but in the eighteenth and nineteenth centuries it was attributed to cold and damp.

4. "a lead mine": Lead mining was common in the period particularly in Derbyshire, Wales and the North. Obviously it was highly profitable, however, the joke is in Austen's use of a base metal rather than gold or silver.

5. "a ticket in the lottery": The first Royal lottery was chartered by Queen Elizabeth I in the year 1566 and drawn in 1569; the final Royal lottery was in 1826. Then, as now, the chances of winning were not high.

6. "one she must have": The heroine of a romance must have a particular friend with whom she can speak of her emotions and suffering. This role is, however, always played by a woman, usually someone of the heroine's own age and certainly of her own social class. Evidently Emma is playing the role she has learned from her reading, but is forced to substitute not only a male but a servant for the girlfriend she does not have. *A Father's Legacy to His Daughters* (1774) by Dr. John Gregory (1724-1773) warns, "Beware of making confidants of your servants ... if you make them your confidants, you spoil them and debase yourself."

7. "Eton": Eton College an elite independent boarding school for boys in Berkshire, England.

8. "Winchester": Winchester College is also an elite independent boarding school for boys in Hampshire.

9. "Queen's Square": An elegant garden square in Bloomsbury, Central London, constructed between 1716 and 1725. Number 31 Queen's Square was an exclusive girls' school known as The Ladies' Eton.

10. "a convent at Brussels": There are a large number of convents in Brussels (now the capital of Belgium but until 1795 under Austrian rule). It does not *necessarily* follow that the Willmots were Catholic; perhaps they wanted their daughter to improve her French or Dutch. There were no convent schools in England.

11. "at college": Given that the list begins with the eldest, this probably means a school not a university.

12. "at nurse": At this time, gentry families sent their babies away from home to live with their wet nurse for up to the first three years of their life. Jane Austen herself spent the first year-and-a-half of her life living away from home in the cottage of her wet nurse.

Commentary:

Edgar and Emma is a withering satire of the presentation of woman's love for a man in sentimental novels. Once again, the male of the title makes no appearance in the story which concentrates on Emma's hopeless love for the absent Edgar. Emily Auerbach's comment on the juvenilia in general seems particularly appropriate to this tale, "They offer a unique glimpse into what Jane Austen rejected: literary conventions that were divorced from real life; social customs that were absurdly affected and hypocritical; ideals about womanhood that were insincere, confining or degrading" (65).

The absurd comic tone is set when Sir Godfrey and Lady Marlow discover that they have been living for two whole years in lodgings, at "'great inconvenience,'" in a "'smoky town'" that neither likes, and that each has been under the impression that it was the other who wanted to live there rather than in one of their three fine country houses! The narrator comments that they are sensible people who, like all sensible people, occasionally do stupid things.

Having returned to Marlhurst, they are visited (as is required by etiquette) by Mr. and Mrs. Willmot. Mr. Willmot is said to be "the representative of a very ancient family and possessed besides his paternal estate, a considerable share in a lead mine and a ticket in the lottery." Notice the list of the visitor's wealth declines into bathos (an anticlimax created by a transition in mood from the sublime to the trivial or ridiculous). To have an ancient family and a family estate is certainly a good start (though the value of the estate is not specified), but lead is the basest of metals and, as a guarantee of wealth, a single lottery ticket must be regarded as a long shot. The narrator asserts that "Their children were too numerous to be particularly described." In fact, twenty children are identified in the story, of whom the Willmots can only take "nine with them alternately" leaving a number "at home."

The heroine of the tale is Emma, youngest daughter of Sir Godfrey and Lady Marlow, who is "attached to their eldest son [Edgar]" – this despite the fact that she has not seen the young man for two years. Emma, who appears to have learned about love from reading rather bad sentimental novels, watches for Edgar from her dressing-room window (just as the Bennet girls look out for Mr. Bingley on his first visit to Longbourn). Heartbroken that Edgar is not amongst the party, "Emma sunk breathless on a sofa" (that is, she fainted). Her heart being "too full to contain its afflictions," Emma knows from her reading that "[a] confidante was necessary." Ideally, of course, this should be an intimate female friend (like Jane and Elizabeth Bennet in *Pride and Prejudice*, or Jane and Cassandra in real life), but having none such, poor Emma has to coerce Thomas, the footman. Embarrassed when "she unbosomed herself without restraint," he declares himself unable to offer advice as to how she should proceed.

In the parlour, Emma resolves to ask about Edgar, but her first effort is in so "faltering a voice that no one knew she spoke." From this extreme of diffidence, the fear that the Willmots are about to leave pushes Emma into melodrama:

> [S]he stepped across the room and, seizing the string, said
> in a resolute manner:
> "Mrs. Willmot, you do not stir from this house till you let
> me know how all the rest of your family do, particularly

your eldest son."

Emma is rewarded with a list of the whereabouts of the eleven absent children which culminates in the information that Edgar is away at college. Emma knows that her life is ruined (or rather that she should *act as if* her life were ruined). We are told that "she remained ... tolerably composed till the Willmots were gone when having no check to the overflowings of her grief, she gave free vent to them, and retiring to her own room, continued in tears the remainder of her life." It seems that, unable to tell the difference between literature and real life, Emma has *become* the heroine in a sentimental novel.

Henry and Eliza – a novel

Is humbly dedicated to Miss Cooper[1] by her obedient humble servant
The Author

As Sir George and Lady Harcourt were superintending the labours of their haymakers, rewarding the industry of some by smiles of approbation, and punishing the idleness of others by a cudgel, they perceived lying closely concealed beneath the thick foliage of a haycock[2], a beautiful little girl not more than three months old[3].

Touched with the enchanting graces of her face and delighted with the infantine though sprightly answers she returned to their many questions, they resolved to take her home and, having no children of their own, to educate her with care and cost.

Being good people themselves, their first and principal care was to incite in her a love of virtue and a hatred of vice, in which they so well succeeded (Eliza having a natural turn that way herself) that when she grew up, she was the delight of all who knew her.

Beloved by Lady Harcourt, adored by Sir George, and admired by all the world, she lived in a continued course of uninterrupted happiness, till she had attained her eighteenth year, when happening one day to be detected in stealing a banknote of fifty pound[4], she was turned out of doors by her inhuman benefactors. Such a transition, to one who did not possess so noble and exalted a mind as Eliza, would have been death, but she, happy in the conscious knowledge of her own excellence, amused herself as she sat beneath a tree with making and singing the following lines:

SONG

Though misfortunes my footsteps may ever attend
I hope I shall never have need of a friend
As an innocent heart I will ever preserve
And will never from virtue's dear boundaries swerve.

Having amused herself ~~with~~ some hours, with this song and her own pleasing reflections, she arose and took the road to M——, a small market town, of which place her most intimate friend kept the Red Lion.

To this friend she immediately went, to whom having recounted her late misfortune, she communicated her wish of getting into some family in the capacity of humble companion.

Mrs. ~~James~~ Wilson, who was the most amiable creature on earth, ~~had~~ was no sooner acquainted with her desire, than she sat down in the bar and wrote the following letter to the Duchess of F——, the woman whom of all others she most esteemed:

> To the Duchess of F——.
> Receive into your family, at my request, a young woman of unexceptionable character, who is so good as to choose your society in preference to going to service[5]. Hasten, and take her from the arms of your
> Sarah Wilson.

The Duchess, whose friendship for Mrs. ~~James~~ Wilson[6] would have carried her any lengths, was overjoyed at such an opportunity of obliging her, and ~~of expressing the love she bore her~~ accordingly sate [i.e., set] out immediately on the receipt of her letter for the Red Lion, which she reached the same evening. The Duchess of F——. was about forty-five and a half; her passions were strong, her friendships firm, and her enmities unconquerable[7]. She was a widow and had only one daughter, who was on the point of marriage with a young man of considerable fortune.

The Duchess no sooner beheld our heroine than throwing her arms around her neck, she declared herself so much pleased with her, that she was resolved they never more should part. Eliza was delighted with such a protestation of friendship, and after taking a most affecting leave of her dear Mrs. Wilson, accompanied her grace the next morning to her seat in Surrey[8].

With every expression of regard did the Duchess introduce her to Lady Harriet, who was so much pleased ~~by~~ with her appearance that she besought her to consider her as ~~his~~ her sister, which Eliza with the greatest condescension promised to do.

Mr. Cecil, the lover of Lady Harriet, being often with the family was often with Eliza. A mutual love took place and Cecil having declared his first, prevailed on Eliza to consent to a private union[9], which was easy to be effected, as the Duchess's chaplain being ~~likewise~~ very much in love with Eliza himself, would, they were certain, do anything to oblige her.

The Duchess and Lady Harriet being engaged one evening to an assembly, they took the opportunity of their absence and were united by the enamoured Chaplain.

When the ladies returned, their amazement was great at finding instead of Eliza the following note:

> Madam,
> We are married and gone.
> Henry and Eliza Cecil

Her Grace, ~~after having read it~~ as soon as she had read the letter, which sufficiently explained the whole affair, flew into the most violent passion and after having spent an agreeable half hour in calling them by all the shocking names her rage could suggest to her, sent out ~~after~~ after them three hundred armed men, with orders not to return without their bodies, dead or alive; intending that if they should be brought to her in the latter condition to have them put to death in some torture-like manner, after a few years confinement[10].

In the meantime, Cecil and Eliza continued their flight to the Continent, which they judged to be more secure than their native land, from the dreadful effects of the Duchess's vengeance which they had so much reason to apprehend.

In France they remained three years, during which time they became the parents of two boys, and at the end of it Eliza became a widow without anything to support either her or her children. They had lived since their marriage at the rate of £~~10~~18,000 a year, of which Mr. Cecil's estate being rather less than the twentieth part, they had been able to ~~scarce~~ save but a trifle, having lived to the utmost extent of their income[11].

Eliza, being perfectly conscious of the derangement in their affairs, immediately on her husband's death set sail for England, in a man-of-war[12] of fifty-five guns, which they had built in their more prosperous days. But no sooner had she stepped on shore at Dover, with a child in each hand, than she was seized by the officers of the Duchess, and conducted by them to a snug little Newgate[13] of their Lady's, which she had erected for the reception of her own private prisoners.

No sooner had Eliza entered her dungeon than the first thought which occurred to her, was how to get out of it again.

She went to the door; but it was locked. She looked at the window; but it was barred with iron. Disappointed in both her expectations, she despaired of affecting her escape, when she fortunately perceived in a corner of her cell, a small saw and ladder of ropes. With the saw, she instantly went to work and in a few weeks had displaced every bar but one to which she fastened the ladder.

A difficulty then occurred, which for some time she knew not how to obviate. Her children were too small to get down the ladder by themselves, nor would it be possible for her to take them in her arms when *she* did. At last, she determined to fling down all her clothes, of which she had a large quantity, and then having given them strict charge not to hurt themselves, threw her children after them. She herself with ease descended by the ladder, at the bottom of which she had the pleasure of finding her little boys in perfect health and fast asleep.

Her el wardrobe she now saw a fatal necessity of selling, both for the preservation of her children and herself. With tears in her eyes, she parted with these last relics of her former glory, and with the money she got for them, bought others more useful, some playthings for her boys, and a gold watch for herself.

But scarcely was she provided with the above-mentioned necessaries, than she began to find herself rather hungry, and had reason to think, by their biting off too two of her fingers, that her children were much in the same situation.

To remedy these unavoidable misfortunes, she determined to return to her old friends, Sir George and Lady Harcourt, whose generosity she had so often experienced and hoped to experience as often again.

She had about forty miles to travel before she could reach their hospitable mansion, of which having walked thirty without stopping, she found herself at the entrance of a town, where often in happier times, she had accompanied Sir George and Lady Harcourt to regale themselves with a cold collation[14] at one of the inns.

The reflections that her adventures since the last time she had partaken of this these happy *junketings* afforded her, occupied her mind, for some time, as she sat on the steps ~~of~~ at the door of a gentleman's house. As soon as these reflections were ended, she arose and determined to take her station at the very inn she remembered with so much delight, from the company of which, as they went in and out, she hoped to receive some charitable gratuity[15].

She had but just taken her post at the inn yard before a carriage drove out of it, and on turning the corner at which she was stationed, stopped to give the postilion an opportunity of admiring the beauty of the prospect. Eliza then advanced to the carriage and was going to request their charity, when on fixing her eyes on the lady, within it, she exclaimed, "Lady Harcourt!"

To which the lady replied, "Eliza!"

"Yes Madam, it is the wretched Eliza herself."

Sir George, who was also in the carriage, but too much amazed to speak, was proceeding to demand an explanation from Eliza of the situation she was then in, when Lady Harcourt in transports of joy, exclaimed:

"Sir George, Sir George, she is not only Eliza our adopted daughter, but our real child."

"Our real child! What, Lady Harcourt, do you mean? You know you never even was with child. Explain yourself, I beseech you."

"You must remember, Sir George, that when you sailed for America, you left me breeding."

"I do, I do, go on, dear Polly."

"Four months after you were gone, I was delivered of this girl, but dreading your just resentment at her not proving the boy you wished, I took her to a haycock and laid her down. A few weeks afterwards, you returned, and fortunately for me, made no enquiries on the subject. Satisfied within myself of the welfare of my child, I soon forgot I had one, insomuch that when we shortly after found ~~this~~ her in the very haycock I had placed her, I had no more idea of her being my own, than you ~~do~~ had, and nothing, I will venture to say, would have recalled the circumstance to my remembrance, but my thus accidentally hearing her voice, which ~~never before struck me with~~ now strikes me as being the very counterpart of my own child's."

"The rational and convincing account you have given of the whole affair," said Sir George, "leaves no doubt of her being our daughter, and as such I freely forgive the robbery she was guilty of."

A mutual reconciliation then took place, and Eliza,

ascending the carriage with her two children, returned to that home from which she had been absent nearly four years.

No sooner was she reinstated in her accustomed power at Harcourt Hall, than she raised an army, with which she entirely demolished the Duchess's Newgate, snug as it was, and by that act, gained the blessings of thousands, and the applause of her own heart.

Finis

Notes

1. "Miss Cooper": Lady Jane Williams, née Cooper, (1771-98) was Austen's cousin and close friend from childhood. In 1783, she attended school first in Oxford and then in Southampton with Jane and Cassandra who acted as witnesses to her 1792 wedding. Cooper took a very active role in the Steventon dramatic performances. She was tragically killed by a runaway horse while on the Isle of Wight.

2. "haycock": A conical mound of hay. Eliza appears to be named after Eliza Hancock, Austen's adventurous and exotic cousin. The word 'haycock' is virtually identical to 'Hancock' – a family joke.

3. "three months old": The foundling was a very common plot device in the fiction of the day.

4. "fifty pound": Worth over $1,500 in today's money.

5. "going to service": That is, hiring oneself out as a domestic servant – definitely a course of last resort. Eliza is seeking to be a companion to the Duchess, a position that (like that of governess) allowed the employee to retain an aura of gentility but which was often abused by the employer.

6. "friendship for Mrs. Wilson": Acquaintance between an innkeeper and a duchess stresses credibility; a friendship where the duchess travels personally to collect an employee is inconceivable.

7. "her passions were strong, her friendships firm, and her enmities unconquerable": Compare Darcy's description of himself, "I cannot forget the follies and vices of others so soon as I ought, nor their offenses against myself. My feelings are not puffed about with every attempt to move them. My temper would perhaps be called resentful. My good opinion once lost, is lost forever" (*Pride and Prejudice*, Ch. 11).

8. "Surrey": A small county in south east England that lies to the south west of London.

9. "a private union": This would require a common license which had to be obtained from a bishop. A common license allowed a couple to marry without the reading of the banns. Of course, no license is mentioned, so the marriage would have been illegal.

10. "Her Grace ... confinement": The entire description of the Duchess's plans for revenge are patently absurd. They reflect the excesses of medieval tyrants in Gothic novels.

11. "at the rate of £18,000 a year, of which Mr. Cecil's estate being rather less than the twentieth part, they had been able to save but a trifle": It seems that Austen originally wrote 10,000 and then changed it to 18,000; she might, however, have intended the new figure to be 12,000. Either way, this is a joke by reversal. In real life, holding assets of £18,000 would give an annual income of about £900 a year (the "twentieth part" or 5%); if one spent the full £900, one would not be able to save anything to add to one's capital. Austen's fictional Henry Cecil spends £18,000 a year (a rather fabulous sum) from a total capital of less than £900, and so is "able to save but a trifle" (Pemberley.com). (These figures have to be adjusted if we take the figure to be £12,000 which would provide a total capital of less than £600.) For comparison, Mr. Darcy's entire income comes to £10,000 a year.

12. "man-of-war": A warship in the British Navy. A huge vessel, the equivalent of a twentieth century battleship. Having an odd number of guns is a fine comic touch – obviously each side should have the same number of guns.

13. "Newgate": A private dungeon (such as did not exist at this date) named after the famous London prison.

14. "collation": A light, informal meal.

15. "charitable gratuity": That is, she is begging.

Commentary

The title of this novel is as unreliable as are the previous ones, since, though Henry does fall in love with and marry Eliza, he hardly appears, and his main contribution to the plot is to die leaving his wife penniless. Eliza is the sole protagonist of this picaresque novel (a fiction in which the hero, a likeable rogue, goes through a series of episodic adventures) which reads like a parody of *The History of Tom Jones, a Foundling* (1749) by Henry Fielding (1707-1754). Austen inverts the gender roles which normally make the adventurous foundling a male and further subverts the genre by making her protagonist constitutionally dishonest, vengeful and vicious, whereas Tom Jones is a fundamentally good-hearted fellow.

Henry and Eliza is the first story in the juvenilia to have a structured plot. There are two plot strands: Eliza's relationship with Sir George and Lady Harcourt, which begins and concludes the circular narrative, and her relationship with the Duchess of F—. Each strand has exactly the same structure: upon first meeting, Eliza appears charming and good; Eliza is taken in and treated very well; Eliza steals from her benefactor(s); Eliza is punished for her theft; and Eliza triumphs over the consequences of her own misdeeds. The resolution (or happy ending) is achieved by reversing the normal foundling plot: it is Eliza who finds her biological parents, rather than they who find her. Though tidily symmetrical, the plot is in other ways perfunctory and frankly slap-dash. Characters enter, perform their function, and arbitrarily disappear from the story: Eliza's "most intimate friend" the landlady of the

Red Lion (in itself an unlikely alliance given Eliza's gentry status) writes the letter that gets the heroine into the household of the Duchess of F— and never features again; Eliza's two infants, having served their comic purpose in being thrown out of the prison cell window and gnawing off two of Eliza's fingers, simply vanish since Sir George and Lady Harcourt appear not to see them.

Henry and Eliza is a satire on contemporary sentimental fiction. Emily Auerbach says of the protagonists of the juvenilia, "The heroines of Austen's juvenilia just do not seem to have read those conduct books advising young women to be pious, modest, silent in company, and self-effacing, ignoring their own inclinations in deference to the needs and wishes of their husbands" (53). To this description of 'girls behaving badly,' we really should add that there is another set of heroines in the juvenilia who appear to have read far too many sentimental novels and to have absorbed uncritically from them how a young woman ought feel, act and react. Eliza is a prime example of Auerbach's description: she breaks all of the rules, and a great many laws, yet by sheer force of personality, together with some novelistic good fortune, she triumphs over ever obstacle and enemy. Nor does Eliza consider herself to be bound by the rules and laws that govern the conduct of ordinary people; as a person of "noble and ... exalted mind" and "conscious knowledge of her own excellence," she considers herself to be above such considerations. We have said that Eliza has certainly not imbibed the conduct of the sentimental female from novels – even faced by the most challenging situations, she does not cry, nor faint, nor run mad even once. She seems, however, to be surrounded by people out of sentimental novels – characters who judge by appearance, make instant intimate friendships, suffer extremes of feeling, and are therefore easy victims for a selfish young woman who puts her own desires above everything and everyone else.

The narrator cannot be trusted because, from the very beginning when we are told that Eliza has "a natural turn" to love virtue and hate vice, the third person narrative is limited to Eliza's own perspective. Thus, when she is caught stealing £50, the narrator puts the discovery of the theft down to simple bad luck ("happening one day to be detected") rather than to bad morals, and her foster parents become the villains. The narrator calls them "inhuman benefactors" – a delightfully comic oxymoron (i.e., a figure of speech in which apparently contradictory terms appear in conjunction). Given the inherently amoral nature of the protagonist, characters must be judged by what they do not by what they say, or by what other characters, or even the narrator, say about them. The narrator's point of view remains that of the heroine for the rest of the story, and therefore readers should bear in mind D. H. Lawrence's advice, "Never trust the teller, trust the tale."

The story begins with one of those absurdly incongruous juxtapositions in which Austen delights, "Sir George and Lady Harcourt were superintending the labours of their haymakers, rewarding the industry of some by smiles of approbation, and punishing the idleness of others by a cudgel." Sir George and his Lady initially seem to be benevolent landowners (Mr. Darcy types), but they instantly metamorphose into brutal tyrants. As usual, the narrator passes over the incongruity without comment as thought there were nothing remarkable about the scene being described.

The three-month-old Eliza immediately makes a good impression: she is beautiful, her face is enchantingly graceful, and she gives "infantine though sprightly answers" to the Sir George and Lady Harcourt's questions. Neither they nor the narrator finds anything remarkable in a talking baby! Their efforts to "incite in her a love of virtue and a hatred of vice" succeed because Eliza has "a natural turn that way herself," which turns out to be the very opposite of the truth. Convinced of the superiority of her "noble and exalted … mind [i.e., sensibility]," Eliza extemporizes a song whose theme is her own virtue and innocence.

The amiable, and gullible, Mrs. Wilson recommends Eliza to the Duchess of F— as "a young woman of unexceptionable character, who is so good as to choose your society in preference to going to service." This makes it appear as though Eliza is doing the Duchess some kind of favor. The reverse is true, since "going into service" would be a painful step down for a young woman brought up in a gentry family.

Instantly upon meeting Eliza, the Duchess (evidently a reader of sentimental novels) "resolved they never more should part"; her daughter, Lady Harriet (with the same reading background), feels the same instant bond and "besought her to consider her as her sister." Eliza's charms, however, extend also to the males; with the help of the Duchess's chaplain, who is besotted with her, she secretly marries and runs off with Mr. Henry Cecil, Lady Harriet's fiancé. The Duchess, out of an excess of sensibility spends "an agreeable half hour in calling them by all the shocking names her rage could suggest" (an activity which she finds "agreeable"), and then, out of an excess of the melodramatic gothic, sends three hundred armed men to arrest the miscreants.

Eliza and Henry escape, but retribution comes when, after three years, Henry dies in France and Eliza, with two young sons, is left penniless, though fortunately with access to a man-of-war, "which they had built in their more prosperous days," on which she sails back to England. Detained in a prison cell which, by pure chance, contains "a small saw and ladder of ropes," she is able to make her escape by throwing down her extensive collection of clothes which make a soft landing for her boys. Austen is here parodying the very common plot device of a cunning escape from imprisonment beloved of authors of Gothic romances. Eliza then sells these same clothes and with the money buys things "more useful, some playthings for her boys, and a gold watch for herself." Eliza's idea of the useful is faulty since she soon perceives herself and her children to be hungry, which she "had reason to think, by their biting off two of her fingers" – a surreal touch. Austen's parody of the use of coincidence and chance in literature takes her well into the absurd world that would be rediscovered in the twentieth century by dramatists such as Samuel Beckett and Harold Pinter and comedians such as the Monty Python team.

Eliza resolves on throwing herself on the mercy of her foster parents and, having walked "thirty [miles] without stopping" (presumably a penance that makes her worthy of being saved by the author's manipulation of the plot) has the good fortune to encounter the coach of Sir George and Lady Harcourt at an inn. At this point, the Lady reveals that the foundling "'is not only Eliza our adopted daughter, but our real child.'" She knows this, she says, because her chance hearing of Eliza's voice has reminded her of the voice of her own two-month old child. Sir George is totally convinced by the "'rational and convincing account'" which his wife proceeds to give. Unlike the reader, it does not seem in any way odd to him that: having left his wife pregnant to go to America, he made no enquiry about the outcome of her pregnancy on his return; his wife, having placed the baby girl in a haycock, then forgot that she had ever had a baby; she did not make the connection between her own baby and the baby they found under the same haycock; the baby survived under this haycock for over three weeks without food; Lady Harcourt did not recognize Eliza's voice as that of her own baby in the eighteen years she lived with the family, but instantly did so when she heard Eliza call out to the coach. Austen is having great fun mocking contrived happy endings.

Eliza is allowed her revenge. She raises an army which demolishes the Duchess's prison, earning the "blessings of thousands, and the applause of her own heart." Eliza's view of herself as a superior being is validated by her status of universal benefactress.

The Adventures of Mr. Harley

a short, but interesting tale, is with all imaginable respect inscribed to Mr. Francis William Austen, Midshipman on board His Majesty's Ship the *Perseverance* by his obedient servant
The Author[1].

Mr. Harley[2] was one of many children. Destined by his father for the church and by his mother for the sea, desirous of pleasing both, he prevailed on Sir John to obtain for him a chaplaincy on board a man-of-war. He accordingly cut his hair and sailed.

In half a year he returned and set off in the stage coach for Hogsworth Green[3], the seat of Emma. His fellow travelers were: a man without a hat, another with two, an old maid, and a young wife.

This last appeared about seventeen, with fine dark eyes and an elegant shape; in short, Mr. Harley soon found out that she was his Emma and recollected he had married her a few weeks before he left England.

Finis

Notes

1. Like her previous dedication of *Jack and Alice* to Francis, this one was added later, squeezed into an inadequate space between the title and the first line of the story. Since two of Austen's brothers (the second being her youngest "particular brother" Charles) went into the Navy (where they were both very successful), this story must reflect discussions had amongst the family about their career choices.

2. "Mr. Hartley": For her protagonist, Austen chooses the name of the hero of *The Man of Feeling* (1777) by Henry Mackenzie (1745-1831). This novel of sentiment presents fragmentary episodes of the life of the sensitive, empathetic protagonist. Austen's Mr. Hartley, in contrast, appears to be deficient in sentiment to say the least!

3. "Hogsworth Green": The name evokes the very opposite of a pastoral idyll. This would be the country seat of Emma's family.

Commentary

The essential joke is the compression of the plot. Apparently Mr. Hartley needs no preparation to become an ordained minister other than cutting his hair and his initial period of service is unrealistically brief.

He appears to have no interest at all in his fellow travelers whom he simply perceives by external details. Almost as forgetful as Lady Harcourt, Mr. Hartley returns from his first voyage as ship's chaplain and does not recognize the young woman whom "he had married … a few weeks before he left England." Critics usually fail to point out that Emma also fails to recognize her husband of six months.

Sir William Montague

an unfinished performance is humbly dedicated to Charles John Austen Esquire[1], by his most obedient humble servant
The Author

Sir William Mountague was the son of Sir Henry Mountague, who was the son of Sir John Mountague, a descendant of Sir Christopher Mountague, who was the nephew of Sir Edward Mountague, whose ancestor was Sir James Mountague, a near relation of Sir Robert Mountague, who inherited the title and estate from Sir Frederic Mountague[2].

Sir William was about seventeen when his father died, and left him a handsome fortune, an ancient house, and a park well stocked with deer[3]. Sir William had not been long in the possession of his estate before he fell in love with the three Miss Cliftons of Kilhoobery Park[4]. These young ladies were all equally young, equally handsome, equally rich and equally amiable – Sir William was equally in love with them all, and knowing not which to prefer, he left the country and took lodgings in a small village near Dover.

In this retreat, to which he had retired in the hope of finding a shelter from the pangs of love, he became enamoured ~~with~~ of a young widow of quality, who came for change of air to the same village, after the death of a husband, whom she had always tenderly loved and now sincerely lamented.

Lady Percival was young, accomplished and lovely. Sir William adored her and she consented to become his wife. Vehemently pressed by Sir William to name the day in which he might conduct her to the altar, she at length fixed on the following Monday, which was the first of September[5]. Sir William was a shot[6] and could not support the idea of losing such a day, even for such a cause. He begged her to delay the wedding a short time. Lady Percival was enraged and returned to London the next morning.

Sir William was sorry to lose her, but ~~it would~~ as he knew that he should have been much more grieved ~~at~~ by the loss of the 1st of September, his sorrow was not without a mixture of happiness, and his affliction was considerably lessened by his joy.

After staying at the village a few weeks longer, he left it and went to a friend's house in Surrey. Mr. Brudenell was a sensible man, and had a beautiful niece with whom Sir William soon fell in love. But Miss Arundel was cruel; she preferred a Mr. Stanhope: Sir William shot Mr. Stanhope[7]; the lady had then no reason to refuse him; she accepted him, and they were to be married on the 27th of October. But on the 25th Sir William received a visit from Emma Stanhope, the sister of the unfortunate victim of his rage. She begged some recompense, some atonement for the cruel murder of her brother. Sir William bade her name her price. She fixed on fourteen shillings[8]. Sir William offered her himself and fortune. They went to London the next day and were there privately married[9]. For a fortnight Sir William was completely happy, but chancing one day to see a charming young woman entering a chariot in Brook Street[10], he became again most violently in love. On enquiring the name of this fair unknown, he found that she was the sister of his old friend Lady Percival, ~~with~~ at which he was much rejoiced, as he hoped to have, by his acquaintance with her Ladyship, free access[11] to Miss Wentworth ...

Finis

Notes

1. "Charles John Austen Esquire": Austen's youngest brother, Charles, (1779-1852) eventually rose to the rank of Rear Admiral in the Royal Navy. At the time this story was written (conjecturally late 1788), Charles would have been nine. Even at the later date on which it was transcribed, "Esquire" is comically premature.

2. The detailed genealogy of the protagonist is a parody of the style of entries in *A New Baronetage of England* (1769) by John Debrett (1753-1822). Its length and detail is in comically inverse proportion to the story.

3. "well stocked with deer": Deer were something of a status symbol since they added beauty to an estate as well as offering the opportunity for hunting.

4. "Kilhoobery Park": Another of Austen's comic names. This one has an Irish feel despite the English setting.

5. "the first of September": This is the first day of the partridge, duck, woodcock and goose shooting season which extends until February 1st.

6. "a shot": That is, one who enjoys and is expert in the sport of shooting.

7. "Sir William shot Mr. Stanhope": Sir William is able to turn his shooting skills to practical use by getting rid of a rival. Perhaps the two fought a duel, but the implication is that Sir William simply murdered Mr. Stanhope.

8. "fourteen shillings": This is an absurdly small price to pay. The legal authorities appear to have no interest in the prosecution of Sir William, though his guilt seems to be generally known.

9. "privately marriage": A private marriage (as opposed to a church marriage following the reading of the banns) needed a common license and to get that the groom needed to be twenty-one or older, which Sir William is not. The marriage is, therefore, illegal.

10. "Brook Street": A very fashionable street in Mayfair, London, which was developed in the first half of the eighteenth century.

11. "free access": This immediately strikes the reader as an odd phrase. It means the legal right of owners of property to some means of access to their property from a road or highway over land belonging to others.

Commentary

In a very short period, Sir William falls in love with: the three Clifton sisters of Kilhoobery Park, with whom he is "equally in love"; Lady Percival, a young, grieving widow; Miss Arundel, who agrees to marry him after he has shot her lover; Emma Stanhope, the sister of the murdered man, whom he actually marries; and Miss Wentworth, who proves to be the sister of Lady Percival. The story thus mocks the literary conventions of love at first sight.

Austen maintained, both in her life and her fiction, that a man and woman must first know and respect each other; love came later. Elizabeth Bennet gets the order of things right when she tells her father, "'I do, I do like him ... I love him.'" (*Pride and Prejudice*, Ch. 59). The story also parodies arbitrary plot twists and inconsistent characters.

If Sir William is entirely selfish, for example in preferring a day's shooting to marrying Lady Percival, some of the ladies emerge with even less credit. We are told that Lady Percival "tenderly loved and now sincerely lamented" her late husband, but she forgets him soon enough when she meets Sir William. Similarly, we are assured that "Miss Arundel was cruel; she preferred a Mr. Stanhope: Sir William shot Mr. Stanhope; the lady had then no reason to refuse him; she accepted him." Notice again Austen's predilection for writing the most outrageous things in the most calm and reasonable manner. There is no suggestion that Miss Arundel is unaware of what Sir William has done but now has no "reason to refuse him." She has, of course, every "reason" for refusing; she accepts because of her feelings. Even worse is Emma Stanhope, the sister of the man Sir William shot, who originally comes to him for "some atonement for the cruel murder of her brother." Finally, she decides on "fourteen shillings" (not a great sum even in those days), but settles instead for the hand of Sir William, who manages to remain faithful to her for a fortnight.

Memoirs of Mr. Clifford – an unfinished tale

To Charles John Austen Esquire
Sir,

~~Permit~~ Your generous patronage[1] of the unfinished tale, I have already taken the liberty of dedicating to you, encourages me to dedicate to you a second, as unfinished as the first.
I am, sir, with every expression of regard for you and your noble family, your most obedient
&c &c ....
The Author

Mr. Clifford lived at Bath; and having never seen London, set off one Monday morning determined to feast his eyes with a sight of that great metropolis. He travelled in his coach and four, for he was a very rich young man and kept a great many carriages of which I do not recollect half. I can only remember that he had a coach, a chariot, a chaise, a landeau, a landeaulet, a phaeton, a gig, a whisky, an Italian chair, a buggy, a curricle and a wheelbarrow[2]. He had likewise an amazing fine stud[3] of horses. To my knowledge he had six greys, four bays, eight blacks and a pony.

In his coach and four bays, Mr. Clifford sate[4] forward about five o'clock on Monday morning the 1st of May for London. He always travelled[5] remarkably expeditiously and contrived therefore to get to Devizes from Bath, which is no less than nineteen miles, the first day. To be sure he did not get in till eleven at night and pretty tight work it was as you may imagine.

However, when he was once got to Devizes, he was determined to comfort himself with a good hot supper and therefore ordered a whole egg to be boiled for him and his servants[6]. The next morning he pursued his journey and in the course of three days hard labour reached Overton, where he was seized with a ~~violent~~ dangerous fever the consequence of too violent exercise.

Five months did our hero remain in this celebrated city under the care of its no less celebrated physician[7], who at length completely cured him of his troublesome disease.

As Mr. Clifford still continued very weak, his first day's journey carried him only to Dean Gate, where he remained a few days and found himself much benefited by the change of air[8].

In easy stages he proceeded to Basingstoke. One day carrying him to Clarken Green, the next to Worting, the third to the bottom of Basingstoke Hill, and the fourth, to Mr. Robins's[9]

...

Finis

Notes

1. "generous patronage": Austen's joke is that her younger brother Charles would be in no position to provide his sister with financial support. Neither were the Austen's a noble family, though on the Leigh side they had some connection with the nobility.

2. It really is not necessary to know the precise nature of each kind of carriage. The joke is that for a young man who never goes anywhere, he has a lot of carriages – remember that those listed are only the half that the narrator can remember. The list ends in bathos (an effect of anticlimax created by an unintentional lapse in mood from the sublime to the trivial or ridiculous) with that most humble of wheeled vehicles, the wheelbarrow.

3. "stud": A collection of fine horses kept for breeding purposes.

4. "sate": An archaic form of the past tense of the verb 'to set out.'

5. Full details of Mr. Clifford's route and his progress (or lack of progress)

along it are given in the Commentary which follows the Notes.

6. "a whole egg ... servants": Mr. Clifford seems to be as slow in spending his money as he is in traveling the roads.

7. "celebrated physician": The idea of a celebrated physician living in a small place like Overton is absurd.

8. "change of air": The air cannot have changed much since he has only gone a few miles.

9. "Mr. Robins's": A historical figure: Thomas Robins was landlord of the Crown Inn and Post House at Basingstoke.

Commentary

The story's essential joke is the contrast between how Mr. Clifford is introduced in the opening paragraph and a half and the way he is described after that. He is a very rich man with an amazing collection of carriages (too many for the narrator to recall them all, but the list ends in "a wheelbarrow" which is a comic anticlimax that prepares us for the greater anticlimax to come) and fine horses, who sets off, at 5 am on Monday morning, "determined to feast his eyes with a sight of that great metropolis" and, we are assured, "always travelled remarkably expeditiously." The problem is that he never gets very far.

Whether consciously of not, Austen makes his journey a comic version of Zeno's dichotomy which states, "That which is in locomotion must arrive at the half-way stage before it arrives at the goal." As a result, a person travelling from Point A to Point B can never actually reach Point B, but must make smaller and smaller movements bisecting the remaining distance, and so *ad infinitum*. This is exactly what happens as Mr. Clifford travels from Bath to London, though appreciating the joke does depend upon a clear knowledge of geography, which Austen could confidently assume that her readers had, since members of her family were very familiar with this region.

On the first stage, from Devizes from Bath, we are told that, though it is "pretty tight work," he achieves "no less than nineteen miles" in eighteen hours. Fairly obviously this is an average pace of little over one mile an hour! He could walk it more quickly. Following his exertions, this rich man "determined to comfort himself with a good hot supper ... ordered a whole egg to be boiled for him and his servants."

The second stage of the journey, from Devizes to Overton, takes "three days hard labour." In this time, he travels a distance of approximately forty-five miles, at an average of around fifteen miles a day. Mr. Clifford here pays the price of such break-neck speed, coming down with a "dangerous fever the consequence of too violent exercise" which detains him in Overton for five months.

The third stage is from Overton to Dean Gate, a distance of two miles travelled in one day, which requires that he rest there "a few days." The fourth stage from Dean Gate to Clarken Green is a distance of two miles; the fifth from Clarken Green to Worting is also two miles; the sixth from Worting to the bottom of Basingstoke Hill is a mile; and the seventh from there to the Crown Inn is also a mile. In total, the distance from Dean to Basingstoke is six miles, which Mr. Clifford covers in four days.

This area would have been very familiar to members of the Austen family, since James Austen, the eldest of the Austen children, was appointed curate of Overton in Hampshire in 1789, Overton being the nearest town next to their father's parish at Steventon. Austen could expect her readers to know that the journey from Bath to London is one hundred and ten miles and that it could be made comfortably in two days.

The Beautiful Cassandra

a novel, in twelve chapters dedicated by permission to Miss Austen[1].

Dedication

Madam,

You are a Phoenix[2]. Your taste is refined; your sentiments are noble; and your virtues innumerable. Your person is lovely, your figure elegant, and your form majestic. Your manners are polished; your conversation is rational; and your appearance singular. If, therefore, the following tale will afford one moment's amusement to you, every wish will be gratified of

Your most obedient humble servant

The Author

Chapter the First

Cassandra was the daughter and the only daughter of a celebrated milliner in Bond Street[3]. Her father was of noble birth, being the near relation of the Duchess of —'s butler.

Chapter the 2nd

When Cassandra had attained her sixteenth year, she was lovely and amiable, and chancing to fall in love with an elegant bonnet her mother had just completed, bespoke[4] by the Countess[5] of —, she placed it on her gentle head[6] and walked from her mother's shop to make her fortune.

Chapter the 3rd

The first person she met, was the Viscount[7] of —, a young man, no less celebrated for his accomplishments and virtues, than for his elegance and beauty. She curtseyed and walked on.

Chapter the 4th

She then proceeded to a pastry-cook's, where she devoured six ices[8], refused to pay for them, knocked down the pastry cook and walked away.

Chapter the 5th

She next ascended a hackney coach[9] and ordered it to Hampstead[10], where she was no sooner arrived than she ordered the coachman to turn round and drive her back again.

Chapter the 6th

Being returned to the same spot of the same street she had set out from, the coachman demanded his pay.

Chapter the 7th

She searched her pockets over again and again; but every search was unsuccessful. No money could she find. The man grew ~~arrogant~~ peremptory. She placed her bonnet on his head and ran away.

Chapter the 8th

Through many a street she then proceeded and met in none the least adventure, till on turning a corner of Bloomsbury Square[11], she met Maria.

Chapter the 9th

Cassandra started and Maria seemed surprised; they trembled, blushed, turned pale and passed each other in a mutual silence.

Chapter the 10th

Cassandra was next accosted by her friend ~~a~~ the widow, who squeezing out her little head through her less window[12], asked her how she did? ~~Miss~~ Cassandra curtseyed and went on.

Chapter the 11th

A quarter of a mile brought her to her paternal roof in Bond Street, from which she had now been absent nearly seven hours.

Chapter the 12th

She entered it and was pressed to her mother's bosom by that worthy woman. Cassandra smiled and whispered to herself, "This is a day well spent."

Finis

Notes

1. "Miss Austen": Cassandra Elizabeth (1773-1845), Jane's beloved elder sister. By convention the eldest daughter is called "Miss ---." Thus, in *Pride and Prejudice*, only Jane is ever addressed as "Miss Bennet" while Elizabeth is "Miss Elizabeth." A family visit to London in August 1788 may have provided inspiration and material for this story.

2. "Phoenix": That is, Cassandra is phoenix-like being a person of uniquely remarkable qualities – the phoenix being the only bird that can renew itself and thus live forever. The Oxford English Dictionary defines this use of the word thus, "a person (or thing) of unique excellence or of matchless beauty; a paragon." Austen is obviously inflating her praise for comic effect. However, throughout her life, Jane had a very real respect and admiration for Cassandra. In response to a letter from her sister (now lost since Cassandra destroyed all of her letters to Jane following her sister's death), Jane wrote, "The letter which I have this moment received from you has diverted me beyond moderation. I could die of laughter at it, as they used to say at school. You are indeed *the finest comic writer of the present age*" (September 1st, 1796, emphasis added).

3. "a celebrated milliner in Bond Street": Milliners made bonnets, caps and other female attire. Bond Street was (and is) a very fashionable part of London.

4. "bespoke": Custom-made for a particular person; made to order.

5. "Countess": The wife or widow of a count or earl who holds that title in her own right.

6. "gentle head": That is, 'belonging to the gentry class' – which Cassandra's head does not since she is the daughter of a tradesperson, albeit one with the nobility for customers.

7. "Viscount": A nobleman in the fourth rank in the British peerage system, above a baron and below an Earl. Bond Street was a well known place where fashionable young gentlemen went to see and to be seen.

8. "six ices": Ice cream and water ices were sold in upper class London confectioners but were very expensive since the ice from which they were made had to be 'harvested' from frozen ponds in winter and preserved in ice houses for later use. Austen wrote of an up-coming visit to Godmersham in Kent where her rich brother, Edward, had an ice house, "I shall eat ice and drink French wine, and be above vulgar economy."

9. "hackney coach": A coach for hire. Hackney coaches first appeared in London in the 1630s. Cassandra would have ridden in an open, four-wheeled coach drawn by two horses with seating for six and a uniformed driver. (The famous Hackney Cab, a two-wheeled coach drawn by a single horse with the driver perched on a seat at the rear, beloved of Sherlock Holmes fans, did not appear in London until 1823.) Peter Sabor estimates that Cassandra would owe "about eight shillings for the eight-mile round-trip to Hampstead"

(*Juvenilia* 408); Kathryn Sutherland agrees on the distance but estimates the fare at about five shillings (*Teenage* 271).

10. "Hampstead": A fashionable, rural suburb four miles north of Bond Street with great views over London.

11. "Bloomsbury Square": One of the earliest of London's squares which attracted wealthy residents.

12. "less window": The widow's head is small, but the window through which she looks out is smaller still. Presumably, it is one in an upper story where windows were smaller and rents were lower.

Commentary

This miniature picaresque novel features Austen's typical inversion of gender stereotypes since novels of this genre typically feature the adventures of a youthful male protagonist. Austen's heroine is another of her 'girls behaving badly.' Natalie Tyler writes that "[Cassandra] delights in flouting convention and in indulging her own impulses no matter what the consequences might be ... [She] determinedly follows her own desires, her own appetites, her own caprices..." (38). She has none of the affectations of those young women in the juvenilia who have bought into the cult of sensibility– it is hard to envisage Cassandra fainting or running mad no matter what the provocation. She is, however, unashamedly egotistical. John Leffel explains what he takes to be Austen's intention in drawing this character:

> [B]y depicting a heroine who boldly and unapologetically flaunts gender boundaries, social codes, and even laws, Austen ultimately challenges her era's stifling restrictions on women's bodies and minds at the same time that she questions exactly what constitutes a "novel." ("Austen's Miniature 'Novel'" 187)

Perhaps quite naturally, some critics have found in Cassandra an early version of the egotistical Lydia Bennet, though the former is certainly the more engaging.

Cassandra is introduced as "lovely and amiable and chancing to fall in love." All three are typical of heroines in sentimental fiction, but they are comically subverted when we learn that the object of Cassandra's love is a bonnet not a man. Simply by walking out unaccompanied, Cassandra is committing an indecorous act: unmarried young women simply did not walk unaccompanied in town – the only women who did *that* were prostitutes. The first person she meets is a young Viscount, "a young man, no less celebrated for his accomplishments and virtues, than for his elegance and beauty." Here is more gender reversal for the four qualities named are those associated with young women rather than young men (who might more normally be praised for their handsome features, impeccable manners, tasteful dress and serious learning).

Next, Cassandra indulges her appetite by going into a pastry shop, "where she devoured six ices, refused to pay for them, knocked down the pastry cook and walked away." Notice the force of the verb "devoured." Cassandra eats in a way that is an act of rebellion against the suppression of bodily appetites stressed in conduct books for young ladies. Similarly, she does not just fail to pay for the ices and run out; Cassandra is much more assertive than that. She "refused" to pay for them and "knocked down" the (presumably male) pastry cook.

The next male to be triumphed over is the driver of a hackney coach. By making him drive out to Hamstead and then return to "the same spot of the same street she had set out from," Cassandra mocks his entire function (which is to take people somewhere they want to go). At last, a male becomes threatening as the driver "demanded his pay" and "grew peremptory." The undaunted Cassandra "placed her bonnet on his head and ran away." The bonnet would, in terms of its value, more than pay her debt (except that it was 'stolen' from her mother's shop), but placing it on the man's head effectively feminizes him – more triumphant role reversal.

To her offence against decorum in walking the streets and hiring a carriage as a lone young woman, Cassandra now adds being bare-headed which was quite improper, yet in this manner, "Through many a street she then proceeded," wording which implies her complete comfort with herself and the image she is projecting. There follow meetings with two females: Maria and her friend the widow. Maria makes quite an impression on Cassandra and Cassandra on her, "Cassandra started and Maria seemed surprised; they trembled, blushed, turned pale and passed each other in a mutual silence." The reactions of both are familiar from sentimental novels, but there they are generally used to describe a woman's feelings of instant attraction toward a man. Just what is happening between the two is unclear: Are they falling in love? Is this, perhaps, a private joke between Austen and her sister? The meeting with the widow is less ambiguous. John Leffel suggests that:

> the widow, seemingly stuck within the confines of her small window, symbolizes the restraints (physical, intellectual, social, and economic) placed upon women in Austen's time – restraints that Cassandra comically flaunts and that the young Jane Austen herself challenges by writing a female mock-picaresque. ("Austen's Miniature 'Novel'" 192)

This might explain why Cassandra does not allow herself to be drawn into conversation with her friend. Indeed, she has spoken to no once since the start of her day out. The only words attributed to her in the entire novel are, "'This is a day well spent.'" Cassandra is self-congratulatory: she has broken the repressive mould of her life as a young woman, got away with it, and been received back into the bosom of her mother's love.

Amelia Webster

an interesting and well written tale is dedicated by permission to Mrs. Austen[1] by her humble servant
The Author.

Letter the first: To Miss Webster.

My Dear Amelia,

You will rejoice to hear of the return of my amiable brother from abroad. He arrived on Thursday, and never did I see a finer form, save that of your sincere friend
Matilda Hervey

Letter the second: To H. Beverley Esquire.

Dear Beverley,

I arrived here last Thursday and met with a hearty reception from my father, mother, and sisters. The latter are both fine girls – particularly Maud, who I think would suit you as a wife well enough. What say you to this? She will have two thousand pounds and as much more as you can get[2]. If you don't marry her you will mortally offend
George Hervey

Letter the third: To Miss Hervey[3].

Dear Maud,

Believe me, I'm happy to hear of your brother's arrival. I have a thousand things to tell you, but my paper will only permit me to add that I am your[4] affect[ionate] friend
Amelia Webster

Letter the fourth: To Miss S. Hervey.

Dear Sally,

I have found a very convenient old hollow oak to put our letters in[5]; for you know we have long maintained a private correspondence. It is about a mile from my house and seven from yours. You may perhaps imagine that I might have made choice of a tree which would have divided the distance more equally – I was sensible of this at the time, but as I considered that the walk would be of benefit to you in your weak and uncertain state of health, I preferred it to one nearer your house, and am your faithful
Benjamin Bar

Letter the fifth: To Miss Hervey.

Dear Maud,

I write now to inform you that ~~we~~ I did not stop at your house in my way to Bath last Monday. – I have many things to inform you of besides; but ~~the con~~ my paper reminds me of concluding[6]; and believe me yours ever andc.

Amelia Webster

Letter the sixth: To Miss Webster.

Saturday

Madam,

An humble admirer now addresses you – I saw you, lovely fair one, as you passed on Monday last, before our house in your way to Bath. I saw you through a telescope[7], and was so struck by your charms that from that time to this I have not tasted human food.

George Hervey

Letter the seventh: To Jack

As I was this morning at breakfast the newspaper was brought me, and in the list of marriages I read the following:

    George Hervey Esquire to Miss Amelia Webster
    Henry Beverley Esquire to Miss Hervey
    and
    Benjamin Bar Esquire to Miss Sarah Hervey

Yours, Tom

Finis

Notes

1. "Mrs. Austen": The author's mother, Cassandra Leigh Austen (1739-1827), had family connections with at least one duke and one lord. As an adult, at least on the evidence of her letters, Austen was often frustrated by what she saw as Mrs. Austen's nervous hypochondria. Nevertheless, she undoubtedly inherited her sense of humor from her mother.

2. George expresses the conviction that either of his sisters, but particularly Maud, "would suit" his friend (Henry) Beverley "as a wife well enough," despite the fact that the two appear never to have met and Maud appears not to have been consulted on the matter. Though this is not strictly speaking a marriage of convenience, economic factors are an important consideration. Maud will have, in her own right, an inheritance of £2,000 which would only generate £100 per annum – not enough for a married couple of the gentry class to live on. The reference to "as much more as you can get" is rather vague. This may refer to Beverley being able to get money from his own sources, but I believe it is a reference to any additional dowry that Beverley

might be able to negotiate with Maud's father.

3. Miss Hervey is Maud, the elder of the two sisters. Susan is Miss S. Hervey. Similarly in *Pride and Prejudice*, Jane is Miss Bennet and Elizabeth is Miss Elizabeth.

4. "my paper will only permit me to add that I am your...": This is a very conventional way of drawing a letter to a close, but here it makes no sense at all since the letter is so very short. It must have been a very small sheet of paper!

5. "to put our letters in": Secret letters placed in hiding places known only to the correspondents (often, as here, lovers) were a common plot device in epistolary novels.

6. "my paper reminds me of concluding": Another conventional turn of phrase that is absurd at the end of such a short letter.

7. "through a telescope": It is impossible to miss the phallic symbolism of the telescope particularly since it occurs in other works of fiction. In *The Summer House: or, The History of Mr. Morton and Miss Bamstead* (1768), which seems to be an erotic novel, a young man "increases the pleasures of vision" when he points his "uplifted tube" on the beautiful Almeria, who in turn "cannot get the telescope out of her head." Austen is a little more subtle in her symbolism.

Commentary

Amelia Webster parodies the Richardsonian novel-in-letters (whose characters seem to have nothing to do in life but to write to each other at inordinate length) except that, instead of filling several volumes, it is finished in two pages. The title is ironic since Amelia is the least active correspondent and her letters the least communicative. Richardson's characters also appear to have an endless supply of fine writing paper, whereas in Austen's novel the writers of two of the seven letters excuse themselves for writing virtually nothing at all on the grounds that they are at the end of their sheet of paper – presumably the only one they have access to. Nor are the contents of these letters of particular import. Amelia writes to Maud to inform her that she "did not stop at your house in my way to Bath last Monday" – something which Maud might have been expected to have noticed for herself.

Common staples of romantic fiction are also mocked. Benjamin Bar feels the need to remind his lover Sally Hervey that they "have long maintained a private correspondence," which one might have thought she would remember. The hidden letter gambit is rendered absurd by Benjamin's conception of "a very convenient old hollow oak to put" their letters in. The oak is certainly "convenient" for him being one mile from his home, but seven miles from Sally's home. The reverse logic of Benjamin's self-justification is delightful, "I considered that the walk would be of benefit to you in your weak and uncertain state of health." Logically, if Sally is ill, she should have the shortest possible walk. Love at first sight is ridiculed by making it happen through a telescope! George Hervey, something of a voyeur, is so smitten by Amelia merely by having seen her at a great distance that since seeing her first he has "not tasted human food," which raises the interesting question of what other kind of food he may have eaten.

The Visit – a comedy in two acts

Dedication: To the Reverend James Austen[1]
Sir,
The following drama, which I humbly recommend to your protection and patronage, though inferior to those celebrated comedies called "The School for Jealousy" and "The Travelled Man,"[2] will I hope afford some amusement to so respectable a *curate* as yourself; which was the end in view when ~~they~~ it was first composed by your humble servant the Author.

Dramatis Personae

Sir Arthur Hampton	Lady Hampton
Lord Fitzgerald	Miss Fitzgerald
Stanly	Sophy Hampton
Willoughby, Sir Arthur's nephew	Cloe Willoughby

The scenes are laid in Lord Fitzgerald's House.

ACT THE FIRST

Scene the First.

A parlour.
Enter LORD FITZGERALD and STANLY.
STANLY: Cousin, your servant.
FITZGERALD: Stanly, good morning to you. I hope you slept well last night.
STANLY: Remarkably well, I thank you.
FITZGERALD: I am afraid you found your bed too short. It was bought in my grandmother's time, who was herself a very short woman and made a point of suiting all her beds to her own length, as she never wished to have any company in the house, on account of an unfortunate impediment in her speech, which she was sensible of being very disagreeable to her inmates[3.].
STANLY: Make no more excuses, dear Fitzgerald.
FITZGERALD: I will not distress you by too much civility – I only beg you will consider yourself as much at home as in your father's house. Remember, "The more free, the more welcome."[4]

Exit FITZGERALD.

STANLY: Amiable youth!

Your virtues, could he imitate

How happy would be Stanly's fate!

Exit STANLY

Scene the Second

STANLY and MISS FITZGERALD, discovered.

STANLY: What company is it you expect to dine with you today, cousin?

MISS FITZGERALD: Sir Arthur and Lady Hampton; their daughter, nephew and niece.

STANLY: Miss Hampton and her cousin are both handsome, are they not?

MISS FITZGERALD: Miss Willoughby is extremely so. Miss Hampton is a fine girl, but not equal to her.

STANLY: Is not your brother attached to the latter?

MISS FITZGERALD: He admires her, I know, but I believe nothing more. Indeed I have heard him say that she was the most beautiful, pleasing, and amiable girl in the world, and that of all others he should prefer her for his wife. But it never went any farther, I'm certain.

STANLY: And yet my cousin never says a thing he does not mean.

MISS FITZGERALD: Never. From his cradle he has ~~ever~~ always been a strict adherent to truth. ~~He never told a lie but once, and that was merely to oblige me. Indeed, I may say there never was such a brother!~~

Exeunt severally.

End of the First Act.

ACT THE SECOND

Scene the First.

The drawing room.

Chairs set round in a row. LORD FITZGERALD, MISS FITZGERALD and STANLY seated.

Enter a Servant.

SERVANT: Sir Arthur and Lady Hampton. Miss Hampton, Mr. and Miss Willoughby.

Exit SERVANT.

Enter the Company.

MISS FITZGERALD: I hope I have the pleasure of seeing your Ladyship well. Sir Arthur, your servant. Yours, Mr. Willoughby.

Dear Sophy, Dear Cloe, –

They pay their compliments alternately.

MISS FITZGERALD: Pray be seated.

They sit.

Bless me! There ought to be eight chairs and there are but six. However, if your Ladyship will but take Sir Arthur in your lap, and Sophy ~~take~~ my brother in hers, I believe we shall do pretty well.

LADY HAMPTON: Oh! with pleasure....

SOPHY: I beg his Lordship would be seated.

MISS FITZGERALD: I am really shocked at crowding you in such a manner, but my grandmother (who bought all the furniture of this room) as she had never a very large party, did not think it necessary to buy more chairs than were sufficient for her own family and two of her particular friends.

SOPHY: I beg you will make no apologies. Your brother is very light.

STANLY (*aside*): What a cherub[5] is Cloe!

CLOE (*aside*): What a seraph[6] is Stanly!

Enter a Servant.

SERVANT: Dinner is on table.

They all rise

MISS FITZGERALD: Lady Hampton, Miss Hampton, Miss Willoughby.

STANLY hands CLOE, LORD FITZGERALD, SOPHY, WILLOUGHBY, MISS FITZGERALD; and SIR ARTHUR, LADY HAMPTON.

Exeunt.

Scene the Second.

The dining parlour.

MISS FITZGERALD at top. LORD FITZGERALD at bottom[7]. Company ranged on each side. Servants waiting.

CLOE: I shall trouble Mr. Stanly for a little of the fried cow heel and onion[8].

STANLY: Oh Madam, there is a secret pleasure in helping so amiable a lady. –

LADY HAMPTON: I assure you, my Lord, Sir Arthur never touches wine; but ~~however~~ Sophy will toss off a bumper[9] I am sure, to oblige your Lordship.

LORD FITZGERALD: Elder wine or mead[10], Miss Hampton?

SOPHY: If it is equal to you, Sir, I should prefer some warm ale with a toast and nutmeg[11].

LORD FITZGERALD: Two glasses of warmed ale with a toast and nutmeg.

MISS FITZGERALD: I am afraid, Mr. Willoughby, you take no care of yourself. I fear you don't meet with anything to your liking.

WILLOUGHBY: Oh! Madam, I can want for nothing while there are red herrings[12] on table.

LORD FITZGERALD: Sir Arthur, taste that tripe[13]. I think you will not find it amiss.

LADY HAMPTON: Sir Arthur never eats tripe; 'tis too savoury for ~~children~~ him, you know, my Lord.

MISS FITZGERALD: Take away the liver and crow[14], and bring in the suet pudding[15].

A short pause.

MISS FITZGERALD: Sir Arthur, shan't I send you a bit of pudding?

LADY HAMPTON: Sir Arthur never eats suet pudding, Ma'am. It is too high a dish[16] for him.

MISS FITZGERALD: Will no one allow me the honour of helping them? Then John, take away the ~~suet~~ pudding, and bring the wine.

SERVANTS take away the things and bring in the bottles and glasses.

LORD FITZGERALD: I wish we had any dessert to offer you. But my grandmother in her lifetime, destroyed the hothouse[17] in order to build a receptacle for the turkeys with its materials; and we have never been able to raise another tolerable one.

LADY HAMPTON: I beg you will make no apologies, my Lord.

WILLOUGHBY: Come girls, let us circulate the bottle[18].

SOPHY: A very good notion, cousin; and I will second it with all my heart. Stanly, you don't drink.

STANLY: Madam, I am drinking draughts of love from Cloe's eyes.

SOPHY: That's poor nourishment truly. Come, drink to her better acquaintance.

MISS FITZGERALD goes to a closet and brings out a bottle.

MISS FITZGERALD: This, Ladies and Gentlemen, is some of my dear grandmother's own manufacture. She excelled in gooseberry wine[19]. Pray taste it, Lady Hampton

LADY HAMPTON: How refreshing it is!

MISS FITZGERALD: I should think, with your Ladyship's permission, that Sir Arthur might taste a little of it.

LADY HAMPTON: Not for worlds. Sir Arthur never drinks

anything so high.

LORD FITZGERALD: And now my amiable Sophia, condescend to marry me.

He takes her hand and leads her to the front.

STANLY: Oh! Cloe, could I but hope you would make me blessed –

CLOE: I will.

They advance.

MISS FITZGERALD: Since you, Willoughby, are the only one left, I cannot refuse your earnest solicitations. – There is my hand.

LADY HAMPTON: And may you all be happy!

Finis

Notes

1. "Reverend James Austen": James (1765-1819) was the eldest of the Austen children. He had the reputation of being the 'literary one' in the family and was the leading light in the family theatricals at Steventon from 1782-1789. This skit might have been part of one of those performances. His publication, with his brother Henry, of the periodical *The Loiterer* must have been a significant influence on Austen. He was ordained at Oxford in 1789, became his father's curate at Deane, and took on the duties at Steventon after his father's retirement.

2. "'The School for Jealousy' and 'The Travelled Man'": No professional plays with these titles are known, so they are most likely plays (now lost) written for the Austen family theatricals probably by Jane herself though just possibly by James.

3. "inmates": He means her guests, the people staying at the house. The word did not yet have its present definition: prisoner.

4. "The more free, the more welcome": Compare *High Life Below Stairs: A Farce in Two Acts* (1759) by James Townley (1714-1778): "Lady Charlotte, pray be free; the more free, the more welcome, as they say in my Country." The phrase seems to have been a well-used aphorism.

5. "cherub": Winged angel attending on God. The second of the nine orders of angels.

6. "seraph": Highest order of angel associated with light, ardor, and purity.

7. As the hosts, Lord and Miss Fitzgerald are seated at the head and foot of the table.

8. "fried cow heel and onion": "Cowheel is the fatty cartilage from around a beast's heel." From *Modern domestic cookery, and useful receipt book* (1819) by Elizabeth Hammond, "having cut the heel into four parts, dip them in yolk of egg, strew grated bread over them, and fry of a nice brown in dripping: fry sliced onions, lay them in the middle of the dish, and the heel round it"

(*Foods of England Project*). As with all of the foods that follow, this is not really a dish served to such exalted company; it is more a dish for laborers and servants.

9. "bumper": A large glass filled to the brim (i.e., the wine literally 'bumping' against the rim). To "toss off a bumper" means to drain a full glass all in one motion – not ladylike at all.

10. "Elder wine or mead": Elderberry wine was a homemade alternative to much more expensive foreign wines. Austen's own family made wine at home. Mead is a traditional English alcoholic drink fermented with three basic ingredients: honey, yeast and water. It was also homemade.

11. "warm ale with a toast and nutmeg": A bit of spiced toast was put in the bottom of a cup or glass of ale or wine to flavor it. Nutmeg was a popular spice to use. Warming the ale (mulled ale) brought out the flavor of the spice. It had the reputation of being a drink for invalids and is therefore inappropriate for the young and sprightly Sophy.

12. "red herrings": A kipper, that is, a herring cured in brine and/or heavily smoked which gives it a red tint. Red herrings were used to lay a trail for hounds to follow, but the modern meaning (i.e., a false clue or trail) did not originate until 1804.

13. "tripe": Tripe is the edible muscle wall of a cow or sheep's stomach.

14. "liver and crow": Liver can be cooked in a variety of ways – fried with onions is a popular way. Eating crows' meat is essentially the same as eating the meat of any other bird, although crows are carrion birds. [The modern figurative sense of 'to eat crow' (i.e., to admit having been proved wrong) did not appear in print until 1850.]

15. "suet pudding": This would be a savory dish made from boiled or steamed suet (beef or mutton fat), mixed with flour and bread with a meat filling.

16. "too high a dish": This means food that is too spicy, or too rich in butter, cream and other ingredients that make it hard to digest. This would not apply to suet pudding which is rather a plain dish.

17. "Dessert... destroyed the hothouse": Because the hothouse (or greenhouse) was pulled down, there is no fruit, traditionally served with nuts for dessert.

18. "Come girls, let us circulate the bottle": Comic gender role reversal. Normally, after a meal, the women would withdraw allowing the men to smoke and drink some more. Here it is the women who drink heavily while the men drink little – Stanly and Sir Arthur abstain entirely.

19. "gooseberry wine": Another popular homemade wine – not at all the thing to serve at a sophisticated dinner party.

Commentary

The text follows exactly the conventions of printed drama, with stage directions, including asides and instructions on the actors' entrances, exits and movements. The playlet itself is a comic parody of society drama. The central joke is that the visit is being hosted by Lord Fitzgerald and his sister Miss

Fitzgerald who are definitely upper class – the sort of society with which Jane and Cassandra mixed when they visited the family of her rich brother, Edward Austen Knight, at Godmersham Park. However, neither the accommodation, the furniture, nor the food – all of which are inadequate – reflect the social position and wealth of the hosts. Austen wrote of being "above vulgar economy" when she visited Godmersham, but vulgar economy is in evidence throughout this play, not that any of the characters draws attention to it because of their good manners. The dialogue is limited to polite clichés.

The hosts blame everything on their dead grandmother. Thus, Lord Fitzgerald explains that the beds are all too short because his grandmother, "who was herself a very short woman ... made a point of suiting all her beds to her own length," with the intention of discouraging company because of her speech impediment "which she was sensible of being very disagreeable to her inmates" – so, of course, she was only doing it for their benefit! It appears not to have occurred to Lord Fitzgerald that, his grandmother now being dead, he might have purchased new beds. Similarly, Miss Fitzgerald blames the shortage of chairs on her grandmother who "did not think it necessary to buy more chairs than were sufficient for her own family and two of her particular friends." It appears not to have occurred to her to count up the number of her invited guests and so know in advance the number of chairs needed. She admits herself "really shocked at crowding [her guests] in such a manner," but her solution leads to a surreal scene of gender reversal in which Sir Arthur sits on Lady Hampton's lap and Lord Fitzgerald on Miss Hampton's lap, and they all "do pretty well." Fortunately, as Sophy reassures Miss Fitzgerald, her brother "is very light"! Austen source for this comic scene is *The Vicar of Wakefield* (1766) by Oliver Goldsmith (1728-1774) in which the vicar is visited by five ladies and gentlemen. He comments, "We happened not to have enough chairs for the whole company, but Mr. Thornhill immediately proposed that every gentleman should sit in a lady's lap" (Ch. 9).

The other comic aspect of the hospitality offered by the Fitzgeralds is that the food they serve is plebian fair: here are no French wines and ices such as Austen looked forward to enjoying when she went to Godmersham Park, but rather the sort of food and drink with which she would have been familiar at home. Just as there is no expensive ice for desserts there are no hothouse fruits, a failure that Lord Fitzgerald once again lays on his late grandmother, who "destroyed the hothouse in order to build a receptacle for the turkeys with its materials." The gooseberry wine is also of their "grandmother's own manufacture," and Lady Hampton feels obliged to compliment it, "How refreshing it is." Poor Lord Hampton seems to be effectively prevented by his wife from eating or drinking anything, but their daughter Sophy, Lady Hampton assures her hosts, "will toss off a bumper," which sounds a little less than refined table manners.

Love affairs amongst the characters provide a second comic element. The feelings of the lovers are deliberately not developed, so that they seem both arbitrary and excessive. Miss Fitzgerald reports that her brother has said of Sophy Hampton that she is, "the most beautiful, pleasing, and amiable girl in the world, and that of all others he should prefer her for his wife," but Miss Fitzgerald declares her not to be the equal of Cloe Willoughby. She is sure that her brother's attraction to Sophy "never went any farther," despite the fact that he always speaks the truth. Cloe Willoughby and Stanly seem to fall in love with each other almost simultaneously, each convinced that the other is an angel. At the conclusion of the dessertless meal, Lord Fitzgerald proposes to, and is accepted by, Sophy Hampton; ditto Stanly and Cloe; and Miss Fitzgerald (more gender role-reversal here) proposes to Willoughby saying, "Since you, Willoughby, are the only one left, I cannot refuse your earnest solicitations. – There is my hand." The first part of this statement is ridiculously arbitrary, and the second half is simply untrue since Willoughby has shown no sign of wanting anything in the play beyond red herrings and wine.

The Mystery – an unfinished comedy

Dedication: To the Reverend George Austen[1]

Sir,
I humbly solicit your patronage ~~of~~ to the following comedy, which though an unfinished one, is I flatter myself as complete a mystery as any of its kind.
I am sir, your most humble servant
The Author

Dramatis Personae

Men	Women
Colonel Elliott	Fanny Elliott
Sir Edward Spangle	Mrs. Humbug
Old Humbug	and Daphne
Young Humbug	
and Corydon	

Act the First

Scene the First

A Garden. *Enter CORYDON.*
CORY: But Hush! I am interrupted.
Exit CORYDON.
Enter OLD HUMBUG and his son, talking.
OLD HUMBUG: It is for that reason I wish you to follow my advice. Are you convinced of its propriety?

100

YOUNG HUMBUG: I am, sir, and will certainly act in the manner you have pointed out to me.

OLD HUMBUG: Then let us return to the house.

Exeunt.

Scene the Second

A parlour in Humbug's house.

MRS. HUMBUG and FANNY discovered at work[2].

MRS. HUMBUG: You understand me, my love?

FANNY: Perfectly ma'am. Pray continue your narration.

MRS. HUMBUG: Alas! It is nearly concluded, for I have nothing more to say on the subject.

FANNY: Ah! Here's Daphne.

Enter DAPHNE.

DAPHNE: My dear Mrs. Humbug, how d'ye do? Oh! Fanny, 'tis all over.

FANNY: It is indeed?!

MRS. HUMBUG: I'm very sorry to hear it.

FANNY: Then t'was to no purpose that I ....

DAPHNE: None upon earth.

MRS. HUMBUG: And what is to become of? .....

DAPHNE: Oh! That's all settled.

Whispers [to] MRS. HUMBUG.

FANNY: And how is it determined?

DAPHNE: I'll tell you.

Whispers [to] FANNY.

MRS. HUMBUG: And is he to? ...

DAPHNE: I'll tell you all I know of the matter.

Whispers [to] MRS. HUMBUG and FANNY.

FANNY: Well! Now I know everything about it, I'll go ~~and dress~~ away.

MRS. HUMBUG and DAPHNE: And so will I.

Exeunt.

Scene the Third

The curtain rises and discovers SIR EDWARD SPANGLE reclined in an elegant attitude on a sofa, fast asleep.

Enter COLONEL ELLIOTT.

COLONEL: My daughter is not here I see ... there lies Sir Edward ... Shall I tell him the secret? ... No, he'll certainly blab it. ... But he is asleep and won't hear me.... So I'll e'en venture.

Goes up to SIR EDWARD, whispers him, and exit.

End of the First Act.

Finis

101

Notes

1. "Reverend George Austen": This is the only item of juvenilia dedicated to Austen's father (1731-1805).

2. "discovered at work": 'Work' in the context of women at home inevitably meant sewing or needlework of some kind.

Commentary

The Mystery has the distinction of being the first of Austen's juvenilia to be published. It was included in James Edward Austen Leigh's *A Memoir of Jane Austen* as an example of those "juvenile effusions ... of the kind of transitory amusement which Jane was continually supplying to the family party," presumably for no other reasons than its brevity and its completely inoffensive content. Brilliant as it is, Austen was on much safer ground in mocking the trope of stage secrecy than in her more shocking conduct stories.

The characters in the three scenes whisper, drop hints, refer to unidentified topics, and tantalizingly leave their sentences unfinished – but nothing material is actually revealed to the audience, justifying Austen's joke in the dedication that her playlet is "as complete a mystery as any of its kind."

[Dedication]

To Edward Austen Esquire[1]
The following unfinished novel is respectfully inscribed by his obedient humble servant
The Author

The Three Sisters – a novel

Introduction to the main characters in *The Three Sisters*:

Mrs. Stanhope, a widow, has three daughters of marriageable age but no sons. In order of age, they are: **Mary**, **Georgiana** and **Sophy**.
Mr. Watts is a local bachelor aged thirty-two who is looking for a wife.
The **Duttons** is a local family familiar with the Stanhopes and Mr. Watts. The family has daughters (**Kitty** and **Jemima**) of marriageable age.
Mr. Brudenell is a very handsome young man who is visiting the Duttons.

Letter [the] First

Miss Stanhope[2] to Mrs. –

My dear Fanny,

I am the happiest creature in the world, for I have received an offer of marriage from Mr. Watts. It is the first I have ever had, and I hardly know how to value it enough. How I will triumph over the Duttons! I do not intend to accept it, at least I believe not, but as I am not quite certain, I gave him an equivocal answer and left him. And now my dear Fanny, I want your advice whether I should accept his offer or not; but that you may be able to judge of his merits and the situation of affairs, I will give you an account of them.

He is quite an old man, about two and thirty, very plain, so plain that I cannot bear to look at him. He is extremely disagreeable, and I hate him more than anybody else in the world. He has a large fortune and will make great settlements on me; but then he is very healthy. In short, I do not know what to do. If I refuse him, he as good as told me that he should offer himself to Sophia, and if she refused him, to Georgiana, and I could not bear to have either of them married before me. If I accept him I know I shall be miserable all the rest of my life, for he is very ill-tempered and peevish, extremely jealous, and so stingy that there is no living in the house with him. He told me he should mention the affair to Mama, but I insisted upon it that he did not, for very likely she would make me marry him whether I would or no; however, probably he has before now, for he never does anything he is desired to do.

I believe I shall have him. It will be such a triumph to be married before Sophy, Georgiana, and the Duttons; And he promised to have a new carriage on the occasion, but we almost quarreled about the colour, for I insisted upon its being blue spotted with silver, and he declared it should be a plain chocolate; and to provoke me more, said it should be just as low as his old one. I won't have him, I declare. He said he should come again tomorrow and take my final answer, so I believe I must get him while I can. I know the Duttons will envy me and I shall be able to chaperone Sophy and Georgiana to all the winter balls. But then, what will be the use of that when very likely he won't let me go myself, for I know he hates dancing, and ~~has a great idea of women never going from home~~ what he hates himself he has no idea of any other person's liking; and besides he ~~has a great idea~~ talks a great deal of women always staying at home and such stuff. I believe I shan't have him; I would refuse him at once if I were certain that neither of my sisters would accept him, and that if they did not, he would not offer to the Duttons. I cannot run such a risk, so, if he will promise to have the carriage ordered as I like, I will have him; if not he may ride in it by himself for me. I hope you like my determination; I can think of nothing better;

And am your ever affectionate

Mary Stanhope

From the same to the same

Dear Fanny,

I had but just sealed my last letter to you, when my mother came up and told me she wanted to speak to me on a very particular subject.

"Ah! I know what you mean," said I. "That old fool Mr. Watts has told you all about it, though I bid him not. However, you shan't force me to have him if I don't like ~~him~~ it."

"I am not going to force you, child, but only want to know what your resolution is with regard to his proposals, and to insist upon your making up your mind one way or t'other, that if you don't accept him, Sophy may."

"Indeed," replied I hastily. "Sophy need not trouble herself, for I shall certainly marry him myself."

"If that is your resolution," said my mother, "why should you be afraid of my forcing your inclinations?"

"Why, because I have not settled whether I shall have him or not."

"You are the strangest girl in the world, Mary. What you say one moment, you unsay the next. Do tell me once for all, whether you intend to marry Mr. Watts or not."

"Law! Mama, how can I tell you what I don't know myself?"

"Then I desire you will know, and quickly too, for Mr. Watts says he won't be kept in suspense."

"That depends upon me."

"No it does not, for if you do not give him your final answer tomorrow when he drinks tea with us, he intends to pay his addresses to Sophy."

"Then I shall tell all the world that he behaved very ill to me."

"What good will that do? Mr. Watts has been too long abused by all the world to mind it now."

"I wish I had a father or a brother, because then they should fight him[3]."

"They would be cunning if they did, for Mr. Watts would run away first; and therefore you must and shall resolve either to accept or refuse him before tomorrow evening."

"But why, if I don't have him, must he offer to my sisters?"

"Why! Because he wishes to be allied to the family and because they are as pretty as you are."

"But will Sophy marry him, Mama, if he offers to her?"

"Most likely. Why should not she? If, however, she does not choose it, then Georgiana must, for I am determined not to let such an opportunity escape of settling one of my daughters so advantageously. So make the most of your time, I leave you to settle the matter with yourself."

And then she went away. The only thing I can think of, my dear Fanny, is to ask Sophy and Georgiana whether they would have him were he to make proposals to them, and if they say they would not, I am resolved to refuse him too, for I hate him more than you can imagine. As for the Duttons, if he marries one of *them*, I shall still have the triumph of having refused him first. So, adieu my dear friend –

Yours ever, M. S.

Miss Georgiana Stanhope to Miss XXX

Wednesday

My dear Anne,

Sophy and I have just been practising a little deceit on our eldest sister, to which we are not perfectly reconciled, and yet the circumstances were such that if anything will excuse it, they must. Our neighbour Mr. Watts has made proposals to Mary: proposals which she knew not how to receive, for though she has a particular dislike to him (in which she is not singular), yet she would willingly marry him sooner than risk his offering to Sophy or me, which, in case of a refusal from refusal herself, he told her should be the case he should do – for you must know the poor girl considers our marrying before her as one of the greatest misfortunes that can possibly befall her, and, to prevent it, would willingly ensure herself everlasting misery by a marriage with Mr. Watts.

An hour ago she came to us to sound our inclinations respecting the affair, which were to determine hers. A little before she came, my mother had given us an account of it, telling us that she certainly would not let him go farther than our own family for a wife.

"And therefore," said she, "if Mary won't have him, Sophy must; and if Sophy won't, Georgiana *shall*."

Poor Georgiana! – We neither of us attempted to alter my mother's resolution, which I am sorry to say is generally mostre strictly kept and, than rationally formed. As soon as she was gone, however, I broke silence to assure Sophy that if Mary should refuse Mr. Watts, I should not expect her to sacrifice *her* happiness by becoming his wife from a motive of generosity to me, which I was afraid her good nature and sisterly affection might induce her to do.

"Let us flatter ourselves," replied she, "that Mary will not refuse him. Yet how can I hope that my sister may accept a man who cannot make her happy."

"*He* cannot, it is true, but his fortune, his name, his house, his carriage will, and I have no doubt but that Mary will marry him; indeed, why should she not? He is not more than two and thirty, a very proper age for a man to marry at. He is rather plain to be sure, but then what is beauty in a man? – if he has but a genteel figure and a sensible looking face, it is quite sufficient."

"This is all very true, Georgiana, but Mr. Watts's figure is unfortunately extremely vulgar and his countenance is very heavy."

"And then as to his temper; it has been reckoned bad, but may not the world be deceived in their judgment of it? There is an open frankness in his disposition which becomes a man. They say he is stingy; we'll call that prudence. They say he is suspicious. That proceeds from a warmth of heart always excusable in youth, and in short, I see no reason why he should not make a very good husband, or why Mary should not be very happy with him."

Sophy laughed.

I continued, "However, whether Mary accepts him or not, I am resolved. My determination is made. I never would marry Mr. Watts, were beggary the only alternative. So deficient in every respect! Hideous in his person, and without one good quality to make amends for it. His fortune, to be sure, is good. Yet not so very large! Three thousand a year[4]. What is three thousand a year? It is but six times as much as my mother's income. It will not tempt me."

"Yet it will be a noble fortune for Mary," said Sophy, laughing again.

"For Mary! Yes indeed, it will give *me* pleasure to see *her* in such affluence."

Thus I ran on, to the great entertainment of my sister, till Mary came into the room, to appearance in great agitation. She sat down. We made room for her at the fire. She seemed at a loss how to begin, and at last said in some confusion:

"Pray Sophy, have you any mind to be married?"

"To be married! None in the least. But why do you ask me? Are you acquainted with anyone who means to make me proposals?"

"I – no, how should I? But mayn't I ask a common question?"

"Not a very common one Mary, surely," said I.

She paused, and after some moments silence went on –

"How should you like to marry Mr. Watts, Sophy?"

I winked at Sophy, and replied for her. "Who is there but must rejoice to marry a man of three thousand a year ~~who keeps a postchaise~~[5] ~~and pair, with silver harness, a boot before, and a window to look out at behind?"~~?"

"Very true," she replied, "That's very true. So you would have him if he would offer, Georgiana, and would *you* Sophy?"

Sophy did not like the idea of telling a lie and deceiving her sister; she prevented the first and saved half her conscience by equivocation.

"I should certainly act just as Georgiana would do."

"Well then," said Mary, with triumph in her eyes, "*I* have had an offer from Mr. Watts."

We were of course very much surprised.

"Oh! do not accept him," said I, "and then perhaps he may have me."

In short, my scheme took, and Mary is resolved to do *that* to prevent our supposed happiness, which she would not have done to ~~have made us really so~~ ensure it in reality. Yet after all, my heart cannot acquit me, and Sophy is even more scrupulous. Quiet our minds, my dear Anne, by writing and telling us you approve our conduct. Consider it well over. Mary will have real pleasure in being a married woman, and able to chaperone us, which she certainly shall do, for I think myself bound to contribute as much as possible to her happiness in a state I have made her choose. They will probably have a new carriage, which will be paradise to her, and if we can prevail on Mr. W. to set up his phaeton[6], she will be too happy. These things, however, would be no consolation to Sophy or me for domestic misery. Remember all this, and do not condemn us.

Friday.

Last night, Mr. Watts by appointment drank tea with us. As soon as his carriage stopped at the door, Mary went to the window.

"Would you believe it, Sophy?" said she. "The old fool wants to have his new chaise[7] just the colour of the old one, and hung as low[8] too. But it shan't – I *will* carry my point. And if he won't let it be as high as the Duttons', and blue spotted with silver, I won't have him. Yes I will too. Here he comes. I know he'll be rude; I know he'll be ill-tempered and won't say one civil thing to me! nor behave at all like a lover."

She then sat down and Mr. Watts entered.

"Ladies, your most obedient[9]."

We paid our compliments, and he seated himself.

"Fine weather, ladies." Then turning to Mary, "Well, Miss Stanhope, I hope you have *at last* settled the matter in your own mind; and will be so good as to let me know whether you will *condescend* to marry me or not."

"I think, sir," said Mary, "you might have asked in a genteeler way than that. I do not know whether I *shall* have you if you behave so odd."

"Mary!" said my Mother.

"Well, Mama, if he will be ~~so angry and~~ so cross ..."

"Hush, hush, Mary, you shall not be rude to Mr. Watts."

"Pray madam, do not lay any restraint on Miss Stanhope by obliging her to be civil. If she does not choose to accept my hand, I can offer it elsewhere, for as I am by no means guided by a particular preference to you above your sisters; it is equally the same to me which I marry of the three."

Was there ever such a wretch! Sophy reddened with anger and I felt so spiteful!

"Well then," said Mary in a peevish accent, "I *will* have you if I *must*."

"I should have thought, Miss Stanhope, that when such settlements are offered as I have offered to you, there can be no great violence done to the inclinations in accepting of them."

Mary mumbled out something, which I who sat close to her could just distinguish to be, "What's the use of a great jointure[10], if men live forever?" And then audibly, "Remember the pin-money[11]; two hundred a year."

"A hundred and seventy-five, madam."

"Two hundred indeed, sir," said my mother.

"And remember, I am to have a new carriage hung as high as the Duttons's, and blue spotted with silver; and I shall expect a new saddle horse, a suit of fine lace[12], and an infinite number of the most valuable jewels. Diamonds such as never were seen, ~~pearls as large as those of the Princess Badroulbadour in the forth volume of the *Arabian Nights*, and rubies, emerald, topazes, sapphires, amethysts, turkeystones[13], agate, beads, bugles[14] and garnets~~ and pearls, rubies, emeralds, and beads out of number. You must set up your phaeton, which must be cream-coloured with a wreath of silver flowers round it; you must buy four of the finest bays[15] in the kingdom, and you must drive me in it every day. This is not all: you must entirely new furnish your house after my taste; you must hire two more footmen to attend me, two women to wait on me; [you] must always let me do just as I please and make a very good husband."

Here she stopped, I believe rather out of breath.

"This is all very reasonable, Mr. Watts, for my daughter to expect."

"And it is very reasonable, Mrs. Stanhope, that your daughter should be disappointed."

He was going on, but Mary interrupted him.

"You must build me an elegant greenhouse and stock it with plants. You must let me spend every winter in Bath, every spring in town, every summer in taking some tour, and every autumn at a watering place, and if we are at home the rest of the year," (Sophy and I laughed.) "you must do nothing but give balls and masquerades. You must build a room on purpose and a theatre to act plays in. The first play we have shall be *Which is the Man?*[16], and I will do Lady Bell Bloomer."

"And pray, Miss Stanhope," said Mr. Watts, "what am I to expect from you in return for all this."

"Expect? Why, you may expect to have me pleased."

"It would be odd if I did not. Your expectations, madam, are too high for me, and I must apply to Miss Sophy, who perhaps may not have raised hers so much."

"You are mistaken, sir, in supposing so," said Sophy, "for though they may not be exactly in the same line, yet my expectations are to the full as high as my sister's; for I expect my husband to be good-tempered and cheerful; to consult my happiness in all his actions, and to love me with constancy and sincerity."

Mr. Watts stared.

"These are very odd ideas, truly, young lady. You had better discard them before you marry, or you will be obliged to do it afterwards."

My mother, in the meantime, was lecturing Mary, who was sensible that she had gone too far, and when Mr. Watts was just turning towards me in order, I believe, to address me, she spoke to him in a voice half humble, half sulky.

"You are mistaken, Mr. Watts, if you think I was in earnest when I said I expected so much. However, I must have a new chaise."

"Yes, sir, you must allow that Mary has a right to expect that."

"Mrs. Stanhope, I *mean* and have always meant to have a new one on my marriage. But it shall be the colour of my present one."

"I think, Mr. Watts, you should pay my girl the compliment of consulting her taste on such matters."

Mr. Watts would not agree to this, and for some time insisted upon its being a chocolate colour, while Mary was as eager for having it blue with silver spots. At length, however, Sophy proposed that to please Mr. W. it should be a dark brown, and to please Mary it should be hung rather high and have a silver border. This was at length agreed to, though reluctantly on both sides, as each had intended to carry their[17] point entire. We then proceeded to other matters, and it was settled that they should be married as soon as the writings could be completed. Mary was very eager for a special licence and Mr. Watts talked of banns. A common licence[18] was at last agreed on. Mary is to have all the family jewels, which are very inconsiderable, I believe, and Mr. W. promised to buy her a saddle horse; but in return, she is not to expect to go to town or any other public place for these three years. She is to have neither greenhouse, theatre, or phaeton; to be contented with one maid without an additional footman. It engrossed the whole evening to settle these affairs; Mr. W. supped with us and did not go till twelve.

As soon as he was gone, Mary exclaimed, "Thank heaven! He's off at last; how I do hate him!"

It was in vain that Mama represented to her the impropriety she was guilty of, in disliking him who was to be her husband, for she persisted in declaring her aversion to him and hoping she might never see him again. What a wedding will this be! Adieu, my dear Anne.

Your faithfully sincere
Georgiana Stanhope

From the same to the same

Saturday

Dear Anne,

Mary, eager to have everyone know of her approaching wedding, and more particularly desirous of triumphing, as she called it, over the Duttons, desired us to walk with her this morning to Stoneham. As we had nothing else to do, we readily agreed, and had as pleasant a walk as we could have with Mary, whose conversation entirely consisted in abusing the man she is so soon to marry, and in longing for a blue chaise spotted with silver. When we reached the Duttons, we found the two girls in the dressing-room with a very handsome young man, who was of course introduced to us. He is the son of Sir Henry Brudenell of Leicestershire[19]. ~~Not related to the family, and even but distantly connected with it. His sister is married to John Dutton's wife's brother. When you have puzzled over this account a little, you will understand it.~~ Mr. Brudenell is the handsomest man I ever saw in my life; we are all three very much pleased with him. Mary, who from the moment of our reaching the dressing-room had been swelling with the knowledge of her own importance, and with the desire of making it known, could not remain long silent on the subject after we were seated, and soon addressing herself to Kitty, said:

"Don't you think it will be necessary to have all the jewels new set?"

"Necessary for what?"

"For what! Why, for my appearance[20]."

"I beg your pardon, but I really do not understand you. What jewels do you speak of, and where is your appearance to be made?"

"At the next ball, to be sure, after I am married."

You may imagine their surprise. They were at first incredulous, but on our joining in the story, they at last believed it.

"And who is it to?" was of course the first question.

Mary pretended bashfulness, and answered in confusion, her eyes cast down, "To Mr. Watts."

This also required confirmation from us, for that anyone who had the beauty and fortune (though small, yet a provision) of Mary would willingly marry Mr. Watts, could by them scarcely be credited. The subject being now fairly introduced, and she found herself the object of ~~general~~ everyone's attention in company, she lost all her confusion and became perfectly unreserved and communicative.

"I wonder you should never have heard of it before, for in general things of this nature are very well known in the neighbourhood."

"I assure you," said Jemima, "I never had the least suspicion of such an affair. Has it been in agitation long?"

"Oh! Yes, ever since Wednesday."

They all smiled, particularly Mr. Brudenell.

"You must know Mr. Watts is very much in love with me, so that it is quite a match of affection on his side."

"Not on his only, I suppose," said Kitty.

"Oh! When there is so much love on one side, there is no occasion for it on the other. However, I do not much dislike him, though he is very plain to be sure."

Mr. Brudenell stared, the Miss Duttons laughed, and Sophy and I were heartily ashamed of our sister.

She went on, "We are to have a new post-chaise, and very likely may set up our phaeton."

This we knew to be false, but the poor girl was pleased at the idea of persuading the company that such a thing was to be, and I would not deprive her of so harmless an enjoyment.

She continued, "Mr. Watts is to present me with the family jewels, which I fancy are very considerable."

I could not help whispering [to] Sophy, "I fancy not."

"These jewels are what I suppose must be new set before they can be worn. I shall not wear them till the first ball I go to after my marriage. If Mrs. Dutton should not go to it, I hope you will let me chaperone you; I shall certainly take Sophy and Georgiana."

"You are very good," said Kitty, "and since you are inclined to undertake the care of young ladies, I should advise you to prevail on Mrs. Edgecumbe to let you chaperone her six daughters, which with your two sisters and ourselves will make your entrée[21] very respectable."

Kitty made us all smile except Mary, who did not understand her meaning and coolly said that she should not like to chaperone so many. Sophy and I now endeavoured to change the conversation, but succeeded only for a few minutes, for Mary took care to bring back their attention to her and her approaching wedding. I was sorry for my sister's sake to see that Mr. Brudenell seemed to take pleasure in listening to her account of it, and even encouraged her in doing so by his questions and remarks, for it was evident that his only aim was to laugh at her. I am afraid he found her very ridiculous. He kept his countenance extremely well, yet it was easy to see that it was with difficulty [that] he kept it. At length, however, he seemed fatigued and disgusted with her ridiculous conversation, as he turned from her to us, and spoke but little to her for about half an hour before we left Stoneham. As soon as we were out of the House, we all joined in praising the person and manners of Mr. Brudenell.

We found Mr. Watts at home.

"So, Miss Stanhope," said he, "you see I am come a courting in a true lover-like manner."

"Well you need not have *told* me that. I knew why you came very well."

Sophy and I then left the room, imagining of course that we must be in the way, if a scene of courtship were to begin. We were surprised at being followed almost immediately by Mary.

"And is your courting so soon over?" said Sophy.

"Courting!" replied Mary. "We have been quarrelling. Watts is such a fool! I hope I shall never see him again."

"I am afraid you will," said I, "as he dines here today. But what has been your dispute?"

"Why, only because I told him that I had seen a man much handsomer than he was this morning, he flew into a great passion and called me a vixen, so I only stayed to tell him I thought him a blackguard[22] and came away."

"Short and sweet," said Sophy, "but pray, Mary, how will this be made up?"

"He ought to ask my pardon; but if he did, I would not forgive him."

"His submission, then, would not be very useful."

When we were dressed[23], we returned to the parlour where Mama and Mr. Watts were in close conversation. It seems that he had been complaining to her of her daughter's behaviour, and she had persuaded him to think no more of it. He therefore met Mary with all his accustomed civility, and except one touch at the phaeton and another at the greenhouse, the evening went off with great harmony and cordiality. Watts is going to town to hasten the preparations for the wedding.

I am your affectionate friend,

G.S.

Notes

1. "Edward Austen": The third eldest of the Austen boys (1768-1852) was adopted by his wealthy relatives Thomas and Catherine Knight (not an unusual arrangement at that time) and eventually became their legal heir. In 1812, he took the surname Knight. The dedication may reflect Edward's part in the genesis of this narrative. On March 1st, 1791, the engagement of Edward Austen and Elizabeth Bridges was announced. Elizabeth had two elder sisters, Fanny and Sophy, who became engaged in the same year.

Indeed, on December 27th there was a double wedding between Edward and Elizabeth and Sophy and William Deedes. These circumstances seem to have been the inspiration for this story.

2. "Miss Stanhope": By convention, the eldest unmarried daughter is referred to as Miss, so "Miss Stanhope" is Mary.

3. "they should fight him": Mary has been reading too many romantic novels if she thinks that a father or brother of hers would fight a duel because Mr. Watts has proposed to her.

4. "'Three thousand a year'": For comparison, Mr. Darcy's income is £10,000 per annum and Mr. Bingley's £4,000 per annum. When Edward Austen inherited Godmersham Park, Chawton Manor, and Steventon they provided an income of between £10,000 and £15,000 a year. In *Patronage* (1814) by Maria Edgeworth (1768-1849), Lady Jane states that "pretty well married" implies that the husband has £2,000 a year while "very well married" implies an annual income in excess of £10,000. Mr. Watts's income, then, is adequate for a comfortable life, but hardly a luxurious one. Peter Sabor points out that it would be "too little for the expenses of a winter season in London, for which at least £5,000 a year was needed; in his negotiations with Mary, Mr. Watts is acutely aware of the limitations of his own wealth" (*Juvenilia* 418).

5. "'postchaise'": A four-wheeled, closed carriage, with one forward-looking seat for two or three passengers.

6. "'phaeton'": A two-horse carriage with a lightly sprung carriage mounted high on large wheels – the sports car of its day.

7. "'chaise'": A two or four wheeled carriage for one or two people who drove the horse(s) themselves.

8. "'hung as low'": High suspension was something of a status symbol. It also tended to make carriages unstable so that they were more likely to overturn on a corner.

9. "'your most obedient'": The word 'servant' is understood in this conventional form of address.

10. "'a great jointure'": Money and/or property set aside for a widow for the period she survives her husband – particularly necessary if the husband was considerably older than his wife.

11. "'pin-money'": A regular sum of money given to a wife by her husband to be spent on things for herself, not on household necessities:

> Aunt Sarah [with her] good sense ... thought it better that young married women should have a fixed income, whatever it might be called, pin-money or allowance. They knew then what they ought to spend, and all their little charities, or any presents they wished to give, would be the fruits of their own self-denial; and she even hinted that [otherwise] the most devoted and liberal husbands would, after a certain term of married life, object to milliners' bills, and become possessed

with an insane idea that their wives were extravagant and always asking for money. (Emily Eden *The Semi-detached House* [1859])

The term "pin-money" did not then carry the present-day connotation of a very small amount of money earned by or given to a woman. The word originated in the sixteenth century, well before the age of mass production, when pins and needles were expensive.

12. "suit of fine lace": A luxurious gown and petticoat in expensive lace.

13. "'~~turkeystones~~'": Turquoises.

14. "'~~bugles~~'": Small, hollow, cylindrical beads.

15. "'bays'": Reddish-brown colored horses.

16. "'*Which is the Man?*'": Mrs. Hannah Cowley (1743-1809) wrote this play which premiered at Covent Garden in London in 1785. On September 8th, 1787, Eliza de Feuillide saw the play at Tunbridge Wells and suggested that it be performed by the Austen family at Steventon, with herself in the leading female role, but other plays were chosen instead.

17. "their": 'Each one' is, of course, singular ('each one was' not 'each one were') hence "their" here must also be singular.

18. "a special license. Banns … common licence…": The banns of a couple planning to marry must be read in their parish church on the three successive Sundays before the proposed date of the marriage. This was to allow members of the congregation who knew the two people to voice any objections. A "common license" meant that proclaiming the banns was not necessary, and named one or two parishes where the wedding could take place. A special license (which must be obtained from a bishop) allowed the wedding to be celebrated at a place other than the couple's parish church at a time of the couple's choosing (traditionally marriages were performed in the morning). A special license was the most expensive and therefore something of a status symbol.

19. "the son of Sir Henry Brudenell of Leicestershire": A. Walton Litz comments that *The Three Sisters* "hovers between burlesque and a more subtle comic form. At several points Jane Austen cannot resist pushing the description or dialogue to the burlesque extreme, but in almost every case these incongruous, though amusing, passages have been erased" (25-26). He singles out the initial description of the jewels and this introduction of Mr. Brudenell as examples of discarded burlesque.

20. "my appearance": Mary's first appearance in public as Mrs. Watts.

21. "'entrée'": The right to enter or join a particular social sphere or group of people. Peter Sabor explains that Mrs. Edgecumbe might be prevailed upon to let Mary chaperone her six daughters "is maliciously portraying Mary Stanhope as a governess or a school-teacher, rather than as the elegant married woman she aspires to be" (*Juvenilia* 421). This clarifies the following comment that "Kitty made us all smile except Mary, who did not understand

her."
22. "blackguard": A shabby, dirty fellow.
23. "dressed": Dressed formally for dinner.

Commentary

It is immediately evident to the reader that *The Three Sisters* (composed 1792 or 1793) is a text very different from the earlier offerings in *Volume the First*. A glance at the facsimile shows that the handwriting of this story, though evidently Austen's, is both more mature and less neat than previously and that the deletions are more thorough, with the evident intention of obscuring the original words. Also, the narrative style is unusual in the juvenilia for its use of direct rather than reported speech, a development which foreshadows one of the aspects of Austen's mature style that made her novels so distinctively dramatic. All of this suggests that there was some considerable period between the transcription of *The Mystery* and this novel.

This text is no skit, but a story of approaching 4,600 words in which character motivates plot. Though no doubt Austen's satire is still informed by her novel reading (as how should it not be), it is clear that the author's target here is less literature per se than the life and values of the society in which she lived; that is, the story marks a point of transition in the author's development from pure literary parody to social commentary. It is Austen's earliest treatment of a calculated and a mercenary marriage for social position rather than for love. Frances Beer writes, "Together, the burlesque and the realistic cooperate to enhance Austen's social and moral message, revealing the corrupt tendencies of her society and allowing for the development of her protagonists" ("A 'little bit of Ivory'" 239). Beer goes on to explain the "impressive range" of the novel's social commentary:

> the ruthless lengths to which the mercenary mother will go to acquire an 'eligible' suitor for the advantage of her family and her own future well-being; the crass misogyny of a system that encourages the selling of a daughter to someone so indisputably repulsive; the pathos of a situation that turns sisters against one another; the implied/underlying fear of what will happen to young women who don't marry; the claustrophobic social scene. (Ibid. 242)

The story satirizes the acquisitive materialism of Mary, but it implicitly criticizes the social realities which lead a weak personality like hers to make the choices that she does. There is more than a hint of Mary Wollstonecraft's thesis in *Rights of Woman* that, with marriage being the sole destiny of young women, and their education being entirely directed to making them attractive as potential mates, then we ought not to wonder that women so often act in a competitive way since they are motivated only by materialism, for they have been presented with no higher value in life to which to aspire. For most gentlewomen (as for Charlotte Lucas in *Pride and Prejudice*) marriage was the only way to escape the parental home, and often the only possible way for a woman to avoid impending quasi-poverty and to have spending money of her own, a house to be mistress of, a carriage, a position in local society, etc.

Jane Austen was quite aware of the limited and limiting choice that many women were forced to make. She presented her own views on marriage in letters to her beloved niece Fanny Knight. When Fanny was uncertain whether to accept a marriage proposal from one Mr. Plumptre, Austen wrote:

> I … entreat you not to commit yourself farther & not to think of accepting [Mr. Plumptre] unless you really do like him. Anything is to be preferred or endured rather than marrying without Affection; and if his deficiencies of Manner &c &c strike you more than all his good qualities, if you continue to think strongly of them, give him up at once. (November 18th, 1814)

However, on another occasion, she pointed to the unavoidable truth that her own spinsterhood exemplified, "Single women have a dreadful propensity for being poor – which is one very strong argument in favor of Matrimony" (March 13th, 1817).

The three young women are caught in a trap between Mr. Watts's determination to have a wife and Mrs. Stanhope's determination that he shall marry *one* of her daughters – to her it does not much matter which one. Since his feelings are not involved in the decision, it is likewise of no importance to Mr. Watts which of the sisters he marries, one being as pretty as the others, and beauty being the only criterion that he appears to be using. Thus, when Mary complains about his "'cross'" manner of love-making, he assures her, "'It is equally the same to me which I marry of the three.'" For her part, Mrs. Stanhope (a prototype of Mrs. Bennet) is decided because he has an income of £3,000 a year. Thus, when Mary expresses doubts about accepting Mr. Watts, her mother tells her that "'If, however, she [Sophy] does not choose it [his proposal], then Georgiana must, for I am determined not to let such an opportunity escape of settling one of my daughters so advantageously. So make the most of your time, I leave you to settle the matter with yourself.'" Later in the novel, Mrs. Stanhope will tell her other two daughters "that she certainly would not let him go farther than our own family for a wife." Early in the story, Mary laments that she has no father or brother to protect her interests and reputation in this situation, but her mother replies that, given the character of Mr. Watts, they would be helpless to do so. In the end, between the two of them, Mrs. Stanhope and Mr. Watts pressure Mary into acquiescing: "in a peevish accent," she tells Mr. Watts, "'Well then … I *will* have you if I *must*.'"

There is no doubt that Mary is a young woman of mean understanding and mercenary motives from the very start of the novel. Beer calls her, "the epitome of the warped and stunted sort of creature that is produced by a materialist, misogynist society" (244). In her first letter, it becomes clear that her feelings tell her that she can never be anything but miserable with a man who is "extremely disagreeable" and whom she hates "more than anybody else in the world." Against this, however, Mary weighs the material advantages of marriage to a man with "a large fortune" and the social prestige that she will gain as a married woman. She simply cannot countenance the humiliation she will feel if one of her younger sisters should marry before her, or (even worse) if one of the Dutton girls should accept Mr. Watts.

Austen extracts fine comedy from Mary's contorted thinking and her inconsistency. More comedy arises from the cunning manipulation of Mary by her two younger sisters. They are able to practice "a little deceit" on Mary because they know that she will not be able to tolerate the idea of either of them accepting Mr. Watts if she should refuse him. By hinting that they each would accept Mr. Watts should he propose (something which, in reality, they would *never* do) they extract from Mary a boast, "'Well then,' said Mary with triumph in her eyes, '*I* have had an offer from Mr. Watts.'"

The witty and intelligent Georgiana is the sister most like Elizabeth Bennet, not least in her desire to protect her more naïve elder sister Sophy, which prefigures Elizabeth's relationship to Jane. She instantly gains the approval of the reader when she tells Sophy, "'never would [I] marry Mr. Watts, were beggary the only alternative.'" It is Georgiana who devises the scheme to trick Mary into accepting Mr. Watts admitting to her correspondent that both she and Sophy "are not perfectly reconciled [to the ploy], and yet the circumstances were such that if anything will excuse it, they must." Georgiana's motivation is to save Sophy, whom she fears will "sacrifice her happiness by becoming his wife from a motive of generosity to me, which I was afraid her good nature and sisterly affection might induce her to do." She chooses to save Sophy at the expense of Mary because she knows that Mary will survive marriage to Mr. Watts, finding consolation in his wealth and her new social status, while Sophy's innocence and genuine sensitivity would make her truly miserable as his wife. She writes, that Mary "will probably have a new carriage," and perhaps a phaeton, "which will be paradise to her … These things however would be no consolation to Sophy or me for domestic misery," and tells Sophy that "He cannot [make Mary happy], it is true, but his fortune, his name, his house, his carriage will…" Sophy has more moral scruples about deceiving her eldest sister, but Georgiana manages to talk her round.

Sophy (who writes none of the letters) shows a misunderstanding of marriage very different from Mary, yet just as fatal to happiness. When Mr. Watts finds Mary's demands too much, he turns to Sophy as the next sister in chronological line. The ensuing dialogue is worth quoting in full:

"Your expectations, madam, are too high for me, and I

must apply to Miss Sophy, who perhaps may not have raised hers so much."

"You are mistaken, sir, in supposing so," said Sophy, "for though they may not be exactly in the same line, yet my expectations are to the full as high as my sister's; for I expect my husband to be good-tempered and cheerful; to consult my happiness in all his actions, and to love me with constancy and sincerity."

Mr. Watts stared.

"These are very odd ideas, truly, young lady. You had better discard them before you marry, or you will be obliged to do it afterwards."

Critics generally find in Sophy a prototype for the character of Elizabeth Bennet, but it would be a mistake to see the above exchange as anything like Elizabeth's rejection of Mr. Collins, even though it is true that Mr. Watts is as arrogant and self-satisfied as that clergyman. Sophy's error is to vest all emotional power within the marriage in the wife, just as Mary attempts to vest all economic power with the wife. What Sophy leaves out is the wife's duty to respect and honor her husband. Elizabeth Bennet does not marry Mr. Darcy on the terms laid out here by Sophy Stanhope, and they do not represent an idea of marriage but entirely unrealistic demands, "full as high as [her] sister's," whose purpose is to get Mr. Watts to withdraw his offer to her as he already has to Mary.

Once the proposal is accepted by Mary, the negotiation begins – what Wollstonecraft refers provocatively to as "marriage as prostitution." Mary is determined to sell herself at the highest possible price; living with Mr. Watts will only be endurable if she is surrounded by luxury. Austen again gets a great deal of comedy out of the extravagant demands that Mary makes (though note where Austen deletes a passage on the jewels that Mary demands because it falls too much into farce). Mary gets quite carried away with demands well above Mr. Watts's relatively modest income, which is ironically made clear by Mrs. Stanhope's unconsciously absurd comment that Mary's demands are, in fact, "'all very reasonable.'"

Sensing herself to be in a powerful negotiating position, Mary tells Mr. Watts that, in return for this lavish expenditure he will "'have me pleased.'" Mary is here either appealing to his male gallantry or promising her sexual compliance, but she has overplayed her hand as her mother makes quite clear to her. Faced with the risk of losing Mr. Watts to a sister or to one of the Dutton girls, Mary concedes every demand but one, "'You are mistaken, Mr. Watts, if you think I was in earnest when I said I expected so much. However, I must have a new chaise.'" Since Mr. Watts maintains that he always intended to buy a new chaise upon getting married, Mary is indeed selling herself cheaply. She does not even succeed in her determination to have it "blue with silver spots." Sophy proposes a compromise: "to please Mr. W. it should be dark brown and to please Mary it should be hung rather high and have a silver border." Effectively, Mary prostitutes herself for high suspension, a silver border and a saddle horse!

Mary embarrasses her sisters when she publicly announces her engagement to Mr. Watts. Georgiana records their mortification at Mary's self-justifying nonsense:

> "You must know Mr. Watts is very much in love with me, so that it is quite a match of affection on his side."
>
> "Not on his only, I suppose," said Kitty.
>
> "Oh! When there is so much love on one side, there is no occasion for it on the other. However, I do not much dislike him, though he is very plain to be sure."
>
> Mr. Brudenell stared, the Miss Duttons laughed, and Sophy and I were heartily ashamed of our sister.

Shame is a very strong emotion. Mary's sisters are as ashamed of her as Elizabeth is of the ill-mannered behavior of members of her own family at the Netherfield ball or of Lydia when she returns in triumph to Longbourn with Wickham. As we have seen, however, we do not feel the same empathy that we feel for Elizabeth because the sisters do not represent an alternative vision of what a marriage *should* be.

The Dutton sisters, Kitty and Jemima, are genuinely shocked at the news of Mary's engagement feeling, "that anyone who had the beauty and fortune (though small yet a provision) of Mary would willingly marry Mr. Watts, could by them scarcely be credited." When Mary boasts that, once married, she will be able to chaperone them, Kitty wittily mocks her, "'You are very good ... and since you are inclined to undertake the care of young ladies, I should advise you to prevail on Mrs. Edgecumbe to let you [also] chaperone her six daughters.'" Mary, of course, does not even realize that she is being mocked, which makes the joke all the funnier for the reader. The handsome Mr. Brudenell has a very different reaction to Mary's absurdity: he leads her on to expose herself more absurdly, causing even Georgiana to feel some sympathy for her sister, "I was sorry for my sister's sake, to see that Mr. Brudenell seemed to take pleasure in listening to her account . . . and even encouraged her by his questions and remarks, for it was evident that his only aim was to laugh at her." Eventually, "he seemed fatigued and disgusted with her ridiculous conversation." There is a great deal of Mr. Bennet's delight in laughing at the absurdities of others (and particularly of women) in the enigmatic Mr. Brudenell.

Austen appears to have planned to continue this story, but really she has written herself into a corner. What more could be said of the marriage of Mary and Mr. Watts that has not already been foreshadowed? How could the rather sinister and manipulative Mr. Brudenell become the love-interest of either Sophy or Georgiana? Austen was still much better at scenes and incidents than she was at plotting.

[Dedication]

To Miss Jane Anna Elizabeth Austen[1]

My dear Niece:

Though you are at this period not many degrees removed from infancy, yet trusting that you will in time be older[2], and that through the care of your excellent parents, you will one day or another be able to read written hand, I dedicate to you the following miscellaneous morsels, convinced that if you seriously attend to them, you will derive from them very important instructions, with regard to your conduct in life[3]. – If such my hopes should hereafter be realized, never shall I regret the days and nights that have been spent in composing these treatises[4] for your benefit. I am, my dear niece,

Your very affectionate aunt,

The Author

June 2nd, 1793

~~A Fragment Written to Inculcate the Practise of Virtue~~[5]

~~We all know that many are unfortunate in their progress through the world, but we do not know all that are so. To seek them out to study their wants, and to leave them unsupplied is the duty, and ought to be the business of man. But few have time, fewer still have inclination, and no one has either the one or the other for such employments. Who amid those that perspire away their evenings in crowded assemblies can have leisure to bestow a thought on such as sweat under the fatigue of their daily labour?~~

A Beautiful Description of the Different Effects of Sensibility on Different Minds

I am but just returned from Melissa's bedside, and in my life, though it has been a pretty long one, and I have during the course of it been at many bedsides, I never saw so affecting an object as she exhibits[6]. She lies wrapped in a book muslin bedgown, a chambray gauze shift, and a French net nightcap[7]. Sir William is constantly at her bedside. The only repose he takes is on the sofa in the drawing room, where for five minutes every fortnight he remains in an imperfect slumber, starting up every moment and exclaiming, "Oh! Melissa, Ah! Melissa," then sinking down again, raises his left arm and scratches his head[8]. Poor Mrs. Burnaby is beyond measure afflicted. She sighs every now and then, that is about once a week; while the melancholy Charles says every moment "Melissa how are you?" The lovely sisters are much to be pitied. Julia is ever lamenting the situation of her friend, while lying behind her pillow and supporting her head. – Maria, more mild in her grief, talks of going to town next week, and Anna is always recurring to the pleasures we once enjoyed when Melissa was well. – I am usually at the fire cooking some little delicacy for the unhappy invalid – perhaps hashing up the remains of an old duck, toasting some cheese or making a curry[9], which are the favourite dishes of our poor friend. – In these situations, we were this morning surprised by receiving a visit from Dr. Dowkins.

"I am come to see Melissa," said he. "How is she?"

"Very weak indeed," said the fainting Melissa. –

"Very weak," replied the punning Doctor, "aye, indeed it is more than a very *week* since you have taken to your bed. – How is your appetite?"

"Bad, very bad," said Julia.

"That *is* very bad," – replied he. "Are her spirits good, madam?"

"So poorly, sir, that we are obliged to strengthen her with cordials[10] every minute." –

"Well then she receives *spirits* from your being with her. Does she sleep?"

"Scarcely ever." –

"And ever scarcely[11], I suppose, when she does. Poor thing! Does she think of dying?"

"She has not strength to think at all."

"Nay, then she cannot think of to have strength."

The Generous Curate
– a moral tale[12], setting forth the advantages of being generous and a curate

In a part little known in the county of Warwickshire, a very worthy clergyman lately resided. – The income of his living, which amounted to about two hundred pounds[13], and the interest of his wife's fortune, which was nothing at all, was entirely sufficient for the wants and wishes of a family who neither wanted [n]or wished for anything beyond what their income afforded them. Mr. Williams has been in possession of his living above twenty years, when this history commences, and his marriage, which had taken place soon after his presentation to it, had made him the father of six very fine children.

The eldest had been placed at the Royal Academy for Seamen at Portsmouth[14] when about thirteen years old, and from thence had been discharged on board one of the vessels of the small fleet destined for Newfoundland, where his promise and amiable disposition had procured him many friends amongst the natives and from whence he regularly sent home a large Newfoundland dog[15] every ~~year~~ month to his family.

The second, who was also a son, had been adopted by a neighboring clergyman with the intention of educating him at his own expense, which would have been a very desirable circumstance had the gentleman's fortune been equal to his generousity, but as he had nothing to support himself and a very large family but a curacy of fifty pound a year[16], Young Williams knew nothing more at the age of eighteen than what a twopenny Dame's School[17] in the village could teach him. His character, however, was perfectly amiable, though his genius[18] might be cramped, and he was addicted to no vice, or ever guilty of any fault beyond what his age and situation rendered perfectly excusable. He had indeed sometimes been detected in flinging stones at a duck or putting brickbats[19] in his benefactor's bed; but these innocent efforts of wit were considered by the good man rather as the effects of a lively imagination, than of anything bad in his nature, and if any punishment were decreed for the offence, it was in general no greater than that the culprit could pick up the stones or take the brickbats away.–

Finis

Notes

1. "Miss Jane Anna Elizabeth Austen": Anna Lefoy (1793 - 1872) was the first daughter of James Austen and Anne Mathew. Having been born on April 15th, 1793, she would have been a little less than seven weeks old when Austen wrote this dedication. Anna stayed with Jane and Cassandra for two years at Steventon after her mother died and before her father James married Mary Lloyd in 1797. (The early death of her mother accounts for the deletion of the 's' from the word "parents" in the original text of the dedication.)

2. "trusting that you will in time be older": This is a joke, since obviously people do grow older with time, but there is a serious undertone, for in an age of high infant mortality there was a significant risk that an infant might not survive to adulthood. In fact, Anna (who inherited the good Austen Leigh genes) lived almost twice as long as Jane herself.

3. "very important instructions, with regard to your conduct in life": Austen presents herself, at age eighteen, as an authority on the proper conduct of young women, thus satirizing the large number of men who claimed the same authority.

4. "the days and nights that have been spent in composing these treatises": There are two jokes here. First, these texts were written well before Anna's birth and so were not in any sense written for her "benefit," and second, the texts are too short to be called "treatises" and would hardly have required days and nights of work in their composition. Austen's comic hyperbole is a parody of the sententious tone of books of advice to young women written by *men* such as James Fordyce (1720-1796) whose *Sermons to Young Women* (1766) Mr. Collins tries (unsuccessfully) to read to the Bennet girls for their edification in *Pride and Prejudice* (Ch. 14).

5. The whole of the "Fragment" is crossed through with vertical and diagonal lines but in a way that leaves the text entirely legible. Who erased it, when and why we do not know. On reflection, somebody (perhaps Austen herself) may have decided that the satire was just too bluntly political.

6. "so affecting an object as she exhibits": This immediately implies that Melissa's suffering is an affectation put on to impress those who see her.

7. "a book muslin bedgown, a chambray gauze shift, and a French net nightcap": Melissa is wearing a housedress made from very fine muslin (the kind that was sold folded in the manner of uncut pages in a book), a shift (undergarment) of fine quality Chambray linen, and a fashionable, elegantly trimmed cap. Melissa's concern for her appearance seems at odds with her apparently serious illness.

8. "scratches his head": One of a number of mundane, realistic details which deliberately undercut the heightened tone of the narrative.

9. "hashing up the remains of an old duck, toasting some cheese or making a curry": None of these dishes could be termed as "little delicacies." They are all simple and inexpensive; the first and last are good ways of using left-

overs; a curry, being spicy-hot, is precisely the wrong thing to give an invalid with a fever.

10. "cordials": Both a comforting and pleasant-tasting medicine and an alcoholic drink – between which there might not have been much difference.

11. "scarcely": Means both 'infrequently' and (as the doctor uses it) 'almost not at all.'

12. "a moral tale": Austen is parodying the didactic fiction written to teach young children to love good and shun evil such as *Moral Tales for Young People* (1806) by Maria Edgeworth (1767-1849).

13. "two hundred pounds": Austen's father was Rector of Steventon and of Deane: the former produced an income (from tithes, land and a rent-free residence) of £100 and the latter £110 annually. However, the tuition fee of £75, plus expenses, would have placed a strain on Mr. William's income.

14. "Royal Academy for Seamen at Portsmouth": Attended by two of Austen's brothers.

15. "Newfoundland dog": The breed was becoming popular at this time and Austen was familiar with it.

16. "a curacy of fifty pound a year": A comic inversion of the social norm in which a poor boy was adopted by a wealthy and childless (or at least son-less) family, which is exactly what happened to Austen's brother Edward. Here, the boy is adopted by a very poor curate who already has a large family.

17. "a twopenny Dame's School": A private school in a village offering a very basic education to the local children normally run by a wife or widow in her own home. The fee would be two pence per week. At the age of eighteen, Williams would be much too old for such a school.

18. "genius": 'Natural disposition' as in Macbeth's comment on Banquo, "There is none but he [Banquo]/ Whose being I do fear, and under him / My genius is rebuked, as it is said Mark Antony's was by Caesar" (3.1).

19. "brickbats": Fragments of hard material (e.g., brick) used as a weapon, with also perhaps a play on the second meaning of the word: a highly critical, insulting remark.

Commentary

The dedication uses the language of a conduct book specifically written for Austen's niece – who is currently an infant and therefore incapable of reading it! Austen's ironic trust that her niece "will in time be older" and that she (if so) will "be able to read written hand" seems a safe enough bet. In fact, the three fragments contain no clear "instructions, with regard to [a young woman's] conduct in life." Nevertheless, we do know that, while she joked about it, the childless Jane and her sister Cassandra took their role as aunts very seriously in an age where children too often lost their natural mother in childbirth.

The "Fragment" is a biting satire on the contemporary misunderstanding of virtue which lacks any of the absurd humor that characterizes the juvenilia in general because it is so undramatic. Austen argues with bitter irony that: knowing there are unfortunate people in the world is enough, since it would clearly be impossible to actually *locate* them all; and that while studying their needs is every man's duty, this duty does not extend to actually *doing* anything to relieve those needs, for to do so would require both motivation and the time, and no one can be expected to have both. Finally, she asks the rhetorical question: Who among those who "*perspire* away their evenings in crowded assemblies" has the leisure (i.e., the time) to give a single thought to those who "*sweat* under the fatigue of their daily labour" (emphasis added)? The antithesis between perspiring because of an over-heated room and sweating because of excessively hard manual labor enforces the repeated implication of the satire that the leisured classes *do* have the time and *should* have the "inclination" to actually do something about poverty – but they don't! This is probably as close as Austen comes to making a radical political statement, and it is perhaps for this reason that it was deleted.

The "Beautiful Description" is a satire on the sentimental novel and the absurd indulgence in feeling that it has encouraged in suggestible young women (an example of life imitating art). A. Walton Litz writes that all Austen's "works must be seen against the background of an eighteenth-century dialectic involving Reason and Feeling, Judgment and Fancy. Her reactions against the debased expressions of feeling and sensibility derived part of its force from her attachment to the genuine expression of these qualities" (8).

The narrative centers on the dying Melissa who is under the care of one Dr. Dowkins. The first person narrator is unidentified but appears to have been a regular visitor to the ailing Melissa. He/she pens this account following one such visit in the form of a journal entry or perhaps a paragraph from a letter. The narrator's tone is immediately ironic: Melissa "exhibits" herself as an "affecting ... object" (i.e., she makes herself the center of attention); she is elegantly dressed for the part (the beauty of her clothes enhancing the pathos of her dying); Sir William, who sleeps only "five minutes every fortnight," plays the part of the grieving father, "every moment ... exclaiming, 'Oh! Melissa...'"; Mrs. Burnaby, "beyond measure afflicted," sighs "about once a week"; and the sisters lament their sibling (except for Maria "more mild in her grief," who seems not to be playing the same silly game everyone else is playing).

The character of Dr. Dowkins is used to point out the absurdity that is going on. Told that his patient is "'Very weak,'" he punningly quips that "'it is more than a very *week* since you have taken to your bed.'" His use of the word 'very' suggests that Melissa has chosen to retire to her bed rather than had the decision forced upon her by real illness. Asking Mrs. Burnaby, "'Are her spirits good, Madam?'" he is told that they have to "'strengthen her with cordials every minute.'" He immediately exploits another comic pun, saying, "'she receives *spirits* [i.e., alcohol] from your being with her.'" Told that

Melissa scarcely ever sleeps, he makes another pun saying that she must sleep "'ever *scarcely* … when she does'" (emphasis added). Finally, he asks if his patient thinks about dying and is told, "'She has not strength to think at all.'" There is no pun this time, but there is a comic inversion of what he has just heard, "'Nay, then she cannot think to have strength.'" The silly young woman seems to Dr. Dowkins to have given up the faculty of reason in order to indulge her sensibility, and in doing so she shows every sign, with the complicity of her friends, of giving up on life and elegantly dying.

It really seems as though Austen originally intended in *The Generous Curate* to write a skit on all of her siblings, not excluding herself, but she stops short having covered her brothers Francis, who joined the Royal Navy in April 1786 at the age of twelve, and Edward, who, also at the age of twelve, was adopted by the rich, childless Thomas and Catherine Knight of Godmersham Park. Francis did not go to Newfoundland and Edward was certainly not adopted by a curate who could no better afford to keep him than his parents; these are comic inventions. I suspect that, having decided not to complete her skit, Austen chose a title for the story whose moral is that there are no advantages to being "generous and a curate."

[Dedication]

To Miss Austen1, the following "Ode to Pity" is dedicated, from a thorough knowledge of her pitiful nature, by her obedient humble servant
The Author

*Ode to Pity*2

1

Ever musing I delight to tread
The paths of honour and the myrtle grove3
Whilst the pale moon her beams doth shed
On disappointed love.
While Philomel4 on airy hawthorn bush
Sings sweet and melancholy, and the thrush
Converses with the dove.

2

Gently brawling down the turnpike road,
Sweetly noisy falls the silent stream5 –
The moon emerges from behind a cloud
And darts upon the myrtle grove her beam.
Ah! then what lovely scenes appear,
The hut, the cot, the grot6, and chapel queer,
And eke the abbey7 too a mouldering heap,

Conceal'd by aged pines her head doth rear
And quite invisible doth take a peep[8.]

Notes:

1. "Miss Austen": Cassandra. The phrase "her pitiful nature" is a comic play on words. It means both that Cassandra is easily moved to pity (compassion, tenderness) by her nature and that Cassandra is to be pitied for her acute sensibility.
2. "Ode to Pity": A reference to the poem of the same title by William Collins (1721-1759).
3. "myrtle grove": Traditionally, the myrtle is associated with love.
4. "Philomel": This female figure from Greek myth was turned into a nightingale.
5. "Sweetly noisy falls the silent stream": The stream can scarcely be "noisy" *and* "silent."
6. "the cot, the grot": The cottage and the grotto.
7. "chapel … abbey": These buildings complete the picturesque landscape.
8. "quite invisible doth take a peep": Quite how the speaker can see an "invisible" tower is not clear.

Commentary

Natalie Tyler comments, "This rustic scene was undoubtedly conjured up to amuse Cassandra with its oxymorons: its stream, which is both silent and noisy, both brawling and gentle, and the abbey, which invisibly rears its head" (37). The "lovely scenes" turn out to be a rather menacing Gothic landscape with mysterious ruins illuminated by the moon. Austen's final joke is that the poem makes no reference to pity at all.

128

Volume the Second

A glance through the facsimile of *Volume the Second* shows obvious differences from *Volume the First*. The second notebook is much thicker, containing 252 numbered pages as compared with 180. The handwriting is more mature, more fluent, and in some ways less neat. *Love and Friendship* is written in small handwriting with a much narrower space between the lines, as though Austen were concerned to conserve paper. Erasures are generally made more thoroughly, sometimes with the evident intention (often successful) of making the words deleted indecipherable. With the exception of the "Scraps" that end the volume (the equivalent of the "Detached Pieces" at the end of the first notebook), the four major texts are longer and more coherent. It is also possible to date the five texts more precisely to the period 1790-1792:

> *Love and Friendship* – June 13th, 1790;
> *Lesley Castle* – January 3rd, 1792 to April 3rd, 1792;
> *The History of England* – November 26th, 1791 (when Jane was fifteen and Cassandra eighteen); transcribed between May and November 1792.
> "A Collection of Letters" – Late 1791 (?)
> "Scraps" – January, 1793.

Kathryn Sutherland comments on the difference that readers will detect between the juvenilia of the first and second notebooks, "Where knockabout humour dominates the first notebook, *Volume the Second* offers more extended studies of female character and motive. The target is manuals of instruction, or conduct books, as they were called, standard schoolroom fare, like Hester Mulso Chapone's *Letters on the Improvement of the Mind, Addressed to a Young Lady*" (*Teenage* xvi).

[Dedication]

For my brother Frank. C.E.A.[1]
Ex dono mei Patris[2]

Notes

1. "C.E.A.": These words are written in ink on a slip of paper pasted to the inner cover that largely obscures the words "For my brother Frank" written in pencil beneath. At her death in 1845, Cassandra Elizabeth Austen left the notebook to her brother, who lived for another twenty years.
2. "Ex dono mei Patris": "From the gift of my father." This Latin phrase is written at the top of the Contents page. Providing his daughter with a second, higher quality notebook in which to transcribe her writings was a very tangible way of encouraging Austen's authorship ambitions.

Introduction to the characters in *Love and Friendship*:

[In the family trees below: – indicates a union without marriage; = indicates a legal marriage.]

The Family of Lord St. Clair, a Scottish nobleman

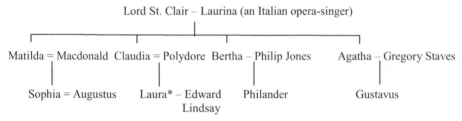

The Family of Sir Edward Lindsay, Baronet

***Laura** (the daughter of Polydore and common law wife of Edward) is the main narrator.

Other Significant Characters

Isabel, a friend of Laura, has a daughter, **Marianne**, to whom Laura's letters are addressed. In the course of the story, Isabel marries an unnamed Irishman and moves to Ireland.

Sir Edward Lindsay's sister, **Philippa** (Edward's aunt) marries a young fortune-hunter.

Macdonald, Scottish landowner, cousin to Sophia, has one daughter, **Janetta**, engaged by her father to Graham, who elopes with **Captain M'Kenzie**.

An unnamed **Scottish cottager** (a widow) with whom Laura and Augusta take shelter has a daughter called **Bridget**.

[Dedication]

To Madame la Comtesse De Fevillide[1] this novel is inscribed by her obliged humble servant
The Author

Love and Friendship – a novel in a series of letters

"Deceived in friendship and betrayed in love."[2]

Letter the First: from Isabel to Laura

How often, in answer to my repeated entreaties that you would give my daughter a regular detail of the misfortunes and adventures of your life, have you said, "No, my friend, never will I comply with your request till I may be no longer in danger of again experiencing such ~~cruel~~ dreadful ones."

Surely that time is now at hand. You are this day fifty-five. If a woman may ever be said to be in safety from the determined perseverance of disagreeable lovers and the ~~reiterated~~ cruel persecutions of obstinate fathers, surely it must be at such a time of life.

Isabel.

Letter 2nd: Laura to Isabel

Although I cannot agree with you in supposing that I shall never again be exposed to misfortunes as unmerited as those I have already experienced, yet to avoid the imputation of obstinacy or ill-nature, I will gratify the curiosity of your daughter; and may the fortitude with which I have suffered the many afflictions of ~~that~~ my past life, prove to her a useful lesson for the support of those which may befall her in her own.

Laura.

Letter 3rd: Laura to Marianne

As the daughter of my most intimate friend, I think you entitled to that knowledge of my unhappy story, which your mother has so often solicited me to give you.

My father was a native of Ireland and an inhabitant of Wales; my mother was the natural daughter[3] of a Scotch peer by an Italian Opera-girl – I was born in Spain, and received my education at a convent in France.

When I had reached my eighteenth year, I was recalled by my parents to my paternal roof in Wales. Our mansion was situated in one of the most romantic parts of the Vale of Usk[4]. Though my charms are now considerably softened and somewhat impaired by the misfortunes I have undergone, I was once beautiful. But lovely as I was, the graces of my person were the least of my perfections. Of every accomplishment accustomary to my sex, I was mistress. When in the convent, my progress had always exceeded my instructions, my acquirements ~~were~~ had been wonderful for my age, and I had shortly surpassed my masters.

In my mind, every virtue that could adorn it was centered; it was the *rendezvous* of every good quality and ~~the place of appointment~~ of every noble sentiment.

A sensibility[5] too tremblingly alive to every affliction of my friends, my acquaintance, and particularly to every affliction of my own, was my ~~own~~ only fault, if a fault it could be called. Alas! how altered now! Though indeed my own misfortunes do not make less impression on me than they ever did, yet now I never feel for those of another. My accomplishments too, begin to fade. – I can neither sing so well nor dance so gracefully as I once did – and I have entirely forgot the *minuet de la cour*[6].

Adieu,

Laura.

Letter 4th: Laura to Marianne

Our neighbourhood was small, for it consisted only of your mother. She may probably have already told you that, being left by her parents in indigent circumstances, she had retired into Wales on economical motives. There it was, our friendship first commenced. Isabel was then one-and-twenty. Though pleasing both in her person and manners, (between ourselves) she never possessed the hundredth part of my beauty or accomplishments. Isabel had seen the world. She had passed two years at one of the first boarding-schools in London, had spent a fortnight in Bath, and had ~~slept~~ supped one night in Southampton.

"Beware, my Laura," she would often say, "Beware of the insipid vanities and idle dissipations of the metropolis of England; beware of the unmeaning luxuries of Bath and of the stinking fish of Southampton[7]."

"Alas!" exclaimed I. "How am I to avoid those evils I shall never be exposed to? What probability is there of my ever tasting the dissipations of London, the luxuries of Bath, or the stinking fish of Southampton? I, who am doomed to waste my days of youth and beauty in an humble cottage in the Vale of Usk."

Ah! little did I then think I was ordained so soon to quit that humble cottage for the deceitful pleasures of the world.

Adieu,

Laura.

Letter 5th: Laura to Marianne

One evening in December, as my father, my mother, and myself were arranged in social converse round our fireside, we were, on a sudden, greatly astonished, ~~considerably amazed and somewhat surprised~~ by hearing a violent knocking on the outward door of our rustic cot[tage].

My father started. –

"What noise is that?" said he.

"It sounds like a loud rapping at the door," – replied my mother.

"It does indeed," cried I.

"I am of your opinion," said my father. "It certainly does appear to proceed from some uncommon violence exerted against our unoffending door."

"Yes!" exclaimed I. "I cannot help thinking it must be somebody who knocks for admittance."

"That is another point," replied he. "~~I cannot pretend to assert that anyone knocks, though for my own part, I own I rather image it is a knock at the door that somebody does. Yet as we have no ocular demonstration...~~ We must not pretend to determine on what motive the person may knock – though that someone does rap at the door, I am partly convinced."[8]

Here, a second tremendous rap interrupted my father in his speech, and somewhat alarmed my mother and me.

"Had we not better go and see who it is?" said she. "The servants are out."

"I think we had," replied I.

"Certainly," added my father, "by all means."

"Shall we go now?" said my mother.

"The sooner the better," answered he.

"Oh! let ~~us go immediately~~ no time be lost!" cried I.

A third, more violent rap than ever, again assaulted our ears.

"I am certain there is somebody knocking at the door," said my mother.

"I think there must," replied my father.

"I fancy the servants are returned," said I. "I think I hear Mary going to the door."

"I'm glad of it," cried my father, "for I long to know who it is."

I was right in my conjecture; for Mary instantly entering the room, informed us that a young gentleman and his servant were at the door who had lost their way, were very cold, and begged leave to warm themselves by our fire.

"Won't you admit them?" said I.

"You have no objection, my dear?" said my father.

"None in the world," replied my mother.

Mary, without waiting for any further commands, immediately left the room and quickly returned, introducing the most beauteous and amiable youth I had ever beheld. The servant, she kept to herself.

My natural sensibility had already been greatly affected by

the sufferings of the unfortunate stranger and no sooner did I first behold him, than I felt ~~myself instantly in love with him~~ that on him the happiness or misery of my future life must depend[9].

Adieu,

Laura.

Letter 6th: Laura to Marianne

The noble youth informed us that his name was Lindsay – for particular reasons, however, I shall conceal it under that of Talbot[10]. He told us that he was the son of an English baronet, that his mother had been many years no more, and that he had a sister of the middle size.

"My father," he continued, "is a mean and mercenary wretch – it is only to such particular friends as this dear party that I would thus betray his failings. Your virtues, my amiable Polydore," addressing himself to my father, "yours dear Claudia, and yours my charming Laura[11], call on me to repose in you my confidence."

We bowed.

"My father, seduced by the false glare of fortune and the deluding pomp of title, insisted on my giving my hand to Lady Dorothea."

"'No, never!' exclaimed I. 'Lady Dorothea is lovely and engaging; I prefer no woman to her; but know, sir, that I scorn to marry her ~~if you wish I should~~ in compliance with your wishes. No! Never shall it be said that I obliged my father.'"[12]

We all admired the noble manliness of his reply. He continued:

"Sir Edward was surprised; he had perhaps little expected to ~~have met~~ meet with so spirited an opposition to his will. 'Where, Edward in the name of wonder,' said he, 'did you pick up ~~these~~ this unmeaning gibberish? You have been studying novels[13], I suspect.'

"I scorned to answer: it would have been beneath my dignity. I mounted my horse and followed by my faithful William, set forwards for my aunt's.

"My father's house is situated in Bedfordshire, aunt's in Middlesex, and though I flatter myself with being a tolerable proficient in geography, I know not how it happened, but I found myself entering this beautiful Vale which I find is in South Wales[14], when I had expected to have reached my aunt's."

"After having wandered some time on the banks of the Usk without knowing which way to go, I began to lament my cruel destiny in the bitterest and most pathetic manner. It was now perfectly dark, not a single star was there to direct my steps, and I know not what might have befallen me, had I not at length discerned through the solemn gloom that surrounded me a distant light, which, as I approached it, I discovered to be the cheerful blaze of your fire. Impelled by the combination of misfortunes under which I laboured, namely fear, cold, and hunger, I hesitated not to ask admittance, which at length I have gained; and now, my adorable Laura," continued he, taking my hand, "when may I hope to receive that reward of all the painful sufferings I have undergone during the course of my attachment to you, to which I have ever aspired. Oh! when will you reward me with yourself?"

"This instant, dear and amiable Edward," replied I.

We were immediately united by my father, who, though he had never taken orders, had been bred to the Church[15].

Adieu,

Laura.

Letter 7th: Laura to Marianne

We remained but a few days after our marriage in the Vale of Usk. After taking an affecting farewell of my father, my mother, and my Isabel, I accompanied Edward to his aunt's in Middlesex. Philippa received us both with every expression of affectionate love. My arrival was indeed a most agreeable surprise to her, as she had not only been totally ignorant of my marriage with her nephew, but had ~~not even the~~ never even had the slightest idea of there being such a person in the world.

Augusta, the sister of Edward, was on a visit to her when we arrived. ~~Her~~ I found her exactly what her brother had described her to be – of the middle size. She received me with equal surprise, though not with equal cordiality, as Philippa. There was a disagreeable coldness and forbidding reserve in her reception of me which was equally distressing and unexpected; none of that interesting sensibility or amiable sympathy[16] in her manners and address to me when we first met, which should have distinguished our introduction to each other. Her language was neither warm nor affectionate, her expressions of regard were neither animated nor cordial; her arms were not opened to receive me to her heart, though my own were extended to press her to mine.

A short conversation between Augusta and her brother, which I accidentally overheard, increased my dislike to her, and convinced me that her heart was no more formed for the soft ties of love than for the endearing intercourse of friendship.

"But do you think that my father will ever be reconciled to this imprudent connection?" said Augusta.

"Augusta," replied the noble youth, "I thought you had a better opinion of me, than to imagine I would so abjectly degrade myself as to consider my father's concurrence in any of my affairs, either of consequence or concern to me. Tell me, Augusta, tell me with sincerity; did you ever know me consult his inclinations, or follow his advice in the least trifling particular, since the age of fifteen?"

"Edward," replied she, "you are surely too diffident in your own praise. Since you were fifteen only! My dear brother, since you were five years old, I entirely acquit you of ever having willingly contributed to the satisfaction of your father. But still, I am not without apprehensions of your being shortly obliged to degrade yourself in your own eyes by seeking a support for your wife in the generosity of Sir Edward."

"Never, never Augusta will I so demean myself," said Edward. "Support! What support will Laura want which she can receive from him?"

"Only those very insignificant ones of victuals and drink," answered she. "None that I know of, so efficacious," ~~replied~~ returned Augusta.

"And did you then never feel the pleasing pangs of love, Augusta?" replied my Edward, "~~Did~~ Does it appear impossible to your vile and ~~vulgar~~ corrupted palate, to exist on love? Can you not conceive the luxury of living in every distress ~~than~~ that poverty can inflict, with the object of your tenderest affection?"

"You are too ridiculous," said Augusta, "to argue with[17]; perhaps, however, you may in time be convinced that..."

Here I was ~~interrupted~~ prevented from hearing the remainder of her speech, by the appearance of a very handsome young woman, who was ushered into the room at the door of which I had been listening. On hearing her announced by the name of "Lady Dorothea," I instantly quitted my post and followed her into the parlour, for I well remembered that she was the lady proposed as a wife for my Edward by the cruel and unrelenting baronet.

Although Lady Dorothea's visit was nominally to Philippa and Augusta, yet I have some reason to imagine that (acquainted with the marriage and arrival of Edward) to see me was a principal motive to it.

I soon perceived that, though lovely and elegant in her person, and though easy and polite in her address, she was of that inferior order of beings with regard to delicate feeling, tender sentiments, and refined sensibility, of which Augusta was once [i.e., one].

She staid but half an hour and neither, in the course of her visit, confided to me any of her secret thoughts, nor requested me to confide in her any of mine. You will easily imagine, therefore, my dear Marianne, that I could not feel any ardent affection or very sincere attachment for Lady Dorothea.

Adieu,

Laura.

Letter 8th: Laura to Marianne, in continuation

Lady Dorothea had not left us long before another visitor, as unexpected a one as her ladyship, was announced. It was Sir Edward, who informed by Augusta of her brother's marriage, came doubtless to reproach him for having dared to unite himself to me without his knowledge. But Edward, foreseeing his design, approached him with heroic fortitude as soon as he entered the room, and addressed him in the following manner:

"Sir Edward, I know the motive of your journey here. – You come with the base design of reproaching me for having entered into an indissoluble engagement with my Laura without your consent. But sir, I glory in the act. – It is my greatest boast, that I have incurred the displeasure of my father!"

So saying, he took my hand and whilst Sir Edward, Philippa, and Augusta were doubtless reflecting with admiration on his undaunted bravery, led me from the parlour to his father's carriage, which yet remained at the door, and in which we were instantly conveyed from the pursuit of Sir Edward[18].

The postilions had at first received orders only to take the London road; as soon as we had sufficiently reflected, however, we ordered them to drive to M—, the seat of Edward's most particular friend, which was but a few miles distant.

At M—, we arrived in ~~less than an hour~~ a few hours; and on sending in our names, were immediately admitted to Sophia, the wife of Edward's friend. After having been deprived during the course of three weeks of a real friend (for such I term your mother), imagine my transports at beholding one most truly worthy of the name. Sophia was rather above the middle size;

most elegantly formed. A soft languor spread over her lovely features, but increased their beauty. – It was the characteristic of her mind. – She was all sensibility and feeling. We flew into each other's arms and after having exchanged vows of mutual friendship for the rest of our lives, instantly unfolded to each other the most inward secrets of our hearts. – We were interrupted in the delightful employment by the entrance of Augustus (Edward's friend), who was just returned from a solitary ramble.

Never did I see such an affecting scene as was the meeting of Edward and Augustus.

"My life! My soul!" exclaimed the former.

"My adorable angel!" replied the latter, as they flew into each other's arms.

It was too pathetic for the feelings of Sophia and myself. – We fainted alternately on a sofa[19].

Adieu,

Laura.

Letter the 9th: From the same to the same

~~When we were somewhat recovered from the overpowering effusions of our~~[20]

Towards the close of the day, we received the following letter from Philippa:

> Sir Edward is greatly incensed by your abrupt departure; he has taken back Augusta with him to Bedfordshire. Much as I wish to enjoy again your charming society, ~~yet~~ I cannot determine to snatch you from that of such dear and deserving friends. – When your visit to them is terminated, I trust you will return to the arms of your
> Philippa

We returned a suitable answer to this affectionate note, and after thanking her for her kind invitation, assured her that we would certainly avail ourselves of it, whenever we might have no other place to go to. Though certainly nothing could, to any reasonable being, have appeared more satisfactory than so grateful a reply to her invitation, yet I know not how it was, but she was certainly capricious enough to be displeased with our behaviour and in a few weeks after, either to revenge our conduct, or relieve her own solitude, married a young and illiterate fortune-hunter. This imprudent step (though we were sensible that it would probably deprive us of that fortune which

Philippa had ever taught us to expect) could not, on our own accounts, excite from our exalted minds a single sigh; yet fearful lest it might prove a source of endless misery to the deluded bride, our trembling sensibility was greatly affected when we were first informed of the event.

The affectionate entreaties of Augustus and Sophia that we would forever consider their house as our home, easily prevailed on us to determine never more to leave them. In the society of my Edward and this amiable pair, I passed the happiest moments of my life. Our time was most delightfully spent, in mutual protestations of friendship, and in vows of unalterable love, in which we were secure from being interrupted by intruding and disagreeable visitors, as Augustus and Sophia had, on their first entrance in the neighbourhood, taken due care to inform the surrounding families, that as their happiness centered wholly in themselves, they wished for no other society.

But alas! my dear Marianne, such happiness as I then enjoyed was too perfect to be lasting. A most severe and unexpected blow at once destroyed every sensation of pleasure. Convinced as you must be from what I have already told you concerning Augustus and Sophia, that there never ~~were were~~ were a happier couple, I need not, I imagine, inform you that their union had been contrary to the inclinations of their cruel and mercenary parents; who had vainly endeavoured with obstinate perseverance to force them into a marriage with those whom they had ever abhorred; but with an heroic fortitude worthy to be related and admired, they had both constantly refused to submit to ~~their~~ such despotic ~~will~~ power.

After having so nobly disentangled themselves from the shackles of parental authority, by a clandestine marriage, they were determined never to forfeit the good opinion they had gained in the world, ~~by~~ in so doing, by accepting any proposals of reconciliation that might be offered them by their fathers. – To this farther trial of their noble independence, however, they never were exposed.

They had been married but a few months when our visit to them commenced, during which time they had been amply supported by a considerable sum of money which Augustus had gracefully purloined from his unworthy father's escritoire[20], a few days before his union with Sophia.

By our arrival, their expenses were considerably increased, though their means for supplying them were then nearly exhausted. But they, exalted creatures! scorned to reflect a moment on their pecuniary distresses, and would have blushed at the idea of paying their debts. – Alas! what was their reward for such disinterested behaviour! The beautiful Augustus was arrested and we were all undone. Such perfidious treachery in the merciless perpetrators of the deed will shock your gentle nature, dearest Marianne, as much as it then affected the delicate sensibility of ~~Augus~~ Edward, Sophia, your Laura, and of Augustus himself[22]. To complete such unparalleled barbarity, we were informed that an execution in the house[23] would shortly take place. Ah! what could we do but what we did! We sighed and fainted on the sofa.

Adeiu,

Laura.

Letter 10th: Laura in continuation

When we were somewhat recovered from the overpowering effusions of our grief, Edward desired that we would consider what was the most prudent step to be taken in our unhappy situation, while he repaired to his imprisoned friend to lament over his misfortunes. We promised that ~~he~~ we would, and he set forwards on his journey to town. During his absence, we faithfully complied with his desire, and after the most mature deliberation, at length agreed that the best thing we could do was to leave the house; of which we every moment expected the officers of justice to take possession.

We waited, therefore, with the greatest impatience for the return of Edward, in order to impart to him the result of our deliberations. But no Edward appeared. In vain did we count the tedious moments of his absence – in vain did we weep – in vain even did we sigh – no Edward returned. – This was too cruel, too unexpected a blow to our gentle sensibility – we could not support it – we could only faint. At length, collecting all the resolution I was mistress of, I arose, and after packing up some necessary apparel for Sophia and myself, I dragged her to a carriage I had ordered, and we instantly set out for London.

As the habitation of Augustus was within ~~six~~ twelve miles of town, it was not long ere we arrived there, and no sooner had we entered ~~Piccadilly~~ Holbourn[24] than, letting down one of the front glasses, I enquired of every decent-looking person that we passed if they had seen my Edward.

But as we drove too rapidly to allow them to answer my repeated enquiries, I gained little, or indeed, no information concerning him.

"Where am I to drive?" said the postilion.

"To Newgate[25], gentle youth," replied I, "to see Augustus."

"Oh! no, no!" exclaimed Sophia. "I cannot go to Newgate; I shall not be able to support the sight of my Augustus in so cruel a confinement. – My feelings are sufficiently shocked by the *recital* of his distress, but to behold it will overpower my sensibility."

As I perfectly agreed with her in the justice of her sentiments, the postilion was instantly directed to return into the country[26]. You may perhaps have been somewhat surprised, my dearest Marianne, that in the distress I then endured, destitute of any support, and unprovided with any habitation, I should never once have remembered my father and mother or my paternal cottage in the Vale of Usk. To account for the seeming forgetfulness, I must inform you of a trifling circumstance concerning them which I have as yet never mentioned. The death of my parents a few weeks after my departure is the circumstance I allude to. By their decease, I became the lawful inheritress of their house and fortune. But alas! the house had never been their own, and their fortune had only been an annuity on their own lives[27]. Such is the depravity of the world!

To your mother, I should have returned with pleasure, should have been happy to have introduced to her my charming Sophia, and should with cheerfulness have passed the remainder of my life in their dear society in the Vale of Usk, had not one obstacle to the execution of so agreeable a scheme, intervened; which was the marriage and removal of your mother to a distant part of Ireland.

Adieu,

Laura.

Letter 11th: Laura in continuation

"I have a relation in Scotland," said Sophia to me as we left London, "who I am certain would not hesitate in receiving me."

"Shall I order the boy to drive there?" said I – but instantly recollecting myself, exclaimed, "Alas, I fear it will be too long a journey for the horses."

Unwilling, however, to act only from my own inadequate knowledge of the strength and abilities of horses, I consulted the postilion, who was entirely of my opinion concerning the affair. We therefore determined to change horses at the next town and to travel post[28] the remainder of the journey. – When we arrived at the last inn we were to stop at, which was but a few miles from the house of Sophia's relation, unwilling to intrude our society on him unexpected and unthought of, we wrote a very elegant and well penned note to him containing an account of our destitute and melancholy situation, and of our intention to spend some months with him in Scotland.

As soon as we had dispatched this letter, we immediately prepared to follow ~~her~~ it in person, and were stepping into the carriage for that purpose, when our attention was attracted by the entrance of a coroneted coach[29] and four into the inn-yard. A gentleman considerably advanced in years, descended from it. At his first appearance my sensibility was wonderfully affected, and ere I had gazed at him a second time, an instinctive sympathy whispered to my heart that he was my grandfather. Convinced that I could not be mistaken in my conjecture, I instantly sprang from the carriage I had just entered, and following the venerable stranger into the room he had been shown to, I threw myself on my knees before him and besought him to acknowledge me as his grandchild. He started, and after having attentively examined my features, raised me from the ground, and throwing his grandfatherly arms around my neck, exclaimed:

"Acknowledge thee! Yes, dear resemblance of my Laurina and Laurina's daughter, sweet image of my Claudia and my Claudia's mother, I do acknowledge thee as the daughter of the one and the granddaughter of the other."

While he was thus tenderly embracing me, Sophia, astonished at my precipitate departure, entered the room in search of me. No sooner had she caught the eye of the venerable peer, than he exclaimed with every mark of astonishment –

"Another granddaughter! Yes, yes, I see you are the daughter of my Laurina's eldest girl; your resemblance to the beauteous Matilda sufficiently proclaims it."

"Oh!" replied Sophia, "when I first beheld you, the instinct of nature whispered me that we were in some degree related – but whether grandfathers, or grandmothers, I could not pretend to determine."

He folded her in his arms, and whilst they were tenderly embracing, the door of the apartment opened and a most beautiful young man appeared. On perceiving him, Lord St. Clair started, and retreating back a few paces, with uplifted

142

hands, said, "Another grandchild! What an unexpected happiness is this! To discover, in the space of three minutes, as many of my descendants! This, I am certain, is Philander the son of my Laurina's third girl, the amiable Bertha; there wants now but the presence of Gustavus to complete the union of my Laurina's grandchildren."

"And here he is," said a graceful youth who that instant entered the room. "Here is the Gustavus you desire to see. I am the son of Agatha, your Laurina's fourth and youngest daughter."

"I see you are indeed," replied Lord St. Clair. – "But tell me," continued he, looking fearfully towards the door, "tell me, have I any other grandchildren in the house."

"None, my Lord."

"Then I will provide ~~with~~ for you all without farther delay. – Here are four banknotes of £50 each. – Take them and remember I have done the duty of a grandfather."

He instantly left the room and immediately afterwards the house[30].

Adieu,

Laura.

Letter the 12th: Laura in continuation

You may imagine how greatly we were surprised by the sudden departure of Lord St. Clair.

"Ignoble grandsire!" exclaimed Sophia.

"Unworthy grandfather!" said I, and instantly fainted in each other's arms.

How long we remained in this situation, I know not; but when we recovered we found ourselves alone, without either Gustavus, Philander, or the banknotes. As we were deploring our unhappy fate, the door of the apartment opened and "Macdonald" was announced. He was Sophia's cousin. The haste with which he came to our relief so soon after the receipt of our note spoke so greatly in his favour that I hesitated not to pronounce him at first sight, a tender and sympathetic friend. Alas! he little deserved the name – for though he told us that he was much concerned at our misfortunes, yet by his own account it appeared that the perusal of them, had neither drawn from him a single sigh, nor induced him to bestow one curse on our vindictive stars. – He told Sophia that his daughter depended on her returning with him to Macdonald Hall, and that, as his cousin's friend, he should be happy to see me there also. To Macdonald Hall, therefore, we went, and were received with great kindness by Janetta, the daughter of Macdonald and the mistress of the mansion.

Janetta was then only fifteen; naturally well disposed, endowed with a susceptible heart, and a sympathetic disposition; she might, had these amiable qualities been properly encouraged, have been an ornament to human nature, but unfortunately her father possessed not a soul sufficiently exalted to admire so promising a disposition, and had endeavoured by every means in his power to prevent its increasing with her years. He had actually so far extinguished the natural noble sensibility of her heart, as to prevail on her to accept an offer from a young man of his recommendation. They were to be married in a few months, and Graham was in the house when we arrived.

We soon saw through his character. He was just such a man as one might have expected to be the choice of Macdonald. They said he was sensible, well-informed, and agreeable; we did not pretend to judge of such trifles, but as we were convinced he had no soul, that he had never read *The Sorrows of Werter*[31], and that his hair bore not the least resemblance to auburn[32], we were certain that Janetta could feel no affection for him, or at least that she ought to feel none. The very circumstance of his being her father's choice too, was so much in his disfavour, that had he been deserving her in every other respect, yet *that* of itself ought to have been a sufficient reason in the eyes of Janetta for rejecting him.

These considerations we were determined to represent to her in their proper light, and doubted not of meeting with the desired success from one naturally so well disposed; whose errors in the affair had only arisen from a want of proper confidence in her own opinion, and a suitable contempt of her father's. We found her, indeed, all that our warmest wishes could have hoped for; we had no difficulty to convince her that it was impossible she could love Graham, or that it was her duty to disobey her father; the only thing at which she rather seemed to hesitate, was our assertion that she must be attached to some other person. For some time, she persevered in declaring that she knew no other young man for whom she had the smallest affection; but upon explaining the impossibility of such a thing, she said that she believed she *did like* Captain M'Kenzie better than anyone she knew besides. This confession satisfied us, and after having enumerated the good qualities of M'Kenzie, and assured her that she was violently in love with him, we desired to know whether he had ever in any wise declared his affection to her.

"So far from having ever declared it, I have no reason to imagine that he has ever felt any for me," said Janetta.

"That he certainly adores you," replied Sophia, "there can be no doubt. – The attachment must be reciprocal. Did he never gaze on you with admiration – tenderly press your hand – drop an involuntary tear – and leave the room abruptly?"

"Never," replied she, "that I remember. – He has always left the room indeed when his visit has been ended, but has never gone away particularly abruptly or without making a bow."

"Indeed my love," said I, "you must be mistaken – for it is absolutely impossible that he should ever have left you but ~~with~~ confusion, despair, and precipitation[33]. Consider but for a moment, Janetta, and you must be convinced how absurd it is to suppose that he could ever make a bow, or behave like ~~other people~~ any other person."

Having settled this point to our satisfaction, the next we took into consideration was, to determine in what manner we should inform M'Kenzie of the favourable opinion Janetta entertained of him ... We at length agreed to acquaint him with it by an anonymous letter which Sophia drew up in the following manner:

> Oh! happy lover of the beautiful Janetta. Oh! enviable possessor of her heart whose hand is destined to another, why do you thus delay a confession of your attachment to the amiable object of it? Oh! consider that a few weeks will at once put an end to every flattering hope that you may now entertain, by uniting the unfortunate victim of her father's cruelty to the execrable and detested Graham.
>
> Alas! why do you thus so cruelly connive at the projected misery of her and of yourself by delaying to communicate that scheme which had doubtless long possessed your imagination? A secret union will at once secure the felicity of both.

The amiable M'Kenzie, whose modesty, as he afterwards assured us, had been the only reason of his having so long concealed the violence of his affection for Janetta, on receiving this billet flew on the wings of love to Macdonald Hall, and so powerfully pleaded his attachment to her who inspired it, that after a few more private interviews, Sophia and I experienced the satisfaction of seeing them depart for Gretna Green[34], which they chose for the celebration of their nuptials, in preference to any other place, as it was a most agreeable drive ... from its wonderful celebrity although it was at a considerable distance from Macdonald Hall.

Adieu,

Laura.

Letter the 13th: Laura in continuation

They had been gone nearly a couple of hours, before either Macdonald or Graham had entertained any suspicion of the affair. And they might not even then have suspected it had it not, but for the following little accident. Sophia, happening one day to open a private drawer in Macdonald's Library with one of her own keys, discovered that it was the place where he kept his papers of consequence, and with amongst them some bank notes of considerable amount. This discovery she imparted to me; and having agreed together that it would be a proper treatment of so vile a wretch as Macdonald to deprive him of money, perhaps dishonestly gained, it was determined that the next time we should either of us happen to go that way, we would take one or more of the bank notes from the drawer. This well-meant plan we had often successfully put in execution; but alas! on the very day of Janetta's escape, as Sophia was majestically removing the fifth banknote from the drawer to her own purse, she was suddenly most impertinently interrupted in her employment by the entrance of Macdonald himself, in a most abrupt and precipitate manner.

Sophia (who though naturally all winning sweetness could, when occasions demanded it, call forth the dignity of her sex) instantly put on a most forbidding look, and darting an angry frown on the undaunted culprit, demanded in a haughty tone of voice, "Wherefore her retirement was thus insolently broken in on?"

The unblushing Macdonald, without even endeavouring to exculpate himself from the crime he was charged with, meanly endeavoured to reproach Sophia with ignobly defrauding him of his money ... The dignity of Sophia was wounded.

"Wretch!" exclaimed she, hastily replacing the banknote in the drawer. "How darest thou to accuse me of an act of which the bare idea makes me blush?"

The base wretch was still unconvinced and continued to

upbraid the justly-offended Sophia in such opprobrious language, that at length he so greatly provoked the gentle sweetness of her nature, as to induce her to revenge herself on him by informing him of Janetta's elopement, and of the active part we had both taken in the affair. At this period of their quarrel, I entered the library and was, as you may imagine, equally offended as Sophia at the ill-grounded accusations of the malevolent and contemptible Macdonald.

"Base miscreant!" cried I. "How canst thou thus undauntedly endeavour to sully the spotless reputation of such bright excellence? Why dost thou not suspect my innocence as soon?"

"Be satisfied, madam," replied he. "I *do* suspect it, and therefore must desire that that you will both leave this house in less than half an hour."

"We shall go willingly," answered Sophia, "our hearts have long detested thee, and nothing but our friendship for thy daughter could have induced us to remain so long beneath thy roof."

"Your friendship for my daughter has indeed been most powerfully exerted by throwing her into the arms of an unprincipled fortune-hunter," replied he.

"Yes!" exclaimed I. "Amidst every misfortune, it will afford us some consolation to reflect that by this one act of friendship to Janetta, we have amply discharged every obligation that we have received from her father."

"It must indeed be a most grateful reflection, to your exalted minds," said he.

As soon as we had packed up our wardrobe and valuables, we left Macdonald Hall, and after having walked about a mile and a half, we sat down by the side of a clear limpid stream to refresh our exhausted limbs. The place was suited to meditation. A grove of full-grown elms sheltered us from the east. – A bed of full-grown nettles from the west. – Before us ran the murmuring brook and behind us ran the turnpike road. We were in a mood for contemplation and in a disposition to enjoy so beautiful a spot. A mutual silence which had for some time reigned between us, was at length broke by my exclaiming:–

"What a lovely scene! Alas, why are not Edward and Augustus here to enjoy its beauties with us?"

"Ah! my beloved Laura," cried Sophia, "for pity's sake forbear recalling to my remembrance the unhappy situation of my imprisoned husband. Alas, what would I not give to learn the fate of my Augustus! to know if he is still in Newgate, or if he is yet hung[35]. But never shall I be able so far to conquer my tender sensibility as to enquire after him. Oh! do not, I beseech you ever, let me again hear you repeat his beloved name. – It affects me too deeply. – I cannot bear to hear him mentioned, it wounds my feelings."

"Excuse me, my Sophia, for having thus unwillingly offended you –" replied I – and then changing the conversation, desired her to admire the noble grandeur of the elms which sheltered us from the eastern zephyr[36].

"Alas! my Laura," returned she, "avoid so melancholy a subject, I entreat you. Do not again wound my sensibility by observations on those elms. They remind me of Augustus. He was like them, tall, majestic. – He possessed that noble grandeur which you admire in them."

I was silent, fearful lest I might any more unwillingly distress her by fixing on any other subject of conversation which might again remind her of Augustus.

"Why do you not speak, my Laura?" said she after a short pause. "I cannot support this silence – you must not leave me to my own reflections; they ever recur to Augustus."

"What a beautiful sky!" said I. "How charmingly is the azure varied by those delicate streaks of white!"

"Oh! my Laura," replied she, hastily withdrawing her eyes from a momentary glance at the sky, "do not thus distress me by calling my attention to an object which so cruelly reminds me of my Augustus's blue satin waistcoat striped with white! In pity to your unhappy friend, avoid a subject so distressing."

What could I do? The feelings of Sophia were at that time so exquisite, and the tenderness she felt for Augustus so poignant that I had not power to start any other topic, justly fearing that it might in some unforeseen manner again awaken all her sensibility by directing her thoughts to her husband. Yet to be silent would be ~~cruel~~ cruel; she had entreated me to talk.

From this dilemma I was most fortunately relieved by an accident truly *apropos*[37]; it was the lucky overturning of a gentleman's phaeton, on the road which ran murmuring behind us. It was a most fortunate accident as it diverted the attention of Sophia from the melancholy reflections ~~of Augustus~~ which she had been before indulging. We instantly quitted our seats and ran to the rescue of those who, but a few moments before, had been in so elevated a situation as a fashionably high phaeton[38], but who were now laid low and sprawling in the dust.

"What an ample subject for reflection on the uncertain enjoyments of this world, would not that phaeton and the life of Cardinal Wolsey[39] afford a thinking mind!" said I to Sophia as we were hastening to the field of action[40].

She had not time to answer me, for every thought was now engaged by the horrid spectacle before us. Two gentlemen, most elegantly attired, but weltering in their blood, was what first struck our eyes. – We approached. – They were Edward and Augustus. – Yes, dearest Marianne, they were our husbands. Sophia shrieked and fainted on the ground. – I screamed and instantly ran mad. – We remained thus mutually deprived of our senses some minutes, and on regaining them were deprived of them again. For an hour and a quarter did we continue in this unfortunate situation – Sophia fainting every moment and I running mad as often.

At length, a groan from the hapless Edward (who alone retained any share of life) restored us to ourselves. Had we indeed before imagined that either of them lived, we should have been more sparing of our grief – but as we had supposed when we first beheld them that they were no more, we knew that nothing could remain to be done but what we were about. No sooner, therefore, did we hear my Edward's groan than postponing our lamentations for the present, we hastily ran to the dear youth and kneeling on each side of him implored him not to die.–

"Laura," said he, fixing his now languid eyes on me, "I fear I have been overturned."

I was overjoyed to find him yet sensible.

"Oh! tell me Edward," said I, "tell me, I beseech you, before you die, what has befallen you since that unhappy day in which Augustus was arrested and we were separated.–"

"I will," said he and, instantly fetching a deep sigh, expired. – Sophia immediately sunk again into a swoon. – My grief was more audible. My voice faltered, my eyes assumed a vacant stare, my face became as pale as death, and my senses were considerably impaired.–

"Talk not to me of phaetons," said I, raving in a frantic, incoherent manner, "– Give me a violin. – I'll play to him and sooth him in his melancholy hours. – Beware ye gentle nymphs of Cupid's thunderbolts, avoid the piercing shafts of Jupiter[41]. – Look at that grove of firs. – I see a leg of mutton. – They told me Edward was not dead; but they deceived me. – They took him for a cucumber.–"

Thus, I continued wildly exclaiming on my Edward's death. – For two hours did I rave thus madly, and should not then have left off, as I was not in the least ~~tired~~ fatigued, had not Sophia who was just recovered from her swoon, entreated me to consider that night was now approaching and that the damps began to fall.

"And whither shall we go," said I, "to shelter us from either?"

"To that white cottage," replied she, pointing to a neat building which rose up amidst the grove of elms, and which I had not before observed. – I agreed, and we instantly walked to it. – We knocked at the door. – It was opened by an old woman; on being requested to afford us a night's lodging, she informed us that her house was but small, that she had only two bedrooms, but that, however, we should be welcome to one of them. We were satisfied and followed the good woman into the house, where we were greatly cheered by the sight of a comfortable fire. – She was a widow and had only one daughter, who was then just seventeen – one of the best of ages; but alas! she was very plain and her name was Bridget[42] ... Nothing, therefore, could be expected from her. – She could not be supposed to possess either exalted ideas, delicate feelings or refined sensibilities. – She was nothing more than a mere good-tempered, civil and obliging young woman; as such we could scarcely dislike her – she was only an object of contempt.–

Adieu,

Laura.

Letter the 14th: Laura in continuation

Arm yourself, my amiable young friend, with all the philosophy you are mistress of; summon up all the fortitude you possess, for alas! in the perusal of the following pages your sensibility will be most severely tried. Ah! what were the misfortunes I had before experienced, and which I have already related to you, to the one I am now going to inform you of. The death of my father, my mother, and my husband, though almost more than my gentle nature could support, were trifles in comparison to the misfortune I am now proceeding to relate.

The morning after our arrival at the cottage, Sophia complained of a violent pain in her delicate limbs, accompanied with a disagreeable headache. She attributed it to a cold caught by her continued faintings in the open air as the dew was falling the evening before. This, I feared, was but too probably

150

the case; since how could it be otherwise accounted for that I should have escaped the same indisposition, but by supposing that the bodily exertions I had undergone in my repeated fits of frenzy had so effectually circulated and warmed my blood as to make me proof against the chilling damps of night, whereas Sophia, lying totally inactive on the ground, must have been exposed to all their severity. I was most seriously alarmed by her illness which, trifling as it may appear to you, a certain instinctive sensibility whispered me, would in the end be fatal to her.

Alas! my fears were but too fully justified; she grew gradually worse – and I daily became more alarmed for her. At length she was obliged to confine herself solely to the bed allotted us by our worthy landlady. – Her disorder turned to a galloping consumption[43] and in a few days carried her off. Amidst all my lamentations for her (and violent you may suppose they were), I yet received some consolation in the reflection of my having paid every attention to her that could be offered, in her illness. I had wept over her every day – had bathed her ~~fair~~ sweet face with my tears and had pressed her fair hands continually in mine.–

"My beloved Laura," said she to me a few hours before she died, "take warning from my unhappy end and avoid the imprudent conduct which had occasioned it ... Beware of fainting-fits ... Though at the time they may be refreshing and agreeable, yet believe me they will in the end, if too often repeated and at improper seasons, prove destructive to your constitution ... My fate will teach you this ... I die a martyr to my grief for the loss of Augustus ... One fatal swoon has cost me my life... Beware of swoons, dear Laura ... A frenzy fit is not one quarter so pernicious; it is an exercise to the body and if not too violent, is, I dare say, conducive to health in its consequences. – Run mad as often as you choose; but do not faint.–"

These were the last words she ever addressed to me ... It was her dying advice to her afflicted Laura, who has ever most faithfully adhered to it.

After having attended my lamented friend to her early grave, I immediately (though late at night) left the detested village ~~where~~ in which she died, and near which expired my husband and Augustus. I had not walked many yards from it before I was overtaken by a stagecoach, in which I instantly took a place, determined to proceed in it to Edinburgh, where I hoped to find some kind, some pitying friend who would receive and comfort me in my afflictions.

It was so dark when I entered the coach that I could not distinguish the number of my fellow-travelers; I could only perceive that they were many. Regardless, however, of anything concerning them, I gave myself up to my own sad reflections. A ~~mutual~~ general silence prevailed ~~amongst us all~~ – a silence, which was by nothing interrupted, but by the loud and repeated snores of one of the party.

"What an illiterate villain must that man be!" thought I to myself. "What a total want of delicate refinement must he have, who can thus shock our senses by such a brutal noise! He must, I am certain, be capable of every bad action! There is no crime too black for such a character!"

Thus reasoned I within myself, and doubtless such were the reflections of my fellow travelers.

At length, returning day enabled me to behold the unprincipled scoundrel who had so violently disturbed my feelings. It was Sir Edward, the father of my deceased husband. By his side sat Augusta, and on the same seat with me were your mother and Lady Dorothea. Imagine my surprise at finding myself thus seated amongst my old acquaintance. Great as was my astonishment, it was yet increased, when on looking out of windows, I beheld the husband of Philippa, with Philippa by his side, on the coachbox, and when on looking behind I beheld, Philander and Gustavus in the basket[44].

"Oh! Heavens," exclaimed I. "Is it possible that I should so unexpectedly be surrounded by my nearest relations and connections?"

These words roused the rest of the party, and every eye was directed to the corner in which I sat.

"Oh! my Isabel," continued I, throwing myself across Lady Dorothea into her arms, "receive once more to your bosom the unfortunate Laura. Alas! when we last parted in the Vale of Usk, I was happy in being united to the best of Edwards; I had then a father and a mother, and had never known misfortunes – But now, deprived of every friend but you—"

"What!" interrupted Augusta. "Is my brother dead, then? Tell us, I entreat you, what is become of him?"

"Yes, cold and insensible nymph," replied I, "that luckless swain your brother, is no more, and you may now glory in being the heiress of Sir Edward's fortune."

Although I had always despised her from the day I had

152

overheard her conversation with my Edward, yet in civility I complied with hers and Sir Edward's entreaties that I would inform them of the whole melancholy affair. They were greatly shocked – even the obdurate heart of Sir Edward and the insensible one of Augusta, were touched with sorrow by the unhappy tale. At the request of your mother, I related to them every other misfortune which had befallen me since we parted. Of the imprisonment of Augustus and the absence of Edward – of our arrival in Scotland – of our unexpected meeting with our grandfather and our cousins – of our visit to Macdonald Hall – of the singular service we there performed towards Janetta – of her father's ingratitude for it ... of his inhuman behaviour, unaccountable suspicions, and barbarous treatment of us, in obliging us to leave the house ... of our lamentations on the loss of Edward and Augustus, and finally, of the melancholy death of my beloved companion.

Pity and surprise were strongly depictured in your mother's countenance, during the whole of my narration, but I am sorry to say, that to the eternal reproach of her sensibility, the latter infinitely predominated. Nay, faultless as my conduct had certainly been during the whole course of my late misfortunes and adventures, she pretended to find fault with my behaviour in many of the situations in which I had been placed. As I was sensible myself that I had always behaved in a manner which reflected honour on my feelings and refinement, I paid little attention to what she said, and desired her to satisfy my curiosity by informing me how she came there, instead of wounding my spotless reputation with ~~unseemly~~ unjustifiable reproaches. As soon as she had complied with my wishes in this particular and had given me an accurate detail of everything that had befallen her since our separation (the particulars of which, if you are not already acquainted with, your mother will give you), I applied to Augusta for the same information respecting herself, Sir Edward, and Lady Dorothea.

She told me that having a considerable taste for the beauties of nature, her curiosity to behold the ~~beautiful~~ delightful scenes it exhibited in that part of the world had been so much raised by Gilpin's *Tour to the Highlands*[45], that she had prevailed on her father to undertake a tour to Scotland and had persuaded Lady Dorothea to accompany them. That they had arrived at Edinburgh a few days before, and from thence had ~~many~~ made daily excursions into the country around in the stagecoach they were then in, from one of which excursions they were at that time returning. My next enquiries were concerning Philippa and her husband, the latter of whom, I learned, having spent all her fortune, had recourse for subsistence to the talent in which, he had always most excelled, namely driving, and that having sold everything which belonged to them except their coach, had converted it into a stage, and in order to be removed from any of his former acquaintance, had driven it to Edinburgh, from whence he went to Sterling[46] every other day; that Philippa, still retaining her affection for her ungrateful husband, had followed him to Scotland and ~~always~~ generally accompanied him in his little excursions to Stirling.

"It has only been to throw a little money into their pockets," continued Augusta, "that my father has always travelled in their coach to view the beauties of the country since our arrival in Scotland – for it would certainly have been much more agreeable to us to visit the Highlands in a post-chaise, than merely to travel from Edinburgh to Sterling and from Sterling to Edinburgh every other day in a crowded and uncomfortable stage."

I perfectly agreed with her in her sentiments on the affair, and secretly blamed Sir Edward for thus sacrificing his daughter's pleasure for the sake of a ridiculous old woman, whose folly in marrying so young a man ought to be punished. His behaviour, however, was entirely of a piece with his general character; for what could be expected from a man who possessed not the smallest atom of sensibility, who scarcely knew the meaning of sympathy, and who actually snored.–

Adieu,
Laura.

Letter the 15th: Laura in continuation

When we arrived at the town where we were to breakfast, I was determined to speak with Philander and Gustavus, and to that purpose, as soon as I left the carriage, I went to the basket and tenderly enquired after their health, expressing my fears ~~for~~ of the uneasiness of their situation[47]. At first, they seemed rather confused at my appearance, dreading no doubt that I might call them to account for the money which our grandfather had left me, and which they had unjustly deprived me of, but finding that I mentioned nothing of the matter, they desired me to step into the basket, as we might there converse with greater ease. Accordingly I entered, and whilst the rest of the party were devouring green tea and buttered toast, we feasted ourselves in a more refined and sentimental manner by a confidential conversation. I informed them of everything which had befallen ~~them~~ me during the course of my life, and at my request they related to me every incident of theirs.

"We are the sons, as you already know, of the two youngest daughters which Lord St. Clair had by Laurina, an Italian opera girl. Our mothers could neither of them exactly ascertain who were our fathers, though it is generally believed that Philander is the son of one Philip Jones, a bricklayer, and that my father was Gregory Staves, a staymaker[48] of Edinburgh. This is, however, of little consequence, for as our mothers were certainly never married to either of them, it reflects no dishonour on our blood, which is of a most ancient and unpolluted kind. Bertha (the mother of Philander) and Agatha (my own mother) always lived together. They were neither of them very rich; their united fortunes had originally amounted to nine thousand pounds, but, as they had always lived upon the principal of it[49], when we were fifteen it was diminished to nine hundred.

This nine hundred, they always kept in a drawer in one of the tables which stood in our common sitting parlour, for the convenience of having it always at hand. Whether it was from this circumstance, of its being easily taken, or from a wish of being independent, or from an excess of sensibility (for which we were always remarkable), I cannot now determine, but certain it is that when we had reached our fifteenth year, we took the nine hundred pounds and ran away.

"Having obtained this prize, we were determined to manage it with economy and not to spend it either with folly or extravagance. To this purpose, we therefore divided it into nine parcels, one of which we devoted to victuals, the second to drink, the third to housekeeping, the forth to carriages, the fifth to horses, the sixth to servants, the seventh to amusements, the eighth to clothes, and the ninth to silver buckles[50]. Having thus arranged our expenses for two months (for we ~~were determined~~ expected to make the nine hundred pounds last as long), we hastened to London, and had the good luck to spend it in seven weeks and a day, which was six days sooner than we had intended.

"As soon as we had thus happily disencumbered ourselves from the weight of so much money, we began to think of returning to our mothers, but accidentally hearing that they were both ~~dead~~ starved to death, we gave over the design and determined to engage ourselves to some strolling company of players, as we had always a turn for the stage. Accordingly we offered our services to one and were accepted; our company was indeed rather small, as it consisted only of the manager, his wife, and ourselves, but there were fewer to pay and the only inconvenience attending it was the scarcity of plays which, for want of people to fill the characters, we could perform. We did not mind trifles, however. – One of our most admired performances was *Macbeth*, in which we were truly great. The manager always played *Banquo* himself, his wife my *Lady Macbeth*. I did the *Three Witches* and Philander acted *all the rest*. To say the truth, this tragedy was not only the best, but the only play we ever performed; and after having acted it all over England, ~~Ireland~~ and Wales, we came to Scotland to exhibit it over the remainder of Great Britain.

"We happened to ~~quit~~ be quartered in that very town, where you came and met your grandfather. – We were in the inn-yard when his carriage entered and perceiving by the arms to whom it belonged, and knowing that Lord St. Clair was our grandfather, we agreed to endeavour to get something from him by discovering the relationship. – You know how well it succeeded. – Having obtained the two hundred pounds, we instantly left the ~~room~~ town, leaving our manager and his wife to act *Macbeth* by themselves, and took the road to Sterling, where we spent our little fortune with great *éclat*[51]. We are now returning to Edinburgh in order to get some preferment in the acting way; and such, my dear cousin, is our history."

I thanked the amiable youth for his entertaining narration, and after expressing my wishes for their welfare and happiness, left them in their little habitation and returned to my other friends who impatiently expected me.

My adventures are now drawing to a close my dearest Marianne; at least for the present.

When we arrived at Edinburgh, Sir Edward told me that as the widow of his son, he desired I would accept from his hands of four hundred a year. I graciously promised that I would, but could not help observing that the unsympathetic Baronet offered it more on account of my being the widow of Edward than in being the refined and amiable Laura.

I took up my ~~lodging~~ residence in a romantic village in the Highlands of Scotland where I have ever since continued, and where I can, uninterrupted by unmeaning visits, indulge in a melancholy solitude my unceasing lamentations for the death of my father, my mother, my husband, and my friend.

Augusta has been for several years united to Graham, the man of all others most suited to her ~~Graham~~; she became acquainted with him during her stay in Scotland.

Sir Edward, in hopes of gaining an heir to his title and estate[52], at the same time married Lady Dorothea. – His wishes have been answered.

Philander and Gustavus, after having raised their reputation by their performances in the theatrical line at Edinburgh, removed to Covent Garden[53], where they still ~~continue to~~ exhibit under the assumed names of Lewis and Quick[54].

Philippa has long paid the debt of nature; her husband, however, still continues to drive the stage-coach from Edinburgh to Stirling. –

Adieu, my dearest Marianne.

Laura.

Finis

~~Sunday~~[55] June 13th, 1790

Notes

1. "Madame la Comtesse De Fevillide": Eliza, Comtesse de Feuillide, née Hancock, (1761-1813) was Austen's cousin, and later her sister-in-law. She was rumored to be the natural daughter of Warren Hastings, the first Governor-General of Bengal, who was officially Eliza's godfather. Eliza's first husband was guillotined in 1794 for treason against the French Republic, and she subsequently married Henry Thomas Austen in December 1797. Eliza was staying at Steventon at the time this story was written in June 1790.

2. "'Deceived in friendship and betrayed in love'": From a glee (unaccompanied song) for three voices by Col. R. Mellish (1777-1817): "Welcome the covert of these aged oaks; / Welcome each cavern of these horrid rocks; / Far from this world's illusion let me rove, / Deceived in friendship and betrayed in love." Love and friendship are often linked together but not always in a positive way. Henry Austen, the author of *The Loiterer* number 27, writes: "The last and most important piece of advice which I have to give, is this. Let every Girl who seeks for happiness conquer both her feelings and her passions. Let her avoid love and friendship as she wishes to be admired and distinguished. For by these means she will always keep her own secrets and prefer her own Interest."

Lady Sarah Pennington, a harsh critic of novels in general and of romances in particular, has some observations upon female friendship which seem to accord with the views of Jane Austen as they emerge through her fiction:

Few people are capable of friendship, and still fewer have all the qualifications one would choose in a friend; the fundamental point is a virtuous disposition – but, to that should be added, a good understanding, solid judgment, sweetness of temper, steadiness of mind, freedom of behavior, and sincerity of heart; – seldom are these to be found united – never make a bosom friend of any one greatly deficient in any. Be slow in contracting friendship, and invariably constant in maintaining it. (*An Unfortunate Mother's Advice to Her Absent Daughter*)

3. "natural daughter": Illegitimate daughter. Opera girls danced in the ballet between the acts. They had a reputation for being sexually 'available' – at the right price.

4. "Vale of Usk": The River Usk flows through south-east Wales into the Severn Estuary. The valley is particularly beautiful.

5. "sensibility": We are all familiar with the opposition between sense and sensibility from the title of Austen's first published novel. By sense is meant reason; by sensibility is meant feeling and emotion. When these are in balance, all is well. As E. M. Forster famously wrote in *Howard's End* (1910), "Only connect! ... Only connect the prose and the passion, and both will be exalted, and human love will be seen at its height. Live in fragments no longer. Only connect, and the beast and the monk, robbed of the isolation that is life to either, will die." What Austen is satirizing is the cult of sensibility, which found its apotheosis in the novel of sensibility, which she criticized as a guide by which to live one's life. It was the debasement of *real* sensibility to which Austen objected.

6. "*Menuet de la cour*": A formal dance of French origin. (For examples see YouTube.)

7. "London ... Bath ... Southampton": On August 23rd, 1796, Austen, newly arrived in London, wrote to Cassandra, "Here I am once more in this Scene of Dissipation & vice, and I begin already to find my morals corrupted. At this point in her life, Austen's knowledge of Bath was largely second-hand but she had been in Southampton (and nearly died there) in the summer of 1793 when the heat must have made the stink of fish unavoidable.

8. "That is another point ... I am partly convinced": The long debate about the origin of the noise is a parody of the philosophy of knowledge (epistemology). Austen's deletion keeps her from going more deeply into the style of academic discourse. Nevertheless, the whole discussion raises the interesting question: How do we know about anything that we do not see with our own eyes? "If a tree falls in a forest and no one is around to hear it, does it make a sound?" is a philosophical question about observation and perception. "If it sounds like someone knocking at the door, are we justified in concluding that someone is knocking at the door even though we have no "'ocular demonstration'"?" is Austen's comic version.

9. "... my future life must depend": This is the clichéd language of sentimental fiction where love is always a sudden impulse accompanied by the conviction that it will be life-long.

10. "conceal it under that of Talbot": The convention of concealing the name of characters by the use of a dash has already been used in the juvenilia. Here Austen takes the mockery one stage further by giving the very name she is pretending to conceal.

11. "Polydore ... Claudia ... Laura": Edward immediately assumes the closest intimacy with his new acquaintances, breaking all rules of good manners and etiquette in addressing them by their first names – though how he knows them is unexplained. Edward's superior sensibility, however, both explains and excuses his forwardness. The names Polydore and Claudia are Latinate, and not at all Welsh.

12. Conflicts between the wishes of parents and their children over the choice of a marriage partner are a staple of eighteenth century romantic fiction, but normally the parent insists on the child marrying for financial gain some person they (quite rightly) detest. Edward suggests that his own father is blinded by "fortune and ... pomp" to select Lady Dorothea (a baronet being the lowest level of the hereditary peerage and Lady Dorothea being the daughter of a duke, marquess or earl), but the fact is that Edward would have chosen the same lady (though for reasons of genuine attachment) if the choice had been left up to him.

13. "studying novels": This charge is normally leveled in fiction by outraged fathers at their rebellious daughters to explain their willful disobedience. Compare *Laura and Augustus: An Authentic Story, in a Series of Letters* (1784) by Eliza Nugent Bromley (died 1803), "'This comes of people suffering their children to read those ridiculous books called novels'" (Letter 11). Once again, Austen engages in gender reversal.

14. "Bedfordshire ... Middlesex ... South Wales": Edward's geographical knowledge is sadly deficient. Bedfordshire lies approximately forty miles north-west of Middlesex; the Vale of Usk lies approximately one hundred and ten miles south-west of Bedfordshire. He is on the wrong side of the country.

15. "bred to the Church": Educated for the service of the Church of England, though he has not actually been ordained a clergyman making the 'marriage' legally invalid – but mere details cannot hinder true love!

16. "interesting sensibility or amiable sympathy": Had Augusta shown true sensibility she would, of course, have thrown her arms around Laura and sworn intimate friendship eternally. Neither Augusta nor Lady Dorothea later in the chapter "confided ... [in Laura] any of her secret thoughts, nor requested ... [Laura] to confide in her any of mine" – a sure sign that both lack sensibility and so are "inferior ... beings."

17. "You are too ridiculous ... to argue with": In this argument between sense and sensibility shows that the two entirely fail to understand each other. Compare the father's words to the heroine in *Laura and Augustus*, "'take

159

yourself off with your beggar's brat, and see if love will support you; you will find it, Madam Heroine, I fancy, damned slender diet'" (Letter 39).

18. "his father's carriage, which yet remained at the door, and in which we were instantly conveyed from the pursuit of Sir Edward": That is, they steal Sir Edward's carriage!

19. "We fainted alternately on a sofa": The meeting between Laura and Sophia and the reunion between Edward and Augustus are described in terms which stress the heightened sensibilities of all four – though there is no doubt that in describing the meeting of the two men in terms that would normally apply only to women, Austen intends mockery. The concluding line comes from a stage direction in *The Critic: or, a Tragedy Rehearsed* by Richard Sheridan (1751-1816), "They faint alternately in each others arms" (3.1).

20. These are the opening words of the next letter. Austen made a copying error.

21. "gracefully purloined from his father's *escritoire*": To a woman of heightened sensibility, the gracefulness of an action outweighs considerations of the action's morality. Augustus had stolen the money from one of the drawers and compartments of his father's small writing desk.

22. "But they ... of Augustus himself": Businessmen, like fathers, are the enemies of sensibility since they are always calculating profits and losses. The person of sensibility is above such degrading practical consideration. In this way, the people who are owed money become the villains and those in debt their victims.

23. "an execution in the house": The people to whom money is owed have obtained a court judgment against the debtors which allows them to enter their house and seize either goods to the value of the debt or (failing that) the persons of the debtors.

24. "Holborn": A London borough just north of the City of London.

25. "Newgate": The London prison, first erected in 1188, had been newly rebuilt by 1782.

26. "As I ... country": Laura and Sophia literally go round in a circle because Sophia's sensibility (her susceptibility to sorrow) makes it impossible for her actually to *do anything* to remove the sorrow under which Augustus is suffering.

27. "an annuity on their own lives": Laura's parents had invested their capital in return for a guaranteed lifetime annual income. On their deaths, the capital was lost and the payments ceased. Of course, Laura blames her parents for the "depravity" of having cheated her out of her inheritance.

28. "to travel post": Scotland is over three hundred miles from London, so Laura is right in suspecting that one team of horses could not make the journey. It is therefore agreed to hire a new team of horses at regular intervals (posts). In this way, a carriage could reach Scotland in three days.

29. "a coroneted coach": A coach with the crest of the family on the side.

30. The discovery of long-lost, frequently illegitimate children or their

descendents was common in the literature of the time. Here Austen probably draws on *Evelina, or the History of a Young Lady's Entrance into the World* (1778) by Frances (Fanny) Burney (1752-1840) and *The Critic* by Richard Sheridan.

31. "The Sorrows of Werter": The German author, Johann Wolfgang von Goethe (1749-1832) wrote the epistolary novel *The Sorrows of Young Werther* (1774). The protagonist is an artistic and sensitive young man who falls in love with a beautiful young woman, Charlotte, who is already betrothed to another man. Despairing of his doomed love, he shoots himself in the head. It is implied that Charlotte subsequently dies of a broken heart. Goethe's novel proved to be very influential throughout Europe. Compare *The Loiterer* number 32, "Miss Louise … began upon Literature, and asked me whether or no, I had ever read The Sorrows of Wetter or the new Rousseau."

32. "auburn": Auburn hair was fashionable and elegant.

33. "precipitation": That is, 'with speed,' although perhaps also 'with tears.'

34. "Gretna Green": The small town just over the Scottish border to which Lydia and Willoughby in *Pride and Prejudice* intend to go to get married (though they never get there) because in Scotland persons under the age of twenty-one (Lydia is sixteen) could be married without parental consent. However, since Janetta and M'Kenzie are *already in* Scotland, they could get married in their home village. Elopement, however, completes the romance of their defiance of her father's wishes.

35. "yet hung": As a debtor, Augustus is in no danger of being hung.

36. "eastern zephyr": 'Zephyr' *may* be used to describe a light wind but in classical mythology, Zephyr is the West wind. This is not the first time that Laura's learning proves faulty.

37. "*apropos*": That is, appropriate to the situation (the impasse Laura has reached on topics of conversation).

38. "a fashionably high phaeton": The higher the suspension, the less stable the carriage was. However, high suspension was something of a status symbol – recall Mary Stanhope's view of its importance.

39. "Cardinal Wolsey": Thomas Wolsey (1473-1530), the son of a butcher, rose to become a Cardinal of the Catholic Church and Lord Chancellor of England in the reign of King Henry VIII. He lost the king's favor, however, when he failed to secure permission from the Pope for Henry to divorce his first wife, Catherine of Aragon. At the time of his death, he was traveling to London to answer charges of treason. Austen was familiar with Shakespeare's play *King Henry VIII*.

40. "field of action": Comic hyperbole since the word is military terminology for a battlefield.

41. "Cupid's thunderbolts, the piercing shafts of Jupiter": Laura's knowledge of Classical mythology is faulty again. Cupid fires arrows of love from his bow, while it is Jupiter (Zeus) hurls thunderbolts.

42. Apparently to be plain and called Bridget is disqualifying of sensibility.

43. "galloping consumption": Tuberculosis is a bacterial infection; lying on the damp ground might not be healthful, but it will not give you tuberculosis. For some reason, consumption has always been an illness with a certain romantic connotation, as though only the most sensitive souls fall victim to it.

44. "on the coachbox ... in the basket": The coachbox was the seat on which the driver and passengers sat, and the basket was a compartment at the rear of the stagecoach used primarily for luggage but also by passengers who valued cheapness over comfort.

45. "Gilpin's *Tour to the Highlands*": *Observations, relative chiefly to picturesque beauty, made in the year 1776, on several parts of Great Britain; particularly the High-lands of Scotland* (1789) by William Gilpin (1724-1804) was one of several books on the landscape of Great Britain. He developed the concept of picturesque beauty, which he defined as "that kind of beauty which is agreeable in a picture." His ideas led to the trend of landowners improving the beauty of their estates in accord with the principles of picturesque beauty – enlarging a lake here, diverting a stream there, making a ruin a little more ruinous, etc. Austen was normally very critical of the cult of the picturesque, but recall that the landscape around Pemberley shows a perfect balance between nature and human improvement.

46. "Edinburgh ... Stirling": Stirling is thirty-seven miles to the west northwest of Edinburgh. Both are in southern Scotland.

47. "the uneasiness of their situation": They are in constant danger of being thrown out of the basket by a sudden motion of the stagecoach.

48. "staymaker": Stays were fully boned laced bodices worn under clothes to pinch in the figure. They were popular in England from the late 16th to the end of the 18th century.

49. "lived upon the principal": They did not invest the money at all. Had they done so the yearly interest would have amounted to £450, which is enough to live off leaving the capital untouched.

50. "silver buckles": Definitely a fashion item – the larger and the fancier the better.

51. "éclat": Flair, brilliance, flamboyance.

52. "an heir to his title and estate": Augusta, being female, cannot inherit the hereditary title of Baronet (the lowest hereditary title, although Austen never portrayed characters higher on the social scale). Perhaps the estate was entailed like Longbourn.

53. "Covent Garden": The Theatre Royal in Covent Garden opened in 1732. In 1741, Handel's oratorio the *Messiah* was performed there. It was almost wholly rebuilt in 1787 and further improved in 1792.

54. "Lewis [Lewes] and Quick": London actors, Charles Lee Lewes (1740-1803) and John Quick (1748-1831) who were in the first productions of Goldsmith's *She Stoops to Conquer* and Sheridan's *The Rivals*.

55. Since the 13th *was* a Sunday, this was not an error. Perhaps Austen did not want to acknowledge that she has been 'working' (i.e., transcribing) on the

Sabbath.

Commentary

Love and Friendship is not a true epistolary novel since it lacks the variety of voices and perspectives on the events described which is provided by a number of interrelated correspondents. The installments of Laura's story are presented in a series of unanswered letters from the protagonist to Marianne, the daughter of her friend Isabel. The result is a first-person picaresque narrative (a story based on an extended journey) from the point of view of Laura, an unreliable narrator who presents herself as the victim of terrible suffering and the heroine of extraordinary adventures. Austen's intention is to parody the novel of sensibility in which, as Todd explains:

> love and hate are sudden and absolute, female friendships immediate and excessive, familial relationships made and unmade, and emotional extremes paralleled only by the extreme nature of the happenings. While sentimental to the core, crying, fainting, palpitating, falling ill and dying, the central characters are entirely amoral, believing that sensation must triumph over commonsense morality and justify any act of theft or betrayal. (*Introduction* 5)

Juliet McMaster states that *Love and Friendship* is "arguably the funniest short work of fiction in the English language. Here we find a young genius gloriously and uninhibitedly letting her hair down, piling joke upon joke, hyperbole on hyperbole" (Barker 138).

Laura, who has internalized all of the values of heightened sensibility, has received the conventional education of a daughter of the gentry class. She tells Marianne, "Of every accomplishment accustomary to my sex, I was mistress." That is, as Mary Wollstonecraft would have put it, Laura's education has developed her emotions at the expense of her reason. Laura is as resourceful, resilient, and totally egotistical as is the heroine of *The Beautiful Cassandra*, but she is altogether less likeable because while Cassandra is clear-sightedly (one might almost say innocently) self-serving, Laura is entirely lacking in self-knowledge and honesty. The former strikes the reader as naively amoral; the latter comes across as hypocritically immoral. Thus, in looking back on her "late misfortunes and adventures," Laura regards all of her "misfortunes as unmerited" and congratulates herself on having met every adversity with "fortitude," which she sees as the only lesson Marianne should learn from her narrative.

Laura admits only that she possesses by nature, "A sensibility too tremblingly alive to every affliction of my friends, my acquaintance, and particularly to every affliction of my own, was my only fault, if a fault it could be called." Evidently, Laura regards her refined sensibility as a sign of her superiority, while the author regards it as a grievous fault. The occasional voices of common sense and rationality (for example Sir Edward and Edward's sister) are presented with derision and contempt. Looking back, Laura regards her own conduct as having been "faultless during the whole course" of her life, whereas the author shows that Laura has been the cause of her own suffering – to say nothing of the sufferings of others with whom she has come into contact with disastrous consequences.

To introduce this novel, I shall draw heavily on the analysis of A. Walton Litz of those narratives in the juvenilia where Austen's main aim is to satirize the sentimental fiction of her day (*Jane Austen: A Study of Her Artistic Development*). Laura is entirely convinced that "the natural noble sensibility of her [own] heart" makes her superior to almost everyone else she encounters (the only exceptions would be Edward, Sophia and Augustus, who are allowed to be her equals in sensibility). She tells Marianne, "In my mind, every virtue that could adorn it was centered; it was the rendezvous of every good quality and of every noble sentiment." Laura's arrogance is insufferable.

Litz argues that the moral center of the novel of sensibility "is a gross equation between value and sentimental *performance*, a direct correlation between the worth of a character and his ability to *display* emotion … In these novels the *physiological* connotations of the word 'sensibility' are emphasized, and delicacy of emotion can only be proved through trembling, tears, hysteria, madness and fainting. *Physical reactions* become an index to virtue…" (Litz 8-9, emphasis added). The reader sees this in Laura's assessment of Graham, the man whom Macdonald has chosen to marry his daughter, Janetta. In recommendation of the man, Laura admits that he has a reputation for being "sensible, well-informed, and agreeable," but Laura dismisses judging a man on "such trifles"; instead, she notes that "he had never read *The Sorrows of Werter*, and that his hair bore not the least resemblance to auburn," which is sufficient evidence on which to decide that he is "execrable and detested" and has "no soul," a conclusion which justifies her (in her own and Sophia's eyes though not the reader's) in sabotaging his proposed wedding to Janetta. Similarly, nothing can be expected in the way of sensibility even of a young woman of seventeen, "one of the best of ages," who is "very plain" and has the name Bridget. A fellow stage coach traveler must be "'an illiterate villain'" because he snores.

Litz goes on to argue that in novels of sentiment "display of emotion is the only index to value, all other standards are jettisoned. Jane Austen shows that the final corruption of the individual 'moral sense' is selfishness, and she demonstrates that false sensibility is founded upon self-interest" (20). Indeed, these novels constitute what he calls a "land of fiction" which has its own rules concerning conduct and manners, which Austen mocks by having her characters follow them to the letter. Thus, *Love and Friendship* contains a number of robberies, each of which is justified in the eyes of Laura by the superior sensibility of the those who steal: Augustus takes "a considerable sum of money" from his father; Edward commandeers his father's carriage;

Philander and Gustavus steal £900 from their mothers and £100 from Laura and Sophia; and Sophia and Laura conspire to rob Macdonald, the former's cousin, who is at that time their host. None of the perpetrators feels any guilt about having stolen because they have complete contempt for the economic values of the society in which they live. Indeed, when Laura or one of her friends is detected in an act of theft, it is their victims who are described as impertinent, base, "malevolent and contemptible."

Love and Friendship is a 'Quixotic' novel in which "the heroine, having received a false view of the world from literature, embarks upon a series of adventures which expose the absurdity of his [her] *idée fixe*; the disparity between idea and reality produces comic-moralistic effects" (Litz 13). Laura is a perfect example since she values sensibility over every other human quality (rationality, good sense, kindness, morality, honesty, etc.) with the result that she goes through life from one self-imposed disaster to the next, yet remains confident that, throughout, her own conduct has been unimpeachable. The central beliefs upon which Laura (and Edward, Sophia and Augustus) base their actions may be summarized thus: all parents (but especially fathers) are "mean and mercenary," and it is therefore the duty of children to oppose their will in all things, but particularly in the choice of the person they will marry; love and friendship are bonds forged between two people of heightened sensibility at the moment they meet and will endure for life; lovers and friends immediately share their most intimate feelings and secrets; and people of true sensibility scorn the economic motives that govern the conduct of others, allowing them to leave bills unpaid and to take money as needed from people they consider unworthy. When his sister, Augusta, tries to impress upon Edward the need to have money with which to support his new wife Laura, he replies, "Victuals and drink!… and dost thou then imagine that there is no other support for an exalted mind (such as is my Laura's) than the mean and indelicate employment of eating and drinking?"

Above all, to those individuals with "delicate feeling, tender sentiments, and refined sensibility," the sufferings that life inevitably brings take a terrible toll particularly on women of feeling who are prone to faint or to run mad rather than to deal rationally with the difficulties. Thus, having gone to London where Augustus is being help in prison, Sophia announces that she cannot, after all, see him, and so she and Laura absurdly turn around to go back home having achieved nothing. The novel has, at fairly regular intervals, such reactions to catastrophes as these, "This was too cruel, too unexpected a blow to our gentle sensibility – we could not support it – we could only faint … It was too pathetic for the feelings of Sophia and myself. – We fainted alternately on a sofa … Sophia shrieked and fainted on the ground. – I screamed and instantly ran mad. – We remained thus mutually deprived of our senses some minutes, and on regaining them were deprived of them again. For an hour and a quarter did we continue in this unfortunate situation – Sophia fainting every moment and I running mad as often." In the latter case, occasioned by the death of their husbands in a carriage accident, the comic-moralistic irony is that while Laura opts for the health-giving activity of running mad, Sophia chooses the consumption-inducing activity of repeatedly fainting on the cold, damn ground, which turns out to be, quite literally, the death of her.

Litz concludes his analysis by commenting:

> *Love and Friendship* is a compendium of all the stock situations and stock responses of the novel of sensibility: exotic parentage, revolt against authority, fantastic recognition scenes, love-at-first-sight, a propensity for self-revelation. But throughout it all Jane Austen manages to maintain a clear awareness of the normal as well as the literary reaction to each situation, so we have a double sense of the characters in relation to the laws of the "land of fiction" had in relation to the standards of probable social behavior. (19)

It is not that Austen was entirely against sensibility; she was against the degraded sensibility presented in second-rate novels.

The themes of the novel are announced, for the first time in the juvenilia, with the two abstract nouns of its title, *Love and Friendship*. In this context 'love' means the romantic love between man and woman and 'friendship' the deep emotional attachment between two people of the same gender. To state the obvious, given the age of the author, Austen's only real experience of romantic love came from the novels she had read (which frequently depicted such love in ways that she found absurd) while she already had personal experience of genuinely profound friendships with other young women (beginning with, but not limited to, the confidential relationship that she had with her sister Cassandra). This being so, it is no surprise that the novel is more concerned with women's friendships than it is with courtship or marriage. The epigram which follows the title, "Deceived in friendship and betrayed in love" represents the author's approach to her themes not those of her protagonist; the spurious emotion and spontaneous attachment of romantic love and sentimental friendship are exposed by Austen's satire, while Laura remains a devotee of romantic love and female friendship despite the disasters into which those relationships lead both her and most other characters in her narrative.

Romantic relationships in the novel always lead to marriage. They are the result of the conviction that love is entirely incompatible with marrying a person deemed suitable by one's parent(s) since these spring from the tyranny of parental authority over the feelings of the off-spring and from the rational motive of wanting to ensure the future economic and social status of the family – both of which are seen to be inimical to genuine love which must originate in instant and mutual attachment. Sir Edward terms such ideas "'unmeaning gibberish'" which he assumes that his son has picked up by "'studying novels.'" Both factors are evident in the case of Laura and Edward and seem to be embodied in the marriage of their friends Sophia and Augustus (whose origin is not described). When Laura first sees Edward, she concludes that he is "the most beauteous and amiable youth I had ever beheld … I felt that on him the happiness or misery of my future life must depend." Laura's love-at-first-sight is matched by Edward's willingness to tell the newly encountered Polydore, Claudia, and Laura that he regards his father as "a mean and mercenary wretch," adding "it is only to such particular friends as this dear party that I would thus betray his failings." In this way he has proved his sensibility.

In the case of both couples, we see how the elevation of love to an ethereal level leads to economic disaster. Following their marriage, Laura and Edward exist only by sponging on the charity of others and by theft, and Sophia and Augustus, having established themselves on money Augustus has stolen from his father, keep their household going by the simple expedient of not paying their bills. Neither strategy has any prospect of success in the long-term since Laura and Edward quickly run out of charitable friends and Sophia and Augustus are prosecuted by those to whom they owe money. The arrest of Augustus provides Austen with a plot mechanism to get rid of the two male characters, which are finally disposed of in a carriage accident.

The disaster of sentimental love and marriage is illustrated in several minor characters: Lord St. Clair has four illegitimate daughters with Laurina, an Italian opera-singer (whose fate is unrecorded): Sir Edward's sister, Philippa, impulsively marries a young fortune-hunter; and Janetta, engaged by her father to the admirable if dull Graham, elopes with Captain M'Kenzie whom her father terms "[an] unprincipled fortune-hunter." In contrast, there are a number of rational marriages which seem to work out rather well: Sir Edward Lindsay, a widower, marries Lady Dorothea and they have a son; and his daughter, Augusta, eventually marries Graham.

Friendships between women are dealt with in much more detail though the mock-sentimental parody of the author is exactly the same as that used in the portrayals of romantic relationships. Indeed, Laura's epistolary narrative is occasioned by her life-long friendship for Marianne's mother – a friendship which endures despite Laura's conviction that she is much more beautiful and accomplished than her friend Isabel, whose defect in sensibility is proved by her having "retired into Wales on economical motives" rather than because of the natural beauties of the region. The most important female friendship is that between Laura and Sophia, the wife of her husband's best friend. When the penniless Edward takes his new bride to the home of his friend Augustus, Laura laments that she has been "deprived during the course of three weeks of a real friend." Indeed. Laura has met two young women who prove quite incapable of sentimental friendship: Edward's sister, Augusta, about whom Laura comments, "There was disagreeable coldness and forbidding reserve in her reception of me which was equally distressing and unexpected. None of that interesting sensibility or amiable sympathy [was seen] in her manners and address to me…"; and Lady Dorothea, Sir Edward Lindsay's choice to be his son's wife, of whom Laura writes, "she was of that inferior order of beings with regard to delicate feeling, tender sentiments, and refined sensibility … She staid but half an hour and neither in the course of her visit, confided to me any of her secret thoughts, nor requested me to confide in her, any of mine." However, at first sight, it is clear to Laura that Sophia has the qualities to be such a sentimental friend, "[she] was all sensibility and feeling. We flew into each other's arms and after having exchanged vows of mutual friendship for the rest of our lives, instantly unfolded to each other the most inward secrets of our hearts." The meeting of Edward and Augustus, which follows that of their wives, is described in the same sentimental (and frankly feminine) terms. Laura describes the "affecting scene":

> "'My life! My soul!' exclaimed the former.
> "'My adorable angel!'" replied the latter, as they flew into
> each other's arms."

Their sentimental behavior prompts the alternate swoons of Laura and Sophia. However, this friendship is not explored in any detail since the two promptly exit the plot, returning only in order to die.

In contrast, the adventures of Laura and Sophia include: journeying to Scotland; the discovery of their (mutual) grandfather, and the loss of his gift of £100; their disastrous intervention in the marriage plans of Janetta Macdonald; their expulsion from the house for theft; the discovery of their dead or dying husbands; and Sophia's death from "galloping consumption" as a result of having swooned once too often on the damp ground. After all of these trials, Laura is fortuitously reunited with the family of her late husband and her friend Isabel. She has learned sufficient vulgar prudence to accept an income from her late husband's father, but remains sufficiently loyal to her values to note with dissatisfaction that "the unsympathetic baronet offered it more on account of my being the widow of Edward than in being the refined and amiable Laura."

Self-evidently, *Love and Friendship* is a longer and more carefully structured narrative than anything in *Volume the First*. Here, character determines action – except where Austen takes aim at the abuse of coincidence and chance in the romantic novels of her day. The most obvious examples are: the accidental encounter with their dead and dying husbands; the amazingly fortuitous meeting of Lord St. Clair with his four grandchildren at a Scottish inn; and Laura's chance reunion with the family of her father-in-law and her cousins in the stagecoach from Stirling to Edinburgh. The other extraneous narrative is the absurd story of the theatrical careers of Laura's cousins, Philander and Gustavus, which allows Austen to indulge her own love of the theater and to provide a satirical, Dickensian description of a very small, and not very good, company of peripatetic thespians. With this story, Austen has once again written herself into a dead end – a common problem with the juvenilia. There are no more adventures or misfortunes for Laura to have since her three accomplices in sensibility (Edward, Sophia and Augustus) are all dead. All Austen can do with her heroine is have her retire to a quiet and solitary life in Wales.

[Dedication]

To Henry Thomas Austen[1] Esquire.
Sir,
I am now availing myself of the liberty you have frequently honoured me with of dedicating one of my novels to you. That it is unfinished, I grieve; yet fear that from me, it will always remain so; that as far as it is carried, it should be so trifling and so unworthy of you, is another concern to your obliged humble servant
The Author

Messrs. Demand and Company – please to pay Jane Austen spinster the sum of one hundred guineas on account of your humble servant
H. T. Austen
£105.0.0.[2]

Lesley Castle - an unfinished novel in letters

Introduction to Significant Characters

This novel is written in letters mostly between Margaret Lesley in Scotland and Charlotte Lutterell in England. The following family trees will help readers to keep track of the various characters and sub-plots.

The Lesley Family (whose family home is Lesley Castle near Perth in Scotland)

Sir George Lesley = First wife (unnamed) = Susan Fitzgerald (Second wife)

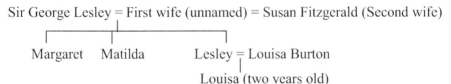

Margaret   Matilda   Lesley = Louisa Burton
                                Louisa (two years old)

Lutterell Family (whose family home is Glenford in Sussex)

Unnamed mother = Deceased father (unnamed)

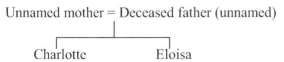

Charlotte   Eloisa

Other Significant Characters

Henry Hervey is engaged to marry Eloisa Lutterell but dies shortly before their marriage following a fall from his horse.

Mrs. Emma Marlowe comes, out of season, to Bristol with her husband and her ailing son. There she is the only person whom the Lesley sisters visit. She becomes a confidential friend to Eloisa Lutterell.

Letter the First is from Miss Margaret Lesley to Miss Charlotte Lutterell

Lesley Castle. January 3rd, 1792.

My brother[3] has just left us.

"Matilda," said he at parting, "you and Margaret will I am certain take all the care of my dear little one that she might have received from an indulgent, and affectionate and amiable mother."

Tears rolled down his cheeks as he spoke these words – the remembrance of her, who had so wantonly disgraced the maternal character and so openly violated the conjugal duties, prevented his adding anything farther; he embraced his sweet child and after saluting Matilda and me, hastily broke from us, and seating himself in his chaise, pursued the road to Aberdeen[4]. Never was there a better young man! Ah! how little did he deserve the misfortunes he has experienced in the marriage state. So good a husband to so bad a wife! For you know, my dear Charlotte, that the worthless Louisa left him, her child and reputation a few weeks ago in company with Danvers and [Austen's footnote: Rakehelly Dishonour Esquire[5]] dishonour.

Never was there a sweeter face, a finer form, or a less amiable heart than Louisa owned! Her child already possesses the personal charms of her unhappy mother! May she inherit from her father all his mental ones! Lesley is at present but five-and-twenty, and has already given himself up to melancholy and despair; what a difference between him and his father! Sir George is fifty-seven and still remains the beau, the flighty stripling, the gay lad, and sprightly youngster, that his son was really about five years back, and that *he* has affected to appear ever since my remembrance. While our father is fluttering about the streets of London, gay, dissipated, and thoughtless at the age of fifty-seven, Matilda and I continue secluded from mankind in our old and mouldering castle, which is situated two miles from Perth on a bold projecting rock, and commands an extensive view of the town and its delightful environs.

But though retired from almost all the world[6] (for we visit no one but the M'Leods, the M'Kenzies, the M'Phersons, the M'Cartneys, the M'Donalds, the M'kinnons, the M'lellans, the M'kays, the Macbeths and the Macduffs), we are neither dull nor unhappy; on the contrary, there never were two more lively, more agreeable or more witty girls, than we are; not an hour in the day hangs heavy on our hands.

We read, we work, we walk, and when fatigued with these employments relieve our spirits, either by a lively song, a graceful dance, or by some smart *bon-mot*[7] and witty *repartee*. We are handsome, my dear Charlotte, very handsome, and the greatest of our perfections is that we are entirely insensible of them ourselves[8]. But why do I thus dwell on myself! Let me rather repeat the praise of our dear little niece, the innocent Louisa, who is at present sweetly smiling in a gentle nap, as she reposes on the sofa. The dear creature is just turned of two years old; as handsome as though two-and-twenty, as sensible as though two-and-thirty, and as prudent as though two-and-forty. To convince you of this, I must inform you that she has a very fine complexion and very pretty features, that she already knows the two first letters in the alphabet, and that she never tears her frocks. – If I have not now convinced you of her beauty, sense and prudence, I have nothing more to urge in support of my assertion, and you will therefore have no way of deciding the affair but by coming to Lesley Castle, and by a personal acquaintance with Louisa, determine for yourself.

Ah! my dear friend, how happy should I be to see you within these venerable walls! It is now four years since my removal from school has separated me from you; that ~~too~~ two such tender hearts, so closely linked together by the ties of sympathy and friendship, should be so widely removed from each other, is vastly moving. I live in Perthshire; you in Sussex[9]. We might meet in London, were my father disposed to carry me there, and were your mother to be there at the same time. We might meet at Bath, at Tunbridge[10], or anywhere else indeed, could we but be at the same place together. We have only to hope that such a period may arrive.

My father does not return to us till autumn; my brother will leave Scotland in a few days; he is impatient to travel. Mistaken youth! He vainly flatters himself that change of air will heal the wounds of a broken heart! You will join with me, I am certain my dear Charlotte, in prayers for the recovery of the unhappy Lesley's peace of mind, which must ever be essential to that of

your sincere friend
M. Lesley.

Letter the Second from Miss C. Lutterell to Miss M. Lesley in answer.

Glenford[11], February 12th

I have a thousand excuses to beg for having so long delayed thanking you, my dear Peggy, for your agreeable letter, which believe me I should not have deferred doing, had not every moment of my time during the last five weeks been so fully employed in the necessary arrangements for my sister's wedding, as to allow me no time to devote either to you or myself. And now what provokes me more than anything else is that the match is broke off, and all my labour thrown away. Imagine how great the disappointment must be to me, when you consider that after having laboured both by night and by day, in order to get the wedding dinner ready by the time appointed, after having roasted beef, broiled mutton, and stewed soup enough to last the new-married couple through the honeymoon, ~~to find that~~ I had the mortification of finding that I had been roasting, broiling and stewing both the meat and myself to no purpose.

Indeed, my dear friend, I never remember suffering any vexation equal to what I experienced on last Monday when my sister came running to me in the store-room with her face as white as a whipped syllabub[12], and told me that Hervey had been thrown from his horse[13], had fractured his skull and was pronounced by his surgeon to be in the most imminent danger.

"Good God!" said I, "you don't say so? Why what in the name of heaven will become of all the victuals! We shall never be able to eat it while it is good. However, we'll call in the surgeon to help us. I shall be able to manage the sirloin myself, my mother will eat the soup, and you and the doctor must finish the rest."

Here I was interrupted, by seeing my poor sister fall down, to appearance lifeless, upon one of the chests, where we keep our table linen. I immediately called my mother and the maids, and at last we brought her to herself again; as soon as ever she was sensible, she expressed a determination of going instantly to Henry, and was so ~~very~~ wildly bent on this scheme, that we had the greatest difficulty in the world to prevent her putting it in execution; at last, however, more by force than entreaty, we prevailed on her to go into her room; ~~where~~ we laid her upon

172

the bed, and she continued for some hours in the most dreadful convulsions.

My mother and I continued in the room with her, and when any intervals of tolerable composure in Eloisa would allow us, we joined in heartfelt lamentations on the dreadful waste in our provisions which this event must occasion, and in concerting some plan for getting rid of them. We agreed that the best thing we could do was to begin eating them immediately, and accordingly we ordered up the cold ham and fowls, and instantly began our devouring plan on them with great alacrity. We would have persuaded Eloisa to have taken a wing of a chicken, but she would not be persuaded. She was, however, much quieter than she had been; the convulsions she had before suffered having given way to an almost perfect insensibility. We endeavoured to rouse her by every means in our power, but to no purpose.

I talked to her of Henry.

"Dear Eloisa," said I, "there's no occasion for your crying so much about such a trifle." (For I was willing to make light of it in order to comfort her.) "I beg you would not mind it. – You see it does not vex me in the least; though perhaps I may suffer most ~~for~~ from it after all; for I shall not only be obliged to eat up all the victuals I have dressed already, but must if Henry should recover (which, however, is not very likely) dress as much for you again; or should he die (as I suppose he will) I shall still have to prepare a dinner for you whenever you marry anyone else. So you see that though perhaps for the present it may afflict you to think of Henry's sufferings, yet I dare say he'll die soon, and then his pain will be over and you will be easy, whereas my trouble will last much longer for, work as hard as I may, I am certain that the pantry cannot be cleared in less than a fortnight."

Thus I did all in my power to console her, but without any effect, and at last as I saw that she did not seem to listen to me, I said no more, ~~I left~~ but leaving her with my mother ~~and~~ I ~~taking~~ took down the remains of the ham and chicken and sent William to ask how Henry did. He was not expected to live many hours; he died the same day. We took all possible care to break the melancholy ~~account~~ event to Eloisa in the tenderest manner; yet in spite of every precaution, her sufferings on hearing it were too violent for her reason, and she continued for many hours in a high delirium. She is still extremely ill, and her ~~physician is~~ physicians are greatly afraid of her ~~being in~~ going into a decline. We are therefore preparing for Bristol[14], where we mean to be in the course of the next week.

And now my dear Margaret let me talk a little of your affairs; and in the first place I must inform you that it is confidently reported your father is going to be married. I am very unwilling to believe so unpleasing a report[15], and at the same time cannot wholly discredit it. I have written to my friend Susan Fitzgerald, for information concerning it, which as she is at present in town, she will be very able to give me. I know not who is the lady. I think your brother is extremely right in the resolution he has taken of travelling, as it will perhaps contribute to obliterate from his remembrance, those disagreeable events, which have lately so much afflicted him. – I am happy to find that, though secluded from all the world, neither you nor Matilda are dull or unhappy – that you may never know what it is to be either is the wish of your sincerely affectionate C.L.

P. S. I have this instant received an answer from my friend Susan, which I enclose to you, and on which you will make your own reflections.

The enclosed letter:

My dear Charlotte,
You could not have applied for information concerning the report of Sir George Lesley's marriage, to any one better able to give it you than I am. Sir George is certainly married; I was myself present at the ceremony, which you will not be surprised at when I subscribe myself
Your affectionate, Susan Lesley[16]

Letter the Third from Miss Margaret Lesley to Miss C. Lutterell

Lesley Castle, February the 16th

I *have* made my own reflections on the letter you enclosed to me, my dear Charlotte, and I will now tell you what those reflections ~~are~~ were. I reflected that if, by this second marriage, Sir George should have a second family, our fortunes must be considerably diminished – that if his wife should be of an extravagant turn, she would encourage him to persevere in that gay and dissipated way of life to which little encouragement would be necessary, and which has, I fear, already proved but too detrimental to his health and fortune – that she would now become mistress of those jewels which once adorned our mother, and which Sir George had always promised us – that if

174

they did not come into Perthshire, I should not be able to gratify my curiosity of beholding my mother-in-law, and that, if they did, Matilda would no longer sit at the head of her father's table[17].–

These, my dear Charlotte, were the melancholy reflections which crowded into my imagination after perusing Susan's letter to you, and which instantly occurred to Matilda when she had perused it likewise. The same ideas, the same fears, immediately occupied her mind, and I know not which reflection distressed ~~us~~ her most, whether the probable diminution of our fortunes, or her own consequence[18]. We both wish very much to know whether Lady Lesley is handsome and what is your opinion of her; as you honour her with the appellation of your friend, we flatter ourselves that she must be amiable.

My brother is already in Paris. He intends to quit it in a few days, and to begin his route to Italy. He writes in a most ~~lively~~ cheerful manner, says that the air of France has greatly recovered both his health and spirits; that he has now entirely ceased to think of Louisa with any degree either of pity or affection, that he even feels himself obliged to her for her elopement, as he thinks it very good fun to be single again. By this, you may perceive that he has entirely regained that cheerful gaiety and sprightly wit, for which he was once so remarkable. When he first became acquainted with Louisa, which was little more than three years ago, he was one of the most lively, the most agreeable young men of the age.–

I believe you never yet heard the particulars of his first acquaintance with her. It commenced at our cousin Colonel Drummond's; at whose house in Cumberland[19] he spent the Christmas, in which he attained the age of two and twenty. Louisa Burton was the daughter of a distant relation of Mrs. Drummond, who dying a few months before in extreme poverty, left his only child, then about eighteen, to the protection of any of his relations who would protect her. Mrs. Drummond was the only one who found herself so disposed – Louisa was therefore removed from a miserable cottage in Yorkshire[20] to an elegant mansion in Cumberland, and from every pecuniary distress that poverty could inflict, to every elegant enjoyment that money could purchase.–

Louisa was naturally ill-tempered and cunning; but she had been taught to disguise her real disposition, under the appearance of insinuating sweetness, by a father who but too well knew, that to be married, would be the only chance she would have of not being starved, and who flattered himself that with such an extraordinary share of personal beauty, joined to a gentleness of manners, and an engaging address, she might stand a good chance of pleasing some young man who might afford to marry a girl without a shilling. Louisa perfectly entered into her father's schemes and was determined to forward them with all her care and attention. By dint of perseverance and application, she had at length so thoroughly disguised her natural disposition under the mask of innocence and softness, as to impose upon everyone who had not, by a long and constant intimacy with her, discovered her real character.

Such was Louisa when the hapless Lesley first beheld her at Drummond-house. His heart which (to use your favourite comparison) was as delicate as sweet and as tender as a whipped syllabub, could not resist her attractions. In a very few days, he was falling in love, shortly after actually ~~felled~~ fell, and before he had known her a month, he had married her. My father was at first highly displeased at so hasty and imprudent a connection; but when he found that they did not mind it, he soon became perfectly reconciled to the match. The estate near Aberdeen[21] which my brother possesses by the bounty of his great uncle independent of Sir George, was entirely sufficient to support him and my sister[-in-law] in elegance and ease.

For the first twelvemonth, no one could be happier than Lesley, and no one more amiable to appearance than Louisa, and so plausibly did she act and so cautiously behave that though Matilda and I often spent several weeks together with them, yet we neither of us had any suspicion of her real disposition. After the birth of Louisa however, which one would have thought would have strengthened her regard for Lesley, the mask she had so long supported was by degrees thrown aside, and as probably she then thought herself secure in the affection of her husband (which did indeed appear if possible augmented by the birth of his child) she seemed to take no pains to prevent that affection from ever diminishing.

Our visits therefore to Dunbeath[22], were now less frequent and by far less agreeable than they used to be. Our absence was, however, never either mentioned or lamented by Louisa, who in the society of young Danvers, with whom she became acquainted at Aberdeen (he was at one of the universities there), felt infinitely happier than in that of Matilda and your friend, though there certainly never were pleasanter girls than

176

we are. You know the sad end of all Lesley's connubial happiness; I will not repeat it.

Adieu my dear Charlotte; although I have not yet mentioned anything of the matter, I hope you will do me the justice to believe that I *think* and *feel*, a great deal for your sister's affliction. I do not doubt but that the healthy air of the Bristol downs will entirely remove it, by erasing from her mind the remembrance of Henry. I am, my dear Charlotte, yours ever

M. L.

Letter the Fourth from Miss C. Lutterell to Miss M. Lesley

Bristol. February 27th

My dear Peggy,

I have but just received your letter, which being directed to Sussex while I was at Bristol[23] was obliged to be forwarded to me here, and from some unaccountable delay, has but this instant reached me. – I return you many thanks for the account it contains of Lesley's acquaintance, love and marriage with Louisa, which has not the less entertained me for having often been repeated to me before.

I have the satisfaction of informing you that we have every reason to imagine our pantry is by this time nearly cleared, as we left particular orders with the servants to eat as hard as they possibly could, and to call in a couple of chairwomen[24] to assist them. We brought a cold pigeon pie, a cold turkey, a cold tongue, and half a dozen jellies with us, which we were lucky enough with the help of our landlady, her husband, and their three children, to get rid of in less than two days after our arrival. Poor Eloisa is still so very indifferent both in health and spirits, that I very much fear, the air of the Bristol downs, healthy as it is, has not been able to drive poor Henry from her remembrance.

You ask me whether your new mother-in-law is handsome and amiable. – I will now give you an exact description of her bodily and mental charms. She is short, and extremely well made; is naturally pale, but rouges a good deal; has fine eyes, and fine teeth, as she will take care to let you know as soon as she sees you, and is altogether very pretty. She is remarkably good-tempered when she has her own way, and very lively when she is not out of humour. She is naturally extravagant and not very affected; she never reads anything but the letters she receives from me, and never writes anything but her answers to them. She plays, sings and dances, but has no taste for either, and excels in none, though she says she is passionately fond of all.

Perhaps you may flatter me so far as to be surprised that one of whom I speak with so little affection should be my particular friend; but to tell you the truth, our friendship arose rather from caprice on ~~herself~~ her side than esteem on mine. We spent two or three days together with a lady in Berkshire[25] with whom we both happened to be connected. – During our visit, the weather being remarkably bad and our party particularly stupid, she was so good as to conceive a violent ~~friendship~~ partiality for me, which very soon ~~turned into~~ settled in a downright friendship and ended in an established correspondence. She is probably by this time as tired of me, as I am of her, but as she is too polite, and I am too civil to say so, our letters are still as frequent and affectionate as ever, and our attachment as firm and sincere as when it ~~was~~ first commenced.

As she had a great taste for the pleasures of London, and ~~the amusements~~ of Brighthelmstone[26], she will, I dare say, find some difficulty in prevailing on herself even to satisfy the ~~certainty~~ curiosity I dare say she feels of beholding you, at the expense of quitting those favourite haunts of dissipation for the melancholy though venerable gloom of the castle you inhabit. Perhaps, however, if she finds her health impaired by too much amusement, she may acquire fortitude sufficient to undertake a journey to Scotland in the hope of its proving at least beneficial to her health, if not conducive to her happiness.

Your fears, I am sorry to say, concerning your father's extravagance, your own fortunes, your mother's jewels and your sister's consequence, I should suppose are but too well founded. My friend herself has four thousand pounds[27], and will probably spend nearly as much every year in dress and public places, if she can get it. – She will certainly not endeavour to reclaim Sir George from the manner of living to which he has been so long accustomed, and there is therefore some reason to fear that you will be very well off[28] if you get any fortune at all. The jewels I should imagine too will undoubtedly be hers, and there is too much reason to think that she will preside at her husband's table in preference to his daughter. But as so melancholy a subject must necessarily extremely distress you, I will no longer dwell on it.–

Eloisa's indisposition has brought us to Bristol at so unfashionable a season of the year[29] that we have actually seen but one genteel family since we came. Mr. and Mrs. Marlowe are very agreeable people; the ill-health of their little boy occasioned their arrival here; you may imagine that being the only family with whom we can converse. We are, of course, on a footing of intimacy with them; we see them indeed almost every day, and dined with them yesterday. We spent a very pleasant day, and had a very good dinner, though to be sure the veal was terribly underdone, and the curry had no seasoning. I could not help wishing all dinner-time that I had been at the dressing it. –

A brother of Mrs. Marlowe, Mr. Cleveland, is with them at present; he is a good-looking young man, and seems to have a good deal to say for himself. I tell Eloisa that she should set her cap at him[30], but she does not at all seem to relish the proposal. I should like to see the girl married and Cleveland has a very good estate. Perhaps you may wonder that I do not consider myself as well as my sister in my matrimonial projects; but to tell you the truth I never wish to act a more principal part at a wedding than the superintending and directing the dinner, and therefore, while I can get any of my ~~friends~~ acquaintance to marry for me, I shall never think of doing it myself, as I very much suspect that I should not have so much time for dressing my own wedding-dinner, as for dressing that of my friends.

Yours sincerely
C. L.

Letter the Fifth: Miss Margaret Lesley and to Miss Charlotte Lutterell

Lesley-Castle, March 18th

On the same day that I received your last kind letter, Matilda received one from Sir George which was dated from Edinburgh, and informed us that he should do himself the pleasure of introducing Lady Lesley to us on the following evening. This, as you may suppose, considerably surprised us, particularly as your account of her Ladyship had given us reason to imagine there was little chance of her visiting Scotland at a time that London must be so ~~giddy~~ gay[31]. As it was our business, however, to be delighted at such a mark of condescension as a visit from Sir George and Lady Lesley, we prepared to return them an answer expressive of the happiness we enjoyed in expectation of such a blessing, when luckily recollecting that as they were to reach the Castle the next evening, it would be impossible for my father to receive it before he left Edinburgh, we ~~therefore~~ contented ourselves with leaving them to suppose that we were as happy as we ought to be.

At nine in the evening on the following day, they came, accompanied by one of Lady Lesley's brothers. Her Ladyship perfectly answers the description you sent me of her, except that I do not think her so pretty as you seem to consider her. She has not a bad face, but there is something so extremely unmajestic in her little diminutive figure, as to render her in comparison ~~to~~ with the elegant height of Matilda and myself, an insignificant dwarf. Her curiosity to see us (which must have been great to ~~have brought us~~ bring her more than four hundred miles) being now perfectly gratified, she already begins to mention their return to town, and has desired us to accompany her. We cannot refuse her request since it is seconded by the commands of our father, and thirded by the entreaties of Mr. Fitzgerald who is certainly one of the most pleasing young men, I ever beheld. It is not yet determined when we are to go, but whenever we do we shall certainly take our little Louisa with us.

Adieu my dear Charlotte; Matilda unites in best wishes to you, and Eloisa, with yours ever

M. L.

Letter the Sixth: Lady Lesley to Miss Charlotte Lutterell

Lesley Castle, March 20th

We arrived here, my sweet friend, about a fortnight ago, and I already heartily repent that I ever left our charming house in Portman Square[32] for such a dismal old weather-beaten castle as this. You can form no idea sufficiently hideous, of its dungeon-like ~~appearance~~ form. It is actually perched upon a rock to appearance so totally inaccessible, that I expected to have been pulled up by a rope; and sincerely repented having gratified my curiosity to behold my daughters at the expense of being obliged to enter their prison in so dangerous and ridiculous a manner. But as soon as I once found myself safely arrived in the inside of this tremendous building, I comforted myself with the hope of having my spirits revived by the sight of two beautiful girls, such as the Miss Lesleys had been represented to me, at Edinburgh. But here again, I met with nothing but disappointment and surprise.

Matilda and Margaret Lesley are two great, tall, out of the

way, over-grown, girls, just of a proper size to inhabit a castle almost as large in comparison as themselves. I wish, my dear Charlotte, that you could but behold these Scotch giants; I am sure they would frighten you out of your wits. They will do very well as foils to myself[33], so I have invited them to accompany me to London where I hope to be in the course of a fortnight. Besides these two fair damsels, I found a little humoured brat here who I believe is some relation to them; they told me who she was, and gave me a long rigmarole story of her father and a Miss *Somebody* which I have entirely forgot. I hate scandal and detest children.

I have been plagued ever since I came here with tiresome visits from a parcel of Scotch wretches, with terrible hard-names; they were so civil, gave me so many invitations, and talked of coming again so soon, that I could not help affronting them. I suppose I shall not see them anymore, and yet as a family party we are so stupid, that I do not know what to do with myself. These girls have no music but Scotch airs, no drawings but Scotch mountains, and no books but Scotch poems – and I hate everything Scotch.

In general, I can spend half the day at my toilette[34] with a great deal of pleasure, but why should I dress here, since there is not a creature in the house whom I have any wish to please. I have just had a conversation with my brother in which he has greatly offended me and which, as I have nothing more entertaining to send you, I will give you the particulars of.

You must know that I have for these four or five days past strongly suspected William of entertaining a partiality to my eldest daughter. I own, indeed, that, had *I* been inclined to fall in love with any woman, I should not have made choice of Matilda Lesley for the object of my passion, for there is nothing I hate so much as a tall woman: but however there is no accounting for some men's taste, and as William is himself nearly six feet high, it is not wonderful that he should be partial to that height. Now as I have a very great affection for my brother and should be extremely sorry to see him unhappy, which I suppose he means to be if he cannot marry Matilda, as moreover I know that his circumstances will not allow him to marry anyone without a fortune, and that Matilda's is entirely dependent on her father, who will neither have his own inclination nor my permission to give her anything at present, I thought it would be doing a good-natured action by my brother to let him know as much, in order that he might choose for himself, whether to conquer ~~her~~ his passion, or love and despair. Accordingly, finding myself this morning alone with him in one of the horrid old rooms of this castle, I opened the cause to him in the following manner.

"Well, my dear William. what do you think of these girls? For my part, I do not find them so plain as I ~~sus~~ expected: but perhaps you may think me partial to the daughters of my husband and perhaps you are right. – They are indeed so very like Sir George that it is natural to think–"

"My dear Susan," cried he in a tone of the greatest amazement. "You do not really think they bear the least resemblance to their father! He is so very plain! – but I beg your pardon – I had entirely forgotten to whom I was speaking.–"

"Oh! pray don't mind me," replied I. "Everyone knows Sir George is horribly ugly, and I assure you I always thought him a fright."

"You surprise me extremely," answered William, "by what you say both with respect to Sir George and his daughters. You cannot think your husband so deficient in personal charms as you speak of, nor can you surely see any resemblance ~~with~~ between him and the Miss Lesleys, who are in my opinion perfectly unlike him and perfectly handsome."

"If that is your opinion with regard to the girls, it certainly is no proof of their father's beauty, for if they are perfectly unlike him and very handsome at the same time, it is natural to suppose that he is very plain."

"By no means," said he, "for what may be pretty in a woman, may be very unpleasing in a man."

"But you yourself," replied I, "but a few minutes ago allowed him to be very plain."

"Men are no judges of beauty in their own sex," said he.

"Neither men nor women can think Sir George tolerable."

"Well, well," said he, "we will not dispute about *his* beauty, but your opinion of his *daughters* is surely very singular, for if I understood you right, you said ~~that~~ you did not find them so plain as you expected to do!"

"Why, do *you* find them plainer then?" said I.

"I can scarcely believe you to be serious," returned he, "when you speak of their persons in so extraordinary a manner. Do not you think ~~that~~ the Miss Lesleys are two very handsome young women?"

"Lord! No!" cried I. "I think them terribly plain!"

"Plain!" replied he. "My dear Susan, you cannot really think so! Why what single feature in the face of either of them can you possibly find fault with?"

"Oh! trust me for that," replied I. "Come I will begin with the eldest – with Matilda. Shall I, William?" (I looked as cunning as I could when I said it, in order to shame him).

"They are so much alike," said he, "that I should suppose the faults of one, would be the faults of both."

"Well, then, in the first place, they are both so horribly tall!"

"They are *taller* than you are indeed," said he with a saucy smile.

"Nay," said I, "I know nothing of that."

"Well, but," he continued, "though they may be above the common size, their figures are perfectly elegant; and as to their faces, their eyes are beautiful."

"I never can think such tremendous, knock-me-down figures in the least degree elegant, and as for their eyes, they are so tall that I never could strain my neck enough to look at them."

"Nay," replied he, "I know not whether you may not be in the right in not attempting it, for perhaps they might dazzle you with their luster."

"Oh! Certainly," said I, with the greatest complacency[35], for I assure you my dearest Charlotte ~~that~~ I was not in the least offended, though by what followed, one would suppose that William was conscious of having given me just cause to be so, for coming up to me and taking my hand, he said, 'You must not look so grave Susan; you will make me fear I have offended you!'"

"Offended me! Dear Brother, how came such a thought in your head!" returned I. "No really! I assure you that I am not in the least surprised at your being so warm an advocate for the beauty of these girls.–"

"Well, but," interrupted William, "remember that we have not yet concluded our dispute concerning them. What fault do you find with their complexion?"

"They are so horridly pale."

"They have always a little colour, and after any exercise it is considerably heightened."

"Yes, but if there should ever happen to be any rain in this part of the world, they will never be able raise more than their common stock[36] – except indeed they amuse themselves with running up and down these horrid old galleries and anti-chambers."

"Well," replied my brother in a tone of vexation, and glancing an impertinent look at me, "if they *have* but little colour, at least, it is all their own."

This was too much my dear Charlotte, for I am certain that he had the impudence by that look, of pretending to suspect the reality of mine. But you, I am sure, will vindicate my character whenever you may hear it so cruelly aspersed, for you can witness how often I have protested against wearing rouge, and how much I always told you I disliked it. And I assure you that my opinions are still the same.–

Well, not bearing to be so suspected by my brother, I left the room immediately, and have been ever since in my own dressing-room writing to you. What a long letter have I made of it! But you must not ~~su~~ expect to receive such from me when I get to town; for it is only at Lesley Castle, that one has time to write even to a Charlotte Lutterell. – I was so much vexed by William's glance, that I could not summon patience enough, to stay and give him that advice respecting his attachment to Matilda which had first induced me ~~to~~ from pure love to him to begin the conversation; and I am now so thoroughly convinced by it, of his violent passion for her, that I am certain he would never hear reason on the subject, and I shall therefore give myself no more trouble either about him or his favourite.

Adieu, my dear girl – Yours affectionately,
Susan L.

Letter the Seventh from Miss C. Lutterell to Miss M. Lesley

Bristol the 27th of March

I have received letters from you and your mother-in-law within this week which have greatly entertained me, as I find by them that you are both downright jealous of each other's beauty. It is very odd that two pretty women, though actually mother and daughter cannot be in the same house without falling out about their faces. Do be convinced that you are both perfectly handsome and say no more of the matter.

I suppose ~~that~~ this letter must be directed to Portman Square where probably (great as is your affection for Lesley Castle) you will not be sorry to find yourself. In spite of all that people may say about green fields and the country, I was always of opinion that London and its amusements must be very agreeable for a while, and should be very happy could my mother's income allow her to jockey us into ~~her~~ its public-places, during winter. I always longed particularly to go to Vauxhall[37], to see whether the cold beef there is cut so thin as it is reported, for I have a sly suspicion that few people understand the art of cutting a slice of cold beef so well as I do: nay it would be hard if I did not know something of the matter, for it was a part of my education that ~~I always took~~ I took by far the most pains with.

Mama always found me *her* best scholar, though when papa was alive Eloisa was *his*. Never, to be sure, were there two more different dispositions in the world. We both loved reading. *She* preferred histories, and *I* receipts[38]. She loved drawing pictures, and I drawing pullets[39]. No one could sing a better song than she; and no one make a better pie than I. – And so it has always continued since we have been no longer children. The only difference is that all disputes on the superior excellence of our employments *then* so frequent are now no more. We have for many years entered into an agreement always to admire each other's works; I never fail listening to *her* music, and she is as constant in eating my pies. Such at least was the case 'till Henry Hervey made his appearance in Sussex.

Before the arrival of his aunt in our neighbourhood, where she established herself you know about a twelvemonth ago, his visits to her had been at stated times, and of equal ~~of~~ and settled duration; but on her removal to the Hall which is within a walk from our house, they became both more frequent and longer. This, as you may suppose, could not be pleasing to Mrs. Diana who is a professed enemy to everything which is not directed by decorum and formality, or which bears the least resemblance to ease and good-breeding. Nay, so great was her aversion to her nephew's behaviour that I have often heard her give such hints of it before his face that, had not Henry at such times been engaged in conversation with Eloisa, they must have caught his attention and have very much distressed him.

The alteration in my sister's behavior, which I have before hinted at, now took place. The agreement we had entered into of admiring each other's productions, she no longer seemed to regard, and though I constantly applauded even every country-dance, she played, yet not even a pigeon pie of my making could obtain from her a single word of ~~praise~~ approbation. This was certainly enough to put anyone in a passion; however, I was as cool as a cream-cheese and having formed my plan and concerted a scheme of revenge, I was determined to let her have her own way and not even to make her a single reproach.

My scheme was to treat her as she treated me, and though she might even draw my own picture or play Malbrook[40] (which was is the only tune I ever really liked) not to say so much as, "Thank you Eloisa," though I had for many years constantly hollowed whenever she played, *bravo, bravissom, encore, da capo, allegretto, con expressione,* and *poco presto*[41] with many other such outlandish words, all of them as Eloisa told me expressive of my admiration; and so indeed I suppose they are, as I see some of them in every page of every music book, being the sentiments, I imagine, of the composer.

I executed my plan with great punctuality. I cannot say success, for alas! my silence while she played seemed not in the least to displease her; on the contrary, she actually said to me one day, "Well Charlotte, I am very glad to find that you have at last left off that ridiculous custom of applauding my execution on the harpsichord[42] till you made my head ache, and yourself hoarse. I feel very much obliged to you for keeping your admiration to yourself."

I never shall forget the very witty answer I made to this speech.

"Eloisa," said I, "I beg you would be quite at your ease with respect to all such fears in future, for be assured that I shall always keep my admiration to myself and my own pursuits and never extend it to yours."

This was the only very severe ~~speech~~ thing I ever said in my life; not but that I have often felt myself extremely satirical, but it was the only time I ever made my feelings public.

I suppose there never were two young people who had a greater affection for each other than Henry and Eloisa; no, the love of your brother for Miss Burton could not be so strong, though it might be more violent. You may imagine therefore how provoked my sister must have been to have him play her such a trick. Poor girl! She still laments his death with undiminished constancy, notwithstanding he has been dead more than six weeks; but some people mind such things more than others. The ill state of health into which his loss has thrown her makes her so weak, and so unable to support the least exertion, that she has been in tears all this morning merely from having taken leave of Mrs. Marlowe who, with her husband, brother and child, are to leave Bristol this morning. I am sorry to have them go because they are the only family with whom we have here any acquaintance, but I never thought of crying; to be sure Eloisa and Mrs. Marlowe have always been more together than with me, and have therefore contracted ~~an~~ a kind of affection for each other, which does not make tears so inexcusable in them as they would be in me.

The Marlowes are going to town; Cleveland accompanies them; as neither Eloisa nor I could catch him, I hope ~~that~~ you or Matilda may have better luck. I know not when we shall leave Bristol: Eloisa's spirits are so low that she is very averse to moving, and yet is certainly by no means mended by her residence here. A week or two will I hope determine our measures – in the meantime believe me and etc.– and etc.–

Charlotte Lutterell.

Letter the Eighth: Miss Lutterell to Mrs. Marlowe

Bristol, April 4th

I feel myself greatly obliged to you, my dear Emma, for such a mark of your affection as I flatter myself was conveyed in the proposal you made me of our corresponding; I assure you that it will be a great relief to me to write to you and as long as my health and spirits will allow me, you will find me a very constant correspondent; I will not say an entertaining one, for you know my situation sufficiently not to be ignorant that in me mirth would be improper, and I know my own heart ~~well enough~~ too well not to be sensible that it would be unnatural.

You must not expect news, for we see no one with whom we are in the least acquainted, or in whose proceedings we have any interest. You must not expect scandal, for by the same rule, we are equally debarred either from hearing or inventing it. – You must expect from me nothing but the melancholy effusions of a broken heart which is ever reverting to the happiness it once enjoyed, and which ill supports its present wretchedness. The possibility of being able to write, to speak, to you of my lost Henry will be a luxury to me, and your goodness will not, I know, refuse to read what it will so much relieve my heart to write.

I once thought that to have what is in general called a friend (I mean one of my own sex to whom I might speak with less reserve than to any other person) independent of my sister, would never be an object of my wishes, but how much was I mistaken! Charlotte is too much engrossed by two confidential correspondents of that sort, to supply the place of one to me, and I hope you will not think me girlishly romantic, when I say that to have some kind and compassionate friend who might listen to my sorrows without endeavouring to console me was what I had for some time wished for, when our acquaintance with you, the intimacy which followed it, and the particular affectionate attention you paid me almost from the first, caused me to entertain the flattering idea of those attentions being improved on a closer acquaintance into a friendship which, if you were what my wishes formed you, would be the greatest happiness I could be capable of enjoying.

To find that such hopes are realized is a satisfaction indeed, a satisfaction which is now almost the only one I can ever experience. – I feel myself so languid that I am sure, were you with me, you would oblige me to leave off writing, and I cannot give you a greater proof of my affection for you than by acting, as I know you would wish me to do, whether absent or present.

I am my dear Emma's sincere friend

E. L.

Letter the Ninth: Mrs. Marlowe to Miss Lutterell

Grosvenor Street, April 10th

Need I say, my dear Eloisa, how welcome your letter was to me? I cannot give a greater proof of the pleasure I received from it, or of the desire I feel that our correspondence may be regular and frequent than by setting you so good an example as I now do in answering it before the end of a the week. – But do not imagine that I claim any merit in being so punctual; on the contrary, I assure you, that it is a far greater gratification to me to write to you, than to spend the evening either at a concert or a ball.

Mr. Marlowe is so desirous of my appearing at some of the public places every evening that I do not like to refuse him, but at the same time so much wish to remain at home, that independent of the pleasure I experience in devoting any portion of my time to my dear Eloisa, yet the liberty I claim from having a letter to write of spending an evening at home with my little boy, you know me well enough to be sensible, will of itself be a sufficient inducement (if one is necessary) to my maintaining with pleasure a correspondence with you.

As to the subject of your letters to me, whether grave or merry, if they concern you they must be equally interesting to me; not but that I think the melancholy indulgence of your own sorrows by repeating them and dwelling on them to me, will only encourage and increase them, and that it will be more prudent in you to avoid so sad a subject; but yet knowing, as I do, what a soothing and melancholy pleasure it must afford you, I cannot prevail on myself to deny you so great an indulgence, and will only insist on your not expecting me to encourage you in it by my own letters; on the contrary, I intend to fill them with such lively wit and enlivening humour as shall even provoke a smile in the sweet but sorrowful countenance of my Eloisa.

In the first place, you are to learn that I have met your sister's three friends, Lady Lesley and her daughters, twice in public since I have been here. I know you will be impatient to hear my opinion of the beauty of three ladies of whom you have heard so much. Now, as you are too ill and too unhappy to be vain, I think I may venture to inform you that I like none of their faces so well as I do your own. Yet they are all handsome – Lady Lesley, indeed, I have seen before; her daughters I believe would in general be said to have a finer face than her Ladyship, and yet what with the charms of a blooming complexion, a little affectation and a great deal of small-talk (in each of which she is superior to the young ladies), she will, I dare say, gain herself as many admirers as the more regular features of Matilda and Margaret.

I am sure ~~that~~ you will agree with me in saying that they can none of them be of a proper size for real beauty, when you know that two of them are taller and the other shorter than ourselves. In spite of this defect (or rather by reason of it), there is something very noble and majestic in the figures of the Miss Lesleys, and something agreeably lively in the appearance of their pretty little mother-in-law. But though one may be majestic and the other lively, yet the faces of neither possess that bewitching sweetness of my Eloisa's, which her present languor is so far from diminishing.

What would my husband and brother say of us, if they knew all the fine things I have been saying to you in this letter? It is very hard that a pretty woman is never to be told she is so by anyone of her own sex without that person's being suspected to be either her determined enemy, or her professed toadeater[43]. How much more amiable are women in that particular! One man may say forty civil things to another without our supposing that he is ever paid for it, and provided he does his duty by our sex, we care not how polite he is to his own.

Mrs. Lutterell will be so good as to accept my compliments, Charlotte my love, and Eloisa the best wishes for the recovery of her health and spirits that can be offered by her affectionate friend

E. Marlowe.

I am afraid ~~that~~ this letter will be but a poor specimen of my powers in the witty way; and your opinion of them will not be greatly increased when I assure you that I have ~~as~~ been as entertaining as I possibly could.

Letter the Tenth from Miss Margaret Lesley to Miss Charlotte Lutterell

Portman Square, April 13th

My dear Charlotte,

We left Lesley Castle on the 28th of last month, and arrived safely in London after a journey of seven days. I had the pleasure of finding your letter here waiting my arrival, for which you have my grateful thanks. Ah! my dear friend, I every day more regret the serene and tranquil pleasures of the castle we have left, in exchange for the uncertain and unequal amusements of this vaunted city. Not that I will pretend to assert that these uncertain and unequal amusements are in the least degree unpleasing to me; on the contrary, I enjoy them extremely and should enjoy them even more, were I not certain that every appearance I make in public but rivets the chains of those unhappy beings whose passion it is impossible not to pity, though it is out of my power to return. In short, my dear Charlotte, it is my sensibility for the sufferings of so many amiable young men, my dislike of the extreme admiration I meet with, and my aversion to being so celebrated both in public, in private, in papers, and in print shops[44], that are the reasons why I cannot more fully enjoy, the amusements so various and pleasing of London.

How often have I wished that I possessed as little personal beauty as you do; that my figure were as inelegant; my face as unlovely; and my appearance as unpleasing as yours! But ah! what little chance is there of so desirable an event; I have had the smallpox[45], and must therefore submit to my unhappy fate.

I am now going to entrust you, my dear Charlotte, with a secret which has long disturbed the tranquility of my days, and which is of a kind to require the most inviolable secrecy from you. ~~On~~ Last Monday ~~sen'nit~~ se'night[46], Matilda and I accompanied Lady Lesley to a rout[47] at the Honourable Mrs. Kickabout's. We were escorted by Mr. Fitzgerald, who is a very amiable young man in the main, though perhaps a little singular in his taste. – He is in love with Matilda. – We had scarcely paid our compliments to the lady of the house and curtseyed to half a score different people, when my attention was attracted by the appearance of a young man the most lovely of his sex, who at that moment entered the room with another gentleman and lady.

From the first moment I beheld him, I was certain that on him depended the future happiness of my life. Imagine my surprise when he was introduced to me by the name of Cleveland. – I instantly recognized him as the brother of Mrs. Marlowe, and the acquaintance of my Charlotte at Bristol. Mr. and Mrs. M. were the gentleman and lady who accompanied him. (You do not think Mrs. Marlowe handsome?) The elegant address of Mr. Cleveland, his polished manners and delightful bow, at once confirmed my attachment. He did not speak, but I can imagine everything he would have said, had he opened his mouth. I can picture to myself the cultivated understanding, the noble sentiments, and elegant language which would have shone so conspicuous in the conversation of Mr. Cleveland.

The approach of Sir James Gower (one of my too numerous admirers) prevented the discovery of any such powers, by putting an end to a conversation we had never commenced, and by attracting my attention to himself. But oh! how inferior are the accomplishments of Sir James to those of his so greatly envied rival! Sir James is one of the most frequent of our ~~most~~ visitors, and is almost always of our parties. We have since often met Mr. and Mrs. Marlowe but no Cleveland – he is always engaged somewhere else. Mrs. Marlowe fatigues me to death every time I see her by her tiresome conversations about you and Eloisa. She is so stupid! I live in the hope of seeing her irresistible brother tonight, as we are going to Lady Flambeau's, who is, I know, intimate with the Marlowes. Our party will be Lady Lesley, Matilda, Fitzgerald, Sir James Gower, and myself.

We see little of Sir George, who is almost always at the gaming-table. Ah! my poor fortune where art thou by this time? We see more of Lady L. who always makes her appearance (highly rouged) at dinner-time. Alas! what delightful jewels will she be decked in this evening at Lady Flambeau's! Yet I wonder how she can herself delight in wearing them; surely she must be sensible of the ridiculous impropriety of loading her little diminutive figure with such superfluous ornaments. Is it possible that she cannot know how greatly superior an elegant simplicity is to the most studied apparel? Would she but present them to Matilda and me, how greatly should we be obliged to her. How becoming would diamonds be on our fine majestic figures! And how surprising it is that such an idea should never have occurred to *her*. I am sure if I have reflected in this manner once, I have fifty times. Whenever I see Lady Lesley dressed in them such reflections immediately come across me. My own mother's jewels too!

But I will say no more on so melancholy a subject – let me entertain you with something more pleasing. – Matilda had a letter this morning from Lesley, by which we have the pleasure of finding that he is at Naples, has turned Roman Catholic, obtained one of the Pope's Bulls for annulling his first marriage, and has since actually married a Neapolitan lady of great rank and fortune. He tells us, moreover, that much the same sort of affair has befallen his first wife the worthless Louisa who is likewise at Naples has ~~obtained another of the Pope's Bulls for annulling~~ turned Roman Catholic, and is soon to be married to a Neapolitan nobleman of great and distinguished merit. He says, that they are at present very good friends, have quite forgiven all past errors and intend in future to be very good neighbours.

He invites Matilda and me to pay him a visit to Italy and to bring him his little Louisa whom both her mother, step-mother, and himself are equally desirous of beholding. As to our accepting his invitation, it is at present very uncertain; Lady Lesley advises us to go without loss of time; Fitzgerald offers to escort us there, but Matilda has some doubts of the propriety of such a scheme. – She owns it would be very agreeable. I am certain she likes the fellow. My father desires us not to be in a hurry, as perhaps if we wait a few months both he and Lady Lesley will do themselves the pleasure of attending us. Lady Lesley says no, that nothing will ever tempt her to forego the amusements of Brighthelmstone for a journey to Italy merely to see our brother.

"No," says the disagreeable woman, "I have once in my life been fool enough to travel I don't know how many hundred miles to see two of the family, and I found it did not answer, so Deuce take me, if ever I am so foolish again."

So says her Ladyship, but Sir George still perseveres in saying that perhaps in a month or two, they may accompany us.

Adieu my dear Charlotte, your faithful
Margaret Lesley.

Notes

1. "Henry Thomas Austen": Jane's favorite brother, Henry (1771-1850), was the fourth son. The date of this story coincides with his completing his B.A. at

Oxford University. In real life, he would help Jane to get published during her life and ensure that *Northanger Abbey* and *Persuasion* were published posthumously.

2. "£105.0.0.": The mock bank draft is in Henry's handwriting. This sum represents Henry's supposed patronage of the author.

3. "my brother": Sir George Lesley has three children: Margaret, Matilda, and a brother referred to only as Lesley (whose wife, Louisa, has just abandoned him and their new-born daughter).

4. "Aberdeen": It is soon clear that Lesley is driving from Perth to Aberdeen, a distance of just under ninety miles.

5. "Rakehelly Dishonour Esquire": This is only the second footnote in the entire juvenilia. It appears that Louisa has left her husband in the company of two men, which adds to the scandal. Perhaps, however, the second name is intended as merely a personification of the dishonor Louisa brings upon herself by her infidelity. 'Rakehelly' means a licentious or dissolute man, a rake or libertine.

6. "retired from almost all the world": The castle is not so isolated as Margaret pretends it to be and the sisters appear to have a wide circle of visitors.

7. "*bon-mot*": A witty remark – a sure sign in Austen of empty minds.

8. "insensible of them ourselves": Absurdly oxymoronic: you cannot describe something of which you are unaware. Margaret Lesley is as self-satisfied as Laura in *Love and Friendship*. In fact, Margaret's life emerges as trivial and empty.

9. "Perthshire ... Sussex": A distance of about five hundred miles.

10. "Bath ... Tunbridge": Two very popular spar towns. Bath is in Somerset in the south west of England and Royal Tunbridge Wells is in western Kent in south eastern England.

11. "Glenford": The fictional home of the Lutterell family.

12. "whipped syllabub": A sweet confection made from whipping together cream, sack (a fortified white wine), two egg whites, and a quarter cup of sugar, orange or lemon, plus flavoring spices.

13. "thrown from his horse": Unfortunately not an unusual occurrence. Anne Lefoy (1749-1804), Austen's great friend, would die in a riding accident on December 16th, Jane's 29th birthday. She was fifty-five.

14. "Bristol": They are going for Eloisa's health to Bristol Hotwells, a spa town less fashionable than Bath.

15. "unpleasing a report": The report would be unpleasing to Miss Lesley partly because the marriage of a man her father's age would seem to a young person inappropriate, but mainly because having a stepmother would impact Miss Lesley's expectations of inheriting from her father's will.

16. "I subscribe myself ... Susan Lesley": That is, she has herself married Sir George Lesley.

17. "her father's table": Matilda, as the oldest daughter, had taken the place of

her late mother at the head of her father's table (with her father at the foot), but Sir Lesley's new wife will take this position from Matilda.

18. "her own consequence": That is, the loss of her current status in the family.

19. "Cumberland": A county in north-west England noted for its natural beauty.

20. "Yorkshire": A county in north-east England also noted for its natural beauty but becoming industrialized in Austen's day.

21. "Aberdeen": This estate is Lesley's own property by inheritance from an uncle. At the start of the story when he took the road to Aberdeen, Lesley was presumably going back to his estate prior to leaving for the Continent.

22. "Dunbeath": The name of Lesley's Aberdeen estate. There is a village of that name in the extreme north-east of Scotland, but it is nowhere near Aberdeen.

23. "Sussex … Bristol": Sussex is a county in south-east England and Bristol a town in south-west England. The distance between is almost two hundred miles.

24. "chairwomen": Char women hired by the day as needed.

25. "Berkshire": A fashionable county in south-east England, west of London.

26. "Brighthelmstone": Daniel Defoe visited Brighton in the early 18th century, noting "Bright Helmston, commonly call'd Bredhemston, [is] a poor fishing town, old built, and on the very edge of the sea." By Austen's time, Brighton had developed as a fashionable seaside resort very popular with the Prince Regent (later King George IV), who constructed the Royal Pavilion there in the Regency era.

27. "four thousand pounds": That capital, invested, would produce an income of £200 per annum, which is not a great deal. Charlotte believes that her friend will spend all of this on herself and seek to augment it by dipping into the family fortune.

28. "very well off": That is, 'You will be very lucky if you get any money at all.'

29. "unfashionable a season of the year": The Bristol season ran from the end of March to the end of September – the warmer months.

30. "set her cap at him": That is, determine to win his love and a proposal of marriage. Any young woman seeking to win a man's affections would wear her best clothes, including her most attractive cap – worn, of course, at the most flattering angle. In *Sense and Sensibility*, Marianne (the sixteen-year-old younger sister who embodies sensibility) objects to Sir John Middleton saying that she will set her cap at Mr. Willoughby. She says, "'That is an expression … which I particularly dislike. I abhor every common-place phrase by which wit is intended; and "setting one's cap at a man" or "making a conquest" are the most odious of all. Their tendency is gross and illiberal; and if their construction could ever be deemed clever, time has long ago destroyed its ingenuity'" (Ch. 9).

31. "London must be so gay": March was the height of the London season which ran from late autumn to early June. In summer, the rich went to their country houses.

32. "Portman Square": Portman Square is built around an extensive private garden. It was built between 1765 and 1784 as part of the Portman Estate and immediately attracted the nobility. Susan Lesley's enthusiasm for her "charming house" is understandable.

33. "foils to myself": That is, their unattractive height will show her own smaller stature to advantage. Hamlet tells Laertes, "I'll be your foil, Laertes. In mine ignorance / Your skill shall, like a star I' th' darkest night, / Stick fiery off indeed" (*Hamlet* 5.2).

34. "at my toilette": That is, attending to her appearance both in terms of cosmetics and dress.

35. "complacency": Lack of concern, equanimity. The word did not then have its modern meaning of self-satisfaction.

36. "common stock": That is, their inherent paleness – with a sarcastic hit at the girls not being born to the English cultured elite.

37. "Vauxhall": An area of Lambeth on the south bank of the River Thames. From 1615 to 1859, it was the site of the famous Vauxhall Pleasure Gardens. Refreshments could be purchased inside the Gardens. Vauxhall waiters were noted for their ability to cut very thin slices of ham (called "sliced cobwebs") and beef (called "book muslin"). This ability, of course, made the meats go further.

38. "receipts": An old spelling of 'recipes.'

39. "drawing pullets": That is, pulling the necks of young hens (less than one year old).

40. "Malbrook": Originally a French tune "*Malbrook s'en va-t-en guerre*" (*Malbrook has left for the war*). Malbrook was a corruption of the name the great English general, Marlborough, whose death was falsely reported in 1709. Subsequently, the tune became very popular in Britain.

41. "*bravo … poco presto*": That is, "good, very good, repeat, at a fairly brisk tempo, from the beginning, with expression, as fast as possible." The first three do express approval, but the rest are the composer's instructions on how the piece should be played, although Charlotte is unaware of this.

42. "harpsichord": A keyboard instrument rather like a piano except that the strings are plucked not hit by little hammers. In the late 18th century, the harpsichord was supplanted by the piano, so Eloisa is a little out of date. Austen herself had a piano.

43. "toadeater": "A fawning, obsequious parasite; a mean sycophant or flatterer" (Wiktionary). The assistant of a showman would eat a supposedly poisonous toad and the showman would miraculously 'cure' him.

44. "in papers, and in printshops": The society pages of newspapers reported on the lives of the people of fashion and the portraits of the rich, the famous and the beautiful were sold by printers.

45. "smallpox": In 1796, English physician Edward Jenner demonstrated the effectiveness of cowpox vaccine to protect humans from smallpox. A person surviving smallpox (and many did not survive) was very likely to have facial scars. In 1771, a smallpox epidemic killed the brother of Austen's close friend Martha Lloyd and left her and her sister scarred for life. Margaret's statement is extremely insensitive.

46. "se'night": Seven days, or a week. It is a shortened form of Middle English 'sevennight.' Compare: "Weary sev'nnights nine times nine. / Shall he dwindle, peak and pine" (*Macbeth* 1.3).

47. "rout": A term for a fashionable gathering, but it is hard to forget that it could also mean a disorganized gathering – something in the nature of a riot.

Commentary

Emily Auerbach writes that in her juvenilia Austen frequently "mocks her era's pension for epistolary novels consisting of a heartfelt, sentimental exchange between unbelievably virtuous and affectionate young women who seem to have nothing to do but write lengthy letters detailing the events of their whole lives" (54). However, *Lesley Castle* marks an important stage of the evolution in Austen's experiments with the epistolary form because, for the first time, the two primary letter writers, Miss Margaret Lesley and her friend Miss Charlotte Lutterell, are clearly differentiated characters with distinctive voices. Margaret and Charlotte are Austen's first attempt to portray the contrasting personalities of sensibility and sense. More than this, the focus of the writing is less on parodying bad epistolary novels than on the exposure of human foibles. A. Walton Litz makes this point, stating that *Lesley Castle* "is Jane Austen's first attempt to create a variety of believable characters, and to place them in a wholly realistic social milieu..." (26).

Margaret lives the vacuous life of a young woman of culture and refinement without perceiving that her live is empty. Writing of herself and her sister, Martha, she says, "We read, we work, we walk, and when fatigued with these employments relieve our spirits, either by a lively song, a graceful dance, or by some smart *bon-mot* and witty *repartee*" – in other words, they do nothing! She is insufferably vain about her and her sister's accomplishments and beauty, "there never were two more lively, more agreeable or more witty girls, than we are ... We are handsome, my dear Charlotte, very handsome, and the greatest of our perfections is that we are entirely insensible of them ourselves." Of course, such a woman must have a confidential female friend with whom to share the secrets of her life and heart, and Charlotte is that friend. Margaret describes them as two "tender hearts ... closely linked together by the ties of sympathy and friendship," despite the fact that they have not seen each other for four years and are unlikely to do so in the future because they live at different ends of the kingdom. Margaret's pretentions make her a prime target for Austen's satire.

In contrast, the sensible Charlotte is a stereotype of the female whose world seems to have contracted to domestic economy: she has no time for refined diversions, nor for heightened sensibility. Apparently incapable of romantic emotion herself, she cannot understand or empathize with the love that her sister Eloisa had for her fiancé Henry Hervey. (The sentimental Margaret, on the other hand, assures her friend, "I *think* and *feel*, a great deal for your sister's affliction.") Seeing all of life in household terms, to Charlotte the wedding feast is a logistical operation to be rationally organized, and her attitude does not change when she learns that the groom-to-be has "been thrown from his horse, had fractured his skull and was pronounced by his surgeon to be in the most imminent danger." At first, she simply laments to Margaret that "the match is broke off" which gives no indication of the tragic accident which led to the cancellation because to Charlotte it is irrelevant *what* caused the cancellation. Describing the face of Eloisa as she ran into the store-room (Charlotte's natural habitat), she uses the simile "her face [was] as white as a whipped syllabub," which may be an accurate comparison as to skin tone but hardly does justice to her sister's suffering since a syllabub is a sweet dessert. When Charlotte does turn to consoling Eloisa, she virtually ignores the dying Hervey to assure her sister that the inconvenience to herself of having to dispose of the perishable food prepared for the wedding feast (and having, at a later date when Eloisa eventually marries someone else, to prepare a second wedding feast) is bearable. She tells the grieving Eloisa, "'You see it does not vex me in the least; though perhaps I may suffer most for from it after all.'" It seems that, taken to the extreme, sense is as apt a target for satire as is sensibility.

The contrast between Margaret and Charlotte is evident in their attitudes to the suffering of Margaret's brother, Lesley, whose unfaithful wife, Louisa, has left him with a two-year-old daughter. Margaret describes him in his grief as a stereotype of the sorrowing man of sentiment, "Lesley is at present but five-and-twenty, and has already given himself up to melancholy and despair." In other words, she describes him as though he were herself. Thus, she dismisses his idea that travel will help him to recover from the treachery of his beloved wife, "Mistaken youth! He vainly flatters himself that change of air will heal the wounds of a broken heart!" The sensible Charlotte, however, who is equally incapable of feeling love herself or of understanding the feelings of lost in others, comments, "your brother is extremely right in the resolution he has taken of travelling, as it will perhaps contribute to obliterate from his remembrance, those disagreeable events, which have lately so much afflicted him." As the story progresses, Charlotte is seen to have been closer to the truth in this case since Lindsay reports that the air of France has an almost immediate effect in removing his melancholy. He will later remarry in Italy where he meets Louisa (also planning to remarry) on friendly terms.

While Charlotte writes obsessively about the practical measures she took to ensure that none of the food prepared for Eloisa's wedding should go to waste, Margaret obsesses about the mercenary rivals who seem intent on getting their hands on the Lesley fortune, which of course she considers to be rightfully hers and her sister's. Louisa she presents as a penniless, conniving gold-digger who hid "her natural disposition under the mask of innocence and softness" in order to entrap her brother, but Susan Lesley, her new step-mother, represents a greater threat to Margaret and Martha's financial security. On first hearing rumors of her father's remarriage, she writes to Charlotte, "I reflected that if, by this second marriage, Sir George should have a second family, our fortunes must be considerably diminished ... she would now become mistress of those jewels which once adorned our mother, and which Sir George had always promised us." Like Laura in *Love and Friendship*, Charlotte considers that her superior sensibility entitles her to wealth and that all those who come between her and that entitlement must be mercenary wretches. It is therefore vital to Margaret to establish her own superiority over Susan Lesley whom she criticizes for being short ("an insignificant dwarf") and for using rouge.

A third voice enters the correspondence in the form of Susan, now Lady Lesley, who writes to Charlotte with the openness and honesty of a confidential friend, unaware of Charlotte's prior friendship with Margaret. Susan returns the criticisms that Margaret has made of her: Margaret and Martha are too tall ("two great, tall, out of the way, over-grown, girls") and their complexion is "'horridly pale.'" Once again, the common-sense of Charlotte provides a welcome corrective. She writes to Margaret, "It is very odd that two pretty women, though actually mother and daughter cannot be in the same house without falling out about their faces." Charlotte them proceeds unconsciously to make *herself* ridiculous. She tells Margaret that she has always wanted to visit London and "longed particularly to go to Vauxhall [Gardens]," but with unintended bathos she reveals that her motive is "to see whether the cold beef there is cut so thin as it is reported, for I have a sly suspicion that few people understand the art of cutting a slice of cold beef so well as I do." Charlotte is as vain about her culinary accomplishments as is Margaret about her social accomplishments and her beauty.

Charlotte's own competition with her sister, which results from their complete dissimilarity, is equal to that between Margaret and Susan. Prior to the advent of Henry Hervey, it has been controlled by an "agreement we had entered into of admiring each other's productions," but this agreement has broken down. It appears to the reader that all this time Eloisa has been making fun of her sister by allowing her to think that the Italian words she spoke in praise of Eloisa's musical performances were "the sentiments ... of the composer" when most of them were not. Neither does Charlotte's elaborate plan to get revenge on her sister for withdrawing her praise for Charlotte's pies produce any satisfaction, since Eloisa pronounces herself pleased that Charlotte has stopped. Disgruntled, a surprised Charlotte observes, "silence while she played seemed not in the least to displease her."

Charlotte remains incapable of emotion. She fails to understand Eloisa's continuing mourning for Hervey because her fiancé "has been dead more than six weeks," and she never thinks of crying when she says good-bye to Mrs. Emma Marlowe, explaining that her sister and Mrs. Marlowe have "a kind of affection for each other, which does not make tears so inexcusable in them as they would be in me." This prepares us for the opening of a confidential correspondence between Eloisa and Emma. In her first letter, the former confides that since the death of Hervey she has sorely wanted, "what is in general called a friend (I mean one of my own sex to whom I might speak with less reserve than to any other person)." Eloisa's letter does not come across, however, as silly or affected in the way that Margaret's confidential letters to Charlotte do. Indeed, she is all too aware that she runs the risk that Emma will feel her to be "girlishly romantic" in seeking to communicate her sorrows to another woman.

Emma's first letter allows the reader to gain a more objective view of the beauties of Lady Lesley and her two step-daughters. In Emma's description, there is none of the bitchiness evident of the earlier letters of Margaret and Susan. Indeed, Emma declares all three to be "handsome," and is generous in expressing the opinion that neither of the three young women is as beautiful as Eloisa. When she adds, "I am sure you will agree with me in saying that they can none of them be of a proper size for real beauty, when you know that two of them are taller and the other shorter than ourselves," there is surely a tone of self-mockery to which neither Margaret nor Susan could aspire. Indeed, Emma's first letter evinces genuine concern for and understanding of Eloisa's mourning and a real (and modest) attempt to take her mind off her sorrows by writing entertainingly. The parody that disappears in the letters of Emma and Eloisa, is arguably disastrous in terms of the novel's development.

Margaret's account of having won the hearts of so many young men in London is vainglorious and affected. She praises her own "sensibility for the sufferings of so many amiable young men," and hypocritically expresses the wish that she was as unattractive as her friend and correspondent Charlotte, "How often have I wished that I possessed as little personal beauty as you do…" She then describes falling in love at first sight with a young man called Cleveland who is described (as romantic fiction dictates) as "the most lovely of his sex." Margaret continues, "From the first moment I beheld him, I was certain that on him depended the future happiness of my life." Although Mr. Cleveland does not speak, Margaret imagines what he would have said, "I can picture to myself the cultivated understanding, the noble sentiments, and elegant language which would have shone so conspicuous in the conversation of Mr. Cleveland." Understandably, what Margaret imagines is precisely what a lover *would* have said in a romantic novel.

Lesley Castle may be described as a narrative in search of a plot. The black comedy of Charlotte's reaction to the cancelation of Eloisa's wedding is brilliant, and the mutual back-biting between Margaret and Lady Lesley is fine satire, but each thread is soon exhausted. The novel ends with the remote possibility of the Lesley family traveling to Italy, but Austen knew nothing of Italy, and besides how could the Lesley/Louisa plot possibly develop? On the other hand, there are the love affairs of Martha and Margaret Lesley, but how could they be brought together and what role could Emma Marlowe play? Put simply, there are too many separate strands for a coherent narrative. Once again, Austen has written herself into a narrative *cul-de-sac*. She had yet to discover that the ending to which all of her novels must come is that of happy marriage.

The History of England
from the reign of Henry the 4th to the death of Charles the 1st

By a partial, prejudiced, and ignorant historian[1].

To Miss Austen[2], eldest daughter of the Rev. George Austen, this work is inscribed with all due respect by
The Author
N.B. There will be very few dates in this History.

Henry the Fourth

Henry the 4th ascended the throne of England much to his own satisfaction in the year 1399, after having prevailed on his cousin and predecessor Richard the 2nd, to resign it to him, and to retire for the rest of his life to Pomfret Castle, where he happened to be murdered[3].

It is to be supposed that Henry was married, since he had certainly four sons, but it is not in my power to inform the reader who was his wife. Be this as it may, he did not live forever, but falling ill, his son the Prince of Wales came and took away the crown; whereupon the King made a long speech, for which I must refer the reader to Shakespeare's plays, and the Prince made a still longer. Things being thus settled between them, the King died and was succeeded by his son Henry who had previously beat Sir William Gascoigne[4].

Henry the Fifth

This prince, after he succeeded to the throne, grew quite reformed and amiable, forsaking all his dissipated companions, and never thrashing Sir William again. During his reign, Lord Cobham was burnt alive, but I forget what for[5]. His Majesty then turned his thoughts to France, where he went and fought the famous Battle of Agincourt[6]. He afterwards married the King's daughter Catherine, a very agreeable woman by Shakespeare's account. In spite of all this, however, he died and was succeeded by his son Henry.

Henry the Sixth

I cannot say much for this monarch's sense. Nor would I if I could, for he was a Lancastrian. I suppose you know all about the wars between him and the Duke of York who was of the right side[7]; if you do not, you had better read some other history, for I shall not be very diffuse in this, meaning by it only to vent my spleen *against*, and show my hatred *to* all those people whose parties or principles do not suit with mine, and not to give information[8].

This king married Margaret of Anjou, a woman whose distresses and misfortunes were so great as almost to make me, who hate her, pity her. It was in this reign that Joan of Arc[9] lived and made such a *row* among the English. They should not have burnt her – but they did. There were several battles between the Yorkists and Lancastrians, in which the former (as they ought) usually conquered. At length they were entirely overcome: the King was murdered – the Queen was sent home – and Edward the 4th ascended the throne.

Edward the Fourth

This monarch was famous only for his beauty and his courage, of *which* the picture we have here given of him, and his undaunted behaviour in marrying one woman while he was engaged to another, are sufficient proofs. His wife was Elizabeth Woodville, a widow who, poor woman! was afterwards confined in a convent by that monster of iniquity and avarice Henry the 7th. One of Edward's mistresses was Jane Shore[10], who has had a play written about her, but it is a tragedy and therefore not worth reading. Having performed all these noble actions, his majesty died, and was succeeded by his son.

Edward the Fifth

This unfortunate prince lived so little a while that nobody had him to draw his picture. He was murdered by his uncle's contrivance[11], whose name was Richard the 3rd.

~~Edward the~~

Richard the Third

The character of this prince has been in general very

severely treated by historians, but as he was a *York*, I am rather inclined to suppose him a very respectable man. It has indeed been confidently asserted that he killed his two nephews and his wife[12], but it has also been declared that he did *not* kill his two nephews, which I am inclined to believe true; and if this is the case, it may also be affirmed that he did not kill his wife, for if Perkin Warbeck was really the Duke of York, why might not Lambert Simnel be the widow of Richard[13]. Whether innocent or guilty, he did not reign ~~for ever~~ long in peace, for Henry Tudor, Earl of Richmond, as great a villain as ever lived, made a great fuss about getting the crown and having killed the King at the battle of Bosworth, he succeeded to it.

Henry the Seventh

This monarch soon after his accession married the Princess Elizabeth of York, by which alliance he plainly proved that he thought his own right inferior to hers, though he pretended to the contrary. By this marriage he had two sons and two daughters, the elder of which daughters was married to the King of Scotland and had the happiness of being grandmother to one of the first characters in the world[14]. But of *her*, I shall have occasion to speak more at large in future. The youngest, Mary, married first the King of France and secondly the Duke of Suffolk, by whom she had one daughter, afterwards the mother of Lady Jane Grey[15], who though inferior to her lovely cousin the Queen of Scots, was yet an amiable young woman and famous for reading Greek while other people were hunting.

It was in the reign of Henry the 7th that Perkin Warbeck and Lambert Simnel before mentioned made their appearance, the former of ~~which~~ whom was set in the stocks, took shelter in Beaulieu Abbey, and was beheaded with the Earl of Warwick, and the latter was taken into the King's kitchen[16]. His majesty died and was succeeded by his son Henry whose only merit was his not being *quite* so bad as his daughter Elizabeth.

Henry the Eighth

It would be an affront to my readers were I to suppose that they were not as well acquainted with the particulars of this king's reign as I am myself. It will therefore be saving *them* the task of reading again what they have read before, and *myself* the trouble of writing what I do not perfectly recollect, by giving only a slight sketch of the principal events which marked his reign. Among these may be ranked Cardinal Wolsey's telling the father Abbott of Leicester Abbey that "he was come to lay his bones among them," the reformation in religion and the King's riding through the streets of London with Anna Bullen[17].

It is however but justice, and my duty to declare that this amiable woman was entirely innocent of the crimes with which she was accused[18] ~~of with~~, and of which her beauty, her elegance, and her sprightliness were sufficient proofs, not to mention her solemn protestations of innocence, the weakness of the charges against her, and the King's character; all of which add some confirmation, though perhaps but slight ones when in comparison with those before alleged in her favour.

Though I do not profess giving many dates, yet as I think it proper to give some and shall of course make choice of those which it is most necessary for the reader to know, I think it right to inform him that her letter to the King was dated on the 6th of May[19]. The crimes and cruelties of this prince, were too numerous to be mentioned, (as this history I trust has fully shown), and nothing can be said in his vindication, but that his abolishing religious houses and leaving them to the ruinous depredations of time has been of infinite use to the landscape of England[20] in general, which probably was a principal motive for his doing it, since otherwise why should a man who was of no religion himself be at so much trouble to abolish one which had for ages been established in the kingdom?

His Majesty's fifth wife was the Duke of Norfolk's niece who, though universally acquitted of the crimes for which she was beheaded, has been by many people supposed to have led an abandoned life before her marriage[21] – of this however I have many doubts, since she was a relation of that noble Duke of Norfolk who was so warm in the Queen of Scotland's cause, and who at last fell a victim to it. The King's last wife contrived to survive him, but with difficulty affected it[22]. He was succeeded by his only son Edward.

Edward the Sixth

As this prince was only nine years old at the time of his father's death, he was considered by many people as too young to govern, and the late king happening to be of the same opinion, his mother's brother, the Duke of Somerset, was chosen Protector of the Realm during his minority[23]. This man was, on the whole, of a very amiable character, and is somewhat of a favourite with me, though I would by no means pretend to affirm that he was equal to those first of men Robert

Earl of Essex, Delamere, or Gilpin[24]. He was beheaded, of which he might with reason have been proud, had he known that such was the death of Mary Queen of Scotland; but as it was impossible that he should be conscious of what had never happened, it does not appear that he felt particularly delighted with the manner of ~~his death~~ it.

After his decease the Duke of Northumberland had the care of the King and the kingdom, and performed his trust of both so well that the King died and the kingdom was left to his daughter-in-law the Lady Jane Grey, who has been already mentioned as reading Greek. Whether she really understood that language or whether such a study proceeded only from an excess of ~~cockylorum~~[25] vanity for which I believe she was always rather remarkable, is uncertain. Whatever might be the cause, she preserved the same appearance of knowledge, and contempt of what was generally esteemed pleasure, during the whole of her life, for she declared herself displeased with being appointed Queen, and while conducting to the scaffold, she wrote a sentence in Latin and another in Greek on seeing the dead body of her husband accidentally passing that way[26].

Mary

This woman had the good luck of being advanced to the throne of England, in spite of the superior pretensions, merit, and *beauty* of her cousins Mary Queen of Scotland and Jane Grey. Nor can I pity the kingdom for the misfortunes they experienced during her reign, since they fully deserved them, for having allowed her to succeed her brother – which was a double piece of folly, since they might have foreseen that as she died without children, she would be succeeded by that disgrace to humanity, that pest of society, Elizabeth.

Many were the people who fell martyrs to the protestant religion during her reign; I suppose not fewer than a dozen[27]. She married Philip King of Spain who in her sister's reign was famous for building Armadas. She died without issue, and then the dreadful moment came in which the destroyer of all comfort, the deceitful betrayer of trust reposed in her, and the murderess of her cousin succeeded to the Throne.–

Elizabeth

It was the peculiar misfortune of this woman to have bad ministers – since wicked as she herself was, she could not have committed such extensive mischief, had not these vile and abandoned men connived at, and encouraged her in her crimes. I know that it has by many people been asserted and believed that Lord Burleigh, Sir Francis Walsingham[28], and the rest of those who filled the chief offices of State were deserving, experienced, and able ministers. But oh! how blinded such writers and such readers must be to true merit, to merit despised, neglected and defamed, if they can persist in such opinions when they reflect that these men, these boasted men were such scandals to their country and their sex as to allow and assist their Queen in confining for the space of nineteen years, a *woman* who if the the claims of relationship and merit were of no avail, yet as a queen, and as one who condescended to place confidence in her, had every reason to expect assistance and protection; and at length in allowing Elizabeth to bring this amiable woman to an untimely, unmerited, and scandalous death.

Can anyone, if he reflects but for a moment on this blot, this everlasting blot upon their understanding and their character, allow any praise to Lord Burleigh or Sir Francis Walsingham? Oh! what must this bewitching princess whose only friend was then the Duke of Norfolk, and whose only ones now [are] Mr. Whitaker, Mrs. Lefroy, Mrs. Knight and myself[29], who was abandoned by her son, confined by her cousin, abused, reproached and vilified by all, what must not her most noble mind have suffered when informed that Elizabeth had given orders for her death!

Yet she bore it with a most unshaken fortitude, firm in her mind; constant in her religion; and prepared herself to meet the cruel fate to which she was doomed, with a magnanimity that would alone proceed from conscious innocence. And yet, could you reader, have believed it possible that some hardened and zealous Protestants have even abused her for that steadfastness in the Catholic Religion which reflected on her so much credit? But this is a striking proof of *their* narrow souls and prejudiced judgments who accuse her. She was executed in the Great Hall at Fortheringay Castle (sacred place!) in North on Wednesday the 8th of February, 1586 – to the everlasting reproach of Elizabeth, her ministers, and of England in general.

It may not be unnecessary before I entirely conclude my account of this ill-fated queen, to observe that she had been accused of several crimes during the time of her reigning in Scotland, of which I now most seriously do assure my reader that she was entirely innocent; having never been guilty of anything more than imprudencies into which she was betrayed by the openness of her heart, her youth, and her education. Having I trust by this assurance entirely done away every suspicion and every doubt which might have arisen in the reader's mind, from what other historians have written of her[30], I shall proceed to mention the remaining events that marked Elizabeth's reign.

It was about this time that Sir Francis Drake the first English navigator who sailed round the world, lived, to be the ornament of his country and his profession. Yet great as he was, and justly celebrated as a sailor, I cannot help foreseeing that he will be equaled in this or the next century by one who though now but young, already promises to answer all the ardent and sanguine expectations of his relations and friends[31], amongst whom I may class the amiable lady to whom this work is dedicated, and my no less amiable self.

Though of a different profession, and shining in a different sphere of life, yet equally conspicuous in the character of an *earl*, as Drake was in that of a *sailor*, was Robert Devereux, Lord Essex. This unfortunate young man was not unlike in character to that equally unfortunate one *Frederic Delamere*. The simile may be carried still farther, and Elizabeth, the torment of Essex, may be compared to the Emmeline of Delamere[32]. It would be endless to recount the misfortunes of this noble and gallant Earl. It is sufficient to say that he was beheaded on the 25th of February, after having been Lord Lieutenant of Ireland, after having clapped his hand on his sword, and after performing many other services to his country. Elizabeth did not long survive his loss, and died so miserable that, were it not an injury to the memory of Mary, I should pity her.

James the First

Though this king had some faults, among which and as the most principal, was his allowing his mother's death, yet considered on the whole I cannot help liking him. He married Anne of Denmark, and had several children; fortunately for him his eldest son, Prince Henry, died before his father or he might have experienced the evils which befell his unfortunate brother[33].

As I am myself partial to the Roman Catholic religion[34], it is with infinite regret that I am obliged to blame the behaviour of any member of it: yet truth being I think very excusable in an historian, I am necessitated to say that in this reign the Roman Catholics of England did not behave like gentlemen to the Protestants. Their behaviour indeed to the Royal Family and both Houses of Parliament might justly be considered by them as very uncivil, and even Sir Henry Percy though certainly the best bred man of the party, had none of that general politeness which is so universally pleasing, as his attentions were entirely confined to Lord Mounteagle[35].

Sir Walter Raleigh flourished in this and the preceding reign, and is by many people held in great veneration and respect – but, as he was an enemy of the noble Essex[36], I have nothing to say in praise of him, and must refer all those who may wish to be acquainted with the particulars of his life, to Mr. Sheridan's play of *The Critic*[37], where they will find many interesting anecdotes as well of him as of his friend Sir Christopher Hatton[38]. – His Majesty was of that amiable disposition which inclines to friendship, and in such points was possessed of a keener penetration[39] in discovering merit than many other people.

I once heard an excellent charade on a carpet, of which the subject I am now on reminds me, and as I think it may afford my readers some amusement to *find it out*, I shall here take the liberty of presenting it to them:

> CHARADE: My first is what my second was to
> King James the 1st, and you tread on my whole[39].

The principal favourites of his Majesty were Carr, who was afterwards created Earl of Somerset and whose name perhaps may have some share in the above mentioned charade, and George Villiers afterwards Duke of Buckingham[40]. On his Majesty's death, he was succeeded by his son Charles.

Charles the First

This amiable monarch seems born to have suffered misfortunes equal to those of his lovely grandmother; misfortunes which he could not deserve since he was her descendant. Never certainly were there before so many detestable characters at one time in England as in this period of its history; never were amiable men so scarce. The number of them throughout the whole kingdom amounting only to *five*, besides the inhabitants of Oxford, who were always loyal to their King and faithful to his interests. The names of this noble five who never forgot the duty of the subject, or swerved from their attachment to his Majesty, were as follows – the King himself, ever steadfast in his own support – Archbishop Laud, Earl of Strafford, Viscount Faulkland and Duke of Ormond, who were scarcely less strenuous or zealous in the cause.

While the *villains* of the time would make too long a list to be written or read; I shall therefore content myself with mentioning the leaders of the gang. Cromwell, Fairfax, Hampden, and Pym may be ~~all~~ considered as the original causers of all the disturbances, distresses, and civil wars in which England for many years was embroiled[41]. In this reign, as well as in that of Elizabeth, I am obliged in spite of my attachment to the Scotch, to consider them as equally guilty with the generality of the English, since they dared to think differently from their sovereign, to forget the adoration which as *Stuarts* it was their duty to pay them, to rebel against, dethrone and imprison the unfortunate Mary; to oppose, to deceive, and to sell the no less unfortunate Charles.

The events of this monarch's reign are too numerous for my pen, and indeed the recital of any events (except what I make myself) is ~~tedious~~ uninteresting to me; my principal reason for undertaking the History of England being to prove the innocence of the Queen of Scotland, which I flatter myself with having effectually done, and to abuse Elizabeth, though I am rather fearful of having fallen short in the latter part of my scheme. – As therefore it is not my intention to give any particular account of the distresses into which this King was involved through the misconduct and cruelty of his Parliament, I shall satisfy myself with vindicating him from the reproach of arbitrary and tyrannical government with which he has often been charged. This, I feel, is not difficult to be done, for with one argument I am certain of satisfying every sensible and well disposed person whose opinions have been properly guided by a good education – and this argument is that he was a *Stuart*.

Finis

Saturday Nov: 26th 1791.

Notes

1. Historians, of course, generally claim to be impartial, unprejudiced and authoritative. Austen turns this on its head. In the preface to his *History*, Goldsmith expresses the confident expectation that "the reader will admit my impartiality," to which Austen responded by writing in the margin, "Oh! Dr. Goldsmith Thou art as partial an Historian as myself!"

2. "Miss Austen": Each of the portraits (with the presumably accidental exception of Henry VIII) is signed "C E Austen pinx [i.e. painted]." It has been convincingly argued by Annette Upfal and Christine Alexander that "seven (possibly eight)" of the portraits are based upon family members and acquaintances. Using her own brothers gives the following identifications: James I = James; Edward VI = Edward; and Henry V = Henry. Two more controversial identifications are: Mary Queen of Scots = Jane; Elizabeth I = Mrs. Austen-Leigh. These two portraits are placed at the bottom of a page: Elizabeth on the left and Mary on the right. The two monarchs face each other in confrontation, and contrast in every possible way, Mary being both beautiful and elegantly dressed and Elizabeth being a grotesquely ugly caricature (perhaps of a witch or an evil step-mother) in both her person and her dress. In *Jane Austen's "The History of England" & Cassandra's Portraits* (2009), Upfal and Alexander use this identification to question the conventional view of Jane's happy childhood and to suggest that her relationship with her mother was more antagonistic that it has been presented as being.

3. Richard II (1367-1400) reigned from 1377 until he was deposed and replaced by Henry Bolingbrook in 1399. Richard was imprisoned first in the Tower of London and then in Pontefract Castle where he died (or was murdered).

4. Sir William Gascoigne (c.1350-1419) was King Henry IV's Chief Justice. The King's son, Prince Hal, had a wild reputation and he is said to have resisted when Gascoigne tried to arrest him. Note that Austen gets a great deal of her 'history' from Shakespeare's plays fully aware that Shakespeare took artistic license with the facts as he found them in the histories of his day.

5. Sir John Oldcastle, Lord Cobham, (?-1417) was an English Lollard convicted of heresy who led a rebellion against the King. The reason for his execution is rather important (because it involved objections to the Church of Rome which would shortly lead to the Protestant Reformation and the resulting Wars of Religion throughout Europe) which is why Austen pretends to have forgotten it.

6. The Battle of Agincourt (October 25th, 1415) was a major English victory in the Hundred Years' War with France. It did not, however, achieve anything lasting for the English.

7. The Wars of the Roses (1455-1485) were a dynastic conflict between the House of Lancaster (the red rose) and the House of York (the white rose). They originated in the weak rule and mental infirmity of Henry VI who came to the throne in 1422 when he was only one year old, ruled in person from the age of sixteen, and suffered a mental breakdown in 1453. The wars only ended with the victory of Richard of Richmond (a Lancastrian) over Richard III (a Yorkist) at Bosworth Field in 1485.

8. Austen's implication is that this is precisely what historians do – despite their assertions to the contrary. Austen openly champions the Yorkists over

the Lancastrians in the Wars of the Roses because the Lancastrians won, in the person of Henry Tudor who became Henry VII, the first of the Tudors whom Austen hated because she favored the Stuarts.

9. Joan of Arc, also known as The Maid of Orléans (c.1412-1431), rallied French forces in the Hundred Years' War. Captured, she was tried and burned for heresy.

10. Edward IV had ten children by Elizabeth Woodville, but they were declared illegitimate in order to clear the way for Edward's brother Richard's claim to the throne. Jane Shore was only one of several mistresses.

11. Edward V (1470-c.1483) and his brother Richard of Shrewsbury, Duke of York (1473-c.1483) were the sons of Edward IV. It is generally believed that Richard III had them murdered in the Tower of London. In 1767, Horace Walpole questioned Richard III's guilt over the murder of the two Princes in the Tower. Austen appears to have left room for a portrait, but after the text. (The other portraits are all after the monarch's name.)

12. Richard married Anne Neville (1456-1485) the widow of Edward, Prince of Wales, the son of Henry VI. The marriage probably took place in 1472. She died a natural death.

13. Lambert Simnel (c. 1477-1525) claimed to be Richard's younger brother Edward.

14. Mary Stuart, Queen of Scots (1542-1587), was the daughter of Mary of Guise (1515-1560) and James V, King of Scotland. In 1787, John Whitaker published *Mary Queen of Scots Vindicated* a contrarian history that sought to clear Mary of the various crimes for which she has traditionally be held to be guilty.

15. Lady Jane Grey (c.1537-1554) would become the "Nine Days' Queen" (July 10th to 19th, 1553) having been proclaimed queen in an attempt to prevent the succession of the Catholic Mary. Queen Mary eventually had her and her husband executed.

16. Perkin Warbeck (c.1474-1499) claimed to be the murdered Richard of Shrewsbury, Duke of York. Both he and Lambert Simnel were figureheads in unsuccessful risings against Henry VII. Warbeck was executed and Simnel (who had never posed a real threat to Henry VII) was relegated to the royal kitchen.

17. Austen encapsulates the entire English Reformation in three incidents: the result of Wolsey's failure to get the Pope to give Henry a dispensation to end his marriage to Catherine; the consequences for the state religion of England; and the reason for Henry's desire to divorce Catherine – his infatuation with Anne.

18. Anne Boleyn (c.1501-1536) was found guilty of committing adultery and incest and beheaded in May, 1536. She was almost certainly innocent of the charges against her which were a pretext to allow Henry to marry Jane Seymour.

19. The author obviously does not think it necessary for the reader to know

the year, just the day and the month.

20. William Gilpin described Tintern Abbey as "a very inchanting piece of ruin. Nature has now made it her own. Time has worn off all traces of the rule: it has blunted the sharp edges of the chisel; and broken the regularity of opposing parts" (*Observations on the River Wye*, 1782). Ruins greatly added to picturesque beauty in Gilpin's view.

21. Catherine Howard (c.1523-1542) was found guilty of committing adultery and beheaded in February 1542. Her promiscuity before her marriage to Henry was used against her in her trial. Unlike Anne, she was almost certainly guilty of the charges against her, though she strongly asserted her innocence.

22. Catherine Parr (1512-1548) outlived Henry by only a year – hence she "with difficulty affected it."

23. Edward Seymour, Duke of Somerset (1500–1552), Edward's first Protector, was overthrown and executed in January 1552.

24. Robert Devereux, Earl of Essex (1565-1601) was executed for treason against Elizabeth I. Delamere is the fictional hero of *Emmeline, The Orphan of the Castle* (1788) by Charlotte Turner Smith (1749-1806). William Gilpin (1724-1804) has already been mentioned.

25. "cockylorum": That is, 'cockalorum' meaning 'a self-important little man,' or in this case young woman.

26. Jane Grey and her husband, Guildford Dudley, were executed on February 12th, 1554. A wagon carrying Dudley's body did pass before the window of her cell before Jane was taken for execution, though that can hardly have been accidental. Goldsmith's *History* records Jane Grey as having written three sentences about it, one in Greek, one in Latin and one in English.

27. Mary, a devout Catholic, attempted to undo her father's Reformation of the Church. In fact, about 275 Protestants were executed for heresy between 1555 and 1558. Mary was given the nickname 'Bloody Mary.'

28. William Cecil, Lord Burleigh (1520-1598) was Elizabeth's most important minister for most of her reign; Sir Francis Walsingham (c.1532-1590) was the minister responsible for Mary Queen of Scots's trial and execution. Austen's view of Elizabeth and her ministers is directly opposite to the position taken by Goldsmith.

29. John Whittaker (1735-1808) was the author of *Mary Queen of Scots Vindicated* (1787). Austen adds the names of herself and two friends.

30. Mary is generally supposed to have conspired in the murder of her second husband, Henry Stuart, Lord Darnley. She also conspired against Elizabeth I while imprisoned in England.

31. Sir Francis Drake became the first Englishman to circumnavigate the earth (1577–1580). Austen humorously refers to her brother Francis who had entered the Royal Naval Academy in April 1786. Francis became Admiral of the Fleet and was knighted, so her prediction was not far wrong.

32. *Emmeline, The Orphan of the Castle* (1788) by Charlotte Turner Smith (1749-1806) tells the story of Lord Delamere's tragically unfulfilled love for

Emmeline who refuses to marry him.

33. James VI of Scotland and I of England (1566-1625) married Anne of Denmark (1574-1619) in 1589. Their eldest son, Henry Frederick, died of typhoid fever in 1612. Thus, his brother, Charles, succeeded.

34. A very good joke, since Austen was the daughter of an Anglican minister! A pro-Catholic perspective also goes against all current histories including Goldsmith's.

35. In 1605, the Gunpowder Plot aimed to kill the King in Parliament. Austen assumes that Thomas Percy (c.1560-1605), one of the conspirators, was the author of the anonymous letter to Lord Monteagle (1575-1622) warning him to stay away from Parliament that led to the discovery of the Plot and the arrest of the conspirators.

36. Sir Walter Raleigh (c.1554-1618) was Essex's bitter rival for the favor of Queen Elizabeth. Perhaps Austen is referring to the rumor that Raleigh stood at a window watching the execution Essex while smoking his pipe.

37. *The Critic: or, a Tragedy Rehearsed* by Richard Brinsley Sheridan (1751-1816), which premiered at Drury Lane Theatre in 1779, is based on George Villiers' satire *The Rehearsal*.

38. Sir Christopher Hatton (1540-1591) was Lord Chancellor of England under Elizabeth I. Until his death, he was Raleigh's main rival for the Queen's favor.

39. Readers who suspect the fifteen-year-old female author is making two jokes here on the subject of sodomy are quite correct. The answer to the charade is 'carpet': Sir Robert *Carr* (c.1587-1645) was James's *pet* (i.e. favorite, lover).

40. Robert Carr, Earl of Somerset and George Villiers, Duke of Buckingham (1592-1628) were two of James's favorites and (almost certainly) his lovers.

41. The English Civil War (1642–1651) between the Parliamentarians and the Royalists led to the defeat and eventual execution of King Charles I on January 30th, 1649. The pro-Royalist view that Austen takes of the conflict is consistent with her marginal comments in Goldsmith's *History*.

Commentary

In *A Memoir of Jane Austen and Other Family Recollections* (1870), James Edward Austen-Leigh makes the following statement about Austen's understanding of history:

> In history she followed the old guides – Goldsmith, Hume, and Robertson. Critical enquiry into the usually received statements of the old historians was scarcely begun … Historic characters lay before the reader's eyes in broad light or shade, not much broken up by details. The virtues of King Henry VIII were yet undiscovered, nor had much light been thrown on the inconsistencies of Queen Elizabeth; the one

was held to be an unmitigated tyrant, and an embodied Blue
Beard; the other a perfect model of wisdom and policy.

As so often, James's determination to present his aunt as conventional and unassuming in all things is simply at odds with the facts. In this case, of the three claims made in James's statement only that about Henry VIII is in any way consistent with Austen's spoof history; the claims that she (like her contemporaries) did not question the "received statements of the old historians" or that she saw Queen Elizabeth as "a perfect model of wisdom and policy" are entirely inconsistent with Austen's text.

Written when Austen was one week short of sixteen, her *History* makes fun of the standard histories of the time such as the six-volume *History of England* (1754-1762) by David Hume (1711-1776), and in particular the four-volume schoolroom text *History of England from the Earliest Times to the Death of George II* (1771) by Oliver Goldsmith (1730-1774). A copy of the latter Austen read at home in Steventon rectory and annotated with over one hundred marginal comments (particularly in volumes three and four). Freya Johnston points out that "Goldsmith's 1771 *History* was itself a compilation and an abridgement of earlier histories, chiefly of Hume's – and it was written with the express 'aim', as he wryly and perhaps wearily acknowledged, 'not to add to our present stock of history, but to contract it'. Austen's text is therefore, among other things, an extreme abridgement of an abridgement..." As an historian, Austen is even more dedicated than Goldsmith to cutting down the number of things that a reader needs to know since, as she readily acknowledges, she does not know these things herself and has no intention of taking the trouble to find them out.

Austen mockingly imitates the style and layout of textbook histories. The Austens' edition of Goldsmith's work includes miniatures of the monarch's heads by the Northumbrian wood engraver, Thomas Bewick (1753-1828), a feature parodied by Cassandra's entirely ahistoric portraits which depict monarchs as very ordinary men and women and generally rather unattractive ones at that. Some of these portraits were evidently based on family and friends. As sources, Austen cites works of fiction such as the plays of Shakespeare and Sheridan, the novel *Emmeline* (1788) by Charlotte Turner Smith, and the opinions of her family and friends, presenting them all as though she thought them reliable.

More fundamentally, Austen's text ridicules historians' pretensions to objectivity. Southam makes an important link with the fictional juvenilia explaining that "the heart of Jane Austen's criticism [is] that popularized history is as false to the nature of reality as the picture of life given in the sentimental novel, and perhaps more seriously false, for it purports to be dealing with the facts of great men and great events" (*Manuscripts* 29). On the title page to her work, Austen proudly announces herself as "a partial prejudiced and ignorant historian." This is in reaction to the claims of impartiality made throughout Goldsmith's history which concludes, "I hope that the reader will admit my impartiality." Evidently Austen was prepared to make no such admission. Goldsmith's critical assessment of James Edward Stuart (the Old Pretender) as showing, "pride ... want of perseverance ... attachment to the catholic religion" and being, "but a poor leader" drew the marginal comment, "Oh! Dr Goldsmith Thou art as partial an Historian as myself!"

A fundamental bias in the histories of her day that Austen identified is the marginalization of women. Natalie Tyler draws attention to the fact that:

> Catherine Morland, in *Northanger Abbey*, Austen's first mature novel, complains that histories are written by men and that they depict "the quarrels of popes and kings, with wars or pestilences, in every page; the men all so good for nothing and hardly any women at all..." Anne Elliot in *Persuasion*, Austen's last complete novel, repeats the lament: "Men have had every advantage of us [women] in telling their own story ... the pen has been in their hands. I will not allow books to prove any thing." ... Jane's history is full of women: not only the wives of each monarch, but Joan of Arc, Jane Shore, and Lady Jane Grey. (41)

In Austen's text, women feature as significant figures in English history: twenty-two women are named and thirty-four men. This is only one aspect of Austen taking the position of a contrarian: she is the advocate of every lost cause and heroic failure. This is most evident in her narrator's support of Joan of Arc, the Yorkists, Mary Queen of Scots, the Stuarts, and the Catholics, losers all and in her championing of Richard III, James I and Charles I, tyrants and/or inept rulers all. This approach is complemented by her highly critical accounts of Henry VIII and Elizabeth I, who are normally presented as successful monarchs. The aim throughout is to vindicate her favorites and vilify her enemies. Freya Johnston comments, "the narrator of the *History* is comically indifferent to evidence, the only authenticity to which she appeals being that of her own feelings, and the inherent nobility of the Stuart cause." By openly presenting her own history as special pleading, Austen is making the point that *all* history is so, despite the pretentions of its authors.

Austen is strongest in support of the Stuarts, "A Family," as she calls them in one of her marginal notes in Goldsmith's *History*, who "were always ill used, Betrayed or Neglected Whose Virtues are seldom allowed while their Errors are never forgotten." It is particularly notable that when she is writing about the way in which Mary Queen of Scots was treated during her life and by historians after her death, the comic tone which pervades the *History* disappears to be replaced by serious outrage.

Austen warns the reader, "N.B. There will be very few dates in this history." This is another cut at Goldsmith whose four-volume history contained just two dates – the exact number that Austen uses: 1399, the accession of Henry IV, and February 8th, 1586, the execution of Mary Queen of Scots'. (Anna Bullen's last letter to Henry VIII is dated on May 6th, but Austen neglects to give the year!). She adds before the first of these, which carefully does not include the year, the mischievous comment, "Though I do not profess giving many dates, yet I think it proper to give some and shall, of course, make choice of those which it is most necessary for the reader to know." In fact, the author's choice is merely capricious, reflecting her personal view of what is worth knowing.

[Dedication]

To Miss Cooper[1]

~~Madam~~ Cousin,

Conscious of the charming character which in every ~~county~~ country, and every clime in Christendom is cried, concerning you, with caution and care I commend to your charitable criticism this ~~short~~ clever collection of curious comments, which have been carefully culled, collected and classed by ~~her~~ your comical cousin

The Author.

A Collection of Letters

Letter the First from a mother to her friend.

My children begin now to claim all my attention in different manner ~~to~~ from that in which they have been used to receive it, as they are now arrived at that age when it is necessary for them in some measure to become conversant with the world. My Augusta is seventeen and her sister scarcely a twelvemonth younger. I flatter myself that their education has been such as will not disgrace their appearance in the world, and that *they* will not disgrace their education I have every reason to believe. Indeed they are sweet girls – sensible yet unaffected – accomplished yet easy – lively yet gentle. – As their progress in everything they have learnt has been always the same, I am willing to forget the difference of age, and to introduce them together into public[2]. This very evening is fixed on as their first entree into life, as we are to drink tea with Mrs. Cope and her daughter.

I am glad that we are to meet no one, for my girls' sake, as it would be awkward for them to enter too wide a circle on the very first day. But we shall proceed by degrees. – Tomorrow, Mr. Stanly's family will drink tea with us, and perhaps the Miss

Phillipses will meet them. On Tuesday, we shall pay morning visits. – On Wednesday, we are to dine at Westbrook. On Thursday, we have company at home. On Friday, we are to be at a private concert at Sir John Wynna's – and on Saturday, we expect Miss Dawson to call in the morning – which will complete my daughters' introduction into life. How they will bear so much dissipation, I cannot imagine; of their spirits I have no fear, I only dread their health.

This mighty affair is now happily over, and my girls *are out*. As the moment approached for our departure, you can have no idea how the sweet creatures trembled with fear and ~~apprehension~~ expectation. Before the carriage drove to the door, I called them into my dressing-room, and as soon as they were seated thus addressed them:

"My dear girls, the moment is now arrived when I am to reap the rewards of all my anxieties and labours towards you during your education. You are this evening to enter a world in which you will meet with many wonderful things; yet let me warn you against suffering yourselves to be meanly swayed by the follies and vices of others, for believe me my beloved children that if you do – I shall be very sorry for it."

They both assured me that they would ever remember my advice with gratitude, and follow it with ~~at~~ attention; that they were prepared to find a world full of things to amaze and to shock them, but that they trusted their behaviour would never give me reason to repent the watchful care with which I had presided over their infancy and formed their minds.–

"With such expectations and such intentions," cried I, "I can have nothing to fear from you – and can cheerfully conduct you to Mrs. Cope's without a fear of your being ~~contaminated~~ seduced by her example, or contaminated by her follies. Come, then my children," added I, "the carriage is driving to the door, and I will not a moment delay the happiness you are so impatient to enjoy."

When we arrived at Warleigh, poor Augusta could scarcely breathe, while Margaret was all life and rapture.

"The long-expected moment is now arrived," said she, "and we shall soon be in the world."–

In a few moments, we were in Mrs. Cope's parlour, where with her daughter she sate ready to receive us. I observed with delight the impression my children made on them. – They were, indeed, two sweet, elegant-looking girls, and though somewhat abashed from the peculiarity of their situation, yet there was an ease in their manners and address which could not fail of pleasing. – Imagine, my dear madam, how delighted I must have been in beholding as I did, how attentively they observed every object they saw, how disgusted with some things, how enchanted with others, how astonished at all! On the whole, however, they returned in raptures with the world, its inhabitants, and manners.

Yours Ever –

A. F.

Letter the Second from a young lady crossed in love to her friend

Why should this last disappointment hang so heavyily on my spirits? Why should I feel it more, why should it wound me deeper than those I have experienced before? Can it be that I have a greater affection for Willoughby than I had for his amiable predecessors? Or is it thant our feelings become more acute from being often wounded? I must suppose, my dear Belle, that this is the case, since I am not conscious of being more sincerely attached to Willoughby than I was to Neville, Fitzowen, or either of the Crawfords, for all of whom I once felt the most lasting affection that ever warmed a woman's heart. Tell me then, dear Belle, why I still sigh when I think of the faithless Edward [Willoughby], or why I weep when I behold his bride, for too surely this is the case. –

My friends are all alarmed for me; they fear my declining health; they lament my want of spirits; they dread the effects of both. In hopes of relieving my melancholy, by directing my thoughts to other objects, they have invited several of their friends to spend the Christmas with us. Lady Bridget Darkwood and her sister-in-law, Miss Jane, are expected on Friday; and Colonel Seaton's family will be with us next week. This is all most kindly meant in by my uncle and cousins; but what can the presence of a dozen indifferent people do to me, but weary and distress me? – I will not finish my letter till some of our visitors are arrived.

Friday evening. –

Lady Bridget came this morning, and with her, her sweet sister[-in-law] Miss Jane. – Although I have been acquainted with this charming woman above fifteen years, yet I never before observed how lovely she is. She is now about thirty-five, and in spite of sickness, sorrow and time, is more blooming than I ever saw a girl of seventeen. I was delighted with her the moment she entered the house, and she appeared equally pleased with me, attaching herself to me during the remainder of the day. There is something so sweet, so mild in her countenance, that she seems more than mortal. Her conversation is as bewitching as her appearance; I could not help telling her how much she engaged my admiration.–

"Oh! Miss Jane," said I – and stopped from an inability at the moment of expressing myself as I could wish – "Oh! Miss Jane," – I repeated – I could not think of words to suit my feelings. – She seemed waiting for my speech. – I was confused – distressed – my thoughts were bewildered – and I could only add – "How do you do?"

She saw and felt for my embarrassment and with admirable presence of mind relieved me from it by saying – "My dear Sophia, be not uneasy at having exposed yourself – I will turn the conversation without appearing to notice it."

Oh! how I loved her for her kindness!

"Do you ride as much as you used to do?" said she.–

"I am advised to ride by my physician. We have delightful rides round us; I have a charming horse, am uncommonly fond of the amusement," replied I, quite recovered from my confusion, "and, in short, I ride a great deal."

"You are in the right, my love," said she.

Then repeateding the following line which was an extempore and equally adapted to recommend both riding and candor –

"Ride where you may, be candid where you can[3]." She added, "I rode once, but it is many years ago." –

She spoke this in so low and tremulous a voice, that I was silent.–

Struck with her manner of speaking, I could make no reply.

"I have not ridden," continued she fixing her eyes on my face, "since I was married."

I was never so surprised.–

"Married, ma'am!" I repeated.

"You may well wear that look of astonishment," said she, "since what I have said must appear improbable to you. – Yet nothing is more true than that I once was married."

"Then why are you called Miss Jane?"

"I married, my Sophia, without the consent or knowledge of my father the late Admiral Annesley. It was therefore necessary to keep the secret from him and from everyone, till some fortunate opportunity might offer of revealing it. – Such an opportunity, alas! was but too soon given in the death of my dear Capt. Dashwood.–

"Pardon these tears," continued Miss Jane wiping ~~my~~ her eyes, "I owe them to my husband's memory. He fell, my Sophia, while fighting for his country in America[4] after a most happy union of seven years. – My children, two sweet boys and a girl, who had constantly resided with my father and me, passing with him and with every one, as the children of a brother (though I had ever been an only child) had as yet been the comforts of my life. But no sooner had I lost my Henry, than these sweet creatures fell sick and died. – Conceive, dear Sophia, what my feelings must have been when, as an aunt, I attended my children to their early grave. – My father did not survive them many weeks. – He died, poor good old man, happily ignorant to his last hour of my marriage[5]."

"But did not you own it, and assume his name at your husband's death?"

"No; I could not bring myself to do it; more especially when in my children I lost all inducement for doing it. Lady Bridget and yourself are the only persons who are in the knowledge of my having ever been either wife or mother. As I could not prevail on myself to take the name of Dashwood (a name which after my Henry's death I could never hear without emotion), and as I was conscious of having no right to that of Annesley, I dropped all thoughts of either[6], and have made it a point of bearing only my ~~Christin~~ Christian one since my father's death." She paused.–

"Oh! my dear Miss Jane," said I, "how infinitely am I obliged to you for so entertaining a story! You cannot think how it has diverted me! But have you quite done?"

"I have only to add, my dear Sophia, that my Henry's elder brother dying about the same time, Lady Bridget became a widow like myself, and as we had always loved each other in idea from the high character in which we had ever been spoken of, though we had never met, we determined to live together. We wrote to one another on the same subject by the same post, so exactly did our feeling and our actions coincide! We both eagerly embraced the proposals we gave and received of becoming one family, and have from that time lived together in the greatest affection."

"And is this all?" said I. "I hope you have not done."

"Indeed I have; and did you ever hear a story more pathetic?"

"I never did – and it is for that reason it pleases me so

much, for when one is unhappy nothing is so delightful to one's sensations as to hear of equal misery."

"Ah! but my Sophia why *are you* unhappy?"

"Have you not heard madam of Willoughby's marriage?"

"But my love why lament *his* perfidy, when you bore so well that of many young men before?"

"Ah! Madam, I was used to it then, but when Willoughby broke his engagements I had not been disappointed for half a year."

"Poor girl!" said Miss Jane.

Letter the Third from a young lady in distressed circumstances to her friend

A few days ago, I was at a private ball given by Mr. Ashburnham. As my mother never goes out, she entrusted me to the care of Lady Greville who did me the honour of calling for me in her way and of allowing me to sit forwards[7], which is a favour ~~for~~ about which I am very indifferent especially as I know it is considered as conferring a great obligation on me.

"So Miss Maria," said her Ladyship as she saw me advancing to the door of the carriage, "you seem very smart to night. – *My* poor girls will appear quite to disadvantage by *you*. – I only hope your mother may not have distressed herself to set *you* off[8]. Have you got a new gown on?"

"Yes ma'am," replied I with as much indifference as I could assume.

"Aye, and a fine one too I think" – feeling it, as by her permission I seated myself by her.

"I dare say it is all very smart. – But I must own, for you know I always speak my mind, that I think it was quite a needless piece of expense. – Why could not you have worn your old striped one? It is not my way to find fault with people because they are poor, ~~because~~ for I always think that they are more to be despised and pitied than blamed for it, especially if they cannot help it, but at the same time I must say that in my opinion your old striped gown would have been quite fine enough for its wearer – for to tell you the truth (I always speak my mind), I am very much afraid that one half of the people in the room will not know whether you have a gown on or not. – But I suppose you intend to make your fortune tonight[9]. – Well, the sooner the better; and I wish you success."

"Indeed, ma'am I have no such intention.–"

"Who ever heard a young lady own that she was a fortune-hunter?"

Miss Greville laughed, but I am sure ~~Fanny~~ Ellen[10] felt for me.

"Was your mother gone to bed before you left her?" said her Ladyship.

"Dear ma'am," said Ellen, "it is but nine o'clock."

"True Ellen, but candles cost money, and Mrs. Williams is too wise to be extravagant."

"She was just sitting down to supper ma'am."

"And what had she got for supper?"

"I did not observe."

"Bread and cheese, I suppose."

"I should never wish for a better supper," said Ellen.

"You have never any reason," replied her mother, "as a better is always provided for you."

Miss Greville[11] laughed excessively, as she constantly does at her mother's wit.

Such is the humiliating situation in which I am forced to appear while riding in her Ladyship's coach. – I dare not be impertinent, as my mother is always admonishing me to be humble and patient if I wish to make my way in the world. She insists on my accepting every invitation of Lady Greville, or you may be certain that I would never enter either her house or her coach with the disagreeable certainty I always have of being abused for my poverty while I am in them.–

When we arrived at Ashburnham, it was nearly ten o'clock, which was an hour and a half later than we were desired to be there; but Lady Greville is too fashionable (or fancies herself to be so) to be punctual. The dancing, however, was not begun as they waited for Miss Greville[12]. I had not been long in the room before I was engaged to dance by Mr. Bernard, but just as we were going to stand up, he recollected that his servant had got his white gloves, and immediately ran out to fetch them. In the meantime ~~Lady Greville~~ the dancing began, and Lady Greville in passing to another room went exactly before me. – She saw me and instantly stopping, said to me, though there were several people close to us:

"Hey day, Miss Maria! What cannot you get a partner? Poor young lady! I am afraid your new gown was put on for nothing. But do not despair; perhaps you may get a hop before the evening is over."

So saying, she passed on without hearing my repeated assurance of being engaged, and leaving me very much provoked at being so exposed before everyone. – Mr. Bernard, however, soon returned and by coming to me the moment he entered the room, and leading me to the dancers, my character, I hope, was cleared from the imputation Lady Greville had thrown on it, in the eyes of all the old ladies who had heard her speech.

I soon forgot all my vexations in the pleasure of dancing and of having the most agreeable partner in the room. As he is, moreover, heir to a very large estate, I could see that Lady Greville did not look very well pleased when she found who had been his choice. – She was determined to mortify me, and accordingly when we were sitting down between the dances, she came to me with more than her usual insulting importance attended by Miss Mason and said loud enough to be heard by half the people in the room:

"Pray Miss Maria, in what way of business was your grandfather? For Miss Mason and I cannot agree whether he was a grocer or a bookbinder[13]."

I saw that she wanted to mortify me, and was resolved if I possibly could to prevent her seeing that her scheme succeeded.

"Neither madam; he was a wine merchant."

"Aye, I knew he was in some such low way. – He broke[14] did not he?"

"I believe not ma'am."

"Did not he abscond?"

"I never heard that he did."

"At least he died insolvent?"

"I was never told so before."

"Why, was not your *father* as poor as a rat?"

"I fancy not ~~but your Ladyship knows best~~."

"Was not he in the King's Bench[15] once?"

"~~Just as your Ladyship chooses it is all the same to me.~~ I never saw him there."

She gave me *such* a look, and turned away in a great passion; while I was half delighted with myself for my impertinence, and half afraid of ~~having~~ being thought too ~~much so~~ saucy[16]. As Lady Greville was extremely angry with me, she took no further notice of me all the evening, and indeed had I been in favour I should have been equally neglected, as she was got into a party of great folks and she never speaks to me when she can to anyone else. Miss Greville was with her mother's party at supper, but Ellen preferred staying with the

Bernards and me. We had a very pleasant dance and, as Lady G— slept all the way home, I had a very comfortable ride.

The next day while we were at dinner, Lady Greville's coach stopped at the door, for that is the time of day she generally contrives it should. She sent in a message by the servant to say that "she should not get out but that Miss Maria must come to the coach-door, as she wanted to speak to her, and that she must make haste and come immediately.–"

"What an impertinent message mama!" said I.–

"Go Maria –" replied she. –

Accordingly, I went and was obliged to stand there at her Ladyship's pleasure though the wind was extremely high and very cold.

"Why I think, Miss Maria, you are not quite so smart as you ~~may~~ were last night. – But I did not come to examine your dress, but to tell you that you may dine with us the day after tomorrow. – Not tomorrow, remember, do not come tomorrow, for we expect Lord and Lady Clermont and Sir Thomas Stanley's family. – There will be no occasion for your being very fine, for I shan't send the carriage. – If it rains you may take an umbrella." – I could hardly help laughing at hearing her give me leave to keep myself dry. – "And pray remember to be in time, for I shan't wait. – I hate my victuals over-done. – But you need not come ~~for~~ before the time. – How does your mother do? She is at dinner is not she?"

"Yes ma'am, we were in the middle of dinner when your Ladyship came."

"I am afraid you find it very cold Maria," said Ellen.

"Yes, it is an horrible East wind," said her mother, "– I assure you I can hardly bear the window down. – But you are used to be blown about by the wind, Miss Maria, and that is what has made your complexion so rudely and coarse. You young ladies who cannot often ride in a carriage never mind what weather you trudge in, or how the wind shows your ~~ankles~~ legs. I would not have my girls stand out of doors as you do in such a day as this. But ~~you sort~~ ~~odd~~ ~~low~~ some sort of people have no feelings either of cold or delicacy. – Well, remember that we shall expect you on Thursday at five o'clock. – You must tell your maid to come for you at night. – There will be no Moon – and you will have an horrid walk home. – My complements to your mother. – ~~Drive on~~. I am afraid your dinner will be cold. – Drive on.–"

And away she went, leaving me in a great passion with her

as she always does.

Maria Williams.

Letter the Fourth from a young lady rather impertinent to her friend

We dined yesterday with Mr. Evelyn where we were introduced to a very agreeable looking girl, his cousin. I was extremely pleased with her appearance, for added to the charms of an engaging face, her manner and voice had something peculiarly interesting in them. So much so, that they inspired me with a great curiosity to know the history of her life, who were her parents, where she came from, and what had befallen her, for it was then only known that she was a relation of Mr. Evelyn, and that her name was Grenville.

In the evening, a favourable opportunity offered to me of attempting at least to know what I wished to know, for everyone played at cards but Mrs. Evelyn, my mother, Dr. Drayton, Miss Grenville and myself, and as the two former were engaged in a whispering conversation, and the Doctor fell asleep, we were of necessity obliged to entertain each other. This was what I wished, and being determined not to remain in ignorance for want of asking, I began the conversation in the following manner:

"Have you been long in Essex ma'am?"

"I arrived on Tuesday."

"You came from Derbyshire?"

"No, ma'am!" appearing surprised at my question. "From Suffolk."

You will think this a good dash of mine[17], my dear Mary, but you know that I am not wanting for impudence when I have any end in view.

"Are you pleased with the country Miss Grenville? Do you find it equal to the one you have left?"

"Much superior, ma'am, in point of beauty."

She sighed. I longed to know for why.

"But the face of any country, however beautiful," said I, "can be but a poor consolation for the loss of one's dearest friends."

She shook her head, as if she felt the truth of what I said. My curiosity was so much raised, that I was resolved at any rate to satisfy it.

"You regret having left Suffolk then Miss Grenville?"

"Indeed I do."

"You were born there I suppose?"

224

"Yes ma'am, I was and passed many happy years there.–"

"That is a great comfort," said I. "I hope, ma'am, that you never spent any unhappy one's there."

"Perfect felicity is not the property of mortals, and no one has a right to expect uninterrupted felicity happiness. – *Some* misfortunes I have certainly met with."

"*What* misfortunes, dear ma'am?" replied I, burning with impatience to know everything.

"*None*, ma'am, I hope that have been the effect of any willful fault in me."

"I dare say not, ma'am, and have no doubt but that any sufferings you may have experienced could arise only from the cruelties of relations or the errors of friends."

She sighed.–

"You seem unhappy, my dear Miss Grenville. – Is it in my power to soften your misfortunes?"

"*Your* power, ma'am," replied she extremely surprised. "It is in *no one's* power to make me happy."

She pronounced these words in so mournful and solemn an accent, that for some time I had not courage to reply. I was actually silenced. Could you have believed it Mary? I recovered myself, however, in a few moments and looking at her with all the affection I could:

"My dear Miss Grenville," said I, "you appear extremely young – and may probably stand in need of someone's advice whose regard for you, joined to superior age, perhaps superior judgment, might authorize her to give it. I am that person, and I now challenge you to accept the offer I make you of my confidence and friendship, in return to which I shall only ask for yours.–"

"You are extremely obliging ma'am," said she, "and I am highly flattered by your attention to me. – But I am in no difficulty, no doubt, no uncertainty of situation in which any advice can be wanted. Whenever I am, however," continued she, brightening into a complaisant smile, "I shall know where to apply."

I bowed, but felt a good deal mortified by such a repulse; still, however, I had not given up my point. I found that by the appearance of sentiment and friendship nothing was to be gained, and determined therefore to renew my attacks by questions and suppositions.

"Do you intend staying long in this part of England, Miss Grenville?"

"Yes ma'am, some time I believe."

"But how will Mr. and Mrs. Grenville bear your absence ~~during a long stay in Essex~~?"

"They are neither of them alive, ma'am."

This was an answer I did not expect. – I was quite silenced, and never felt so awkward in my life.–

Letter the Fifth from a young lady very much in love to her friend

My uncle gets more stingy, my aunt more particular, and I more in love every day. What shall we all be at this rate by the end of the year! I had this morning the happiness of receiving the following letter from my dear Musgrove.

Sackville Street[18]: January 7th

It is a month to day since I first beheld my lovely Henrietta, and the sacred anniversary must and shall be kept in a manner becoming the day – by writing to her. Never shall I forget the moment when her beauties first broke on my sight. – No time, as you well know, can erase it from my memory. It was at Lady Scudamore's. Happy Lady Scudamore to live within a mile of the divine Henrietta! When the lovely creature first entered the room, oh! what were my sensations? The sight of you was like the sight of a wonderful fine thing. I started. – I gazed at her with admiration. – She appeared every moment more charming, and the unfortunate Musgrove became a captive to your charms before I had time to look about me.

Yes madam, I had the happiness of adoring you, an happiness for which I cannot be too grateful.

"What," said he to himself, "is Musgrove allowed to die for Henrietta? Enviable mortal! And may he pine for her who is the object of universal admiration, who is adored by a Colonel, and toasted by a Baronet! Adorable Henrietta, how beautiful you are! I declare you are quite divine! You are more than mortal. You are an angel. You are Venus herself. In short, madam you are the prettiest girl I ever saw in my life – and her beauty is increased in her Musgrove's eyes, by permitting him to love her and allowing me to hope. And ah! Angelic Miss Henrietta, Heaven is my witness how ardently I do hope for the death of your villainous uncle and his abandoned wife, since my fair one will not consent to be mine till their decease has placed her in affluence above what my fortune can procure. – Though it is an improvable estate."–

Cruel Henrietta to persist in such a resolution! I am at present with my sister where I mean to continue till my own house which, though an excellent ~~house~~ one, is at present somewhat out of repair, is ready to receive me. Amiable princess of my heart farewell. – Of that heart which trembles while it signs itself Your most ardent admirer and devoted humble servant,

T. Musgrove.

~~May I hope to receive an answer to this e'er many days have tortured me with suspense! Any letter (post paid[19]) will be most welcome.~~

There is a pattern for a love-letter, Matilda! Did you ever read such a master-piece of writing? Such sense, such sentiment, such purity of thought, such flow of language, and such unfeigned love in one sheet? No, never I can answer for it, since a Musgrove is not to be met with by every girl. Oh! how I long to be with him! I intend to send him the following in answer to his letter tomorrow:

My dearest Musgrove—,

Words cannot express how happy your letter made me; I thought I should have cried for joy, for I love you better than anybody in the world. I think you the most amiable, and the handsomest man in England, and so to be sure you are. I never read so sweet a letter in my life. Do write me another just like it, and tell me you are in love with me in every other line. I quite die to see you. How shall we manage to see one another? For we are so much in love that we cannot live asunder.

Oh! my dear Musgrove, you cannot think how impatiently I wait for the death of my uncle and aunt. – If they will not die soon, I believe I shall run mad, for I get more in love with you every day of my life.

~~How fond we shall be of one another when we are married! Oh! do not you long for the time?~~ How happy your sister is to enjoy the pleasure of your company in her house, and how happy everybody in London must be because you are there.

I hope you will be so kind as to write to me again soon, for I never read such sweet letters as yours. I am, my dearest Musgrove, most truly and faithfully yours forever and ever

Henrietta Halton.

I hope he will like my answer; it is as good a one as I can write though nothing to his; indeed, I had always heard what a dab[20] he was at a love-letter. I saw him, you know, for the first time at Lady Scudamore's. – And when I saw her Ladyship afterwards she asked me how I liked her cousin Musgrove?

"Why upon my word," said I, "I think he is a very handsome young man."

"I am glad you think so," replied she, "for he is distractedly in love with you."

"Law! Lady Scudamore," said I, "how can you talk so ridiculously?"

"Nay, 'tis very true," answered she, "I assure you, for he was in love with you from the first moment he beheld you."

"I wish it may be true," said I, "for that is the only kind of love I would give a farthing for. – There is some sense in being in love at first sight."

"Well, I give you joy of your conquest," replied Lady Scudamore, "and I believe it to have been a very complete one; I am sure it is not a contemptible one, for my cousin is a charming young fellow, has seen a great deal of the world, and writes the best love-letters I ever read."

This made me very happy, and I was excessively pleased with my conquest. However, I thought it was ~~best~~ proper to give myself a few airs – so I said to her –

"This is all very pretty Lady Scudamore, but you know that we young ladies who are heiresses must not throw ourselves away upon men who have no fortune at all."

"My dear Miss Halton," said she, "I am as much convinced of that as you can be, and I do assure you that I should be the last person to encourage your marrying anyone who had not some pretensions to expect a fortune with you. Mr. Musgrove is so far from being poor that he has an estate of several hundreds an year[21] which is capable of great improvement, and an excellent house, though at present it is not quite in repair."

228

"If that is the case," replied I, "I have nothing more to say against him, and if, as you say, he is an informed young man and can write a good love-letter, I am sure I have no reason to find fault with him for admiring me, though perhaps I may not marry him for all that Lady Scudamore."

"You are certainly under no obligation to marry him," answered her Ladyship, "except that which love himself will dictate to you, for if I am not greatly mistaken you are at this very moment unknown to yourself, cherishing a most tender affection for him."

"Law, Lady Scudamore," replied I blushing, "how can you think of such a thing?"

"Because every look, every word betrays it," answered she. "Come, my dear Henrietta, consider me as a friend, and be sincere with me. – Do not you prefer Mr. Musgrove to any man of your acquaintance?"

"Pray do not ask me such questions, Lady Scudamore," said I turning away my head, "for it is not fit for me to answer them."

"Nay, my love," replied she, "now you confirm my suspicions. But why, Henrietta, should you be ashamed to own a well-placed love, or why refuse to confide in me?"

"I am not ashamed to own it," said I taking courage. "I do not refuse to confide in you or blush to say that I do love your cousin Mr. Musgrove, that I am sincerely attached to him, for it is no disgrace to love a handsome man. If he were plain, indeed, I might have had reason to be ashamed of a passion which must have been mean, since the object would have been unworthy. But with such a figure and face, and such beautiful hair as your cousin has, why should I blush to own that such superior merit has made an impression on me?"

"My sweet girl," said Lady Scudamore embracing me with great affection, "what a delicate way of thinking you have ~~on~~ in these matters, and what a quick discernment for one of your years! Oh! how I honour you for such noble sentiments!"

"Do you ma'am?" said I. "You are vastly obliging. But pray, Lady Scudamore, did your cousin himself tell you of his affection for me? I shall like him the better if he did, for what is a lover without a confidante?"

"Oh! my love," replied she, "you were born for each other. Every word you say more deeply convinces me that your minds are actuated by the invisible power of sympathy, for your opinions and sentiments so exactly coincide. Nay, the colour of your hair is not very different. Yes, my dear girl, the poor despairing Musgrove did reveal to me the story of his love. – Nor was I surprised at it. – I know not how it was, but I had a kind of presentiment that he *would* be in love with you."

"Well, but how did he break it to you?"

"It was not till after supper. We were sitting round the fire together talking on indifferent subjects, though to say the truth the conversation was chiefly on my side for he was thoughtful and silent, when on a sudden, he interrupted me in the midst of something I was saying, by exclaiming in a most theatrical tone –

"Yes I'm in love. I feel it now. And Henrietta Halton has undone me."

"Oh! What a sweet way," replied I, "of declaring his passion! To make such a couple of charming lines about me! What a pity it is that they are not in rhyme!"

"I am very glad you like it," answered she. "~~Indeed~~ To be sure, there was a great deal of taste in it. 'And are you in love with her, cousin?' said I. 'I am very sorry for it, for unexceptionable as you are in every respect, with a pretty estate capable of great improvements, and an excellent house though somewhat out of repair, yet who can hope to aspire with success to the adorable Henrietta who has had an offer from a Colonel and been toasted by a Baronet?'" –

"*That* I have–" cried I.

Lady Scudamore continued.

"'Ah dear cousin,' replied he, 'I am so well convinced of the little chance I can have of winning her who is adored by thousands, that I need no assurances of yours to make me more thoroughly so. Yet surely neither you [n]or the fair Henrietta herself will deny me the exquisite gratification of dying for her, of falling a victim to her charms. And when I am dead...'" – continued he –

"Oh Lady Scudamore," said I, wiping my eyes, "that such a sweet creature should talk of dying!"

"It is an affecting circumstance indeed," replied Lady Scudamore. "'When I am dead,' said he, 'let me be carried and lain at her feet, and perhaps she may not disdain to drop a pitying tear on my poor remains.'"

"Dear Lady Scudamore," interrupted I, "say no more on this affecting subject. I cannot bear it."

"Oh! how I admire the sweet sensibility of your soul, and, as I would not for worlds wound it too deeply, I will be silent."

"Pray go on." said I.

She did so.

"And then, added he, 'Ah! cousin, imagine what my transports will be when I feel the dear precious drops trickle on my face! Who would not die to haste such ecstasy! And when I am interred, may the divine Henrietta bless some happier youth with her affection. May he be as tenderly attached to her as the hapless Musgrove and while *he* crumbles to dust, may they live an example of ~~conjugal~~ felicity in the conjugal state!'"

Did you ever hear anything so pathetic? What a charming wish, to be lain at my feet when he was dead! Oh! what an exalted mind he must have to be capable of such a wish!

Lady Scudamore went on.

"'Ah! my dear cousin,' replied I to him, 'such noble behaviour as this, must melt the heart of any woman, however obdurate it may naturally be, and could the divine Henrietta but hear your generous wishes for her happiness, all gentle as is her mind, I have not a doubt but that she would pity your affection and endeavour to return it.'"

"'Oh! cousin,' answered he, 'do not endeavour to raise my hopes by such flattering assurances. No, I cannot hope to please this angel of a woman, and the only thing which remains for me to do, is to die.' 'True love is ever desponding,' replied I, 'but I, my dear ~~cousin~~ Tom, will give you even greater hopes of conquering this fair one's heart, than I have yet given you, by assuring you that I watched her with the strictest attention during the whole day, and could plainly discover that she cherishes in her bosom, though unknown to herself, a most tender affection for you.'"

"Dear Lady Scudamore," cried I. "This is more than I ~~never~~ knew!"

"Did not I say that it was unknown to yourself? 'I did not,' continued I to him, 'encourage you by saying this at first, that surprise might render the pleasure still greater.' 'No cousin,' replied he in a languid voice, 'nothing will convince me that I can have touched the heart of Henrietta Halton, and if you are deceived yourself, do not attempt deceiving me.' In short, my love, it was the work of some hours for me to persuade the poor despairing youth that you had really a preference for him; but when at last he could no longer deny the force of my arguments, or discredit what I told him, his transports, his raptures, his ecstasies are beyond my power to describe."

"Oh! the dear creature," cried I, "how passionately he loves me! But, dear Lady Scudamore, did you tell him that I was totally dependent on my uncle and aunt?"

"Yes, I told him everything."

"And what did he say?"

"He exclaimed with virulence against uncles and aunts; accused the laws of England for allowing ~~him~~ them to possess their estates when wanted by their nephews or nieces, and wished *he* were in the House of Commons, that he might reform the legislature, and rectify all its abuses."

"Oh! the sweet man! What a spirit he has!" said I.

"He could not flatter himself, he added, that the adorable Henrietta would condescend for his sake to resign those luxuries and that splendor to which she had been used, and accept only in exchange the comforts and elegancies which his limited income could afford her, even supposing that his house were in readiness to receive her. I told him that it could not be expected that she would, 'It would be doing her an injustice to suppose her capable of giving up the power she now possesses and so nobly uses of doing such extensive good to the poorer part of her fellow creatures, merely for the gratification of you and herself.'"

"To be sure," said I, "I *am* very charitable every now and then. ~~I gave away two pence this morning.~~ And what did Mr. Musgrove say to this?"

"He ~~said~~ replied that he was under a melancholy necessity of owning the truth of what I said, and that therefore, if he should be the happy creature destined ~~as~~ to be the husband of the beautiful Henrietta, he must bring himself to wait, however impatiently, for the fortunate day, when she might be freed from the power of worthless relations and able to bestow herself on him."

What a noble creature he is! Oh! Matilda what a fortunate one I am, who am to be his wife! My aunt is calling me to come and make the pies, so adieu my dear friend, and believe me yours etc—

H. Halton.

Finis

Notes

1. "Miss Cooper": In the spring of 1783, Jane (aged seven), Cassandra, and their cousin Jane Cooper were sent to Mrs. Cawley's school in Oxford. Because of a measles outbreak, Mrs. Cawley moved the school to Southampton but then there was an outbreak of typhus in that town. The three girls became very ill, and Mrs. Austen and Mrs. Cooper went together to

Southampton to rescue them. The girls recovered, but sadly Mrs. Cooper caught the disease and died. In the autumn of 1792, Cooper was staying at Steventon following the death of her father in August. In December, she married Captain Williams, so this dedication must predate that event.

2. "introduce them together into public": The idea of a young woman 'coming out' into society originally meant the she was old enough to be married and therefore ready to meet socially with eligible young men. Mary Wollstonecraft, in her *Rights of Woman*, termed this "to bring to market a marketable miss."

3. "'Ride where you may, be candid where you can'" is Austen's parody of the line, "Laugh where you *must*, be candid where you *can*" by Alexander Pope (1688-1744) in *An Essay on Man* (1732-1734).

4. "in America": This would have been in the War of Independence, 1775-1783.

5. "ignorant … of my marriage": It seems strange that Admiral Annesley did not recall that he had only ever had one child, a daughter, when he was presented with two children supposedly born to a son of his.

6. "I dropped all thoughts of either": The plot thickens: it now appears that Miss Jane is the illegitimate daughter of Admiral Annesley and that her 'marriage' to Capt. Dashwood might not have been legal.

7. "who did me … to sit forwards": Evidently it is Lady Greville who considers that she is conferring two honors upon Maria. The truth is, however, that taking Maria to the ball does not require Lady Greville to go out of her way at all, and that letting Maria sit in her carriage facing forward is a deliberate ploy to make Maria feel obliged to her (since facing in the direction one is going is much preferable to facing behind).

8. "to set *you* off": That is, spent too much money in dressing you up so attractively. Lady Greville is offended by Maria dressing above her station.

9. "make your fortune tonight": That is, get someone rich to propose to her.

10. "Ellen": In each place it occurs, the name "Ellen" replaces the deleted "Fanny."

11. "Miss Greville": There are two of Lady Greville's daughters in the carriage: Miss Greville is the elder and Ellen the younger.

12. "they waited for Miss Greville": Because of her high status, Miss Greville has the honor of the first dance. Thus, in being fashionably late, Lady Greville has willfully delayed everyone's pleasure.

13. "a grocer or a bookbinder": To be 'in trade' was to be below the rank of 'gentleman' and generally looked down upon. A wine merchant would be a superior sort of tradesman.

14. "He broke": That is, went bankrupt.

15. "the King's Bench": A debtors' prison in Southwark, London.

16. "too saucy": The exchange between Lady Greville and Maria obviously caused Austen some problems because she revised it heavily to get the balance right: Maria must appear spirited in defense of her father without

actually being rude.

17. "a good dash of mine": It seems that the writer suggested Derbyshire (a county roughly 150 miles from Suffolk) just to get a reaction from Miss Grenville.

18. "Sackville Street": A fashionable street in Central London.

19. "post-paid": At this time, the cost of a letter was paid by the person *receiving* the letter not by the person sending it. Postage stamps were not introduced until 1840.

20. "a dab": Short for 'dab hand' which means an expert, someone skilled. The origin of the expression is the use of a dab to apply ink to typeface in printing, an operation which needed a delicate and precise touch to get just the right amount of ink on the type.

21. "estate of several hundreds an year": A very small income! One suspects that the house so frequently referred to is in a very poor state of repair and the estate too.

Commentary

Southam writes that the "Collection of Letters" "mocks the tradition of the moral and didactic epistle, perfected by Richardson and subsequently used as an editorial device in the periodicals" – a device that was constantly parodied by *The Loiterer* (Baker ed. 33).

The comedy of the first letter rests on the contrast between the high seriousness with which the mother regards the "mighty affair" of her daughters' coming-out and the absolute triviality of the whole process: "their first entrée into life ... [their] introduction into life" turns out to involve nothing more than a series of conventional social calls on and by neighboring friends. Even more absurd is A.F's concern that her daughters will not be able to "bear so much dissipation," that they will "be meanly swayed by the follies and vices of others," and "seduced ... or contaminated" by what they meet in the adult world. Fortunately, the girls' education has sufficiently inoculated them, and they avoid contamination while they take tea.

The second letter, written by Sophia to a confidential friend, seems to illustrate the aphorism that 'misery seeks company.' The writer is (or rather, *imagines* herself to be) in deep melancholy about having been jilted by the latest of a string of lovers. She seeks out Miss Jane with whom she feels an instinctive sympathy and the two fall into a confidential conversation. Miss Jane's causes of sorrow are many: her secret marriage, the death of her husband and three children, the death of her father, and her own illegitimacy. Hearing of her friend's greater suffering certainly diverts Sophia from her own sorrow. She explains, "'Oh! my dear Miss Jane ... how infinitely am I obliged to you for so entertaining a story! You cannot think how it has diverted me! ... [W]hen one is unhappy nothing is so delightful to one's sensations as to hear of equal misery.'" This statement is wildly inappropriate. The truth is that neither Sophia nor Miss Jane has any capacity for empathy nor any genuine concern for the sufferings of others. Each one is entirely wrapped up in her own feelings.

Critics identify Lady Greville in "Letter the Third" as a prototype of Lady Catherine de Bourgh in *Pride and Prejudice*. Both women are terrible snobs who have an exaggerated view of their own preeminent position in local society and a determination to keep those of inferior family in their place. In her letter, Maria Williams details a number of insults she has received lately from Lady Greville who seems determined to "mortify" (humiliate) the young woman whom she considers to be dressing and acting above her station. Maria, however, has much of Elizabeth Bennet's spirit, and defends herself and her family whenever she can; she is at once "delighted with myself for my impertinence, and half afraid of being thought too saucy." In another incident that prefigures *Pride and Prejudice*, Lady Greville attempts to detach Maria from her handsome dancing partner, Mr. Bernard, by speaking "loud enough to be heard by half the people in the room" of Maria's father having been in trade and in prison for bankruptcy (the former being true and the latter, apparently, a malicious invention).

The very next day, Lady Greville calls in her carriage and, entirely indifferent to the cold and to the fact that Maria's interrupted dinner is getting cold on the table, keeps the young woman talking outside. The incident recurs in *Pride and Prejudice* when Miss De Bough is, in Elizabeth's opinion, "abominably rude to keep Charlotte out of doors in all this wind" (Ch. 28). Ignoring the hurt that she has caused Maria the previous evening, Lady Greville invites her to dine at the hall on a day when she has no other visitors – yet another incident that prefigures the behavior of Lady Catherine. What makes this short narrative important is that Austen's satire is here against how *people* behave rather than against how *characters* behave in novels. In addition, the story contains at least one character (two if one includes the shadowy Ellen) who has *real* sensibility and with whom the reader can entirely identify and sympathize.

The fourth letter is from a "rather impertinent" young woman who gets her comeuppance for prying too deeply into the sorrows of Miss Grenville. The unnamed writer tells her friend of her efforts to gain the confidence of "a very agreeable looking girl" who has just come into Essex to stay with her cousin, Mr. Evelyn. In this, the writer is assertive to the point of rudeness, but she takes pride in her determination "not to remain in ignorance for want of asking." The result is a parody of a woman seeking the instant female friendship so common in novels of sensibility – friendships which often begin with a request that the new friend should tell the entire history of her life and adventures. Despite Miss Grenville's attempts to discourage her advances, the narrator perseveres until Miss Grenville tells her that she has left Suffolk because of the death of her parents. This sudden intrusion of genuine sorrow upon the false sensibility of the writer leaves her rightly embarrassed. She concludes her letter, "This was an answer I did not expect. – I was quite silenced, and never felt so awkward in my life. –" A. Walton Litz concludes, "The climax ... is shocking ... and the impact is a product of the realistic social situation Jane Austen has so skillfully established ... [T]he death of Miss Grenville's parents is represented realistically, her grief is like our own..." (30). The unnamed "impertinent" young woman richly deserves the discomfort she feels when real grief intrudes into her false world of sensibility.

The writer of the fifth letter is Henrietta Halton, a beautiful young woman who is "very much in love" with Tom Musgrove, whom she appears to have met only once and never to have spoken with directly. Her love, however, makes her blind to faults in her lover of which the reader is only too keenly aware. Henrietta shares with her confidential female friend the full text of Musgrove's latest letter which she describes as "a pattern for a love-letter ... a master-piece of writing ... Such sense, such sentiment, such purity of thought, such flow of language, and such unfeigned love in one sheet." This is hardly an accurate description of the formulaic letter presented in which Musgrove describes in very conventional terms falling in love with Henrietta at first sight and wanting only to be allowed to die for her. Henrietta, however, is delighted by the letter and begs for a second; she is in love with being in love.

In her love-blindness, Henrietta fails to notice certain troubling features about her lover (which prefigures Elizabeth Bennet's initial blind infatuation with Mr. Wickham). For example, he ends his letter by requesting a reply from Henrietta "post-paid," which suggests that he is short of money. This is confirmed by Lady Scudamore who assures Henrietta that "Mr. Musgrove is so far from being poor that he has an estate of several hundreds an year which is capable of great improvement, and an excellent house, though at present it is not quite in repair." The implication is clear to the reader: Tom Musgrove is a fortune-hunter who is attracted to Henrietta at least as much by the size of her inheritance (although she will not inherit until her uncle and aunt die) as he is by the beauty of her person.

Henrietta is too steeped in the values of sensibility to suspect what is going on. She is as conventional as Musgrove, threatening to "run mad" if her aunt and uncle do not "die soon." Regarding Lady Scudamore as her intimate friend, Henrietta does not see how she is being manipulated. With that reversal of morality typical of persons of superior sensibility in the juvenilia, Henrietta sees the villains of the piece as her aunt and uncle who keep her from her inheritance (and therefore from being free to marry a man without wealth) because they refuse to die. Lady Scudamore describes Musgrove's reaction to being told of the problem with Henrietta's inheritance, "'He exclaimed with virulence against uncles and aunts; accused the laws of England for allowing them to possess their estates when wanted by their nephews or nieces, and wished he were in the House of Commons, that he might reform the legislature, and rectify all its abuses.'" To the reader, this is empty nonsense, but Henrietta responds, "'Oh! the sweet man! What a spirit he has!'"

Henrietta is called back into the real world by her aunt calling her "to come and make the pies." Thus her letter ends in bathos (i.e., anticlimax created by an unintentional change in mood from the sublime to the trivial or ridiculous).

Scraps

To Miss Fanny Catherine Austen[1]
My dear Niece,
As I am prevented by the great distance between Rowling and Steventon[2] from superintending your education myself, the care of which will probably on that account devolve on your father and mother[3], I think it is my particular duty to prevent your feeling, as much as possible, the want of my personal instructions, by addressing to you on paper my opinions and admonitions on the conduct of young women, which you will find expressed in the following pages. – I am, my dear niece,
Your affectionate Aunt[4],
The Author.

The Female Philosopher: a letter

My Dear Louisa,

Your friend Mr. Millar called upon us yesterday in his way to Bath, whither he is going for his health; two of his daughters were with him, but the eldest and the three boys are with their mother in Sussex. Though you have often told me that Miss Millar was remarkably handsome, you never mentioned anything of her sisters' beauty; yet they are certainly extremely pretty. I'll give you their description. – Julia is eighteen, with a countenance in which modesty, sense and dignity are happily blended; she has a form which at once presents you with grace, elegance and symmetry. Charlotte, who is just sixteen, is shorter than her sister, and though her figure cannot boast the easy dignity of Julia's, yet it has a pleasing plumpness which is in a different way as ~~pleasing~~ estimable. She is fair and her face is expressive sometimes of softness the most bewitching, and at others of vivacity the most striking. She appears to have infinite wit and a good humour unalterable; her conversation during the half hour they set with us, was replete with humourous sallies, *bon mots* and repartees; while the sensible, the amiable Julia uttered sentiments of morality worthy of a heart like her own.

Mr. Millar appeared to answer the character I had always received of him. My father met him with that look of love, that social [hand]shake, and cordial kiss which marked his gladness at beholding an old and valued friend from whom, through various circumstances, he had been separated nearly twenty years. Mr. Millar observed (and very justly too) that many events had befallen each during that interval of time, which gave occasion to the lovely Julia for making most sensible reflections on the many changes in their situation which so long a period had occasioned, on the advantages of some, and the disadvantages of others.

From this subject she made a short digression to the instability of human pleasures and the uncertainty of their duration, which led her to observe that all earthly joys must be imperfect. She was proceeding to illustrate this doctrine by examples from the lives of great men when the carriage came to the door and the amiable moralist with her father and sister was obliged to depart; but not without a promise of spending five or six months with us[5] on their return. We, of course, mentioned you, and I assure you that ample justice was done to your merits by all.

"Louisa Clarke," said I, "is in general a very pleasant girl, yet sometimes her good humour is clouded by peevishness, envy and spite. She neither wants understanding nor is without some pretensions to beauty, but these are so very trifling, that the value she sets on her personal charms, and the adoration she expects them to be offered, are at once a striking example of her vanity, her pride, and her folly."

So said I, and to my opinion everyone added weight by the concurrence of their own.

Your affectionate,
Arabella Smythe.

The First Act of a Comedy

Characters

POPGUN	MARIA
CHARLES	PISTOLETTA
POSTILION	HOSTESS
CHORUS of PLOUGHBOYS	COOK
And STREPHON	And CHLOE

238

Scene – An Inn

Enter HOSTESS, CHARLES, MARIA, and COOK.

HOSTESS to MARIA: If the gentry in the Lion[6] should want beds, show them number nine.

MARIA: Yes Mistress.

Exit MARIA.

HOSTESS to COOK*:* If their honours in the Moon ask for the bill of fare, give it them.

COOK*:* I wull, I wull.

Exit COOK.

HOSTESS to CHARLES: If their ladyships in the Sun ring their bell – answer it.

CHARLES: Yes Madam.

Exeunt severally.

SCENE CHANGES TO THE MOON, and discovers Popgun and Pistoletta.

PISTOLETTA: Pray papa, how far is it to London?

POPGUN: My girl, my darling, my favourite of all my children, who art the picture of thy poor mother who died two months ago, with whom I am going to town to marry ~~you to~~ to Strephon, and to whom I mean to bequeath my whole estate, it wants seven miles.

SCENE CHANGES TO THE SUN –

Enter CHLOE and a chorus of ploughboys.

CHLOE: Where am I? At Hounslow. – Where go I? To London. – What to do? To be married. – Unto whom? Unto Strephon. Who is he? A youth. Then I will sing a song.

> SONG
> I go to town
> And when I come down,
> I shall be married to Streephon[7]
> And that to me will be fun.
> CHORUS: Be fun, be fun, be fun,
> And that to me will be fun.

Enter COOK.

COOK: Here is the bill of fare.

CHLOE (*reads*): Two ducks, a leg of beef, a stinking partridge[8], and a tart. – I will have the leg of beef and the partridge.

Exit COOK.

And now I will sing another song.

SONG

I am going to have my dinner,
After which I shan't be thinner,
I wish I had here Strephon
For he would carve the partridge if it should be a
tough one.
CHORUS: Tough one, tough one, tough one,
For he would carve the partridge if it should be a
tough one.

Exit CHLOE and CHORUS.
SCENE CHANGES TO THE INSIDE OF THE LION.
Enter STREPON and POSTILION.
STREPON: You drove me from Staines to this place, from
whence I mean to go to town to marry Chloe. How much is your
due?
POST: Eighteen pence.
STREPON: Alas, my friend, I have ~~not~~ but a bad guinea[9] with
which I mean to support myself in town. But I will pawn to you
an undirected letter[10] that I received from Chloe.
POST: Sir, I accept your offer.

End of The First Act.

**A Letter from a Young Lady, whose feelings being too
strong for her judgment led her into the commission
of ~~several faults~~ errors which her heart disapproved.**

Many have been the cares and vicissitudes of my past life,
my beloved Ellinor, and the only consolation I feel for their
bitterness is that on a close examination of my conduct, I am
convinced that I have strictly deserved them. I murdered my
father at a very early period of my life, I have since murdered
my mother, and I am now going to murder my sister. I have
changed my religion so often that at present I have not an idea
of any left. I have been a perjured witness in every public trial
for these last twelve ~~months~~ years; and I have forged my own
will[11].

In short there is scarcely a crime that I have not committed.
– But I am now going to reform. Colonel Martin of the Horse
guards has paid his addresses to me, and we are to be married
in a few days. As there is something singular in our courtship, I
will give you an account of it. Colonel Martin is the second son
of the late Sir John Martin who died immensely rich, but
bequeathing only one hundred thousand pound apiece to ~~her~~

his three younger children, left the bulk of his fortune, about eight million to the present Sir Thomas. Upon his small pittance[12] the Colonel lived tolerably contented for nearly four months when he took it into his head to determine on getting the whole of his eldest brother's estate.

A new will was forged and the Colonel produced it in court – but nobody would swear to its being the right will except himself, and he had sworn so much that nobody believed him. At that moment, I happened to to be passing by the door of the court, and was beckoned in by the judge who told the Colonel that I was a lady ready to witness anything for the cause of justice, and advised him to apply to me. In short, the affair was soon adjusted. The Colonel and I swore to its being the right will, and Sir Thomas has been obliged to resign all his ill-gotten wealth.

The Colonel in gratitude waited on me the next day with an offer of his hand. – I am now going to murder my sister.

Yours Ever,
Anna Parker.

A Tour Through Wales – in a letter from a young lady

My Dear Clara,

I have been so long on the ramble that I have not 'till now had it in my power to thank you for your letter.– We left our dear home on last Monday month; and proceeded on our tour through Wales, which is a principality contiguous to England and gives the title to the Prince of Wales. We travelled on horseback by preference. My mother rode upon our little pony, and Fanny and I walked by her side or rather ran, for my mother is so fond of riding fast that she galloped all the way. You may be sure that we were in a fine perspiration when we came to our place of resting. Fanny has taken a great many drawings of the country, which are very beautiful, though perhaps not such exact resemblances as might be wished, from their being taken as she ran along.

It would astonish you to see all the shoes we wore out in our tour. We determined to take a good stock with us and therefore each took a pair of our own besides those we set off in. However, we were obliged to have them both capped and heel-pieced at Carmarthen[13], and at last when they were quite gone, mama was so kind as to lend us a pair of blue satin slippers, of which we each took one and hopped home from Hereford[14] delightfully.–

I am your ever affectionate
Elizabeth Johnson.

A Tale

A gentleman, whose family name I shall conceal, bought a small cottage in Pembrokeshire[15] about two years ago. This daring action was suggested to him by his elder brother who promised to furnish two rooms and a closet[16] for him, provided he would take a small house near the borders of an extensive forest, and about three miles from the sea. Wilhelminus[17] gladly accepted the offer and continued for some time searching after such a retreat, when he was, one morning, agreeably relieved from his suspense by reading this advertisement in a newspaper:

> To be let: A neat cottage on the borders of an extensive forest and about three miles from the sea.
> It is ready furnished except two rooms and a closet.

The delighted Wilhelminus posted away immediately to his brother, and showed him the advertisement. Robertus[17] congratulated him and sent him in his carriage to take possession of the cottage.

After travelling for three days and six nights without stopping[18], they arrived at the forest and following a track which led by its side down a steep hill over which ten rivulets meandered, they reached the cottage in half an hour. Wilhelminus alighted, and after knocking for some time without receiving any answer or hearing anyone stir within, he opened the door which was fastened only by a wooden latch and entered a small room, which he immediately perceived to be one of the two that were unfurnished. – From thence he proceeded into a closet equally bare. A pair[19] of stairs that went out of it led him into a room above, no less destitute, and these apartments he found composed the whole of the house[20].

He was by no means displeased with this discovery, as he had the comfort of reflecting that he should not be obliged to lay out anything on furniture ~~her~~himself. – He returned immediately to his brother, who took him the next day to every shop in town, and bought whatever was requisite to furnish the two rooms and the closet.

In a few days everything was completed, and Wilhelminus returned to take possession of his cottage. Robertus accompanied him, with his lady, the amiable ~~siste~~ Cecilia, and her two lovely sisters, Arabella and Marina[17], to whom

Wilhelminus was tenderly attached, and a large number of attendants.–

An ordinary genius[21] might probably have been embarrassed, in endeavouring to accommodate so large a party, but Wilhelminus with admirable presence of mind gave orders for the immediate erection of two noble tents in an open spot in the forest adjoining to the house. Their construction was both simple and elegant. – A couple of old blankets, each supported by four sticks, gave a striking proof of that taste for architecture and that happy ease in overcoming difficulties which were some of Wilhelminus's most striking virtues.

Finis

End of the Second Volume

Notes

1. "Fanny Catherine Austen": Frances ('Fanny') Catherine Knight (1793-1882) was the eldest child of Jane's brother Edward, who had been adopted by the wealthy Thomas and Catherine Knight. Jane was seventeen when Fanny was born and she quickly became her favorite niece. On February 20th, 1816, Jane wrote to Fanny, "You are inimitable, irresistible. You are the delight of my life." Edward changed the family name to Knight in 1812, a stipulation in Catherine Knight's will, though this did not go down too well amongst the remaining Austens.

2. "Rowling and Steventon": Fanny was living at Rowling House in Goodnestone, Kent, while Jane was living at the parsonage in Steventon, Hampshire – a distance of about 135 miles and a two-day journey.

3. "father and mother": Edward Austen Knight (1768-1852) married Elizabeth Bridges (1791–1808) on December 27th, 1791. They had eleven children, but Elizabeth died in giving birth to her last child when Fanny was about fifteen.

4. The dedication appears to be a direct parody of the opening of *Letters on the Improvement of the Mind, Addressed to a Young Lady* (1773) by Hester Mulso Chapone (1727-1801):

LETTER I.
ON THE FIRST PRINCIPLES OF RELIGION.

MY DEAREST NIECE,

> Though you are so happy as to have parents, who are both capable and desirous of giving you all proper instruction, yet I, who love you so tenderly, cannot help fondly wishing to contribute something, if possible, to your improvement and welfare: and, as I am so far separated from you, that it is only by pen and ink I can offer you my sentiments, I will hope that your attention may be engaged, by seeing on paper, from the

hand of one of your warmest friends, Truths of the highest importance, which, though you may not find new, can never be too deeply engraven on your mind. Some of them perhaps may make no great impression at present, and yet may so far gain a place in your memory as readily to return to your thoughts when occasion recalls them. And, if you pay me the compliment of preserving my letters, you may possibly re-peruse them at some future period, when concurring circumstances may give them additional weight:—and thus they may prove more effectual than the same things spoken in conversation. But, however this may prove, I cannot resist the desire of trying in some degree to be useful to you on your setting out in a life of trial and difficulty; your success in which must determine your fate for ever.

Chapone's unnamed aunt writes letters of advice to her similarly unnamed niece, who is fifteen years old. In parody, the seventeen-year-old Austen, asserting herself to be adult enough to dispense advice "on the conduct of young women," dedicates her conduct pieces to her infant niece. The other element of the parody is that the contents of "Scraps" do not, in fact, contain Austen's "opinions and admonitions on the conduct of young women" at all.

5. "spending five or six months with us": This is an absurdly long time for a visit, particularly since Julia appears to have invited herself.

6. "the Lion": The name of one of the public rooms in the inn. The other public rooms are the Moon and the Sun. Bedrooms are identified by numbers.

7. "Streephon": Note the two e's to make the rhyme.

8. "a stinking partridge": Game birds were hung after being killed for a week or more to enhance their flavor.

9. "a bad guinea": A guinea was a coin worth £1/1/0 (one pound and one shilling). It was used until 1816. Presumably a 'bad' guinea is a forgery.

10. "an undirected letter": A letter bearing no address. This would be of no commercial value (unlike the bonnet that the heroine of *The Beautiful Cassandra* gives to her driver), so it is unclear why the driver takes it as a guarantee of his debt.

11. "forged my own will": It is not actually possible to forge one's own will! You can only forge someone else's will, for example, to make it seem that the deceased left you all of their money.

12. "pittance": Sir John Martin actually dies impossibly rich; in fact, as Sabor points out, he would have been "by far the richest man in eighteenth century Britain" (*Juvenilia* 479). Nor can £100,000 in capital (which would generate an annual income of £5,000) be regarded as a pittance. Colonel Martin has been well provided for by his father.

13. "Carmarthen": The historic county town of Carmarthenshire in south-west Wales.

14. "Hereford": It is slightly less than one hundred miles from Carmarthen to Hereford and sixteen miles from the Welsh border to Hereford.

15. "Pembrokeshire": A county in south-west Wales.

16. "closet": Not a piece of furniture but a small private room used for washing and dressing.

17. "Wilhelminus ... Robertus ... Arabella and Marina": The names Wilhelminus and Robertus are Latinized versions of the names Wilhelm and Robert, and the names Arabella and Marina are also derived from the Latin. These names give a fairy tale atmosphere to the tale.

18. "three days and six nights without stopping": This is, of course, mathematically impossible – the most one could achieve would be to travel four nights and three days without stopping.

19. "pair": Flight or set.

20. "composed the whole of the house": Thus it appears that the cottage "ready furnished except two rooms and a closet" actually *has* only two rooms and a closet.

21. "ordinary genius": That is, a person of average disposition or personality (not a comment on that person's intellect).

Commentary

The concept of a female philosopher was brought into existence by Mary Wollstonecraft's *A Vindication of the Rights of Woman* (1792). "The Female Philosopher" was also the title of a poem by Charlotte Dacre (c.1771-1825), the author of Gothic novels. Austen is, then, using a phrase that was in vogue when she chose it for the title of this letter. Peter Sabor goes further stating that Austen intends the phrase to be understood as "an oxymoron" (*Juvenilia* 477). Certainly this letter exposes female triviality. Arabella describes to her friend Louisa meeting the Millar sisters, Julia and Charlotte, a pair who seem respectively to embody the absurd extremes of sense and sensibility. The former exudes "modesty, sense and dignity," while the latter is characterized by her "vivacity ... wit and a good humour ... [and her] humourous sallies." Julia (the only character who might claim to be a female philosopher and an early sketch for Mary Bennet) takes the smallest opportunity to expound at length on "the instability of human pleasures and the uncertainty of their duration" and is only prevented from saying more by the arrival of the carriage so that she has to leave. The letter then takes an unexpected turn as Arabella reports the unflattering account that she gave the company of the "merits" of Louisa herself whom she actually condemns for "peevishness, envy and spite ... vanity ... pride, and ... folly."

The parody of a musical comedy contains many of the dramatic devices and even lines of dialogue that Austen's audience would have recognized – as when Popgun gives his daughter Pistoletta all sorts of information about the background to and the purpose of their journey to London that she already knows, but the audience does not. The comic plot involves the fact that both

Chloe and Pistoletta are going to London in order to marry the same man, Strephon, who happens by chance to turn up at the very inn in which they are staying. The audience is left to imagine the comic potential of this farce.

Anna Parker writes as a repentant sinner troubled by her conscience and determined to reform – the very stuff of conduct books and sermons. The trouble is that this determination comes from her reason while the impulse to commit crime stems from her "feelings" which are entirely amoral. Although she claims to have suffered "cares and vicissitudes" in her past as a result of her crimes and admits that she "strictly deserved" the bitterness that these occasioned, there is no actual evidence of such suffering in her letter. Anna's claim that she is "now going to reform," may be taken with a pinch of salt. She is, in fact, a remarkably successful criminal who has, by her lies, become the fiancée of the richest man in England. Rather than repentance, the tone of the letter is one of defiance. She tells us, "I murdered my father at a very early period of my life, I have since murdered my mother, and I am now going to murder my sister." No reason is given for the murder of her sister, but then Anna needs no other reason that her own feelings.

In an age when travel was both expensive and inconvenient, accounts of the tours of others to distant parts of the kingdom were very popular. *Observations on the River Wye, and several parts of South Wales, etc. relative chiefly to picturesque beauty; made in the summer of the year 1770* (1782) by William Gilpin (1724-1804) is the most obvious model for this short parody which is part travel guide (note the formal explanation of the status of Wales) and part journal. Austen's comedy frequently rests on her ability to describe the most outrageous and absurd things as though they were commonplace and unremarkable. Here Elizabeth finds nothing odd in her mother's decision to gallop through Wales while she and her sister run alongside her in a fine sweat. She compliments the beauty of her sister's landscapes before adding that they are unfortunately not particularly accurate representations since she was running while drawing them. The ultimate absurdity is that when their second set of shoes fall apart (despite having been repaired in Carmarthen) their mother "was so kind as to lend" ("lend" not 'give') her daughters a pair of light formal "slippers" with which they both "hopped home from Hereford delightfully." The alliteration here suggests the abrupt action of hopping.

The tale of the cottage, a story riddled with improbabilities and impossibilities, is once again narrated as though everything in the story were perfectly natural. This time the perspective is that of the third person narrator (the narrative voice Austen would use in her novels) which allows full scope for irony. Thus, Robertus's conditions for offering to furnish some rooms in his brother's house are both unexplained and arbitrary, as is Wilhelminus happening to find a newspaper advertisement describing just such a cottage. It seems not to strike Wilhelminus that the advertisement was dishonest given that the cottage *has* only two rooms and a closet; he is merely pleased that he will not have any additional outlay on furniture. For the housewarming there are five people present and in addition to "a large number of attendants." Only then does it seem to occur to Wilhelminus that his small cottage will not accommodate so many, so he cleverly erects two tents. Added to the dead-pan irony of these comic details is the narrator's unconscious use of comic hyperbole. The relatively mundane purchase of a small cottage is described as a "daring action," and two tents constructed from a "couple of old blankets, each supported by four sticks" are called "noble tents … simple and elegant" and said to be proof of Wilhelminus's "taste for architecture." Remembering Austen's spoof dedication, one might point out that this story has nothing to teach a young girl about correct conduct since it contains not a single female character who actually *does* anything.

Taken together, the "Scraps" show that Austen's genius for comic sketches and incidents significantly exceeds her ability to develop plots to tie such scenes together into a meaningful narrative. That will be the triumph of her mature novels.

Volume the Third

Effusions of fancy
by a very young lady
consisting of tales
in a style entirely new[1].

For James Edward Austen Leigh[2]
Jane Austen – May 6th 1792[3]

Evelyn

To Miss Mary Lloyd[4],
The following novel is by permission dedicated, by
her obedient, humble servant
The Author

In a retired part of the county of Sussex, there is a village
(for what I know to the contrary) called Evelyn, perhaps one of
the most beautiful spots in the south of England. A gentleman
passing through it on horseback about twenty years ago was so
entirely of my opinion in this respect, that he put up at the little
alehouse in it and enquired with great earnestness whether
there were any house to be let in the parish. The landlady, who
as well as everyone else in Evelyn was remarkably amiable,
shook her head at this question but seemed unwilling to give
him any answer. He could not bear this uncertainty – yet knew
not how to obtain the information he desired. To repeat a
question which had already appear'd to make the good woman
uneasy was impossible. – He turned from her in visible
agitation.

"What a situation am I in!" said he to himself as he walked
to the window and threw up the sash.

He found himself revived by the air, which he felt to a much
greater degree when he had opened the window than he had
done before. Yet it was but for a moment.– The agonizing idea
pain of doubt and suspense again weighed down his spirits.
The good woman, who had watched in eager silence every turn
of his countenance with that benevolence which characterizes
the inhabitants of Evelyn, entreated him to tell her the cause of
his uneasiness.

"Is there anything, sir, in my power to do that may relieve
your griefs. – Tell me in what manner I can sooth them, and
believe me that the friendly balm of comfort and assistance

shall not be wanting, for indeed, sir, I have a sympathetic soul."

"Amiable woman," said Mr. Gower, affected almost to tears by this generous offer. "This greatness of mind in one to whom I am almost a stranger, serves but to make me the more warmly wish for a house in this sweet village. – What would I not give to be your neighbour, to be blessed with your acquaintance, and with the farther knowledge of your virtues! Oh! with what pleasure would I form myself by such an example! Tell me then, best of women, is there no possibility? – I cannot speak. – You know my meaning.–"

"Alas! sir," replied Mrs. Willis, "there is none. Every house in this village, from the sweetness of the situation, and the purity of the air, in which neither misery, ill health, or vice are ever wafted, is inhabited. And yet," (after a short pause) "there is a family, who though warmly attached to the spot, yet from a peculiar generosity of disposition would perhaps be willing to oblige you with ~~the remainder of their lease~~[5] their house."

He eagerly caught at this idea, and having gained a direction to the ~~house~~ place, he set off immediately on his walk to it. As he approached the house, he was delighted with its situation. It was in the exact centre of a small circular paddock, which was enclosed by a regular paling and bordered with a plantation of Lombardy poplars, and spruce firs alternatively placed in three rows. A gravel walk ran through this beautiful shrubbery, and as the remainder of the paddock was unencumbered ~~by~~ with any other timber, the surface of it perfectly even and smooth, and grazed by four white cows ~~who~~ which were disposed at equal distances from each other, the whole appearance of the place as Mr. Gower entered the paddock was uncommonly striking[6]. A beautifully-rounded, gravel road without any turn or interruption led immediately to the house. Mr. Gower rang – the door was soon opened.

"Are Mr. and Mrs. Webb at home?"

"My good sir, they are," replied the servant, and leading the way, conducted Mr. Gower upstairs into a very elegant dressing room, where a lady rising from her seat, welcomed him with all the generosity which Mrs. Willis had attributed to the family.

"Welcome best of men. – Welcome to this house, and to everything it contains. William, tell your master of the happiness I enjoy – invite him to partake of it. – Bring up some chocolate immediately; spread a cloth in the dining parlour, and carry in the venison pasty. – In the meantime, let the gentleman have some sandwiches, and bring in a basket of fruit. – Send up some ices and a basin of soup, and do not forget some jellies and cakes[7]."

Then, turning to Mr. Gower, and taking out ~~a~~ her purse, "Accept this, my good sir. Believe me, you are welcome to everything that is in my power to bestow. – I wish my purse were weightier, but Mr. Webb must make up my deficiencies. – I know he has cash in the house to the amount of an hundred pounds, which he shall bring you immediately."

Mr. Gower felt overpowered by her generosity as he put the purse in his pocket, and from the ~~effusions~~ excess of his gratitude, could scarcely express himself intelligibly when he accepted her offer of ~~a~~ the hundred pounds. Mr. Webb soon entered the room, and repeated every protestation of friendship and cordiality which his lady had ~~before expressed~~ already made. The chocolate, the sandwiches, the jellies, the cakes, the ice, and the soup soon made their appearance, and Mr. Gower, having tasted something of all and pocketed the rest, was conducted into the dining parlour, where he eat a most excellent dinner and partook of the most exquisite wines, while Mr. and Mrs. Webb stood by him still pressing him to eat and drink a little more.

"And now, my good sir," said Mr. Webb when Mr. Gower's repast was concluded, "what else can we do to contribute to your happiness and express the affection we bear ~~for~~ you. Tell us what you wish more to receive, and depend upon our gratitude for the communication of your wishes."

"Give me then your house and grounds; I ask for nothing else."

"It is yours!" exclaimed both at once. "From this moment it is yours."

The agreement concluded on, and the present accepted by Mr. Gower, Mr. Webb rang to have the carriage ordered, telling William at the same time to call the young ladies.

"Best of men," said Mrs. Webb, "we will not long intrude upon your time."

"Make no apologies, dear madam," replied Mr. Gower. 'You are welcome to stay this half hour if you like it."

They both burst forth into raptures of admiration at his politeness, which they agreed served only to make their conduct appear more inexcusable in trespassing on his time.

The young ladies soon entered the room. The eldest of them was about seventeen, the other, several years younger. Mr. Gower had no sooner fixed his eyes on Miss Webb than he felt that something more was necessary to his happiness than the house he had just received. Mrs. Webb introduced him to her daughter.

"Our dear friend Mr. Gower, my love. – He has been so good as to accept of this house, small as it is, and to promise to keep it forever."

"Give me leave to assure you, sir," said Miss Webb, "that I am highly sensible of your kindness in this respect, which from the shortness of my father's and mother's acquaintance with you, is more than usually flattering."

Mr. Gower bowed.–

"You are too obliging, ma'am. – I assure you that I like the house extremely – and if they would complete their generosity by giving me their eldest daughter in marriage with a handsome portion[8], I should have nothing more to wish for."

This compliment brought a blush into the cheeks of the lovely Miss Webb, who seemed, however, to refer herself to her father and mother. *They* looked delighted at each other.–

At length, Mrs. Webb breaking silence, said:

"We bend under a weight of obligations to you which we can never repay. Take our girl, take our Maria, and on her must the difficult task fall, of endeavouring to make some return to so much beneficence."

Mr. Webb added, "Her fortune is but ten thousand pounds[9], which is almost too small a sum to be offered."

This objection, however, being instantly removed by the generosity of Mr. Gower, who declared himself satisfied with the sum mentioned, Mr. and Mrs. Webb, with their youngest daughter, took their leave, and on the next day, the nuptials of their eldest with Mr. Gower were celebrated.–

This amiable man now found himself perfectly happy; united to a very lovely and deserving young woman, with an handsome fortune, an elegant house, settled in the village of Evelyn, and by that means enabled to cultivate his acquaintance with Mrs. Willis[10], could he have a wish ungratified? – For some months he found that he could *not*, till one day as he was walking in the shrubbery with Maria leaning on his arm, they observed a rose full-blown lying on the gravel; it had fallen from a rose tree which with three others had been planted by Mr. Webb to give a pleasing variety to the walk. These four rose trees served also to mark the quarters of the shrubbery, by which means the traveler might always know how far in his progress round the paddock he was got. – Maria stooped to pick up the beautiful flower, and with all her family generosity presented it to her husband.

"My dear Frederic," said she, "pray take this charming rose."

"Rose!" exclaimed Mr. Gower. – "Oh! Maria, of what does not that remind me! Alas, my poor sister, how have I neglected you!"

The truth was that Mr. Gower was the only son of a very large family, of which Miss Rose Gower was the thirteenth daughter. This young lady, whose merits deserved a better fate than she met with, was the darling of her relations. – From the clearness of her skin and the brilliancy of her eyes, she was fully entitled to all their partial affection. Another circumstance contributed to the general love they bore her, and that was one of the finest heads of hair in the world. A few months before her brother's marriage, her heart had been engaged by the attentions and charms of a young man whose high rank and expectations seemed to foretell objections from his family to a match which would be highly desirable to theirs. Proposals were made on the young man's part, and proper objections on his father's. – He was desired to return from Carlisle where he was with his beloved Rose, to the family seat in Sussex[11].

He was obliged to comply, and the angry father then finding from his conversation how determined he was to marry no other woman, sent him for a fortnight to the Isle of Wight under the care of the family chaplain, with the hope of overcoming his constancy by time and absence in a foreign country[12]. They accordingly prepared to bid a long adieu to England. – The young nobleman was not allowed to see his Rosa. They set sail. – A storm arose which baffled the arts of the seamen. The vessel was wrecked on the coast of Calshot[13] and every soul on board perished.

This sad event soon reached Carlisle, and the beautiful Rose was affected by it beyond the power of expression. It was to soften her affliction by obtaining a picture of her unfortunate lover that her brother undertook a journey into Sussex, where he hoped that his petition would not be rejected, by the severe yet afflicted father. When he reached Evelyn, he was not many miles from —— Castle, but the pleasing events which befell him in that place had for a while made him totally forget the object of his journey and his unhappy sister. The little incident of the rose, however, brought everything concerning her to his recollection again, and he bitterly repented his neglect. He returned to the house immediately and agitated ~~with~~ by grief,

252

apprehension and shame wrote the following letter to Rosa:

July 14th –. Evelyn

My dearest sister,

As it is now four months since I left Carlisle, during which period I have not once written to you, you will perhaps unjustly accuse me of neglect and forgetfulness. Alas! I blush when I own the truth of your accusation[14]. Yet if you are still alive, do not think too harshly of me, or suppose that I could for a moment forget the situation of my Rose. Believe me, I will forget you no longer[15], but will hasten as soon as possible to —— Castle, if I find by your answer that you are still alive.

Maria joins me in every dutiful and affectionate wish, and I am yours sincerely

F. Gower.

He waited in the most anxious expectation for an answer to his letter, which arrived as soon as the great distance from Carlisle would admit of[16]. – But alas, it came not ~~for~~ from Rosa:

Carlisle, July 17th

Dear Brother,

My mother has taken the liberty of opening your letter to poor Rose, as she has been dead these six weeks. Your long absence and continued silence gave us all great uneasiness and hastened her to the grave. Your journey to — Castle therefore may be spared. You do not tell us where you have been since the time of your quitting Carlisle, nor in any way account for your tedious absence, which gives us some surprise.

We all unite in compliments to Maria, and beg to know who she is. –

Your affectionate sister

M. Gower.

This letter, by which Mr. Gower was obliged to attribute to his own conduct his sister's death, was so violent a shock to his feelings, that in spite of his ~~life~~ living at Evelyn where illness was scarcely ever heard of, he was attacked by a fit of the gout[17], which confining him to his own room, afforded an opportunity to Maria of shining in that favourite character of Sir Charles Grandison's, a nurse[18]. No woman could ever appear more amiable than Maria did under such circumstances, and at last by her unremitting attentions had the pleasure of seeing him gradually recover the use of his feet.

It was a blessing by no means lost on him, for he was no sooner in a condition to leave the house, that he mounted his horse, and rode to —— Castle, wishing to find whether his lordship softened by his son's death, might have been brought to consent to the match, had both he and Rosa been alive[19]. His amiable Maria followed him with her eyes till she could see him no longer, and then sinking into her chair overwhelmed with grief, found that in his absence she could enjoy no comfort.

Mr. Gower arrived late in the evening at the castle, which was situated on a woody eminence commanding a beautiful prospect of the sea. Mr. Gower did not dislike the situation, though it was certainly greatly ~~superior~~ inferior to that of his own house. There was an irregularity in the fall of the ground, and a profusion of old timber which appeared to him ill-suited to the style of the castle, for it being a building of a very ~~old~~ ancient date, he thought it required the paddock of Evelyn lodge to form a contrast, and enliven the structure[20]. The gloomy appearance of the old castle, frowning on him as he followed its winding approach, struck him with terror[21]. Nor did he think himself safe, till he was introduced into the drawing room where the family were assembled to tea.

Mr. Gower was a perfect stranger to everyone in the circle, but though he was always timid in the dark and easily terrified when alone, he did not want that more necessary and more noble courage which enabled him without a blush to enter a large party of superior rank, whom he had never seen before, and to take his seat amongst them with perfect indifference. The name of Gower was not unknown to Lord ——. He felt distressed and astonished; yet rose and received him with all the politeness of a well-bred man. Lady ——, who felt a deeper sorrow at the loss of her son, than his Lordship's harder heart was capable of, could hardly keep her seat when she found that he was the brother of her lamented ~~Charles~~ Henry's Rosa.

"My Lord," said Mr. Gower as soon as he was seated, "you are perhaps surprised at receiving a visit from a man whom you could not have the least expectation of seeing here. But my sister, my unfortunate sister, is the real cause of my thus troubling you. That luckless girl[22] is now no more – and though *she* can receive no pleasure from the intelligence, yet for the satisfaction of her family, I wish to know whether the death of this unhappy pair has made an impression on your heart sufficiently strong to obtain that consent to their marriage, which in happier circumstances, you would not be persuaded to give, supposing that they now were both alive."

His Lordship seemed lost in astonishment. Lady —— could not support the mention of her son, and left the room in tears; the rest of the family remained attentively listening, almost persuaded that Mr. Gower was distracted.

"Mr. Gower," replied his Lordship, "this is a very odd question. – It appears to me that you are supposing an impossibility. – No one can more sincerely regret the death of my son than I have always done, and it gives me great concern to know that Miss Gower's was hastened by his. – Yet to suppose them alive is destroying at once the motive for a change in my sentiments concerning the affair[23]."

"My Lord," replied Mr. Gower in anger, "I see that you are a most inflexible man, and that not even the death of your son can make you wish his future life happy. I will no longer detain your Lordship. I see, I plainly see, that you are a very vile man. – And now I have the honour of wishing all your Lordships, and Ladyships a goodnight."

He immediately left the room, forgetting in the heat of his anger the lateness of the hour, which at any other time would have made him tremble, and leaving the whole company unanimous in their opinion of his being mad. When, however, he had mounted his horse and the great gates of the castle had shut him out, he felt an universal tremor throughout his whole frame. If we consider his situation indeed, alone, on horseback, as late in the year as August[24], and in the day, as nine o'clock, with no light to direct him but that of the moon almost full, and the stars which alarmed him by their twinkling[25], who can refrain from pitying him? – No house within a quarter of a mile, and a gloomy castle blackened by the deep shade of walnuts and pines, behind him. – He felt indeed almost distracted with his fears, and shutting his eyes till he arrived at the village to prevent his seeing either gypsies or ghosts[26], he rode on a full gallop all the way[27].

On his ["On his" initially erased and then restored] return home, he rang the house bell, but no one appeared; a second time he rang, but the door was not opened; a third and a fourth with as little success, when observing the dining parlour window open̶e̶d̶–he leapt in, and pursued his way through the house 'till he reached Maria's dressing room, where he found all the servants assembled at tea. Surprised at so very unusual a sight, he fainted; on his recovery, he found himself on the sofa, with his wife's maid kneeling by him, chafing his temples with Hungary water[28]. – From her he learned that his beloved Maria had been so much grieved at his departure that she died of a broken heart about three hours after his departure.

He then became sufficiently composed to give necessary orders for her funeral which took place the Monday following, this being the Saturday. – When Mr. Gower had settled the order of the procession, he set out himself to Carlisle, to give vent to his sorrow in the bosom of his family. – He arrived there in high health and spirits, after a delightful journey of three days and a half. – What was his surprise on entering the breakfast parlour to see Rosa, his beloved Rosa, seated on a ~~chaise long~~ sofa; at the sight of him she fainted and would have fallen had not a gentleman sitting with his back to the door, started up and saved her from sinking to the ground. – She very soon came to herself and then introduced this gentleman to her brother as her husband a Mr. Davenport. –

"But my dearest Rosa," said the astonished Gower, "I thought you were dead and buried."

"Why, my dear Frederick," replied Rosa, "I wished you to think so, hoping that you would spread the report about the country, and it would thus by some means reach —— Castle. – By this I hoped somehow or other to touch the hearts of its inhabitants. It was not till the day before yesterday that I heard of the death of my beloved Henry which I learned from Mr. Davenport who concluded by offering me his hand. I accepted it with transport, and was married yesterday.–"

Mr. Gower, embraced his sister and shook hands with Mr. Davenport, he then took a stroll into the town. – As he passed by a public house, he called for a pot of beer, which was brought him immediately by his old friend Mrs. Willis.–

Great was his astonishment at seeing Mrs. Willis in Carlisle. But not forgetful of the respect~~ful~~ he owed her, he dropped on one knee, and received the frothy cup from her, more grateful to *him* than nectar. – He instantly made her an offer of his hand and heart, which she graciously condescended to accept, telling him that she was only on a visit to her cousin, who kept the *Anchor* and should be ready to return to Evelyn, whenever he chose. – The next morning they were married and immediately proceeded to Evelyn.–

256

When he reached home, he recollected that he had never written to Mr. and Mrs. Webb to inform them of the death of their daughter, which he rightly supposed they knew nothing of, as they never took in any newspapers[29]. – He immediately dispatched the following letter:

Evelyn – August 19th, 1809

Dearest Madam,

How can words express the poignancy of my feelings! Our Maria, our beloved Maria, is no more: she breathed her last on Saturday the 12th of August. – I see you now in an agony of grief lamenting not your own, but my loss. – Rest satisfied I am happy: possessed of my lovely Sarah what more can I wish for?–

I remain respectfully yours

F. Gower

Westgate Buildings August 22nd

Generous, best of men,

How truly we rejoice to hear of your present welfare and happiness! and how truly grateful are we for your unexampled generosity in writing to condole with us on the late unlucky accident which befell our Maria. – I have enclosed a draught on our banker for thirty pounds, which Mr. Webb joins with me in entreating you and the amiable Sarah to accept. –

Your most grateful

Anne Augusta Webb

Mr. and Mrs. Gower resided many years at Evelyn enjoying perfect happiness, the just reward of their virtues. The only alteration which took place at Evelyn was that Mr. and Mrs. Davenport settled there in Mrs. Willis's former abode and were for many years the proprietors of the White Horse Inn.–[30]

On re-entering his circular domain, his round-robin of perpetual piece, where enjoyment had no end and calamity no commencement, his spirits became wonderfully composed, and a delicious calm extended itself through every nerve. With his pocket handkerchief (once hemmed by the genius of the too susceptible Rosa), he wiped the morbid moisture from his brow – then flew to the boudoir of his Maria. And did *she* not fly to meet her Frederick? Did she not dart from the couch on which she had so gracefully reclined, and, bounding like an agile fawn over the intervening foot stool, precipitate herself into his arms? Does she not, though fainting between every syllable, breathe forth, as it were by installments, her Frederick's adored name?

Who is there of perception so obtuse as not to realize the touching scene? Who, of ear so dull as not to catch the soft murmur of Maria's voice? Ah! Who? The heart of every sympathetic reader repeats: Ah! Who? Vain echo! Vain sympathy! There is not meeting – no murmur – no Maria. – It is not in the ~~language~~ power of language, however potent, nor in that of style, however diffuse, to render justice to the astonishment of Mr. Gower.–

Arming himself with a mahogany ruler which some fatality had placed on Maria's writing table, and calling repeatedly on her beloved name, he rushed forward to examine the adjacent apartments. – In the dressing room of his lost one, he had the melancholy satisfaction of picking up a curl paper, and a gust of wind, as he reentered the boudoir, swept from the table, and placed at his feet a skein of black sewing silk[31]. – These were the only traces of Maria!!

Carefully locking the doors of these now desolate rooms, burying the key deep in his waistcoat pocket, and the mystery of Maria's disappearance yet deeper in his heart of hearts, Mr. Gower left his once happy home, and sought a supper, and a bed, at the house of the hospitable Mrs. Willis. – There was an oppression on his chest which made him extremely uncomfortable; he regretted that instead of the skein of silk carefully wrapped up in a curl paper ~~which~~ and placed beneath his pillow, he had not rather swallowed laudanum[32]. It would have been, in all probability, more efficacious.

At last Mr. Gower slept a troubled sleep, and in due course of time he dreamt a troubled dream. He dreamed of Maria, as how could he less? She stood by his bedside, in her dressing gown. – One hand held an open book, with the forefinger of the other she pointed to this ominous passage – "*Tantôt c'est un vide; ~~tantôt~~ qui nous ennuie; tantôt c'est un poids qui nous oppresse*[33]." – The unfortunate Frederick uttered a deep groan – and as the vision closed the volume, he observed these characters strangely imprinted on the cover – Rolandi – Berners Street[34]. Who was this ~~mysterious~~ dangerous Rolandi? Doubtless a bravo or a monk[35] – possible both – and what was he to Maria? Vainly he would have dared the worst and put the fatal question. – The semblance of Maria raised her monitory finger, and interdicted speech. Yet some words she spoke, or seemed to speak herself; Mr. Gower could distinguish only these: "Search – cupboard – top shelf." – Once more he assayed to speak, but it was all bewilderment. – He heard strange demon-like sounds; hissing and spitting. – He smelt an unearthly smell. The agony became unbearable, and he awoke.–

Maria had vanished; the rush light[36] was expiring in the socket; and the benevolent Mrs. Willis entering his room, threw open the shutters, and in accordance with her own warmth of heart admitted the full blaze of a summer morning's sun. –

J.A.E.L.

But what found he on re-entering that ~~abode~~ circle of peace, that round robin of perpetual peace[?][37]

[Finis]

Notes

1. This commendation is written on the inside front cover of the notebook in pencil. It is generally accepted that it was written by Jane's father, the Reverend George Austen, although some have found the handwriting consistent with that of either Cassandra or Jane herself.

2. At the top of the Contents page, written in pencil by Cassandra, is the name James Edward Austen (1798-1894), the son of her eldest brother James and his second wife, Mary Lloyd. The surname was amended by the addition of 'Leigh' in a different hand. This must have been done in or after 1837 when James added 'Leigh' to his family surname. James Edward Austen was Jane's favorite nephew. He was the author of *A Memoir of Jane Austen* (1869), the first full-length biography of Jane Austen and the only one written by someone who knew her personally.

3. "May 6th, 1792": This represents the date on which Austen began transcribing *Evelyn*, which had probably been written in late 1791. At this point, Austen entered the title *Kitty, or the Bower* on the Contents page. Although she subsequently changed her heroine's name to Catharine, she did not correct the title on the Contents page.

4. "Miss Mary Lloyd": Mary Lloyd (c.1771-1843) was the second daughter of Rev. Noyes Lloyd and his wife, Martha Craven. When Rev. Lloyd died in 1789, his widow and two daughters, Martha (ten years Jane's senior) and Mary (about four years Jane's senior) moved into the vacant Deane parsonage which had been offered by Rev. Austen. Only a mile and a half from Steventon, the Lloyd sisters became firm friends with the two Austen girls. In 1797, Mary became the second wife of Jane's eldest brother James and bore him two children: James Edward (Austen's first biographer) in 1798 and Caroline Mary Craven in 1805.

5. "~~lease~~": Austen's revision makes the Webbs the owners of the house that

they give to Gower not merely its tenants. This change makes their sacrifice all the greater and their gift much more significant to Mr. Gower.

6. "As he approached the house ... uncommonly striking": According to contemporary theory and practice in landscape gardening, just about everything is wrong with the situation of the Webbs' house. Specifically: the trees are too close to the house, obscuring the views from its windows; the gravel path that runs through the shrubbery seems too definite, unlike the preferred informal, winding, irregular walks; the four cows equidistant from each other offend against Gilpin's definition of the picturesque which requires groupings of three; and the gravel drive leading to the house without any turn or interruption, lacks the winding curves designed to show off the park and the house. In fact, given that there is a great difference of scale, the Webbs' house lacks every feature of improved landscaping that Pemberley exhibits to the eye of Elizabeth Bennet when she visits the house. For all its faults (perhaps *because* of its faults), the Webbs' house is perfect.

7. "Bring up some chocolate ... some jellies and cakes": The foods named are expensive luxuries (in contrast with the food served in the play *The Visit* in *Volume the First*) and are offered in absurd abundance.

8. "a handsome portion": That is, a dowry (property or money brought by a bride to her husband on their marriage).

9. "ten thousand pounds": As earlier notes have made clear, £10,000 is sufficient money to maintain a very comfortable, if not lavish, way of life.

10. "to cultivate his acquaintance with Mrs. Willis": Whether Austen intended this to suggest some sexual motivation on Mr. Gower's part seems to me unlikely. On the other hand, if she did envisage Gower eventually marrying Mrs. Willis (and if she did then *she* never wrote about that), it makes perfectly good sense to talk of his appreciation of the lady.

11. "Carlisle ... Sussex": The distance from Carlisle in Cumberland, north-west England, to Brighton in Sussex, south-east England, is about three hundred miles.

12. "a foreign country": The Isle of Wight is not (and has never been) a foreign country; it is part of England.

13. "the coast of Calshot": The ship would have been sailing from Southampton to Cowes. Calshot is on the west bank of the estuary where Southampton Water reaches The Solent which divides the mainland from the Isle of White. These are calm waters not noted for storms.

14. "your accusation": The charge that he imagines Rosa as making could hardly be "unjust" *and* true.

15. "no longer": Impossibly, Gower claims that he could not "for a moment forget the situation of my Rose" and then that he will forget her "no longer."

16. "would admit of": Gower's letter takes three days to arrive at Carlisle.

17. "gout": Inflammation of the joints, particularly in the leg. At the time, this was attributed to excessive eating and drinking of wine, both of which Gower has been guilty of since his arrival.

18. "a nurse": In Richardson's novel, the eponymous hero, Sir Charles, is an able nurse himself, but he sees women as more natural nurses and praises their skill.

19. "Rosa been alive": This seems like an absurdly hypothetical question.

20. "Mr. Gower ... the structure": Every judgment that Gower makes on the appearance of the castle is nonsense. The description of the castle meets Gilpin's demands for the picturesque.

21. "struck him with terror": Suddenly the picturesque castle is transformed in Gower's mind into a brooding, dark Gothic castle right out of the novels of Mrs. Radcliffe.

22. "luckless girl": Recall that Rosa is the thirteenth daughter.

23. "Yet to ... the affair'": Lord —— points out the logical absurdity of Gower's question. He is being asked if, knowing them to both be dead, he would now agree to their marriage, supposing them to still be alive. His point is that he objected to the marriage because they *were* both alive so if they were both alive still he would *still* object to the marriage, and if they are dead then the question has no meaning.

24. "August": August is, of course, not at all "late in the year"; it is summer in England. In mid-August, in Sussex, sunset would be at about 8.30 pm. It would not, however, be fully dark until about an hour later.

25. "the moon ... their twinkling": A full moon and a starry night would provide plenty of light. When the obnoxious Lady Greville invites Maria Williams to walk over to her house for dinner ("Letter the Third: From a Young Lady in Distressed Circumstances" *Volume the Second*) she warns her that "'There will be no moon'" which will make her walk home "'horrid.'" Writing to Cassandra on September 15th, 1796, Jane begins, "We have been very gay since I wrote last; dining at Nackington, returning by moonlight, and everything quite in style…"

26. "gypsies or ghosts": These two entities were generally feared by travelers. In *Emma*, Harriet Smith is genuinely frightened by an encounter with gypsies, "she trembling and conditioning, they lour and insolent" (Ch. 41).

27. "full gallop all the way": Galloping at night puts Gower in much greater danger than gypsies of ghosts could. At this point Austen's transcription ends, but she left the next nine pages blank. The story is continued in handwriting believed to be that of James Edward Austen Leigh writing in 1815 or 1816.

28. "Hungary water": "Hungary water (sometimes called 'the Queen of Hungary's Water', Eau de la Reine de Hongary, or 'spirits of rosemary') was one of the first alcohol-based perfumes in Europe, primarily made with rosemary" (Wikipedia article). It was thought to have restorative and health-giving effects.

29. "took in any newspapers": It was normal for the deaths of prominent people to be placed in the 'Death notices' sections of newspapers.

30. "the White Horse Inn.–" At this point James Edward's continuation ends. On four loose sheets of paper is an alternative continuation of Austen's

manuscript written by James's sister, Jane Anna Austen Lefroy (1793-1872). Since Jane Anna married Benjamin LeFroy in 1814, this contribution cannot have been made until after that date and may thus have post-dated Austen's death.

31. "a skein of black sewing silk": "a loosely coiled length of yarn or thread wound on a reel" (Merriam-Webster)

32. "swallowed laudanum": Laudanum, a tincture of opium, was developed in the 1660s by the English physician Thomas Sydenham (1624–1689). It rapidly became a very popular cure-all medicine since (largely due to its morphine content) it effectively provided relief from pain, coughing, diarrhea and other symptoms of acute and chronic illness and induced sleep. The dangers of this easily-available medicine included dependence, accidental overdose and intentional suicide (which Gower does not appear to have in mind here), though it is only fair to add that, used appropriately, it was a very effective palliative.

33. "'*Tantôt c'est un vide; qui nous ennuie; tantôt c'est un poids qui nous oppresse.*'": "Sometimes it's a void; which bores us; sometimes it is a weight that oppresses us."

34. "Rolandi – Berners Street": Pietro Rolandi, an Italian émigré, was a famous bookseller, editor and publisher with premises at 20 Berners Street in the City of Westminster in the West End which was a meeting-place for the Italian community in London.

35. "a bravo or a monk": A "bravo" meant a brave, aggressive, quarrelsome person which you might think would be the very opposite of a monk, a man leading a contemplative, prayerful life in a monastery. However, there is a reference here to *The Monk: A Romance* (1796) a Gothic novel by Matthew Gregory Lewis (1775-1818). The novel, set "in the sinister monastery of the Capuchins in Madrid, … is a violent tale of ambition, murder, and incest. The struggle between maintaining monastic vows and fulfilling personal ambitions tempts its main character into breaking his vows" (goodreads.com).

36. "the rush light": "A rushlight is a type of candle or miniature torch formed by soaking the dried pith of the rush plant in fat or grease. For several centuries rushlights were a common source of artificial light for poor people throughout the British Isles" (Wikipedia article). Presumably this accounts for the awful smell Gower detects.

37. This is a draft of the first sentence of Anna Lefroy's continuation of *Evelyn*. It is written on the reverse of the final leaf.

Commentary

The fantasy *Evelyn* is the last of Austen's parodies of the popular fiction of her time; it has nothing to do with real life and everything to do with sending up bad writing. The novel is really two entirely different narratives stitched together in a rather arbitrary fashion: the first is the story of Frederic Gower's arrival in the fairy tale village of Evelyn and his subsequent marriage, and the second is the tale of Rosa's tragic love for Henry and Frederic's consequent visit to Lord —. Put together, these plots allow Austen to parody romantic fiction with its clichéd situations (love at first sight, instant proposals, and oppressive parents preventing marriage) and Gothic novels with their clichéd features (fearful settings, incredible plot twists, and inhuman cruelties). In addition, every character in the novel, with the exception of the "'very vile'" Lord —, embodies the faults of excessive sensibility: absurd acts of generosity, heightened sensitivity to beauty, fainting fits, and death from the pangs of separation and lost love.

Frederic Gower enters an enchanted (or at least enchanting) village such as only exist in fairy tales, a place unique for "'the sweetness of the situation, and the purity of the air, in which neither misery, ill health, or vice ever wafted.'" His superior sensibility makes him hypersensitive not only to the beauties of the village but also to its capacity to foster the physical and psychological health of those who live there. He immediately identifies the amiable landlady of the local public house (Mrs. Willis) as one of the superior inhabitants of Evelyn – a person upon whose virtues and example he might form himself in future. Mrs. Willis in turn self-identifies as one who has "'a sympathetic soul,'" and her sensitivity to Mr. Gower's desire to live in the village leads her to name a family noted for its "'peculiar generosity of disposition.'"

In her depiction of Mr. and Mrs. Webb, Austen mocks sensibility unchecked by sense, or as A. Walton Litz puts it, "emotional and irrational generosity, Benevolence uncontrolled by Judgment ... a parody of the indiscriminate Benevolence so often displayed in the novel of sensibility" (34). Immediately upon his being introduced, Mrs. Webb intuitively knows Frederic to be the "'best of men,'" and proceeds to provide an impossibly excessive banquet such as might even have satisfied Miss Charlotte Lutterell (*Lesley Castle*). Not content with this, however, Mrs. Webb forces on the not at all reluctant Frederic her purse and promises to add the hundred pounds that she knows her husband to have in the house. Far from putting a stop to this nonsense when he enters, Mr. Webb compounds it by repeating "every protestation of friendship and cordiality which his lady had already made," and by giving Frederic his house and grounds simply because Frederic asks for them.

Ironically, the Webbs are now guests in Mr. Gower's house and feel the need to apologize for intruding on his time. Frederic assures them that they "'are welcome to stay this half hour,'" which draws from the couple ridiculous "raptures of admiration at his politeness." The entrance of Miss Maria Webb (who has a younger sister but this is the first and last we hear of her) similarly fails to impose a return to sanity: she is impressed not by her parents' generosity in giving away their house, but in Mr. Gower's kindness in accepting it given "'the shortness of [her] father's and mother's acquaintance with [him].'" This, of course, turns the entire situation on its head. When Frederic asks for the hand of Maria, both she and her parents are overwhelmed by his "'beneficence.'" Mr. Webb apologizes obsequiously for the fact that Maria's dowry amounts only to £10,000, but with his typical "generosity ... Mr. Gower ... declared himself satisfied with the sum" – as well he might.

There follow several months of idyllic happiness for Frederic and Maria. He not only has a beautiful house in a charming village, but also a "very lovely and deserving young" wife and the means to "cultivate his acquaintance with Mrs. Willis," which may strike the reader as a euphemism for rather more than social visits. A chance encounter with a fallen rose, however, reminds the self-involved Frederic of the reason he was travelling in the first place – his sister Rosa. In a letter to Rosa, he attempts to explain his delay claiming that she may "unjustly accuse me of neglect and forgetfulness" and then accepting that he has indeed been guilty of both. Although he learns that his delay has hastened Rosa's death, he yet determines to visit — Castle, and that effectively ends the novel's first narrative, for Austen abandons the story before Frederic's return to his house and his wife.

Rosa Gower is introduced as a stereotypical heroine, beautiful and esteemed by all – and having "one of the finest heads of hair in the world" – a sure indication of her superior sensibility. Her love affair with Henry has been ended by the unfeeling, mercenary motives of Henry's titled father whose efforts to separate the two have led to his son's death by drowning. The purpose of Frederic's original journey, to soften his sister's "affliction by obtaining a picture of the unfortunate lover," seems almost reasonable in a story in which nothing that has happened so far has been in any way reasonable. News of his sister's death, however, brings on "a fit of the gout" – a disease associated with over-indulgence rather than grief.

When Frederic sets out from his home to — Castle, the second narrative begins. This is a parody of the knightly quest. Frederic, leaving behind his fair lady, Maria, is cast in the role of medieval heroes such as Sir Percival, Sir Galahad and Sir Lancelot. Traditionally, the hero's way leads through a pathless, bewildering forest. Here, Frederic encounters a "woody eminence" on which irregular ground there is a winding path and "a profusion of old timber." Far from being confused as to his route, Frederic reflects that the setting of this castle lacks the order of the landscape around his own house in Evelyn. Yet, suddenly and inexplicably, the castle takes on the frightening aspect appropriate to castles in Gothic novels, "The gloomy appearance of the old castle, frowning on him as he followed its winding approach, struck him with terror."

So vivid is the description of Frederic's near approach to the castle, that the reader may miss the fact that the goal of his original quest (made pointless by the apparent death of his sister) has changed: where once he wanted only a picture of the late Henry to console Rosa, now he wants to know, "whether his lordship softened by his son's death, might have been brought to consent to the match, had both he [Henry] and Rosa been alive." Since they are, Frederic believes, *both* dead, this is a nonsensical question. It is no surprise that "His Lordship seems lost in astonishment," or that everyone else in the room concludes that Frederic is "distracted" (i.e., insane). Lord —'s reaction is shockingly normal: he regrets the death of his son and its part in hastening the death of Rosa. He adds, speaking perfectly logically, "Yet to suppose them alive is destroying at once the motive for a change in my sentiments concerning the affair." In other words, 'I might regret not allowing their marriage because doing so resulted in the deaths of the two lovers, but if the two lovers were not dead, then I would have no reason for regret and would now allow their marriage.' Since this logic is unanswerable, Frederic abuses Lord — as a "'very vile man'" and storms out "leaving the whole company unanimous in their opinion of his being mad."

There is now a return to the gothic atmosphere, for Frederic has forgotten that it is night and that he is afraid of the dark. The entire description is absurd since the hour (9 pm) is not particularly late, and the almost full moon and many stars would give a good deal of light. Nevertheless, feeling the "gloomy castle" as a malevolent being shutting him out, Frederic must continue on his way to Evelyn. Fearful of seeing ghosts or gypsies, he makes the reckless decision to ride "on a full gallop all the way [home]" with his eyes shut!

At this point, Austen finishes, though she left several pages blank for a possible continuation. The problem she has set herself is how to unite the Sussex plot with the Carlisle plot, particularly since Frederic has gained nothing from his quest with which to comfort his own family. The first continuation does this audaciously: Maria, whom Frederic expected to find alive, is dead; Rosa, whom he expected to find dead, is alive and happily married; and in Carlisle, quite by chance, he meets Mrs. Willis, immediately proposes and is accepted. The small matter of Maria being dead and buried, but his never having informed her parents (a second example of Frederic's appalling memory), is dealt with by a letter which makes her passing all about him. However, the ever-sensitive Webbs find the letter to be another example of Frederic's "unexampled generosity" and enclose thirty pounds to show their appreciation. Even Frederic's sister moves into the White Horse Inn with her new husband, and everyone lives happily ever after. One cannot help but detect Austen's mind, if not her hand, behind this comically contrived resolution.

The alternative ending, written on loose leaves of paper, is so entirely different from, and inferior to, Austen's story that little need be said of it. It begins with Frederic's melodramatic discovery that Maria is dead (or at least that she has disappeared) and moves to a deliberately over-written description of his vivid, laudanum-induced dream of Maria's spirit in which appear many of the main elements of Gothic fiction (the fevered dream, the spirit of the dead woman appearing to the bereaved lover, an enigmatic message from the ghost, the secret villain, etc.). Even in this version, however, Frederic's future appears to lie with "the benevolent Mrs. Willis."

~~Kitty~~ Catharine[1], or the Bower[2]

To Miss Austen[3]
Madam
Encouraged by your warm patronage of *The Beautiful Cassandra* and *The History of England*, which through your generous support, have obtained a place in every library in the kingdom, and run through threescore editions[4], I take the liberty of begging the same exertions in favour of the following novel, which I humbly flatter myself, possesses merit beyond any already published, or any that will ever in future appear, except such as may proceed from the pen of
Your most grateful humble servant
The Author
Steventon, August 1792

Kitty had the misfortune, as many heroines have had before her, of losing her parents when she was very young, and of being brought up under the care of a maiden aunt[5], who while she tenderly loved her, watched over her conduct with so scrutinizing a severity, as to make it very doubtful to many people, and to Kitty amongst the rest, whether she loved her or not. She had frequently been deprived of a real pleasure through this jealous caution had been sometimes obliged to relinquish a ball because an officer was to be there, or to dance with a partner of her aunt's introduction in preference to one of her own choice. But her spirits were naturally good, and not easily depressed, and she possessed such a fund of vivacity and good humour as could only be damped by some very serious vexation.–

Besides these antidotes against every disappointment, and consolations under them, she had another, which afforded her constant relief in all her misfortunes, and that was a fine shady bower, the work of her own infantine labours assisted by those of two young companions who had resided in the same village. – To this ~~garden~~ bower, which terminated a very pleasant and retired walk in her aunt's garden, she always wandered whenever anything disturbed her, and it possessed such a charm over her senses, as constantly to tranquillize her mind and quiet her spirits. – Solitude and reflection might perhaps have had the same effect in her bed chamber, yet habit had so strengthened the idea which fancy had first suggested, that such a thought never occurred to Kitty who was firmly persuaded that her bower alone could restore her to herself.

Her imagination was warm, and in her friendships, as well as in the whole tenure of her mind, she was enthusiastic[6]. This beloved bower had been the united work of herself and two amiable girls, for whom since her earliest years she had felt the tenderest regard. They were the daughters of the clergyman of the parish with whose family, while it had continued there, her aunt had been on the most intimate terms, and the little girls though separated for the greatest part of the year by the different modes of their education, were constantly together during the holidays of the Miss Wynnes[7] ; they were companions in their walks, their schemes and amusements, and while the sweetness of their dispositions had prevented any serious quarrels, the trifling disputes which it was impossible wholly to avoid, had been far from lessening their affection. In those days of happy childhood, now so often regretted by Kitty, this arbour had been formed, and separated perhaps forever from these dear friends, it encouraged more than any other place the tender and melancholy recollections of hours rendered pleasant by *them*, at on[c]e so sorrowful, yet so soothing!

It was now two years since the death of Mr. Wynne and the consequent dispersion of his family who had been left by it in great distress. They had been reduced to a state of absolute dependence on some relations, who though very opulent and very nearly connected with them, had with difficulty been prevailed on to contribute anything towards their support. Mrs. Wynne was fortunately spared the knowledge and participation of their distress by her release from a painful illness a few months before the death of her husband.–

The eldest daughter had been obliged to accept the offer of one of her cousins to equip her for the East Indies, and though infinitely against her inclinations had been necessitated to embrace the only possibility that was offered to her, of a maintenance. Yet it was *one*, so opposite to all her ideas of propriety, so contrary to her wishes, so repugnant to her feelings, that she would almost have preferred servitude to it, had choice been allowed her. – Her personal attractions had gained her a husband as soon as she had arrived at Bengal, and she had now been married nearly a twelve month.

Splendidly, yet unhappily married[8]. United to a man of double of her own age, whose disposition was not amiable, and whose manners were unpleasing, though his character was respectable. Kitty had heard twice from her friend since her marriage, but her letters were always unsatisfactory, and though she did not openly avow her feelings, yet every line proved her to be unhappy. She spoke with pleasure of nothing but of those amusements which they had shared together and which could return no more, and seemed to have no happiness in view but that of returning to England again.

Her sister had been taken by another relation, the Dowager[9] Lady Halifax, as a companion to her daughters, and had accompanied her family into Scotland about the same time of Cecilia's leaving England. From Mary therefore Kitty had the power of hearing more frequently, but her letters were scarcely more comfortable. – There was not indeed that hopelessness of sorrow in her situation as in her sister's. She was not married and could yet look forward to a change in her circumstances, but situated for the present without any immediate hope of it, in a family where, though all were her relations she had no friend, she wrote usually in depressed spirits, which her separation from her sister and her sister's marriage had greatly contributed to make so.–

Divided thus from the two she loved best on earth, while Cecilia and Mary were still more endeared to her by their loss, everything that brought a remembrance of them was doubly cherished, and the shrubs they had planted, and the keepsakes they had given were rendered sacred.–

The living of Chetwynde[10] was now in the possession of a Mr. Dudley, whose family, unlike the Wynnes, were productive only of vexation and trouble to Mrs. ~~Peterson~~ Percival[11] and her niece. Mr. Dudley, who was the younger son of a very noble family, of a family more famed for their pride than their opulence, tenacious of his dignity and jealous of his rights, was forever quarrelling, if not with Mrs. Peterson herself, with her steward and tenants concerning tithes[12], and with the principal neighbours themselves concerning the respect and parade[13], he exacted. ~~This~~ His wife, an ill-educated, untaught woman of ancient family, was proud of that family almost without knowing why, and like him too was haughty and quarrelsome, without considering for what. Their only daughter, who inherited the ignorance, the insolence, and pride of her parents, was from that beauty of which she was unreasonably vain, considered by them as an irresistible creature, and looked up to as the future restorer, by a splendid marriage, of the dignity which their reduced situation, and Mr. Dudley's being obliged to take orders for a country living had so much lessened.

They at once despised the Petersons as people of ~~no~~ mean family, and envied them as people of fortune. They were jealous of their being more respected than themselves and while they affected to consider them as of no consequence, were continually seeking to lessen them in the opinion of the neighbourhood by scandalous and malicious reports. Such a family as this was ill-calculated to console Kitty for the loss of the Wynnes, or to fill up by their society those occasionally irksome hours which in so retired a situation would sometimes occur ~~to her~~ for want of a companion.

Her aunt was most excessively fond of her, and miserable if she saw her for a moment out of spirits. Yet she lived in such constant apprehension~~s~~ of her marrying imprudently if she were allowed the opportunity of choosing, and was so dissatisfied with her behaviour when she saw her with young men, for it was, from her natural disposition remarkably open and unreserved, that though she frequently wished for her niece's sake, that the neighbourhood were larger, and that she had used herself to mix more with it, yet the recollection of there being young men in almost every family in it, always conquered the wish.

The same fears that prevented Mrs. Peterson's joining much in the society of her neighbours, led her equally to avoid inviting her relations to spend any time in her house. – She had therefore constantly regretted the annual attempt of a distant relation to visit her at Chetwynde, as there was a young man in the family of whom she had heard many traits that alarmed her. This son was, however, now on his travels, and the repeated solicitations of Kitty, joined to a consciousness of having declined with too little ceremony the frequent ~~endeavours~~ overtures of her friends to be admitted, and a real wish to see them herself, easily prevailed on her to press with great earnestness the pleasure of a visit from them during the summer.

Mr. and Mrs. Stanley were accordingly to come, and Kitty, in having an object to look forward to, a something to expect that must inevitably relieve the dullness of a constant *tête à tête* with her aunt, was so delighted, and her spirits so elevated, that for the three or four days immediately preceding their arrival, she could scarcely fix herself to any employment. In this point, Mrs. Peterson always thought her defective, and frequently complained of a want of steadiness and perseverance in her occupations, which were by no means congenial to the eagerness of Kitty's disposition, and perhaps not often met with in any young person. The tediousness too of her aunt's conversation and the want of agreeable companions greatly increased this desire of change in her employments, for Kitty found herself much sooner tired of reading, working, or drawing, in Mrs. Peterson's parlour than in her own arbour, where Mrs. Peterson, for fear of its being damp, never accompanied her.

As her aunt prided herself on the exact propriety and neatness with which everything in her family was conducted, and had no higher satisfaction than that of knowing her house to be always in complete order, as her fortune was good, and her establishment[14] ample, few were the preparations necessary for the reception of her visitors. The day of their arrival so long expected, at length ~~arrived~~ came, and the noise of the coach and as it drove round the sweep[15], was to Kitty a more interesting sound, than ~~an~~ the music of an Italian opera, which to most heroines is the height of enjoyment.

Mr. and Mrs. Stanley were people of large fortune and high fashion. He was a member of the House ~~and~~ of Commons, and they were therefore most agreeably necessitated to reside half the year in town[16]; where Miss Stanley had been attended by the most capital masters from the time of her being six years old to the last spring, which comprehending a period of twelve years had been dedicated to the acquirement of accomplishments which were now to be displayed and in a few years entirely neglected. She was ~~about Kitty's age not in~~elegant in her appearance, rather handsome, and naturally not deficient in abilities; but those years which ought to have been spent in the attainment of useful knowledge and mental improvement, had been all bestowed in learning drawing, Italian and music, more especially the latter, and she now united to these accomplishments, an understanding unimproved by reading and a mind totally devoid either of taste or judgement[17]. Her temper was by nature good, but unassisted by reflection, she had neither patience under disappointment, nor could sacrifice her own inclinations to promote the happiness of others. All her ideas were towards the elegance of her appearance, the fashion of her dress, and the admiration she wished them to excite. She professed a love of books without reading, was lively without wit, and generally good humoured without merit.

Such was Camilla Stanley; and Kitty, who was prejudiced by her appearance, and who from her solitary situation was ready to like anyone, though her understanding and judgement would not otherwise have been easily satisfied, felt almost convinced when she saw her, that Miss Stanley would be the very companion she wanted, and in some degree make amends for the loss of Cecilia and Mary Wynne. She therefore attached herself to Camilla from the first day of her arrival, and from being the only young people in the house, they were by inclination constant companions. Kitty was herself a great reader, though perhaps not a very deep one, and felt therefore highly delighted to find that Miss Stanley was equally fond of it. Eager to know that their sentiments as to books were similar, she very soon began questioning her new acquaintance on the subject; but though she was well read in modern history herself, she chose rather to speak first of books of a lighter kind, of books universally read and admired ~~and that had given rise perhaps to more frequent arguments than any other of the same sort~~.

"You have read Mrs. Smith's novels[18], I suppose!" said she to her companion. –

"Oh! Yes," replied the other, "and I am quite delighted with them. – They are the sweetest things in the world.–"

"And which do you prefer of them?"

"Oh! dear, I think there is no comparison between them.– *Emmeline* is *so much* better than any of the others.–"

"Many people think so, I know, but there does not appear so great a disproportion in their merits to me. Do you think it is better written?"

"Oh! I do not know anything about *that* – but it is better ~~all together~~ in *everything*. – Besides, *Ethelinde* is so long.–"

"That is a very common objection I believe," said Kitty, "but for my own part, if a book is well written, I always find it too short."

"So do I, only I get tired of it before it is finished."

"But did not you find the story of *Ethelinde* very interesting? And the descriptions of Grasmere[19], are not the[y] beautiful?"

"Oh! I missed them all, because I was in such a hurry to know the end of it. –" Then from an easy transition she added, "We are going to the Lakes this autumn, and I am quite mad with joy; Sir Henry Devereux has promised to go with us, and that will make it so pleasant, you know.–"

"I dare say it will, but I think it is a pity that Sir Henry's powers of pleasing were not reserved for an occasion where they might be more wanted. – However, I quite envy you the pleasure of such a scheme."

"Oh! I am quite delighted with the thoughts of it; I can think of nothing else. I ~~shall~~ assure you I have done nothing for this last month but plan ~~what clothes~~ what clothes I should take with me, and I have at last determined to take very few indeed besides my travelling dress, and so I advise you to do, whenever you go; for I intend in case we should fall in with any races[20], or stop at Matlock or Scarborough, to have some things made for the occasion."

"You intend then to go into Yorkshire?"

"I believe not – indeed I know nothing of the route, for I never trouble myself about such things. I only know that we are to go from Derbyshire to Matlock and Scarborough[21], but to which of them first, I neither know nor care. – I am in hopes of meeting some particular friends of mine at Scarborough. – Augusta told me in her last letter that Sir Peter talked of going, but then you know that is so uncertain. I cannot bear Sir Peter; he is such a horrid creature.–

"He *is*, is he?" said Kitty, not knowing what else to say.

"Oh! he is quite shocking."

Here the conversation was interrupted, and Kitty was left in a painful uncertainty as to the particulars of Sir Peter's character; she knew only that he was horrid and shocking, but why, and in what, yet remained to be discovered. She could scarcely resolve what to think of her new acquaintance; she appeared to be shamefully ignorant as to the geography of England, if she had understood her right, and equally devoid of taste and information. Kitty was, however, unwilling to decide hastily. She was at once desirous of doing Miss Stanley justice, and of having her own wishes in her answered; she determined therefore to suspend all judgement for some time.

After supper, the conversation turning on the state of affairs in the political world. Mrs. Peterson, who was firmly of opinion that the whole race of mankind were degenerating, said that for her part, everything she believed was going to rack and ruin, all order was destroyed over the face of the world, the House of Commons she heard did not break up sometimes till five in the morning, and depravity never was so general before[22];

concluding with a wish that she might live to see the manners of the people in Queen Elizabeth's reign, restored again.

"Well, ma'am," said her niece, "~~I believe you have as good a chance of it as anyone else,~~ but I hope you do not mean with the times to restore Queen Elizabeth herself."

"Queen Elizabeth," said Mrs. Stanley, who never hazarded a remark on history that was not well founded, "lived to a good old age, and was a very clever woman."

"True, ma'am," said Kitty, "but I do not consider either of those circumstances as meritorious in herself, and they are very far from making me wish her return, for if she were to come again with the same abilities and the same good constitution, she might do as much mischief and last as long as she did before.–"

Then turning to Camilla who had been sitting very silent for some time, she added, "What do *you* think of Elizabeth, Miss Stanley? I hope you will not defend her."

"Oh! dear," said Miss Stanley. "I know nothing of politics, and cannot bear to hear them mentioned."

Kitty started at this repulse, but made no answer; that Miss Stanley must be ignorant of what she could not distinguish from ~~history~~ politics, she felt perfectly convinced. – She retired to her own room, perplexed in her opinion about her new acquaintance, and fearful of her being very unlike Cecilia and Mary. She arose the next morning to experience a fuller conviction of this, and every future day increased it. – She found no variety in her conversation. She received no information from her but in fashions and no amusement but in her performance on the harpsichord; and after repeated endeavours to find her what she wished, she was obliged to give up the attempt and to consider it as fruitless.

There had occasionally appeared a something like humour in Camilla which had inspired her with hopes that she might at least have a natural genius, though not an improved one, but these sparklings of wit happened so seldom, and were so ill-supported, that she was at last convinced of their being merely accidental. All her stock of knowledge was exhausted in a very few days, and when Kitty had learnt from her, how large their house in town was, when the fashionable amusements ~~again~~ began, who were the celebrated beauties and who the best milliner, Camilla had nothing further to teach, except the characters of any of her acquaintance as they occurred in conversation, which was done with equal ease and brevity, by saying that the person was either the sweetest creature in the world, and one of whom she was dotingly fond, or horrid, shocking and not fit to be seen.

As Kitty was very desirous of gaining every possible information as to the characters of the Halifax family and concluded that Miss Stanley must be acquainted with them, as she seemed to be so with every one of any consequence, she took an opportunity as Camilla was one day enumerating all the people of rank that her mother visited, of asking her whether Lady Halifax were among the number.

"Oh! Thank you for reminding me of her; she is the sweetest woman in the world, and one of our most intimate acquaintance. I do not suppose there is a day passes during the six months that we are in town, but what we see each other in the course of it. – And I correspond with all the girls."

"They *are* then a very pleasant family!" said Kitty. "They ought to be so indeed, to allow of such frequent meetings, or all conversation must be at end."

"Oh! dear, not at all," said Miss Stanley, "for sometimes we do not speak to each other for a month together. We meet perhaps only in public, and then, you know, we are ~~not always~~ often not able to get near enough; but in that case we always nod and smile."

"Which does just as well. – But I was going to ask you whether you have ever seen a Miss Wynne with them?"

"I know who you mean perfectly – she wears a blue hat. – I have frequently seen her in Brook Street, when I have been at Lady Halifax's balls – she gives one every month during the winter. – But only think how good it is in her to take care of Miss Wynne, for she is a very distant relation, and so poor that, as Miss Halifax told me, her mother was obliged to find her in clothes. Is not it shameful?"

"That she should be so poor? It is indeed, with such wealthy connections as the family have."

"Oh! no; I mean, was not it shameful in Mr. Wynne to leave his children so distressed, when he had actually the living of Chetwynde and two or three curacies[23], and only four children to provide for. – What would he have done if he had had ten, as many people have?"

"He would have given them all a good education and have left them all equally poor."

"Well I do think there never was so lucky a family. Sir George Fitzgibbon you know sent the eldest girl to India entirely at his own expense, where they say she is most nobly married and the happiest creature in the world. – Lady Halifax, you see, has taken care of the youngest and treats her as if she were her daughter. She does not go out ~~wit~~ into public with her to be sure, but then she is always present when her Ladyship gives her balls, and nothing can be kinder to her than Lady Halifax is. She would have taken her to Cheltenham ~~to~~ last year, if there had been room enough at the lodgings, and therefore I do not think that *she* can have anything to complain of. The~~re~~ there are the two sons: one of them the Bishop of M—— has ~~sent to sea~~ got into the army[24] as a lieutenant I suppose; and the other is extremely well off I know, for I have a notion that somebody puts him to school somewhere in Wales[25]. Perhaps you knew them when they lived here?"

"~~Slightly~~ Very well, we met as often as your family and the Halifaxes do in town, but as we seldom had any difficulty in getting near enough to speak, we seldom parted with merely a nod and a smile. They were indeed a most charming family, and I believe have scarcely their equals in the world; the neighbours we now have at the Parsonage, appear to more disadvantage in coming after them."

"Oh! horrid wretches! I wonder you can endure them."

"Why, what would you have one do?"

"Oh! Lord, if I were in your place, I should abuse them all day long."

"So I do, but it does no good."

"Well, I declare it is quite a pity that they should be suffered to live. I wish my father would propose knocking all their brains out, some day or other when he is in the House. So abominably proud of their family! And I dare say, after all, that there is nothing particular in it."

"Why yes, I believe they *have* reason to value themselves on it, if anybody has, for you know he is Lord Amyatt's brother."

"Oh! I know all that very well, but it is no reason for their being so horrid. I remember I met Miss Dudley last spring with Lady Amyatt at Ranelagh[26], and she had such a frightful cap on, that I have never been able to ~~w~~bear any of them since. – And so you used to think the Wynnes very pleasant?"

"You speak as if their being so were doubtful! Pleasant! Oh! they were everything that could interest and attach. It is not in my power to do justice to their merits, though not to feel them, I think, must be impossible. They have unfitted me for any society but their own!"

"Well, that is just what I think of the Miss Halifaxes. By the bye, I must write to Caroline tomorrow, and I do not know what to say to her. The ~~Barkers~~ Barlows too are just such other sweet girls, but I wish Augusta's hair was not so dark. I cannot bear Sir Peter – horrid wretch! He is *always* laid up with the gout, which is exceedingly disagreeable to the family."

"And perhaps not very pleasant to *himself*. – But as to the Wynnes, do you really think them very fortunate?"

"Do I? Why, does not everybody? Miss Halifax and Caroline and Maria all say that they are the luckiest creatures in the world. So does Sir George Fitzgibbon and so do everybody."

"That is, everybody who have themselves conferred an obligation on them. But do you call it lucky, for a girl of genius and feeling to be sent in quest of a husband to Bengal, to be married there to a man of whose disposition she has no opportunity of judging till her judgement is of no use to her, who may be a tyrant, or a fool or both for what she knows to the contrary. Do you call *that* fortunate?"

"I know nothing of all that; I only know that it was extremely good in Sir George to fit her out and pay her passage, and that she would not have found many who would have done the same."

"I wish she had not found *one*," said Kitty with great eagerness. "She might then have remained in England and been happy."

"Well, I cannot conceive the hardship of going out in a very agreeable manner with two or three sweet girls for companions, having a delightful voyage to Bengal or Barbados or wherever it is, and being married soon after one's arrival to a very charming man, immensely rich. – I see no hardship in all that[27]."

"Your representation of the affair," said Kitty laughing, "certainly gives a very different idea of it from mine. But supposing all this to be true, still, as it was by no means certain that she would be so fortunate either in her voyage, her companions, or her husband, in being obliged to run the risk of their proving very different, she undoubtedly experienced a great hardship. – Besides, to a girl of any delicacy, the voyage in itself, since the object of it is so universally known, is a punishment that needs no other to make it very severe."

"I do not see that at all. She is not the first girl who has gone to the East Indies for a husband, and I declare I should think it very good fun if I were as poor."

"I believe you would think very differently *then*. But at least

276

you will not defend her sister's situation! Dependant, even for her clothes, on the bounty of others who, of course, do not pity her as, by your own account, they consider her as very fortunate."

"You are extremely nice[28] upon my word. Lady Halifax is a delightful woman, and one of the sweetest tempered creatures in the world; I am sure I have every reason to speak well of her, for we are under most amazing obligations to her. She has frequently chaperoned me when my mother has been indisposed, and last spring she lent me her own horse three times, which was a prodigious favour, for it is the most beautiful creature that ever was seen, and I am the only person she ever lent it to.

~~"If so, *Mary Wynne* can receive very little advantage from her having it."~~

"And then," continued she, "the Miss Halifaxes are quite delightful. Maria is one of the cleverest girls that ever were known – draws in oils[29], and plays anything by sight. She promised me one of her drawings before I left town, but I entirely forgot to ask her for it. I would give anything to have one."

~~"Why indeed, if Maria will give my friend a drawing, she can have nothing to complain of, but as she does not write in spirits, I suppose she has not yet been fortunate enough to be so distinguished."~~

"But was not it very odd," said Kitty, "that the Bishop should send Charles Wynne to sea[30], when he must have had a much better chance of providing for him in the Church, which was the profession that Charles liked best, and the one for which his father had intended him? The Bishop I know had often promised Mr. Wynne a living, and as he never gave him one, I think it was incumbent on him to transfer the promise to his son."

"I believe you think he ought to have resigned his Bishopric to him; you seem determined to be dissatisfied with everything that has been done for them."

"Well," said Kitty, "this is a subject on which we shall never agree, and therefore it will be useless to continue it farther, or to mention it again.–"

She then left the room, and running out of the house was soon in her dear bower where she could indulge in peace all her affectionate anger against the relations of the Wynnes, which was greatly heightened by finding from Camilla that they were in general considered as having acted particularly well by them. – She amused herself for some time in abusing, and hating them all, with great spirit, and when this tribute to ~~the~~ her regard for the Wynnes was paid, and the bower began to have its usual influence over her spirits, she contributed towards settling them, by taking out a book, for she had always one about her, and reading.–

She had been so employed for nearly an hour, when Camilla came running towards her with great eagerness, and apparently great pleasure.–

"Oh! my dear Kitty," said she, half out of breath, – "I have such delightful news for you – But you shall guess what it is. – We are all the happiest creatures in the world; would you believe it, the Dudleys have sent us an invitation to a ball at their own house. – What charming people they are! I had no idea of there being so much sense in the whole family. – I declare I quite dote upon them. – And it happens so fortunately too, for I expect a new cap from town tomorrow which will just do for a ball – gold net. – It will be a most angelic thing – everybody will be longing for the pattern.–"

The expectation of a ball was indeed very agreeable intelligence to Kitty who, fond of dancing and seldom able to enjoy it, had reason to feel even greater pleasure in it than her friend, for to *her*, it was now no novelty. – Camilla's delight, however, was by no means inferior to Kitty's, and she rather expressed the most of the two. The cap came and every other preparation was soon completed; while these were in agitation, the days passed gaily away, but when directions were no longer necessary, taste could no longer be displayed, the difficulties no longer overcome, the short period that intervened before the day of the ball hung heavily on their hands, and every hour was too long. The very few times that Kitty had ever enjoyed the amusement of dancing was an excuse for her impatience, and an apology for the idleness it occasioned to a mind naturally very active; but her friend without such a plea was infinitely worse than herself. She could do nothing but wander from the house to the garden, and from the garden to the avenue, wondering when Thursday would come, which she might easily have ascertained, and counting the hours as they passed, which served only to lengthen them.–

They retired to their rooms in high spirits on Wednesday night, but Kitty awoke the next morning with a violent toothache. It was in vain that she endeavoured at first to deceive herself; her feelings were witnesses too acute of its reality. With as little success did she try to sleep it off, for the pain she suffered prevented her closing her eyes. – She then summoned her maid and with the assistance of the housekeeper, every remedy that the receipt book[31], or the head of the latter contained, was tried, but ineffectually, for though for a short time relieved by them, the pain still returned. She was now obliged to give up the endeavour, and to reconcile herself not only to the pain of a toothache, but to the loss of a ball; and though she had with so much eagerness looked forward to the day of its arrival, had received such pleasure in the necessary preparations, and promised herself so much delight in it, yet she was not so totally void of philosophy as many girls of her age might have been in her situation. She considered that there were misfortunes of a much greater magnitude than the loss of a ball, experienced every day by some part of mortality, and that then time might come when she would herself look back with wonder and perhaps with envy on her having known no greater vexation. By such reflections as these, she soon reasoned herself into as much resignation and patience as the pain she suffered would allow of which, after all, was the greatest misfortune of the two, and told the sad story when she entered the breakfast room, with tolerable composure.

Mrs. Peterson, more grieved for her toothache than her disappointment, as she feared that it would not be possible to prevent her dancing with a *man* if she went, was eager to try everything that had already been applied to alleviate the pain, while at the same time she declared it was impossible for her to leave the house. Miss Stanley, who, joined to her concern for her friend, felt a mixture of dread lest her mother's proposal that they should all remain at home might be accepted, was very violent in her sorrow on the occasion, and though her apprehensions on the subject were soon quieted by Kitty's protesting that, sooner than allow anyone to stay with her, she would herself go, she continued to lament it with such unceasing vehemence as at last drove Kitty to her own room. Her fears for herself being now entirely dissipated left her more than ever at leisure to pity and persecute her friend who though safe when in her own room, was frequently removing from it to some other in hopes of being more free from pain, and then had no opportunity of escaping her.–

"To be sure, there never was anything so shocking," said

Camilla. "To come on such a day too! For one would not have minded it, you know, had it been at *any other* time. But it always is so. I never was at a ball in my life, but what something happened to prevent somebody from going! I wish there were no such things as teeth in the world; they are nothing but plagues to one, and I dare say that people might easily invent something to eat with instead of them; poor thing! What pain you are in! I declare it is quite shocking to look at you. But you won't have it out, will you! For Heaven's sake don't, for there is nothing I dread so much. I declare I have rather undergo the greatest tortures in the world than have a tooth drawn[32]. Well! how patiently you do bear it! How can you be so quiet! Lord, if I were in your place I should make such a fuss, there would be no bearing me. I should torment you to death."

"So you do, as it is," thought Kitty.

"For my own part, Kitty," said Mrs. Peterson, "I have not a doubt but that you caught this toothache by sitting so much in that arbour, for it is always damp. I know it has ruined your constitution entirely, and indeed I do not believe it has been of much service to mine. I sat down in it last May to rest myself, and I have never been quite well since. – I shall order John to pull it all down I assure you."

"I know you will not do that, ma'am," said Kitty, "as you must be convinced how unhappy it would make me."

"You talk very ridiculously, child; it is all whim and nonsense. Why cannot you fancy this room an arbour!"

"Had this room been built by Cecilia and Mary, I should have valued it equally, ma'am, for it is not merely the name of an arbour, which charms me."

"Why indeed, Mrs. Peterson," said Mrs. Stanley, "I must think that Kitty's affection for her bower is the effect of a sensibility that does her credit. I love to see a friendship between young ~~ladies~~ persons and always consider it as a sure mark ~~of their being disposed to like one another~~ of an amiable, affectionate disposition. I have from Camilla's infancy taught her to think the same, and have taken great pains to introduce her to young people of her own age who were likely to be worthy of her regard. ~~There is something mighty pretty, I think, in young ladies corresponding with each other, and~~ Nothing forms the taste more than sensible and elegant letters. – Lady Halifax thinks just like me. – Camilla corresponds with her daughters, and I believe I may venture to say that they are none of them the *worse for* it."

These ideas were too modern to suit Mrs. Peterson, who considered a correspondence between girls as productive of no good, and as the frequent origin of imprudence and error by the effect of pernicious advice and bad example. She could not, therefore, refrain from saying that, for her part, she had lived fifty years in the world without having ever had a correspondent, and did not find herself at all the less respectable for it.–

Mrs. Stanley could say nothing in answer to this, but her daughter, who was less governed by propriety, said in her thoughtless way, "But who knows what you might have been, ma'am, if you *had* had a correspondent; perhaps it would have made you quite a different creature. I declare I would not be without those I have for all the world. It is the greatest delight of my life, and you cannot think how much their letters have formed my taste as mama says, for I hear from them generally every week."

"You received a letter from Augusta Barlow today, did not you, my love?" said her mother. – "She writes remarkably well I know."

"Oh! Yes ma'am, the most delightful letter you ever heard of. She sends me a long account of the new ~~pierrot~~ Regency walking dress[33] Lady Susan has given her, and it is so beautiful that I am quite dying with envy for it."

"Well, I am prodigiously happy to hear such pleasing news of my young friend; I have a high regard for Augusta, and most sincerely partake in the general joy on the occasion. But does she say nothing else? It seemed to be a long letter. – Are they to be at Scarborough?"

"Oh! Lord, she never once mentions it, now I recollect it; and I entirely forgot to ask her when I wrote last. She says nothing indeed except about the ~~jacket~~ Regency dress."

"She *must* write well," thought Kitty, to make a long letter upon a ~~jacket and petticoat~~ bonnet and pelisse[34].

She then left the room tired of listening to a conversation which, though it might have diverted her had she been well, served only to fatigue and depress her while in pain. Happy was it for *her*, when the hour of dressing came, for Camilla, satisfied with being surrounded by her mother and half the maids in the house, did not want her assistance, and was too agreeably employed to want her society. She remained, therefore, alone in the parlour, till joined by Mr. Stanley and her aunt who, however, after a few enquiries, allowed her to ~~remain~~ continue undisturbed and began their usual conversation on politics.

This was a subject on which they could never agree, for Mr. Stanley who considered himself as perfectly qualified by his seat in the House to decide on it without hesitation, resolutely maintained that the kingdom had not for ages been in so flourishing and prosperous a state, and Mrs. Peterson, with equal warmth, though perhaps less argument, as vehemently asserted that the whole nation would speedily be ruined and everything, as she expressed herself, be at sixes and sevens[35]. It was not, however, unamusing to Kitty to listen to the dispute, especially as she began then to be more free from pain, and without taking any share in it herself, she found it very entertaining to observe the eagerness with which they both defended their opinions, and could not help thinking that Mr. Stanley would not feel more disappointed if her aunt's expectations were fulfilled, than her Aunt would be mortified by their failure.

After waiting a considerable time, Mrs. Stanley and her daughter appeared, and Camilla, in high spirits and perfect good humour with her own looks, was more violent than ever in her lamentations over her friend as she practised her Scotch steps[36] about the room. – At length they departed, and Kitty better able to amuse herself than she had been the whole day before, wrote a long account of her misfortunes to Mary Wynne.

When her letter was concluded, she had an opportunity of witnessing the truth of that assertion which says that sorrows are lightened by communication, for her toothache was then so much relieved that she began to entertain an idea of following her friends to Mr. Dudley's. They had been gone ~~but half~~ an hour, and as everything relative to her dress was in complete readiness, she considered that in ~~an hour and a half~~ another hour since there was so little a way to go, she might be there. – They were gone in Mr. Stanley's carriage and therefore she might follow in her aunt's. As the plan seemed so very easy to be executed, and promising so much pleasure, ~~in itself~~ it was after a few minutes deliberation finally adopted, and running up stairs, she rang in great haste for her maid. The bustle and hurry which then ensued for ~~about~~ nearly an hour was at last happily concluded by her finding herself very well dressed and in high beauty. ~~Nanny~~ Anne was then dispatched in the same haste to order the carriage, while her mistress was putting on her gloves, and arranging the folds of her dress~~, and providing~~

herself with lavender water.

In a few minutes, she heard the carriage drive up to the door, and though at first surprised at the expedition with which it had been got ready, she concluded, after a little reflection, that the men had received some hint of her intentions beforehand, and was hastening out of the room, when ~~Nanny~~ Anne came running into it in the greatest hurry and agitation, exclaiming, "Lord, ma'am! Here's a gentleman in a chaise and four[37] come, and I cannot for the life conceive who it is! I happened to be crossing the hall when the carriage drove up, and ~~as~~ I knew nobody would be in the way to let him in but Tom, and he looks so awkward you know, ma'am, now his hair is just done up, that I was not willing the gentleman should see him, and so I went to the door myself. And he is one of the handsomest young men you would wish to see; I was almost ashamed of being seen ~~because you know ma'am I am all over powder~~ in my apron, ma'am, but however, he is vastly handsome and did not seem to mind it at all. – And he asked me whether the family were at home; and so I said everybody was gone out but you, ma'am, for I would not deny you because I was sure you would like to see him. And then he asked me whether Mr. and Mrs. Stanley were not here, and so I said yes, and then–"

"Good Heavens!" said Kitty, "What can all this mean! And who can it possibly be! Did you never see him before! And did not he tell you his name!"

"No, ma'am, he never said anything about it. – So then I asked him to walk into the parlour, and he was prodigious agreeable, and–"

"Whoever he is," said her mistress, "he has made a great impression upon you, Nanny. – But where did he come from? And what does he want here?"

"Oh! ma'am, I was going to tell you, that I fancy his business is with you, for he asked me whether you were at leisure to see anybody, and desired I would give his compliments to you, and say he should be very happy to wait on you. – However, I thought he had better not come up into your dressing room, especially as everything is in such a litter[38], so I told him if he would be so obliging as to stay in the parlour, I would run up stairs and tell you he was come, and I dared to say that you would wait upon *him.* Lord, ma'am, I'd lay anything that he is come to ask you to dance with him tonight, and has got his chaise ready to take you to Mr. Dudley's."

Kitty could not help laughing at this idea, and only wished it might be true, as it was very likely that she would be too late for any other partner.–

"But what, in the name of wonder, can he have to say to me! Perhaps he is come to rob the house. – He comes in style at least, and it will be some consolation for our losses to be robbed by a gentleman in a chaise and four. – What livery has his servants?"

"Why that is the most wonderful thing about him, ma'am, for he has not a single servant with him, and came with hack horses[39]; but he is as handsome as a prince for all that, and has quite the look of one. Do, dear ma'am, go down, for I am sure you will be delighted with him.–"

"Well, I believe I must go; but it is very odd! What can he have to say to me?"

Then, giving one look at herself in the glass, she walked with great impatience, though trembling all the while from not knowing what to expect, down stairs, and, after pausing a moment at the door to gather courage for opening it, she resolutely entered the room. The stranger, whose appearance did not disgrace the account she had received of it from her maid, rose up on her entrance, and laying aside the newspaper he had been reading, advanced towards her with an air of the most perfect ease and vivacity, and said to her:

"It is certainly a very awkward circumstance to be thus obliged to introduce myself, but I trust that the necessity of the case will plead my excuse, and prevent your being prejudiced by it against me. – *Your* name, I need not ask, ma'am. – Miss Peterson is too well known to me by description to need any information of that."

Kitty, who had been expecting him to tell his own name, instead of hers, and who, from having been little in company, and never before in such a situation, felt herself unable to ask it, though she had been planning her speech all the way down stairs, was so confused and distressed by this unexpected address that she could only return a slight curtsy to it, and accepted the chair he reached her, without knowing what she did. The gentleman then continued:

"You are, I dare say, surprised to see me returned from France so soon, and nothing indeed but business could have brought me to England; a very melancholy affair has now occasioned it, and I was unwilling to leave it without paying my respects to the family in Devonshire whom I have so long wished to be acquainted with.–"

Kitty, who felt much more surprised at his supposing her *to be so*, than at seeing a person in England whose having ever left it was perfectly unknown to her, still continued silent from wonder and perplexity, and her visitor still continued to talk.

"You will suppose, madam, that I was not the less desirous of waiting on you, from your having Mr. and Mrs. Stanley with you. – I hope they are well? And Mrs. Peterson, how does she do?" Then without waiting for an answer he gaily added, "But my dear Miss Peterson, you are going out I am sure, and I am detaining you from your appointment. How can I ever expect to be forgiven for such injustice! Yet how can I, so circumstanced, forbear to offend! You seem dressed for a ball! But this is the land of gaiety I know; I have for many years been desirous of visiting it. You have dances I suppose at least every week. – But where are the rest of your party gone, and what kind angel, in compassion to me, has excluded you from it?"

"Perhaps sir," said Kitty extremely confused by his manner of speaking to her, and highly displeased with the freedom of his conversation towards one who had never seen him before and did not *now* know his name, "perhaps sir, you are acquainted with Mr. and Mrs. Stanley, and your business may be with *them*?"

"You do me too much honour, ma'am," replied he laughing, "in supposing me to be acquainted with Mr. and Mrs. Stanley; I merely know them by sight; very distant relations; only my father and mother. Nothing more I assure you."

"Gracious Heaven!" said Kitty. "Are *you* Mr., Stanley then? – I beg a thousand pardons – though really, upon recollection, I do not know for what – for you never told me your name.–"

"I beg your pardon. – I made a very fine speech when you entered the room, all about introducing myself; I assure you it was very great for *me*."

"The speech had certainly great merit," said Kitty smiling. "I thought so at the time; but as since you never mentioned your name in it, as an *introductory one* it might have been better."

There was such an air of good humour and gaiety in Stanley, that Kitty, though perhaps not authorized to address him with so much familiarity on so short an acquaintance, could not forbear indulging the natural unreserve and vivacity of her own disposition in speaking to him as he spoke to her. She was intimately acquainted too with his family, who were her relations, and she chose to consider herself entitled by the connection to forget how little a while they had known each other.

"Mr. and Mrs. Stanley and your sister are extremely well," said she, "and will, I dare say, be very much surprised to see you. – But I am sorry to hear that your return to England has been occasioned by an unpleasant circumstance."

"Oh, don't talk of it," said he. "It is a most confounded shocking affair, and makes me miserable to think of it; but where are my father and mother, and your aunt gone? Oh! Do you know that I met the prettiest little waiting maid in the world, when I came here; she let me into the house; I took her for you at first."

"You did me a great deal of honour, and give me more credit for good nature than I deserve, for I *never* go to the door when anyone comes."

"Nay, do not be angry; I mean no offence. But tell me, where are you going to so smart? Your carriage is just coming ~~to th~~ round."

"I am going to a dance at a neighbour's ~~of ours~~, where your family and my aunt are already gone."

"Gone, without you! What's the meaning of *that*? But I suppose you are like myself, rather long in dressing."

"I must have been so indeed, if that were the case for they have been gone nearly these two hours; the reason, however, was not what you suppose. – I was prevented going by a pain–"

"By a pain!" interrupted Stanley. "Oh! heavens, that is dreadful indeed! No matter where the pain was. But, my dear Miss Peterson, what do you say to my accompanying you! And suppose you were to dance with me too? *I* think it would be very pleasant."

"I can have no objection to either I am sure," said Kitty laughing to find how near the truth her maid's conjecture had been. "On the contrary, I shall be highly honoured by both, and I can answer for your being extremely welcome to the family who give the ball."

"Oh! hang them; who cares for that; they cannot turn me out of the house. But I am afraid I shall cut a sad figure among all your Devonshire beaux in this dusty, travelling apparel, and I have not wherewithal to change it. You can ~~lend~~ procure me some powder perhaps, and I must get a pair of shoes from one of the men, for I was in such a devil of a hurry to leave Lyons that I had not time to ~~pack up anything~~ have anything pack'd up but some linen."

286

Kitty very readily undertook to procure for him everything he wanted, and telling the footman to show him into Mr. Stanley's dressing room, gave Nanny[40] orders to send in some powder and pomatum[41], which orders Nanny chose to execute in person. As Stanley's preparations in dressing were confined to such very trifling articles, Kitty, of course, expected him in about ten minutes; but she found that it had not been merely a boast of vanity in saying that he was dilatory in that respect, as he kept her waiting for him above half an hour, so that the clock had struck ten before he entered the room and the rest of the party had gone ~~before~~ by eight.

"Well," said he as he came in, "have not I been very quick! I never hurried so much in my life before."

"In that case you certainly have," replied Kitty, "for all merit you know is comparative."

"Oh! I knew you would be delighted with me for making so much ["must" in text] haste. – But come, the carriage is ready; so, do not keep me waiting."

And so saying he took her by the hand, and led her out of the room.

"Why, my dear cousin," said he when they were seated, "this will be a most agreeable surprise to everybody to see you enter the room with such a smart young fellow ~~I~~ as I am. – I hope your aunt won't be alarmed."

"To tell you the truth," replied Kitty, "I think the best way to prevent it, will be to send for her, or your mother, before we go into the room, especially as you are a perfect stranger, and must, of course, be introduced to Mr. and Mrs. Dudley.–"

"Oh! Nonsense," said he. "I did not expect *you* to stand upon such ceremony; our acquaintance with each other renders all such prudery ridiculous. Besides, if we go in together, we shall be the whole talk of the country.–"

"To *me*," replied Kitty, "that would certainly be a most powerful inducement, but I scarcely know whether my aunt would consider it as such. – Women at her time of life, have odd ideas of propriety you know."

"Which is the very thing that you ought to break them of. And why should you object to entering a room with me where all our relations are, when you have done me the honour to admit me without any chaperone into your carriage? Do not you think your aunt will be as much offended with you for one, as for the other of these mighty crimes?"

"Why really," said Kitty, "I do not know but that she may;

however, it is no reason that I should offend against decorum a second time, because I have already done it once."

"On the contrary, that is the very reason which makes it impossible for you to prevent it, since you cannot offend for the *first time* again."

"You are very ridiculous," said she laughing, "but I am afraid your arguments divert me too much to convince me."

"At least they will convince you that I am very agreeable, which after all, is the happiest conviction for me, and as to the affair of propriety, we will let that rest till we arrive at our journey's end. – This is a monthly ball[42] I suppose. Nothing but dancing here.–"

"I thought I had told you that it was given by a Mr. and Mrs. Dudley.–"

"Oh! aye so you did, but why should not Mr. Dudley give one every month! By the bye who is that man? Everybody gives balls now I think; I believe I must give one myself soon. – Well, but how do you like my father and mother? And poor little Camilla too, has not she plagued you to death with the Halifaxes?"

Here the carriage fortunately stopped at Mr. Dudley's, and Stanley was too much engaged in handing her out of it, to wait for an answer, or to remember that what he had said required one. They entered the small vestibule which Mr. Dudley had raised to the dignity of a hall, and Kitty immediately desired the footman who was leading the way upstairs, to inform either Mrs. Peterson, or Mrs. Stanley of her arrival, and beg them to come to her, but Stanley, unused to any contradiction and impatient to be amongst them, would neither allow her to wait, or listen to what she said, and forcibly seizing her arm within his, overpowered her voice with the rapidity of ~~hers~~ his own, and Kitty, half angry and half laughing, was obliged to go with him up stairs, and could even with difficulty prevail on him to relinquish her hand before they entered the room.

Mrs. Peterson was at that very moment engaged in conversation with a lady at the upper end of the room, to whom she had been giving a long account of her niece's unlucky disappointment, and the dreadful pain that she had with so much fortitude, endured the whole day.–

"I left her, however," said she, "thank heaven, a little better, and I hope she has been able to amuse herself with a book, poor thing! for she must otherwise be very dull. She is probably in bed by this time, which while she is so poorly, is the best place for her you know, ma'am."

The lady was going to give her assent to this opinion, when the noise of voices on the stairs, and the footman's opening the door as if for the entrance of company, attracted the attention of everybody in the room; and as it was in one of those intervals between the dances when everyone seemed glad to sit down, Mrs. Peterson had a most unfortunate opportunity of seeing her niece, whom she had supposed in bed, or amusing herself as the height of gaiety with a book, enter the room most elegantly dressed, with a smile on her countenance, and a glow of mingled cheerfulness and confusion on her cheeks, attended by a young man uncommonly handsome, and who without any of her confusion, appeared to have all her vivacity. Mrs. Peterson, colouring with anger and astonishment, rose from her seat, and Kitty walked eagerly towards her, impatient to account for what she saw appeared wonderful to everybody, and extremely offensive to *her*, while Camilla on seeing her brother ran instantly towards him, and very soon explained who he was by her words and actions.

Mr. Stanley, who so fondly doted on his son that the pleasure of seeing him again after an absence of three months prevented his feeling for the time any anger against him for returning to England without his knowledge, received him with equal surprise and delight; and soon comprehending the cause of his journey, forbore any further conversation with him, as he was eager to see his mother, and it was necessary that he should be introduced to Mr. Dudley's family. This introduction, to anyone but Stanley, would have been highly unpleasant, for they considered their dignity injured by his coming uninvited to their house, and received him with more than their usual haughtiness. But Stanley, who ~~joined to~~ with a vivacity of temper seldom subdued, and a contempt of censure not to be overcome, possessed an opinion of his own consequence, and a perseverance in his own schemes which were not to be damped by the conduct of others, appeared not to perceive it. The civilities therefore which they coldly offered, he received with a gaiety and ease peculiar to himself, and then attended by his father and sister walked into another room where his mother was playing at cards, to experience another meeting, and undergo a repetition of pleasure, surprise and explanations.

While these were passing, Camilla eager to communicate all she felt to someone who would attend to her, returned to Kitty, and seating herself by her, immediately began, "Well, did you ever know anything so delightful as this! But it always is so; I never go to a ball in my life but what something or other happens unexpectedly that is quite charming!"

"A ball," replied Kitty, "seems to be a most eventful thing to you.–"

"Oh! Lord, it is indeed – but only think of my brother's returning so suddenly – and how shocking a thing it is that has brought him over! I never heard anything so dreadful!–"

"What is it pray that has occasioned his leaving France! I am sorry to find that it is a melancholy event."

"Oh! it is beyond anything you can conceive! His favourite hunter who was turned out in the park on his going abroad, somehow or other fell ill. – No, I believe it was an accident, but however it was something or other, or else it was something else, and so they sent an express immediately to Lyons ~~to my~~ where my brother was, for they knew that he valued this mare more than anything else in the world besides; an[d] so my brother set off directly for England, and without packing up another coat. I am quite angry with him about it; it was so shocking you know to come away without a change of clothes.–"

"Why indeed," said Kitty, "it seems to have been a very shocking affair from beginning to end."

"Oh! it is beyond anything you can conceive! I would rather have had *anything* happen than that he should have lost that mare."

"Except ~~your brother's~~ his coming away without another coat."

"Oh! yes, that has vexed me more than you can imagine. – Well, and so Edward got to Brampton just as the poor thing was dead; but as he could not bear to remain there *then*, he came off directly to Chetwynde on purpose to see us. – I hope he may not go abroad again."

"Do you think he will not?"

"Oh! dear, to be sure he must, but I wish he may not with all my heart. – You cannot think how fond I am of him! By the bye are not you in love with him yourself?"

"To be sure I am," replied Kitty laughing. "*I* am in love with every handsome man I see."

"That is just like me. – *I* am always in love with every handsome man in the world."

"There you outdo me," replied Kitty, "for I am only in love with those I *do* see."

Mrs. Peterson, who was sitting on the other side of her, and who began now to distinguish the words, "*love*" and "*handsome man*," turned hastily towards them and said, "What are you talking of, Kitty!"

To which Kitty immediately answered, with the simple artifice of a child, "Nothing, ma'am."

She had already received a very severe lecture from her aunt on the imprudence of her behaviour during the whole evening; she blamed her for coming to the ball, for coming in the same carriage with Edward Stanley, and still more for entering the room with him. For the last-mentioned offence, Kitty knew not what apology to give, and though she longed in answer to the second to say that she had not thought it would be civil to make Mr. Stanley *walk*, she dared not so to trifle with her aunt, who would have been but the more offended by it. The first accusation, however, she considered as very unreasonable, as she thought herself perfectly justified in coming.

This conversation continued till Edward Stanley entering the room came instantly towards her, and telling her that every one waited for *her* to begin the next dance led her to the top of the room, for Kitty, impatient to escape from so unpleasant a companion, without the least hesitation, or one civil scruple at being so distinguished, immediately gave him her hand, and joyfully left her seat. This conduct, however, was highly resented by several young ladies present, and among the rest by Miss Stanley whose regard for her brother, though *excessive*, and whose affection for Kitty, though *prodigious*, were not proof against such an injury to her importance and her peace. Edward had, however, only consulted his own inclinations in desiring Miss Peterson to begin the dance[43], nor had ~~an~~ he any reason to know that it was either wished or expected by anyone else in the party. As an heiress, she was certainly of consequence, but her birth gave her no other claim to it, for her father had been a merchant[44].

It was this very circumstance which rendered this unfortunate affair so offensive to Camilla, for though she would sometimes boast in the pride of her heart, and her eagerness to be admired that she did not know who her grandfather had been, and was as ignorant of everything relative to genealogy as to astronomy (and, she might have added, geography), yet she was really proud of her family and connections, and easily offended if they were treated with neglect.

"I should not have minded it," said she to her mother, "if she had been *anybody* else's daughter, but to see her pretend to be above *me*, when her father was only a tradesman, is too bad! It is such an affront to our whole family! I declare, I think Papa ought to interfere in it, but he never cares about anything but politics. If I were Mr. Pitt, or the Lord Chancellor, he would take care I should not be insulted, but he never thinks about me, and it is so provoking that *Edward* should let her stand there. I wish with all my heart that he had never come to England! I hope she may fall down and break her neck, or sprain her ankle."

Mrs. Stanley perfectly agreed with her daughter concerning the affair, and though with less violence, expressed almost equal resentment at the indignity. Kitty, in the meantime, remained insensible of having given anyone offence, and therefore, unable either to offer an apology or make a reparation, her whole attention was occupied by the happiness she enjoyed in dancing with the most elegant young man in the room, and everyone else was equally unregarded. The evening, indeed to *her*, passed off delightfully; he was her partner during the greatest part of it[45], and the united attraction that he possessed of person, address and vivacity, had easily gained that preference from Kitty which they seldom fail of obtaining from everyone. She was too happy to care either for her aunt's ill-humour, which she could not help ~~observing~~ remarking, or for the alteration in Camilla's behavior, which forced itself at last on her observations. Her spirits were elevated above the influence of displeasure in anyone, and she was equally indifferent as to the cause of Camilla's, or the continuance of her aunt's.

Though Mr. Stanley could never be really offended by any imprudence or folly in his son that had given him the pleasure of seeing ~~his~~ him, ~~son,~~ he was yet perfectly convinced that Edward ought not to remain in England, and was resolved to hasten his leaving it as soon as possible; but when he talked to Edward about it, he found him much less ~~disposing~~ed towards returning to France, than to accompany them in their projected tour, which he assured his father would be infinitely more pleasant to him, and that as to the affair of travelling he considered it of no importance, and what might be pursued at any little odd time, when he had nothing better to do. He advanced these objections in a manner which plainly showed that he had scarcely a doubt of their being complied with, and appeared to consider his father's arguments in opposition to them as merely given with a view to keep up his authority, and

292

such as he should find little difficulty in combating.

He concluded at last by saying, as the chaise in which they returned together from Mr. Dudley's reached Mrs. Peterson's, "Well sir, we will settle this point some other time, and fortunately it is of so little consequence, that an immediate discussion of it is unnecessary."

He then got out of the chaise and entered the house without waiting for his father's reply.

It was not till their return that Kitty could account for that coldness in Camilla's behaviour to her which had been so pointed as to render it impossible to be entirely unnoticed. When, however, they were seated in the coach with the two other ladies, Miss Stanley's indignation was no longer to be suppressed from breaking out into words, and found the following vent.

"Well, I must say *this*, that I never was at a stupider ball in my life! But it always is so; I am always disappointed in them for some reason or other. I wish there were no such things."

"I am sorry, Miss Stanley," said Mrs. Peterson drawing herself up, "that you have not been amused; everything was meant for the best I am sure, and it is a poor encouragement for your mama to take you to another if you are so hard to be satisfied."

"I do not know what you mean, ma'am, about Mama's *taking* me to another. You know I am come out."

"Oh! dear Mrs. Peterson," said Mrs. Stanley, "you must not believe everything that my lively Camilla says, for her spirits are prodigiously high sometimes, and she frequently speaks without thinking. I am sure it is impossible for *anyone* to have been at a more elegant or agreeable dance, and so she wishes to express herself I am certain."

"To be sure I do," said Camilla very sulkily, "only I must say that it is not very pleasant to have anybody behave so rude to one as to be quite shocking! I am sure I am not at all offended, and should not care if all the world were to stand above me, but still it is extremely abominable, and what I cannot put up with. It is not that I mind it in the least, for I had just as soon stand at the bottom as at the top all night long, if it was not so very disagreeable. – But to have a person come in the middle of the evening and take everybody's place is what I am not used to, and though I do not care a pin about it myself, I assure you I shall not easily forgive or forget it."

This speech, which perfectly explained the whole affair to

Kitty, was shortly followed on her side by a very submissive apology, for she had too much good sense to be proud of her family, and too much good nature to live at variance with anyone. The excuses she made were delivered with so much real concern for the offence, and such unaffected sweetness, that it was almost impossible for Camilla to retain that anger which had occasioned them. She felt indeed most highly gratified to find that no insult had been intended and that Kitty was very far from forgetting the difference in their birth for which she could now only pity her, and her good humour being restored with the same ease in which it had been affected, she spoke with the highest delight of the evening, and declared that she had never before been at so pleasant a ball.

The same endeavours that had procured the forgiveness of Miss Stanley ensured to her the cordiality of her mother, and nothing was wanting but Mrs. Peterson's good humour to render the happiness of the others complete, but she, offended with Camilla for her affected superiority, still more so with her brother for coming to Chetwynde, and dissatisfied with the whole evening, continued silent and gloomy and was a restraint on the vivacity of her companions. She eagerly seized the very first opportunity which ~~offered~~ the next morning offered to her of speaking to Mr. Stanley on the subject of his son's return, and after having expressed her opinion of its being a very silly affair that he came at all, concluded with desiring him to inform Mr. Edward Stanley that it was a rule with her never to admit a young man into her house as a visitor for any length of time.

"I do not speak, sir," she continued, "out of any disrespect to you, but I could not answer it to myself to allow of his stay; there is no knowing what might be the consequence of it, if he were to continue here, for girls nowadays will always give a handsome young man the preference before any other, though for why, I never could discover, for what after all is youth and beauty! ~~Why, in fact, it is nothing more than being young and handsome – and that.~~ It is but a poor substitute for real worth and merit. Believe me, cousin, that whatever people may say to the contrary, there is certainly nothing like virtue for making us what we ought to be, and as to a ~~handsome~~ young man's being young and handsome and having an agreeable person, it is nothing at all to the purpose for he had much better be respectable. I always *did* think so, and I always *shall*, and therefore you will oblige me very much by desiring your son to leave Chetrynde, or I cannot be answerable for what may happen between him and my niece.

"You will be surprised to hear *me* say it," she continued, lowering her voice, "But truth will out, and I must own that Kitty is one of the most impudent[46] girls that ever existed. ~~Her intimacies with young men are abominable. And it is all the same to her; who it is, no one comes amiss to her~~ I assure you, sir, that I have seen her sit and laugh and whisper with a young man whom she has not seen above half a dozen times. Her behaviour indeed is scandalous, and therefore I beg you will send your son away immediately, or everything will be at sixes and sevens."

Mr. Stanley, who from one part of her speech had scarcely known to what length her insinuations of Kitty's impudence were meant to extend, now endeavoured to quiet her fears on the occasion by assuring her that, on every account, he meant to allow only of his son's continuing that day with them, and that she might depend on his being more earnest in the affair from a wish of obliging her. He added also that he knew Edward to be very desirous himself of returning to France, as he wisely considered all time lost that did not forward the plans in which he was at present engaged, though he was but too well convinced of the contrary himself.

His assurance in some degree quieted Mrs. Peterson, and left her tolerably relieved of her cares and alarms, and better disposed to behave with civility towards his son during the short remainder of his stay at Chetwynde. Mr. Stanley went immediately to Edward, to whom he repeated the conversation that had passed between Mrs. Peterson and himself, and strongly pointed out the necessity of his leaving Chetwynde the next day, since his world was already engaged for it. His son, however, appeared struck only by the ridiculous apprehensions of Mrs. Peterson, and highly delighted at having occasioned them himself, seemed engrossed alone in thinking how he might increase them, without attending to any other part of his father's conversation. Mr. Stanley could get no determinate answer from him, and though he still hoped for the best, they parted almost in anger on his side.

His son, though by no means disposed to marry, or any otherwise attached to Miss Peterson than as a good natured lively girl who seemed pleased with him, took infinite pleasure in alarming the jealous fears of her aunt by his attentions to her, without considering what effect they might have on the lady herself. He would always sit by her when she was in the room, appear dissatisfied if she left it, and was the first to enquire whether she meant soon to return. He was delighted with her drawings, and enchanted with her performance on the harpsichord; everything that she said, appeared to interest him; his conversation was addressed to her alone; and she seemed to be the sole object of his attention.

That such efforts should succeed with one so tremblingly alive to every alarm of the kind as Mrs. Peterson is by no means unnatural, and that they should have equal influence with her niece whose imagination was lively, and whose disposition romantic, who was already extremely pleased with him, and of course desirous that he might be so with her, is as little to be wondered at.

Every moment as it added to the conviction of his liking her, made him still more pleasing, and strengthened in her mind a wish of knowing him better. As for Mrs. Peterson, she was in tortures the whole day. Nothing that she had ever felt before on a similar occasion was to be compared to the sensations which then distracted her; her fears had never been so strongly, or indeed so reasonably excited. ~~before~~ Her dislike of Stanley, her anger at her niece, her impatience to have them separated, conquered every idea of propriety and good breeding, and though he had never mentioned any intention of leaving them the next day, she could not help asking him after dinner, in her eagerness to have him gone, at what time he meant to set out.

"Oh! ma'am," replied he, "if I am off by twelve at night, you may think yourself lucky; and if I am not, you can only blame yourself for having left so much as the *hour* of my departure to my own disposal."

Mrs. Peterson coloured very highly at this speech, and without addressing herself to anyone in particular, immediately began a long harangue on the shocking behaviour of modern young men, and the wonderful alteration that had taken place in them, since her time, which she illustrated with many instructive anecdotes of the decorum and modesty which had marked the characters of those whom she had known, when she had been young. This, however, did not prevent his walking in the garden with her niece, without any other companion for nearly an hour in the course of the evening. They had left the room for that purpose with Camilla at a time when Mrs. Peterson had been out of it, nor was it for some time after her return to it that she could discover where they were.

Camilla had taken two or three turns with them in the walk

which led to the arbour, but soon growing tired of listening to a conversation in which she was seldom invited to join, and from its turning occasionally on books, very little able to do it, she left them together in the arbour, to wander alone to some other part of the garden, to eat the fruit, and examine Mrs. Peterson's greenhouse. Her absence was so far from being regretted that it was scarcely noticed by them, and they continued conversing together on almost every subject, for Stanley seldom dwelt long on any, and had something to say on all, till they were interrupted by her aunt.

Kitty was, by this time, perfectly convinced that both in natural abilities, and acquired information, Edward Stanley was infinitely superior to his sister. Her desire of knowing that he was so, had induced her to take every opportunity of turning the conversation on history and they were very soon engaged in an historical dispute, for which no one was more calculated than Stanley, who was so far from being really of any party thant he had scarcely a fixed opinion on the subject. He could therefore always take either side, and always argue with temper. In his indifference on all such topics, he was very unlike his companion, whose judgement being guided by her feelings, which were eager and warm, was easily decided, and though it was not always infallible, she defended it with a spirit and enthusiasm which marked her own reliance on it.

They had continued therefore for sometime conversing in this manner on the character of Richard the Third, which he was warmly defending when he suddenly seized hold of her hand, and exclaiming with great emotion, "Upon my honour you are entirely mistaken," pressed it passionately to his lips[47], and ran out of the arbour. Astonished at this behaviour, for which she was wholly unable to account, she continued for a few moments motionless on the seat where he had left her, and was then on the point of following him up the narrow walk through which he had passed, when on looking up the one that lay immediately before the arbour, she saw her aunt walking towards her with more than her usual quickness.

This explained at once the reason for his leaving her, but his leaving her in such manner was rendered still more inexplicable by it. She felt a considerable degree of confusion at having been seen by her in such a place with Edward, and at having that part of his conduct, for which she could not herself account, witnessed by one to whom all gallantry was odious. She remained therefore confused, distressed and irresolute, and suffered her aunt to approach her, without leaving the arbour.

Mrs. Peterson's looks were by no means calculated to animate the spirits of her niece, who in silence awaited her accusation, and in silence meditated her defence. After a few moment's suspense, for Mrs. Peterson was too much fatigued to speak immediately, she began with great anger and asperity, the following harangue:

"Well, *this* is beyond anything I could have supposed. *Profligate*[48] as I *knew* you to be, I was not prepared for such a sight. This is beyond anything you ever did *before*; beyond anything I ever heard of in my life! Such impudence, I never witnessed before in such a girl! And this is the reward for all the cares I have taken in your education; for all my troubles and anxieties; and Heaven knows how many they have been! All I wished for was to breed you up virtuously; I never wanted you to play upon the harpsichord, or draw better than anyone else; but I had hoped to see you respectable and good; to see you able and willing to give any example of modesty and virtue to the young people hereabouts.

"I bought you Blair's *Sermons*, and ~~Seccar's Explanation of the Catechism~~ *Coelebs In Search of a Wife*. I gave you the key to my own library, and borrowed a great many good books of my neighbours for you[49], all to this purpose. But I might have spared myself the trouble. – Oh! Kitty, you are an abandoned creature, and I do not know what will become of you. I am glad, however," she continued softening into some degree of mildness, "to see that you have some shame for what you have done, and if you are really sorry for it, and your future life is a life of penitence and reformation perhaps you may be forgiven. But I plainly see that everything is going to sixes and sevens, and all order will soon be at an end throughout the kingdom[50]."

"Not, however, ma'am, the sooner, I hope, from any conduct of mine," said Kitty in a tone of great humility, "for upon my honour I have done nothing this evening that can contribute to overthrow the establishment of the kingdom."

"You are mistaken, child," replied she. "The welfare of every nation depends upon the virtue of its individuals, and anyone who offends in so gross a manner against decorum and propriety is certainly hastening its ruin. You have been giving a bad example to the world, and the world is but too well disposed to receive such."

"Pardon me, madam," said her niece, "but I *can* have given an example only to *you*, for you alone have seen the offence.

Upon my world, however, there is no danger to fear from what I have done; Mr. Stanley's behaviour has given me as much surprise, as it has done to you, and I can only suppose that it was the effect of his high spirits, authorized in his opinion by our relationship. But do you consider, madam, that it is growing very late! Indeed you had better return to the house."

This speech, as she well knew, would be unanswerable with her aunt, who instantly rose, and hurried away under so many apprehensions for her own health, as banished for the time all anxiety about her niece, who walked quietly by her side, revolving within her own mind the occurrence that had given her aunt so much alarm.

"I am astonished at my own imprudence," said Mrs. Peterson. "How could I be so forgetful as to sit down out of doors at such a time of night! I shall certainly have a return of my rheumatism after it. – I begin to feel very chill already. I must have caught a dreadful cold by this time. – I am sure of being lain-up all the winter after it.–"

Then reckoning with her fingers, "Let me see. This is July; the cold weather will soon be coming in – August – September – October – November – December – January – February – March – April. – Very likely I may not be tolerable again before May. I must and will have that arbour pulled down. – It will be the death of me; who knows *now*, but what I may never recover. – Such things *have* happened. – My particular friend Miss Sarah Hutchinson's death was occasioned by nothing more. – She stayed out late one evening in April, and got wet through, for it rained very hard, and never changed her clothes when she came home. – It is unknown how many people have died in consequence of catching cold! I do not believe there is a disorder in the world, except the smallpox, which does not spring from it."

It was in vain that Kitty endeavoured to convince her that her fears on the occasion were groundless; that it was not yet late enough to catch cold, and that even if it were, she might hope to escape any other complaint, and to recover in less than ten months. Mrs. Peterson only replied that she hoped she knew more of ill-health than to be convinced in such a point by a girl who had always been perfectly well, and hurried up stairs leaving Kitty to make her apologies to Mr. and Mrs. Stanley for going to bed.–

Though Mrs. Peterson seemed perfectly satisfied with the goodness of the apology herself, yet Kitty felt somewhat embarrassed to find that the only one she could offer to their visitors was that her aunt had *perhaps* caught cold, for Mrs. Peterson charged her to make light of it for fear of alarming them. Mr. and Mrs. Stanley, however, who well knew that their cousin was easily terrified on that score, received the account of it with very little surprise, and all proper concern.

Edward and his sister soon came in, and Kitty had no difficulty of in gaining an explanation of his conduct from him, for he was too warm on the subject himself, and too eager to learn its success, to refrain from making immediate enquiries about it; and she could not help feeling both surprised and offended at the ease and indifference with which he owned that all his intentions had been to frighten her aunt by pretending an affection for *her*, a design so very compatible incompatible with that partiality which she had, at one time, been almost convinced of his feeling for her. It is true that she had not yet seen enough of him to be actually in love with him, yet she felt greatly disappointed that so handsome, so elegant, so lively a young man should be so perfectly free from any such sentiment as to make it his principal sport.

There was a novelty in his character which to *her* was extremely pleasing; his person was uncommonly fine, his spirits and vivacity suited to her own, and his manners at once so animated and gentle insinuating, that she thought it must be impossible for him to be otherwise than amiable, and was ready to give him credit for being completely perfectly so. He knew the powers of them himself: to them he had often been indebted for his father's forgiveness of faults which had he been awkward and inelegant would have appeared very serious; to them, even more than to his person or his fortune, he owed the regard which almost everyone was disposed to feel for him, and which young women in particular were disposed to feel inclined to entertain.

Their influence was acknowledged on the present occasion by Kitty, whose anger they entirely dispelled, and whose cheerfulness they had power not only to restore, but to raise. – The evening passed off as agreeably as the one that had preceded it; they continued talking to each other, during the chief part of it, and such was the power of his address, and the brilliancy of his eyes, that when they parted for the night, though Kitty had but a few hours before totally given up the idea, yet she felt almost convinced again that he was really in love with her. She reflected on their past conversation, and though it had been on various and indifferent subjects, and she could not exactly recollect any speech on his side expressive of such a partiality, she was still, however, nearly certain of its being so. But, fearful of being vain enough to suppose such a thing without sufficient reason, she resolved to suspend her final determination on it, till the next day, and more especially till their parting, which she thought would infallibly explain his regard if any he had.–

The more she had seen of him, the more inclined was she to like him, and the more desirous that he should like *her*. She was convinced of his being naturally very clever and very well disposed, and that his thoughtlessness and negligence, which, though they appeared to *her* as very becoming in *him*, she was aware would by many people be considered as defects in his character, merely proceeded from a vivacity always pleasing in young men, and were far from testifying a weak or vacant understanding. Having settled this point within herself, and being perfectly convinced by her own arguments of its truth, she went to bed in high spirits; determined to study his character, and watch his behaviour still more the next day.

She got up with the same good resolutions, and would probably have put them in execution, had not ~~Nanny~~ Anne informed her as soon as she entered the room that Mr. Edward Stanley was already gone. At first, she refused to credit the information, but when her maid assured her that he had ordered a carriage the evening before to be there at seven o'clock in the morning, and that she herself had actually seen him depart in it a little after eight, she could no longer deny her belief to it.

"And this," thought she to herself, blushing with anger at her own folly, "this is the affection for me of which I was so certain. Oh! what a silly thing is woman! How vain, how unreasonable! To suppose that a young man would be seriously attached in the course of four and twenty hours, to a girl who has nothing to recommend her but a good pair of eyes! And he is really gone! Gone perhaps without bestowing a thought on me! Oh! why was not I up by eight o'clock! But it is a proper punishment for my laziness and folly, and I am heartily glad of it. I deserve it all, and ten times more for such insufferable vanity. It will at least be of service to me in that respect; it will teach me in future *not* to think everybody is in love with me. Yet I *should* like to have seen him before he went, for perhaps it may be many years before we meet again. By his manner of leaving us, however, he seems to have been perfectly indifferent about it.

How very odd, that he should go without giving us notice of it, or taking leave of anyone! But it is just like a young man, governed by the whim of the moment, or actuated merely by the love of doing anything odd! Unaccountable beings indeed! And young women are equally ridiculous! I shall soon begin to think like my aunt that everything is going to sixes and sevens, and that the whole race of mankind are degenerating."

She was just dressed, and on the point of leaving her room to make her personal enquires after Mrs. Peterson, when Miss Stanley knocked at her door, and on her being admitted began in her usual strain a long harangue upon her father's being so shocking as to make Edward go at all, and upon Edward's being so horrid as to leave them at such an hour in the morning.

"You have no idea," said she, "how surprised I was, when he came into my room to bid me good bye.–"

"Have you seen him then, this morning?" said Kitty.

"Oh yes! And I was so sleepy that I could not open my eyes. And so he said, 'Camilla, goodbye to you for I am going away. – I have not time to take leave of anybody else, and I dare not trust myself to see Kitty, for then you know I should never get away.'"

"Nonsense," said Kitty; "he did not say that, or he was in joke if he did."

"Oh! no I assure you he was as much in earnest as he ever was in his life; he was too much out of spirits to joke *then*. And he desired me when we all met at breakfast to give his compliments to your aunt, and his love to you, for you was a nice girl[51], he said, and he only wished it were in his power to be more with you. You were just the girl to suit him, because you were so lively and good-natured, and he wished with all his heart that you might not be married before he came back, for there was nothing he liked better than being here. Oh! You have no idea what fine things he said about you, till at last I fell asleep and he went away. But he certainly is in love with you – I am sure he is – I have thought so a great while I assure you."

"How can you be so ridiculous?" said Kitty smiling with pleasure. "I do not believe him to be so easily affected. But he *did* desire his love to me then? And wished I might not be married before his return? And said I was a nice girl, did he?"

"Oh! dear, yes, and I assure you it is the greatest praise in his opinion, that he can bestow on any~~one~~body; I can hardly ever persuade him to call *me* one, though I beg him sometimes for an hour together."

"And do you really think that he was sorry to go?"

"Oh! you can have no idea how wretched it made him. He would not have gone this month, if my father had not insisted on it; Edward told me so himself yesterday. He said that he wished with all his heart he had never promised to go abroad, for that he repented it more and more every day; that it interfered with all his other schemes, and that since papa had spoke to him about it, he was more unwilling to leave Chetwynde than ever."

"Did he really say all this? And why would your father insist upon his going?"

"His leaving England interfered with all his other plans, and his conversation with Mr. Stanley had made him still more averse to it."

"What can this mean!"

"Why that he is excessively in love with you to be sure; what other plans can he have? And I suppose my father said that if he had not been going abroad, he should have wished him to marry you immediately. – But I must go and see your aunt's plants. – There is one of them that I quite dote on – and two or three more besides.–"

"Can Camilla's explanation be true?" said Kitty to herself, when her friend had left the room. "And after all my doubts and uncertainties, can Stanley really be averse to leaving England for *my sake* only? 'His plans interrupted.' And what indeed can his plans be, but towards marriage. Yet *so soon* to be in love with *me*! – But it is the effect perhaps only of the warmth of heart which to *me* is the highest recommendation in anyone. A heart disposed to love – And such under the appearance of so much gaiety and inattention, is Stanley's. Oh! how much does it endear him to me! But he is gone – gone perhaps for years – obliged to tear himself from what he most loves; his happiness is sacrificed to the vanity of his father! In what anguish he must have left the house! Unable to see me, or to bid me adieu, while I, senseless wretch, was daring to sleep. This, then, explained his leaving us at such a time of day. – He could not trust himself to see me. – Charming young man! How much must you have suffered! I *knew* that it was impossible for one so elegant, and so well bred, to leave any family in such a manner, but for a motive like this unanswerable."

Satisfied, beyond the power of change, of this, she went in

high spirits to her aunt's apartment, without giving a moment's recollection on the vanity of young women, or the unaccountable conduct of young men[52].

Kitty continued in this state of satisfaction during the remainder of the Stanleys' visit – who took their leave with many pressing invitations to visit them in London when, as Camilla said, she might have an opportunity of becoming acquainted with that sweet girl Augusta Halifax – Or rather (thought Kitty), of seeing my dear Mary Wynne again. – Mrs. Peterson, in answer to Mrs. Stanley's invitation, replied – that she looked upon London as the hot house of vice where virtue had long been banished from society and wickedness of every description was daily gaining ground – that Kitty was of herself sufficiently inclined to give way to, and indulge in vicious inclinations – and therefore was the last girl in the world to be trusted in London, as she would be totally unable to withstand temptation.–

After the departure of the Stanleys, Kitty returned to her usual occupations, but alas! they had lost their power of pleasing. Her bower alone retained its interest in her feelings, and perhaps that was owing to the particular remembrance it brought to her mind of Edward Stanley[53].

The summer passed away unmarked by any incident worth narrating, ~~save one~~ or any pleasure to Kitty save one, which arose from the receipt of a letter from her friend Cecilia, now Mrs. Lascelles, announcing ~~their~~ the speedy return of herself and husband to England.

A correspondence productive indeed of little pleasure to either party had been established between Camilla and Kitty. The latter had now lost the only satisfaction she had ever received from the letters of Miss Stanley, as that young lady having informed her friend of the departure of her brother to Lyons now never mentioned his name – her letters seldom contained any intelligence except ~~the account~~ a description of some new article of dress, an enumeration of various engagements, a panegyric on Augusta Halifax and perhaps a little abuse of ~~Sir~~ the unfortunate Sir Peter.–

The Grove, for so was the mansion of Mrs. Peterson at Chetwynde denominated, was situated within five miles from ~~the town~~ Exeter, but though that lady possessed a carriage and horses of her own, it was seldom that Kitty could prevail on her to visit that town for the purpose of shopping, on account of the many officers perpetually quartered there and who infested the principal streets. – A company of strolling players on their way from some neighbouring races having opened a temporary theatre there, Mrs. Peterson was prevailed on by her niece to indulge her by attending the performance ~~and an~~ once during their stay. – Mrs. Peterson insisted on paying Miss Dudley the compliment of inviting her to join the party, when a new difficulty arose, from the necessity of having some gentleman ~~of their party~~ to attend them. —

Notes

1. Austen's original name for her heroine, Kitty, is replaced by the more formal Catharine three times on the first page (though she never corrected it on the Contents page). In the remainder of the manuscript, Kitty is sometimes changed to Catharine and sometimes not, but this version of the text uses Kitty throughout for consistency and because I believe it more accurately indicates Austen's original intention.

2. "the Bower": An arbor is a sheltered garden retreat with its sides and a roof formed by trees or climbing plants trained over and woven into a wooden framework. Undoubtedly, Austen was familiar with the description of a bower in the Elizabethan poem *The Fairie Queen* (1590-1596) by Edmund Spencer (1552/3-1599):

> His dearest Dame is that Enchaunteresse,
> The vile Acrasia, that with vaine delightes,
> And idle pleasures in her Bowre of Blisse,
> Does charme her louers, and the feeble sprightes
> Can call out of the bodies of frailes wights:
> Whom then she does transforme to mo[n]strous hewes,
> And horribly misshapes with ugly sightes,
> Captiu'd eternaly in yron mewes (V.XXII.1-8)

In Spencer, the Bower of Blisse is the place from which the enchantress Acrasia calls men to her; those who fall in love with her subsequently lose their souls. It is a place of seeming natural beauty, but it is, in fact, a false Eden. The hero, Guyon, the Knight of Temperance, is tempted by the place, but finally he puts Acrasia in chains, releases from her spell her latest victim, and destroys the bower. In Austen, Kitty's Bower is a space of private tranquility where the young girl can be the person whom she wants to be – an escape from the adult world that she is about to enter which constrains her identity and takes away her agency. Mrs. Peterson feels threatened by it and promises to tear it down.

3. "Miss Austen": Cassandra.

4. "in every library in the kingdom, and run through threescore editions": Comic hyperbole. Booksellers often advertised their books as being 'in every

circulating library in the country' (or similar phrases) but not in 'every library,' and even the most popular novels did not achieve sixty editions.

5. "losing her parents ... care of a maiden aunt": The orphaned heroine brought up by a tyrannical or unsympathetic relative is common in sentimental and Gothic fiction.

6. "she was enthusiastic": This identifies Kitty as by nature passionate and given to imagination and fancy, qualities which, taken to excess, might become the defects of heightened sensibility.

7. "during the holidays of the Miss Wynnes": Her two friends are sent away to school (as were Austen and Cassandra) whereas Kitty is home-schooled.

8. "Splendidly, yet unhappily married": Austen's own aunt, the beautiful Philadelphia Hancock (1730-1792), sailed to Madras, India, in 1752 where she married Tysoe Saul Hancock (1711-1775) in February 1753. He was a surgeon, and therefore a good match for Philadelphia, but he was seven years older than she and there were rumors that Philadelphia conducted a love affair with Warren Hastings, later to be the first Governor-General of Bengal, and that he was the father of her daughter, Eliza.

9. "Dowager": Title given to a widow who retains the whole or a portion of her husband's estate for the rest of her life.

10. "Chetwynde": There is no village of this name in Devonshire, though one exists in Gloucestershire.

11. "Mrs. Percival": This change is indicated (with a very few exceptions) throughout the manuscript. The name Percival has a long association with myth and romance going back to the tales of King Arthur. The change from Kitty Peterson to Catharine Percival was made (presumably with Austen's approval) by her nephew James Edward Austen (afterwards Austen-Leigh). The effect of this and of other changes that he made to the manuscript (including his continuation of the story) is to 'gentrify' the text: the revisions "reveal a failure to understand or a shying away from the story's political implications" (Sutherland, "From Kitty to Catharine"). In this version, I have restored Peterson throughout for the same reason that I have restored Kitty throughout.

12. "tithes": A tax of one tenth of annual produce or earnings paid to the rector for the support of the church and clergy.

13. "parade": Ostentation, show.

14. "establishment": Number of servants to prepare for and cater to guests.

15. "sweep": The winding drive from the road to the house.

16. "He was ... in town": Although members were elected to the Commons, there was nothing really democratic about their election since voting was restricted to adult male landowners. The terms of the Commons (i.e., the dates when the House was in session) coincide roughly with the London season when everyone who was anyone was in London.

17. "She was ... taste or judgement": Austen might have taken this criticism of the type of education provided for girls right out of *A Vindication of the*

Rights of Woman: with Strictures on Political and Moral Subjects (1792), written by Mary Wollstonecraft (1759-1797).

18. "Mrs. Smith's novels": Charlotte Turner Smith (1749-1806) was both a Romantic poet and a novelist in the Gothic and sentimental genres. She wrote ten novels: *Emmeline* (1788), *Ethelinde* (1789), *Celestina* (1791), *Desmond* (1792), *The Old Manor House* (1793), *The Wanderings of Warwick* (1794), *The Banished Man* (1794), *Montalbert* (1795), *Marchmont* (1796), and *The Young Philosopher* (1798). Smith was politically active in the fight against class and gender inequality which made her a controversial figure.

19. "Grasmere": *Emmeline* opens with a description of Grasmere Water. The beauties of The Lake District were described in Gilpin's *Observations, relative chiefly to picturesque beauty, made in the year 1772, on several parts of England; particularly the mountains, and lakes of Cumberland, and Westmoreland* (1786) and were just being discovered by tourists such as the Gardiners in *Pride and Prejudice*, who plan to take Elizabeth Bennet with them to The Lakes (though they only get as far as Derbyshire).

20. "races": Horse races – a fine place to see and be seen, especially for young ladies in search of a husband.

21. "Derbyshire to Matlock and Scarborough": Matlock is in Derbyshire in the north Midlands and Scarborough is in Yorkshire. Yorkshire is on the east coast, while The Lake District is on the west coast. Miss Stanley's knowledge of the geography of England is faulty.

22. "the whole race … so general before": Mrs. Peterson's fears stem from the French Revolution which, having overthrown an oppressive monarchy degenerated into a bloodbath. In *Reflections on the Revolution in France* (1790), Edmund Burke (1730-1797) warned of the dangers posed to England by the revolutionary movement.

23. "the living of Chetwynde and two or three curacies": Mr. Wynne would thus have the living of more than one parish. In the parishes other than Chetwynde, he would employ a curate leaving himself with a profit from the living. Camilla may be overestimating his income.

24. "~~sent to sea~~ got into the army": Two of Austen's own brothers had been "sent to sea," so perhaps she felt that being sent to sea was not so bad after all.

25. "school somewhere in Wales": Welsh schools were cheaper than, and generally inferior to, those in England.

26. "Ranelagh": Ranelegh Gardens in Chelsea (admission two shillings and sixpence) was considered more fashionable than the older Vauxhall Gardens (admission one shilling).

27. "I see no hardship in all that": Camilla has no idea of world geography either (Barbados is in the West Indies not the East Indies) and no conception of the living conditions on board passenger sailing ships – which were no "fun" at all.

28. "nice": Precise, pernickety.

29. "draws in oils": Oils painting was considered a higher skill than

watercolors or crayon. It was also much more expensive.

30. "send Charles Wynne to sea": Austen has forgotten to change this to the Army.

31. "the receipt book": Every house would have its own recipe book(s) for food as well as medicines.

32. "than have a tooth drawn": It was at this time possible to fill teeth with metal, but the usual treatment for bad teeth was to have them out. Since this operation was performed without the benefit of anesthetic, it was very painful. Also, it left a permanent gap! Having poor teeth was the main reason people did not smile in their portraits.

33. "~~pierrot~~ Regency walking dress": "A pierrot is a jacket style that became very popular in the 1780s and 90s. It consisted of a bodice with a ruffled "tail" in back. Sometimes pierrot jackets [were] closed in front, and sometimes were made in a zone front style [i.e., leaving the upper chest exposed]. The ruffled skirting in back could be various lengths, with any sort of trimming…" (thedreamstress.com). This revision brings the fashions of the story right up to date for the 1810s. It must have been made after February 5th, 1811, the date of the passage of the Regency Act under which the Prince of Wales ruled in the place of his 'mad' father. A walking dress was shorter than an evening dress.

34. "pelisse": A pelisse is a finely trimmed woman's cloak with armholes or sleeves, reaching to the ankles.

35. "this was a … sixes and sevens": William Pitt the Younger became Prime Minister in 1783. Stanley is expressing his confidence in Pitt's government. 'At sixes and sevens' is an English idiom dating back to the last decades of the fourteenth century whose origin is obscure. It is used to describe a condition of confusion or disarray.

36. "Scotch steps": Scottish dances were extremely popular and, for that very reason, looked down upon as in bad taste by those who regarded themselves as cultured.

37. "a chaise and four": A light, elegant carriage pulled by four horses.

38. "in such a litter": In such an untidy, disorganized state.

39. "hack horses": Horses hired at various stages of his journey, not horses owned by him. The driver and servants are also, presumably, hired which is why they do not wear Mr. Stanley's uniform (livery).

40. "Nanny": Austen has neglected to change the name to Anne.

41. "powder and pomatum": Use of hair powder was widespread throughout the 18th century; social etiquette required it. Lotion, known as pomade or pomatum, was first applied to the hair to help the powder to stick. It was a messy operation which normally took place in a special powder room. In 1795, the Prime Minister, Pitt the Younger, introduced a tax on hair powder which led to a rapid decline in its use.

42. "a monthly ball": Stanley assumes that Kitty is going to a public ball, funded by subscription. Kitty informs him that it is a private ball in a private

home.

43. "to begin the dance": Stanley takes Kitty to the position of honor in the room and, in beginning the next dance with her, breaks all of the rules of etiquette since neither he nor she has the social status to take that preeminent position.

44. "As an heiress ... been a merchant": Kitty (like the Bingleys in *Pride and Prejudice*) is one of the *nouveau riche*, those whose wealth has been acquired within their own (or in this case the previous) generation, usually through business, rather than by inheritance of wealth in the form of land ownership. Such people (think of Jay Gatsby in *The Great Gatsby* by F. Scott Fitzgerald) are perceived as ostentatious or lacking in good taste by people whose wealth is 'old money.'

45. "he was her partner during the greatest part of it": Another breach of etiquette. Gentlemen were supposed to engage themselves for two dances with the same partner and then move onto another young lady. Ladies carried cards to record the names of men who had asked them to dance.

46. "impudent": This word (meaning utterly immodest, shameless) is a serious charge. In the next two sentences, Mrs. Peterson elaborates. Austen deleted these probably because they are too critical of Kitty's rather innocent errors.

47. "pressed it passionately to his lips": It appears that Stanley has seen Mrs. Peterson approaching and that the kiss is designed to outrage her by confirming her suspicions of Kitty's relationship with him. Stanley is, however, being totally insensitive to the effect that such an action will have on the young and impressionable Kitty.

48. "*Profligate*": Lost to virtue and decency, shameless – another very hard term.

49. "I bought you Blair's ... neighbours for you." As Ross writes, "Literary taste, in Jane Austen's world, is an invariable guide to character" (106). The five-volume *Sermons* (1777-1801) of Hugh Blair (1718-1800), a Presbyterian preacher, proved to be extremely popular. His message was one of conservative morality stressing female modesty and obedience to parental authority. *Lectures on the catechism of the Church of England: with a discourse on confirmation* (1769) by Thomas Secker (1693-1768), Archbishop of Canterbury, is replaced by the more up-to-date *Coelebs in Search of Wife: Comprehending Observations on Domestic Habits and Manners, Religion and Morals* (1809), a didactic novel by Hannah More (1745-1833). On Tuesday, January 24th, 1809, Jane wrote to Cassandra, "You have by no means raised my curiosity after Caleb; – My disinclination for it before was affected, but now it is real. I do not like the evangelicals. Of course I shall be delighted when I read it, but till I do [so] I dislike it." Six days later in her next letter, Jane added, "the only merit it [the novel] could have was in the name of Caleb, which has an honest, un-pretending sound, but in Coelebs there is pedantry and affectation. Is it written only to classical

scholars?"

50. "Oh Kitty ... throughout the kingdom": Mrs. Peterson's criticism of Kitty's conduct echo fears of chaos and disorder expressed in Edmund Burke's *Reflections on the Revolution in France* (1790). She is making a 'slippery slope' argument that once moral standards decline the entire structure of the nation will follow.

51. "a nice girl": The word had recently come to mean pleasing, agreeable, virtuous, and respectable.

52. "conduct of young men": At this point Austen's transcription ends. The story is continued in a different hand. Scholars date this addition to 1809 and generally assume the author to have been James Edward Austen Leigh "writing as a child under Jane Austen's supervision" (McMaster in Baker ed. 29).

53. "brought to her mind of Edward Stanley.": The first continuation is followed by a further continuation also by James-Edward Austen-Leigh but written after 1845.

Commentary

A comparison of handwriting in this manuscript suggests that most of the revisions to the original text were made by James Edward in 1816 or 1817 when he was sixteen or seventeen, though evidently the changes were made with Austen's permission. Kathryn Sutherland comments that "These alterations, all tending to gentrify or upgrade the tone of the story, diminish its political thrust as it was originally written in 1792, a time when championship of wider civil rights and educational opportunities were linked to a reappraisal of vernacular English" (*Teenage* xxii).

Since dating the original composition of *Kitty, or The Bower* and *The Three Sisters* is purely hypothetical, they must share the accolade of being Austen's first sustained experiment in realistic social comedy and in more complex plot development. To be sure, this unfinished novel has its share of parody/burlesque which led Austen's niece, Caroline, to dismiss the work as formally and stylistically one of the young Jane's "betweenities" when she was asked by James Edward her opinion on the publication of any of the juvenilia. In fact, the text touches on the themes that would be central to Austen's novels: the education of young women; friendship between women; women's motivation for marrying; the abuse of social position; and absurd affectation in contrast to good manners. The novel's main theme is, however, the vulnerability of young women in a society determined to disempower them. Catharine (hereafter Kitty) "is Jane Austen's first full-scale attempt to place a heroine in a completely realistic social situation and probe her reactions to the complex (and often contradictory) demands of conventional morality and social custom" (Litz 37).

Kitty, or The Bower is an exploration of the ways in which young women's minds and bodies (specifically their sexuality) are regulated and stifled by a repressive and oppressive patriarchal culture. Through the character of Mrs. Peterson, a self-appointed guardian of female virtue (i.e., virginity) who fears that unconstrained female sexuality constitutes a revolutionary threat to the very foundations of English society, Austen satirizes the conservative argument, found in the sermons of James Fordyce and the novels of Hannah More, "that strict governance of the female sexual body equates with proper governance of the state" (Leffel "'Everything is Going...'").

Against these forces of personal and sexual repression stands Kitty's bower "where she could indulge in peace ... and amuse herself for some time in abusing and hating [the people around her]." The author of "Jane Austen's Bower" argues that the bower is:

> a physical sanctuary from social expectations in which she can freely explore her sexuality and intellectualism [that] can be read as a metaphor for the entire Juvenilia and its importance to the adolescent Austen. The Juvenilia is Austen's literary "Bower". As an unpublished series, it was Austen's private sanctuary, with which she flouted the rigid cultural expectations of women and female writers by parodying the social stereotypes of femininity. In the same way that Catharine retreats from society to her Bower ... Austen retreated to the freedom of her private literary sanctuary of bawdy and subversive tales: the *Juvenilia* ... As Austen matured and her work entered the public literary realm, her content became less critical and less subversive in an effort to conform to the social expectations of her time and become marketable. The external pressures of socially acceptable female literature took the freedom of short, private fiction from Austen and replaced it with the more "quiet [and] subservient" (Doody 9) literary medium of the novel which was considered "safe for women to write."

This is an ingenious and (I think) highly productive way of looking at this novel, for although the above quotation underestimates the subversive, even radical, tendency of Austen's mature novels, it is nevertheless true that the bower does not represent a viable long-term solution for Kitty's problems. Similarly, the juvenilia were merely a preparation for published authorship. Both Austen and her heroine would have to write/live in the adult world.

Kitty, or The Bower marks the first appearance in Austen's fiction of the sympathetic but flawed heroine and of the third person limited narrator who is inside this young woman's mind, showing the reader how the world appears when seen through her eyes. Kitty, the clichéd orphaned heroine brought up by a severe aunt, Mrs. Peterson, is "a charming ingénue of about sixteen or seventeen" (McMaster) given to sentimental emotion; her "imagination was warm, and in her friendships, as well as in the whole tenure of her mind, she was enthusiastic." Her childhood companions, the Wynne sisters, with whom Kitty enjoyed that real sympathy between female friends that we have seen so often mocked in the juvenilia, are gone, pulled from Kitty's orbit by the poverty of their family – Cecilia to a splendid but loveless marriage in Bengal and Mary to be the put-upon companion of the daughters of Lady Halifax.

Kitty's life, then, now allows no outlet for her romantic notions with the exception of the "fine shady bower, the work of her own infantine labours assisted by those of two young companions who had resided in the same village." Evidently the attraction of the bower is less its beauty that its association with her two lost childhood friends. The description that it "terminated a very pleasant and retired walk in her Aunt's Garden" suggests that the bower is secluded far from Aunt Peterson's country house in Chetwynde, and thus hidden from her censorious eyes, but also that it is a kind of trap – a literal *cul-de-sac*. It represents a private space where Kitty is unlikely to be seen or interrupted by others to which she can retreat to find "constant relief in all her misfortunes … whenever anything disturbed her," a place to which she can retire from the adult world that she must inevitably inhabit and all of those she encounters there who fall short of her ideals because they lack true sensibility. Some critics have gone further, interpreting the bower symbolically as "a masturbatory realm of private sexual exploration" ("Jane Austen's Bower"). That seems to me to strain the text too much. It is possible to agree with John Leffel's memorable description of Aunt Peterson, is a "sexually anaesthetized spinster" whose ceaseless "emphasis on propriety" constricts Kitty's ability to explore or understand her budding sexuality without going so far as to claim that Kitty goes to the bower to gain knowledge about her sexuality through self-pleasuring ("'Everything is Going…'").

From an excess of "jealous caution," Mrs. Peterson sees it as her duty to protect Kitty from men. Thus, her niece is often not taken to a ball simply "because an officer was to be there," and when allowed to attend, she must dance with a partner of her aunt's "introduction in preference to one of her own choice." Mrs. Peterson's greatest fear is of Kitty "marrying imprudently if she were allowed the opportunity of choosing." Thus is Kitty denied agency in the one sphere where choice was so important to Austen – the choice of a husband. Mrs. Peterson will not even invite her relations, the Stanleys, "people of large fortune and high fashion," to visit her until their son, Stanley, is safely off on the Continent because of this young man she has "heard many traits that alarmed her."

Although this visit of the Stanley family to Chetwynde holds out to Kitty no prospect of romance, it does seem to promise a confidential friendship with an educated and cultured young woman of her own age, Camilla, whom Kitty hopes will "in some degree make amends for the loss of Cecilia and Mary." She is soon disappointed, however, for Camilla (termed by Juliet McMaster a "ditzy airhead") is shallow and superficial, the victim (the narrator assures us) of a perverse system of education which has not strengthened her mind but merely allowed free rein to her emotions (that is, it has reinforced sensibility over sense):

> She was ... naturally not deficient in abilities; but those years which *ought* to have been spent in the attainment of *useful knowledge* and *mental improvement*, had been all bestowed in learning drawing, Italian and music, more especially the latter, and she now united to these accomplishments, *an understanding unimproved by reading* and a mind totally devoid either of taste or judgement. Her temper was by nature good, but *unassisted by reflection*, she had neither patience under disappointment, nor could sacrifice her own inclinations to promote the happiness of others. All her ideas were towards the elegance of her appearance, the fashion of her dress, and the admiration she wished them to excite. (Emphasis added)

Camilla's 'education' has merely prepared her for marriage. In her conversation, she is superficial and affected, being entirely ignorant of and uninterested in literature, geography, politics and history, but willing to talk for hours about clothes, excursions, parties and gossip. In contrast, Kitty (taking full advantage of the keys to her aunt's library to read widely and 'inappropriately') is desperate to discuss ideas:

> [Kitty] found no variety in her conversation; she received no information from her but in fashions, and no amusement but in her performance on the harpsichord ... and when Kitty had learnt from her, how large their house in town was, when the fashionable amusements began, who were the celebrated beauties and who the best milliner, Camilla had nothing further to teach...

As Mary Waldron writes, "Camilla ... cannot experience real feeling; though she sometimes gives way to emotion, it is all expressed through meaningless formulae and empty hyperbole..." (24). Kitty is forced back to her bower.

The blackest mark against Camilla is that she defends the treatment of the Wynne sisters by the Halifax family. The narrator has already given us the true details (i.e., Kitty's version) of the fate of these two excellent, sensitive young women who have each been imposed upon because of their relative poverty. Camilla, however, defends the indefensible:

> Sir George Fitzgibbon you know sent the eldest girl to India entirely at his own expense, where they say she is most nobly married and the happiest creature in the world. – Lady

> Halifax, you see, has taken care of the youngest and treats her
> as if she were her daughter.

The reader knows that Cecilia is miserable in her marriage and that Mary is simply being exploited; both have been denied agency in deciding their own fate. Camilla herself admits that Lady Halifax does not go into public with Mary and did not take her to Cheltenham, but against even her own evidence, she insists that Lady Halifax (surely a prototype of Lady Catherine de Bourgh) is "a delightful woman, and one of the sweetest tempered creatures in the world."

While Mrs. Peterson represents the entirely unreasonable repression of natural feeling (both in herself and in her niece), Mrs. Stanley and Camilla represent false sensibility. The contrast can be seen in their different attitudes to the custom of friendship and correspondence between young women. Kitty's aunt judges "a correspondence between girls as productive of no good, and as the frequent origin of imprudence and error by the effect of pernicious advice and bad example." The defense of letter writing by Camilla and her mother is, however, entirely unconvincing because, by her own account, the letters between Camilla and her London friends are trivial, indeed vacuous. Camilla remonstrates with her hostess, "'But who knows what you might have been ma'am, if you *had* had a correspondent; perhaps it would have made you quite a different creature.'" On the evidence of the novel, there is some truth in this for Mrs. Peterson is deficient in sensibility, but it would only have been true had she written the kinds of letters that Kitty continues to exchange with Cecilia and Mary Wynne, not if they had resembled Camilla's letters with the Halifax girls which seem to be about nothing other than fashionable clothes.

When Camilla's brother, Edward Stanley, arrives unexpectedly, he finds Kitty alone and (her toothache having gone) ready to go on to the ball at the Dudleys. Edward is all "good humour and gaiety," and the result is some very witty conversation in which the spirited Kitty (surely a precursor of Elizabeth Bennet) more than holds her own. As A. Walton Litz points out, "Edward Stanley ... bursts into [Kitty's] narrow world in fulfillment of her daydreams and temporarily overcomes all her scruples" (37). It is immediately clear to the reader, however, that Edward is not seriously attracted to Kitty, despite finding her beautiful and delightful company. He accompanies her to the private ball, and Kitty allows him to do so because she "chose to consider herself entitled by the [family] connection to forget how little a while they had known each other." In presenting Kitty's view of the matter in this way, the narrator implies criticism of her self-justification.

When Edward says to Kitty, "'I hope your aunt won't be alarmed'" by his accompanying her to the ball, he is showing his prior knowledge of Mrs. Peterson's censorious attitude towards him; knowing how easily shocked Kitty's aunt is, Edward sets out to shock her – the narrator speaks quite openly of "his schemes." Once at the Dudleys, he refuses to bow to "'ceremony'" and "'prudery,'" going out of his way to behave in ways that offend against good manners and "'propriety.'" He enters the ball in Kitty's company without any introduction creating quite a stir (though not so great a stir as he would have had not Kitty, with some difficulty, prevailed "on him to relinquish her hand before they entered"), and when introduced to the haughtily offended hosts, he displays "a vivacity of temper seldom subdued, and a contempt of censure." He manages to offend "several young ladies present," including his own sister, by taking Kitty to the head of the room and beginning the next dance with her (which is a social offence given that she is merely the daughter of a merchant and that he was not even invited to the ball) and by dancing almost exclusively with her for the remainder of the evening. Our heroine falls under Stanley's spell quite as thoroughly as will Elizabeth Bennet fall under that of the equally plausible George Wickham and for much the same reason: she lacks the experience to resist a handsome young man who speaks and acts with total self-confidence.

Following his father's account of his conversation with Kitty's aunt and his ultimatum, Edward "appeared struck only by the ridiculous apprehensions of Mrs. Peterson, and highly delighted at having occasioned them himself, seemed engrossed alone in thinking how he might increase them…" This he does by paying Kitty the sort of attentions and compliments that a lover would, leaving the poor heroine (though not the reader) in the dark about whether his actions really do indicate that he is falling in love with her or that he regards Kitty is no more than "a good natured lively girl who seemed pleased with him," whom he never intends should take his attentions seriously. Kitty is caught between her attraction to Edward and her awareness of his defects, uncertain whether they "merely proceeded from a vivacity always pleasing in young men" or testify "a weak or vacant understanding." The truth ought to dawn on Kitty when she notices that, in their discussion of literature and history, Edward displays intelligence *without* emotion: he is indifferent on every topic, in contrast to Kitty who combines intelligence *with* feeling, making her passionate in defense of her positions.

The kiss in the bower is a fine piece of comedy at our heroine's expense. Seeing Mrs. Peterson approaching, Edward "suddenly seized hold of [Kitty's] hand … pressed it passionately to his lips, and ran out of the arbour." We are told that Kitty (who has not perceived the approach of her aunt) is "astonished" by this behavior and "wholly unable to account" for Edward's action. When she does see her aunt, Kitty only understands that Edward left her so suddenly because of being discovered by Mrs. Peterson in the bower with Kitty; she does not understand (as the reader does) that the kiss was an action designed solely to inflame Mrs. Peterson. Edward's stratagem succeeds entirely, though unfortunately the innocent Kitty has to bear the weight of her aunt's anger – which to the reader is an inexcusable fault in Edward. Only later that evening does Kitty learn the truth behind the kiss in the bower and then she "could not help feeling both surprised and offended at the ease and indifference" with which Edward ignores the effect of his scheme upon her own feelings: "she felt greatly disappointed that so handsome, so elegant, so lively a young man should be so perfectly free from any such sentiment as to make it his principal sport."

As with the venal George Wickham, it is Edward's "uncommonly fine [person], his spirits and vivacity ... and his manners at once so animated and insinuating," that dispels Kitty's anger and "almost convinced" her to be "nearly certain" that he loves her. In both cases, the reader sees the folly into which a naïve, inexperienced young woman of genuine sensibility falls when confronted by a more experienced, cynical and manipulative young man – particularly one who just happens to have fine eyes and a handsome face. It seems that Kitty has learned a lesson when she discovers that Edward has left without even bidding her goodbye for she thinks, "Oh! what a silly thing is woman! How vain, how unreasonable!" However, it is certainly not to Kitty's credit that she allows Camilla's gossip to persuade her again that Edward loves her. Reporting that Edward told her that "leaving England interfered with all his other plans," Camilla assures Kitty that this means that "he is excessively in love with you to be sure; what other plans can he have?" The question hangs in the air, and would undoubtedly have been answered in a surprising way (a way that has *nothing* to do with Kitty) had Austen completed the novel.

The story breaks off with Kitty having convinced herself, despite the evidence of her own eyes, that Edward's plans were to marry her immediately had not his father intervened to force him against his will to return to France. Thus Kitty prides herself on being able to look beneath the surface of Edward's speech and actions to discover, what every young woman of true sensibility hopes to discover, "warmth of heart which ... is the highest recommendation in anyone. A heart disposed to love..." At this point, the nadir of Kitty's fortunes (exactly parallel to the point at which Elizabeth Bennet, having completely misread the character of Wickham, considers him to be in love with her and herself to be in love with him), Austen stopped. Once again, the writer had got herself into a narrative dead end: Edward is in France, Cecilia in India; Mary in Scotland, and Kitty is stuck immovably in Chetwynde where she is pretty much confined to the house and its garden by her aunt. By contrast, Elizabeth Bennet is a much more mobile heroine, one who not only walks alone and in company for miles in the countryside to visit Meryton and Netherfield, and travels to Hunsford and to London, but also goes, with her aunt and uncle, on a tour of Derbyshire where she visits Pemberley and, quite by chance, encounters Darcy.

The most plausible guess (it is not more than that) I have read about the intended plot is that Edward's "plans" are to find and marry Mary Wynne and that Kitty will meet, be courted by and marry Charles Wynne (who, of course, she already knows from childhood). If this, or anything like it, was in

Austen's mind, then somehow she would have to get Edward back from France (or prevent him from returning thence) and included in Lady Halifax's tour of Derbyshire, Yorkshire and Cumberland so that he could connect with Mary, and find some way to bring together Charles and Kitty. The continuation by James Edward seems to grapple with solutions to these problems. The Stanleys' invitation to Mrs. Peterson and Kitty to visit them in London (although Kitty's aunt rejects the idea on the grounds of needing to protect her niece's morals), the anticipated return of Cecilia (now Mrs. Lascelles) to England, and the visit to the theater in Exeter (a town with many army officers) which necessitates having some gentleman accompany them, each holds out the possibility of plot development.

Meanwhile, Kitty is thrown back on her bower which "alone retained its interest in her feelings, and perhaps that was owing to the particular remembrance it brought to [Kitty's] mind of Edward Stanley." Far from developing her sense, through the course of the novel Kitty has moved closer to sensibility; she appears to have learned nothing from her experiences and to have regressed rather than developed. In her isolation, she retreats into her bower which represents "the illusory world of daydreams and romantic fiction" (Litz 36).

This is, above all, a novel about young women who have no control of their own lives. Because of their relative poverty, Cecilia is shipped off to India to become the unhappy Mrs. Lascelles and her sister Mary has no choice but to become the companion (neither equal nor servant) to two self-centered girls. Camilla, by nature lacking in reason and judgment, has been further shaped by her education into a silly, husband-hunting butterfly. In Kitty herself:

> Austen created an extremely honest representation of budding femininity ... and uses the heroine to interrogate the negative impact that unrealistic patriarchal expectations can have on an innocent and developing young woman. This is emphasized by the victimization Catharine experiences at the hands of Edward Stanley, who invades the secure sanctuary of Catharine's bower and unexpectedly kisses her, thus dashing the heroine's innocence and damaging her reputation. ("Jane Austen's Bower")

Kitty has lost her bower (symbolically, we might argue, her innocence, her childhood, and/or her virginity). She must move forward into adulthood, but at the point at which the novel leaves her, there is no obvious route by which she might do so.

Appendix: Guide to Further Reading

Biography and Social Background

Penelope Hughes-Hallett, *Jane Austen: My Dear Cassandra*: The selection of letters will satisfy all but the research scholar and the carefully selected illustrations bring to life Austen's world.

Harold Bloom's *Classic Critical Views*: An excellent collection of historic literary criticism ranging from 1813 to 1913.

Mary Wollstoncraft's *A Vindication of the Rights of Woman* contends that women have the capacity to reason because they have a soul. This being so, the failure of society to educate women in ways that would develop their judgment is responsible for the triviality, acquisitiveness and bitchy rivalry that characterizes the lives of women. Published in 1792, this controversial work could not have been read by the adolescent Jane, and whether she ever read it as an adult I do not know. Nevertheless, it seems evident from what she wrote and from the way in which she lived her life that Austen was intellectually and emotionally in sympathy with the views on the nature of women and their rightful place in society that Wollstoncraft sets out so forcefully in this early feminist work.

Lucy Worsley's *Jane Austen at Home: A Biography* gives a very full account of Austen's life and works placing emphasis on her relationship with the several places where she lived through her life. The author avoids speculation preferring to explain clearly what we can know and admit frankly what we probably never will know about Jane.

Criticism

Helena Kelly's *Jane Austen: The Secret Radical* deconstructs the received image that readers in the twenty-first century have of sweet, modest, entirely conventional Aunt Jane, the natural literary genius entirely immured from the commercial world of publication and from the social and political issues of her day. What emerges is part biography and part literary criticism as Kelly demolishes some of the 'established facts' about Jane's life and offers a reading of her fiction which shows a writer who "reflects back to her readers their world as it really is – complicated, messy, filled with error and injustice" (33). Sadly, Kelly does not include the Juvenilia in her analysis.

Connie Kirk's *A Student's Guide to Jane Austen* is a useful entry-level text for middle and high school students.

Alistair Duckworth's *The Improvement of the Estate* has an Introduction that sets Austen's novels in their literary context.

Emily Auerbach's *Searching for Jane Austen* effectively dismisses the myth of 'sweet and saintly Aunt Jane' and celebrates the acerbic wit of this self-confident writer. The chapter on the *Juvenilia* is the most insightful I have come across.

Ashley Tauchert's *Romancing Jane Austen*: Examines the relationship between Austen's realism and her use of the "romance narrative paradigm" (12). Not always easy reading, but worth the effort.

Bibliography

Works by Jane Austen

Austen, Jane. *Jane Austen's Fiction Manuscripts Digital Edition.* Arts and Humanities Research Council, 2018. August 30, 2018. Web.

---, *Volume the First by Jane Austen: In Her Own Hand.* New York: Abbeville Press, 2013. Print.

---, *Volume the Second by Jane Austen: In Her Own Hand.* New York: Abbeville Press, 2014. Print.

---, *Volume the Third by Jane Austen: In Her Own Hand.* New York: Abbeville Press, 2014. Print.

---, *Teenage Writings: Jane Austen.* Kathryn Sutherland ed. Oxford: Oxford UP, 2017. Print.

---, *The Cambridge Edition of the Works of Jane Austen: Juvenilia.* Peter Sabor ed. Cambridge: Cambridge UP, 2002. Print.

Biography

Le Faye, Deirdre, William Austen-Leigh, and Richard Austen-Leigh. *Jane Austen A Family Record.* Boston: G.K.Hall, 1989. Print.

Galperin, William. *The Historical Austen.* Philadelphia: University of Pennsylvania, 2005. Print.

Shields , Carol. *Jane Austen: A Penguin Life.* New York: Penguin, 2001. Print.

Worsley, Lucy. *Jane Austen at Home: A Biography.* London: Hodder and Stoughton, 2017. Print.

Jane Austen in Context

Austen, Jane. *Jane Austen: My Dear Cassandra.* Hughes-Hallettt, Penelope ed. London: Collins and Brown, 1991. Print.

Bradbrook, Frank. *Jane Austen and Her Predecessors.* London: Cambridge University, 1966. Print.

Butler, Marilyn. *Jane Austen and the War of Ideas.* Oxford: Clarendon, 1975. Print.

Carson, Susannah, editor. *A Truth Universally Acknowledged: 33 Great Writers on Why We Read Jane Austen.* New York: Random House, 2009. Print.

Craik, Wendy. *Jane Austen in her Time.* London: Nelson, 1969. Print.

Galperin, William. *The Historical Austen.* Philadelphia: University of Pennsylvania, 2005. Print.

Geng, Li-Ping. "The *Loiterer* and Jane Austens Literary Identity." *Eighteenth-Century Fiction*, Vol. 13, No. 4, 2001, pp. 579–592.

Harman, Claire. *Jane's Fame: How Jane Austen Conquered the World*. New York: Henry Holt, 2009. Print.

Kelly, Helena. *Jane Austen: The Secret Radical*. London: Icon Books, 2016. Print.

Kirk, Connie. *A Student's Guide to Jane Austen*. Berkeley Heights: Enlsow, 2008. Print.

Konigsberg, Ira. *Narrative Technique in the English Novel: Defoe to Austen*. Hamden: Archon, 1985. Print.

Lerner, Laurence. *The Truthtellers: Jane Austen, George Eliot, D. H. Lawrence*. New York: Schocken, 1967. Print.

Looser, Devoney. *The Making of Jane Austen*. Baltimore: Johns Hopkins University Press, 2017. Print.

Mitton, G.E. *Jane Austen and Her Times*. 1905. Port Washington: Kennikat, 1970. Print.

Richetti, John. ed. *The Cambridge Companion to the Eighteenth Century Novel*. Cambridge: Cambridge UP, 1996. Print.

Ross, Josephine. *Jane Austen A Companion*. New Jersey: Rutgers University Press, 2003. Print.

Todd, Janet. *Jane Austen in Context*. Cambridge: Cambridge University Press, 2005. Print.

Tyler, Natalie. *The Friendly Jane Austen*. New York: Viking Penguin, 1999. Print.

Waldron, Mary. *Jane Austen and the Fiction of Her Time*. Cambridge: Cambridge UP, 1999. Print.

Wollstoncraft, Mary. *A Vindication of the Rights of Woman*. London, Everyman's Library, 1992. Print.

General Criticism of Austen's Work

Auerbach, Emily. *Searching for Jane Austen*. University of Wisconsin, 2004. Print.

Baker, William. ed. *Critical Companion to Jane Austen: A Literary Reference to Her Life and Work*. New York: Infobase Publishing, 2008. Print.

Bloom, Harold, ed. *Bloom's Classic Critical Views: Jane Austen*. New York: Infobase, 2008. Print.

---. *Modern Critical Views: Jane Austen*. New York: Chelsea House, 1986. Print.

Duckworth, Alistair. *The Improvement of the Estate: A Study of Jane Austen's Novels*. John Hopkins, 1971. Print.

Jenkyns, Richard. *A Fine Brush on Ivory: An Appreciation of Jane Austen*. Oxford: Oxford University, 2004. Print.

Litz, A. Walton. *Jane Austen: A Study of Her Artistic Development*. New York: Oxford University, 1965. Print.

Pinion, F. B. *A Jane Austen Companion: A Critical Survey and Reference Book*. London: MacMillan, 1973. Print.

Rees, Joan. *Jane Austen: Woman and writer*. New York: St. Martin's Press, 1976. Print.

Southam, Brian, ed. *Jane Austen: The Critical Heritage*. London: Routledge and Kegan Paul, 1968. Print.

---. *Jane Austen's Literary Manuscripts: A Study of the Novelist's Development through the Surviving Papers*. Oxford: Oxford UP, 1964. Print.

Tauchert, Ashley. *Romancing Jane Austen: Narrative, Realism and the Possibility of a Happy Ending*. New York: Palgrave Macmillan, 2005. Print.

Todd, Janet. *The Cambridge Introduction to Jane Austen*. 2nd edition. Cambridge: Cambridge UP, 2015. Print.

Watt, Ian. *Jane Austen: A Collection of Critical Essays*. 2nd printing. Englewood Cliffs: Prentice-Hall, 1964. Print.

Watt, Ian. *The Rise of the Novel: Studies in Defoe, Richardson and Fielding*. 5th printing. Berkeley and Los Angeles: University of California, 1967. Print.

Weldon, Fay. *Letters to Alice on First Reading Jane Austen*. New York: Taplinger, 1985. Print.

Criticism of the Juvenilia

Beer, Frances. "'The three Sisters': A 'little bit of Ivory.'" *JANSA: Jane Austen Society of North America. Persuasions,* No. 28. 2008. June 18, 2018. Web.

Johnston, Freda. "Jane Austen's Past Lives." *The Cambridge Quarterly*, Vol. 39, Issue 2. June 1, 2010. July 5, 2018. Web.

Knuth, Deborah. "'We fainted Alternately on a Sofa': Female Friendship in Jane Austen's Juvenilia.' *JANSA: Jane Austen Society of North America. Persuasions* No. 9. 1987. August 3, 2018. Web.

Leffel, John C. "'Everything is Going to Sixes and Sevens': Governing the Female Body (Politic) in Jane Austen's *Catharine, Or the Bower* (1792)." *Studies in the Novel*, Vol. 43 No. 2, 2011, pp. 131-151. *Project MUSE*. July 18, 2018. Web.

---. "Jane Austen's Miniature 'Novel': Gender, Politics, and Form in *The Beautifull Cassandra*." *JANSA: Jane Austen Society of North America. Persuasions,* No. 32, 2010. June 13, 2018. Web.

McMaster, Juliet. "'Destined for the Sea': The Hero of 'Catharine, or the Bower'?" *JANSA: Jane Austen Society of North America. Persuasions,* Vol. 38. No. 1. 2017. July 13, 2018. Web.

Sutherland, Kathryn. "From Kitty to Catharine: James Edward Austen's hand in Volume the Third." *The Review of English Studies*, Vol. 66, Issue 273. June 3, 2014. July 18, 2018.

Upfal, Annette, and Christine Alexander. "Are We Ready for New Directions? Jane Austen's *The History of England* & Cassandra's Portraits." *JANSA: Jane Austen Society of North America. Persuasions,* Vol. 30, No. 2. 2010. June 13, 2018. Web.

About the Author

Ray Moore was born in Nottingham, England. He obtained his Master's Degree in Literature from Lancaster University and taught in secondary education for twenty-eight years before relocating to Florida with his wife. There he taught English and Information Technology in the International Baccalaureate Program at a High School in Florida. He is now a full-time writer and fitness fanatic.

Website: http://www.raymooreauthor.com

Ray strives to make his texts the best that they can be. If you have any comments or question about this book please contact the author through his email: villageswriter@gmail.com

Also by Ray Moore:

All books are available from amazon.com and from barnesandnoble.com as paperbacks and at most online eBook retailers.

Fiction:

The **Lyle Thorne Mysteries**: each book features five tales from the Golden Age of Detection:

Investigations of The Reverend Lyle Thorne
Further Investigations of The Reverend Lyle Thorne
Early Investigations of Lyle Thorne
Sanditon Investigations of The Reverend Lyle Thorne
Final Investigations of The Reverend Lyle Thorne
Lost Investigations of The Reverend Lyle Thorne
Official Investigations of Lyle Thorne
Clerical Investigations of The Reverend Lyle Thorne

Non-fiction:

The **Critical Introduction** series is written for high school teachers and students and for college undergraduates. Each volume gives an in-depth analysis of a key text:

"The General Prologue" by Geoffrey Chaucer: A Critical Introduction
"The Great Gatsby" by F. Scott Fitzgerald: A Critical Introduction
"Pride and Prejudice" by Jane Austen: A Critical Introduction
"The Stranger" by Albert Camus: A Critical Introduction (Revised Second Edition)

The **Text and Critical Introduction** series differs from the Critical introduction series as these books contain the original text and in the case of the medieval texts an interlinear translation to aid the understanding of the text. The commentary allows the reader to develop a deeper understanding of the text and themes within the text.

"Sir Gawain and the Green Knight": Text and Critical Introduction

"The General Prologue" by Geoffrey Chaucer: Text and Critical Introduction

"Heart of Darkness" by Joseph Conrad: Text and Critical Introduction

"Henry V" by William Shakespeare: Text and Critical Introduction

"Oedipus Rex" by Sophocles: Text and Critical Introduction

"A Room with a View" By E.M. Forster: Text and Critical Introduction

"The Sign of Four" by Sir Arthur Conan Doyle Text and Critical Introduction

"The Wife of Bath's Prologue and Tale" by Geoffrey Chaucer: Text and Critical Introduction

Study Guides - listed alphabetically by author
Study Guides offer an in-depth look at aspects of a text. They generally include an introduction to the characters, genre, themes, setting, tone of a text. They also may include activities on helpful literary terms as well as graphic organizers to aid understanding of the plot and different perspectives of characters.

* denotes also available as an eBook

"ME and EARL and the Dying GIRL" by Jesse Andrews: A Study Guide

Study Guide to "Alias Grace" by Margaret Atwood*

Study Guide to "The Handmaid's Tale" by Margaret Atwood*

"Pride and Prejudice" by Jane Austen: A Study Guide

"Moloka'i" by Alan Brennert: A Study Guide

"Wuthering Heights" by Emily Brontë: A Study Guide *

Study Guide on "Jane Eyre" by Charlotte Brontë*

"The Myth of Sisyphus" by Albert Camus: A Study Guide

"The Stranger" by Albert Camus: A Study Guide

"The Myth of Sisyphus" and "The Stranger" by Albert Camus: Two Study Guides *

Study Guide to "Death Comes to the Archbishop" by Willa Cather

"The Awakening" by Kate Chopin: A Study Guide

Study Guide to Seven Short Stories by Kate Chopin

Study Guide to "Ready Player One" by Ernest Cline

Study Guide to "Disgrace" by J. M. Coetzee

"The Meursault Investigation" by Kamel Daoud: A Study Guide

Study Guide on "Great Expectations" by Charles Dickens*

"The Sign of Four" by Sir Arthur Conan Doyle: A Study Guide *

Study Guide to "Manhattan Beach" by Jennifer Egan

"The Wasteland, Prufrock and Poems" by T.S. Eliot: A Study Guide

Study Guide on "Birdsong" by Sebastian Faulks*

"The Great Gatsby" by F. Scott Fitzgerald: A Study Guide

"A Room with a View" by E. M. Forster: A Study Guide

"Looking for Alaska" by John Green: A Study Guide

"Paper Towns" by John Green: A Study Guide

Study Guide to "Turtles All the Way Down" by John Green
Study Guide to "Florida" by Lauren Groff
Study Guide on "Catch-22" by Joseph Heller *
"Unbroken" by Laura Hillenbrand: A Study Guide
"The Kite Runner" by Khaled Hosseini: A Study Guide
"A Thousand Splendid Suns" by Khaled Hosseini: A Study Guide
"The Secret Life of Bees" by Sue Monk Kidd: A Study Guide
Study Guide on "The Invention of Wings" by Sue Monk Kidd
Study Guide to "Fear and Trembling" by Søren Kierkegaard
"Go Set a Watchman" by Harper Lee: A Study Guide
Study Guide to "Pachinko" by Min Jin Lee
"On the Road" by Jack Keruoac: A Study Guide
Study Guide on "Life of Pi" by Yann Martel*
Study Guide to "Death of a Salesman" by Arthur Miller
Study Guide to "The Bluest Eye" by Toni Morrison
Study Guide to "Reading Lolita in Tehran" by Azir Nafisi
Study Guide to "The Sympathizer" by Viet Thanh Nguyen
"Animal Farm" by George Orwell: A Study Guide
Study Guide on "Nineteen Eighty-Four" by George Orwell
Study Guide to "The Essex Serpent" by Sarah Perry
Study Guide to "Selected Poems" and Additional Poems by Sylvia Plath*
"An Inspector Calls" by J.B. Priestley: A Study Guide
Study Guide to "Cross Creek" by Marjorie Kinnan Rawlings
"Esperanza Rising" by Pam Munoz Ryan: A Study Guide
Study Guide to "The Catcher in the Rye" by J.D. Salinger
"Where'd You Go, Bernadette" by Maria Semple: A Study Guide
"Henry V" by William Shakespeare: A Study Guide
Study Guide on "Macbeth" by William Shakespeare *
"Othello" by William Shakespeare: A Study Guide *
Study Guide on "Antigone" by Sophocles*
"Oedipus Rex" by Sophocles: A Study Guide
"Cannery Row" by John Steinbeck: A Study Guide
"East of Eden" by John Steinbeck: A Study Guide
"The Grapes of Wrath" by John Steinbeck: A Study Guide
"Of Mice and Men" by John Steinbeck: A Study Guide*
"The Goldfinch" by Donna Tartt: A Study Guide
Study Guide to "The Hate U Give" by Angie Thomas
"Walden; or, Life in the Woods" by Henry David Thoreau: A Study Guide
Study Guide to "Cat's Cradle" by Kurt Vonnegut
"The Bridge of San Luis Rey" by Thornton Wilder: A Study Guide *
Study Guide on "The Book Thief" by Markus Zusak

Study Guides available only as e-books:

Study Guide on "Cross Creek" by Marjorie Kinnan Rawlings.
Study Guide on "Heart of Darkness" by Joseph Conrad:
Study Guide on "The Mill on the Floss" by George Eliot
Study Guide on "Lord of the Flies" by William Golding
Study Guide on "Nineteen Eighty-Four" by George Orwell
Study Guide on "Henry IV Part 2" by William Shakespeare
Study Guide on "Julius Caesar" by William Shakespeare
Study Guide on "The Pearl" by John Steinbeck
Study Guide on "Slaughterhouse-Five" by Kurt Vonnegut

Readers' Guides

Readers' Guides offer an introduction to important aspects of the text and questions for personal reflection and/or discussion. Guides are written for individual readers who wish to explore texts in depth and for members of Reading Circles who wish to make their discussions of texts more productive.

A Reader's Guide to Becoming by Michelle Obama
A Reader's Guide to Educated: A Memoir by Tara Westover

New titles are added regularly.

Teacher resources:

Ray also publishes many more study guides and other resources for classroom use on the 'Teachers Pay Teachers' website:
http://www.teacherspayteachers.com/Store/Raymond-Moore

Printed in Great Britain
by Amazon

25939665R00185